Pro DLR in .NET 4

Chaur Wu

Pro DLR in .NET 4

ISBN-13 (pbk): 978-1-4302-3066-3

ISBN-13 (electronic): 978-1-4302-3067-0

Printed and bound in the United States of America (POD)

President and Publisher: Paul Manning
Lead Editor: Jonathan Gennick
Technical Reviewer: Scott Isaacs
Editorial Board: Steve Anglin, Mark Beckner, Ewan Buckingham, Gary Cornell, Jonathan Gennick, Jonathan Hassell, Michelle Lowman, Matthew Moodie, Duncan Parkes, Jeffrey Pepper, Frank Pohlmann, Douglas Pundick, Ben Renow-Clarke, Dominic Shakeshaft, Matt Wade, Tom Welsh
Coordinating Editor: Jennifer L. Blackwell
Copy Editor: Sharon Terdeman
Compositor: Bytheway Publishing Services
Indexer: Brenda Miller
Artist: Integra Software Services Pvt. Ltd.
Cover Designer: Anna Ishchenko

Distributed to the book trade worldwide by Springer Science+Business Media, LLC., 233 Spring Street, 6th Floor, New York, NY 10013. Phone 1-800-SPRINGER, fax (201) 348-4505, e-mail orders-ny@springer-sbm.com, or visit www.springeronline.com.

For information on translations, please e-mail rights@apress.com, or visit www.apress.com.

Apress and friends of ED books may be purchased in bulk for academic, corporate, or promotional use. eBook versions and licenses are also available for most titles. For more information, reference our Special Bulk Sales–eBook Licensing web page at www.apress.com/info/bulksales.

I want to dedicate this book to Sarah, Everett, Cedric, and Chiachi

Contents at a Glance

Contents

About the Author

Chaur Wu is an author and developer with a passion for model-based, language-oriented software development. He works extensively with .NET, with experience going back to the initial beta release in 2000. He has two successful books to his credit: *Professional Design Patterns in VB.NET* and *Professional UML with Visual Studio .NET*, both published by Wrox Press.

Wu has implemented a number of domain-specific and general-purpose languages—for work, for study, and for fun. All of the projects he developed for *Pro DLR in .NET 4* are collectively hosted on an open source project site at `http://code.google.com/p/dpier/`. You are welcome to visit the web site and check out the latest development there.

About the Technical Reviewer

Scott Isaacs spent the first 25 years of his life in California's Central Valley. He has long since moved to southeast Wisconsin, where he designs software. He also runs the WI .NET Users Group, one of the oldest and largest .NET community groups around.

Isaacs lives in a Milwaukee suburb with his wife and children. He occasionally blogs at http://tapmymind.com/, and can also be found online at http://twitter.com/daughtkom/.

Acknowledgments

I'd like to thank the fabulous folks at Apress, especially Jonathan Gennick and Jennifer Blackwell for their support throughout the writing of the book. There were times when it was impossible for me to make any progress on the writing and I really appreciated Jonathan and Jennifer's understanding and encouragement during those tough periods. I'd also like to thank Scott Isaacs for reviewing the book and providing valuable feedback. Throughout my career as a software engineer, I've continually benefited from the many people I work with, and from open source communities. For this book, I'd like to express my thanks to the DLR forum and the wonderful folks who provided prompt answers to the questions I posted on the forum. A great part of this book was written when I was in Taiwan at my parents' place. I enjoyed my time with them and I want them to know that I love them very much. The rest of the book was written in Fremont, California with the love and support of my wife. Without that love and support, this book would not be what it is.

Introduction

The book you're holding focuses on Microsoft's Dynamic Language Runtime (DLR) and what it can do for you in your day-to-day programming work. Many think the DLR is an esoteric platform that matters only if you happen to be one of the very few who are implementing languages such as Python and Ruby atop the .NET Framework. That belief is far from the truth. The DLR puts a number of exciting capabilities at your disposal. Implementing languages is actually pretty far down on that list.

One of the most obvious things to do with the DLR is to mix and match code and objects from different languages. Do you have an object in Python that does what you need? Use the DLR to make that object usable from your C# code.

Going further, you can mix and match dynamic and compiled languages in ways that are convenient, that allow you to choose the best tool for the job at hand within your overall application. This ability to mix and match leads directly to using dynamic languages as scripting languages within your applications. Going even further, you can dive in and make the DLR your basis for implementing application- and domain-specific scripting languages.

Aspect-oriented programming and runtime code generation are two other techniques made possible by the DLR. You'll find examples of both in this book. You'll also find clear examples that show the details of using the DLR. You'll learn about core components such as LINQ expressions, call sites, binders, and dynamic objects. You'll see how to apply those components to the problem of combining dynamic and compiled languages into a single application. You'll end up with the ability to apply whatever language or language-library is most productive given the programming problem you're trying to solve at any given moment. You'll truly be able to apply the best tool to the job at hand.

Prerequisites

Chapter 1 describes the prerequisites in detail, explaining the software you need to install in order to mimic my own configuration so you can run the examples in this book. In general, though, you should be comfortable programming in C#. You should also know at least one of the common scripting languages, such as Python or Ruby. If you can compile and run a C# program and you can execute Python or Ruby code, you have what it takes to get the most out of this book.

Structure of the Book (or How this Book is Organized...)

This book consists of two parts:

Part I deals with the fundamentals. You are introduced to the DLR, and to the core functionality that the API provides. This is where you'll learn the mechanics of using the DLR.

Part II explores applying the DLR to various ends. You'll find chapters devoted to such topics as aspect-oriented programming, application scripting, domain-specific languages, meta-programming, and more.

Part I consists of six chapters. Chapter 1 stands out in that it gives you a whirlwind tour — code included! — showing all you can accomplish using the DLR. If you want to get the lay of the land, to know what the possibilities are, Chapter 1 is what you should read. Chapters 2-6 then go into detail on the various mechanics of using the DLR.

Part II also consists of six chapters. Here the emphasis is on applying the DLR to specific programming techniques. You'll begin, for example, by learning how the DLR helps enable aspect-oriented programming. You'll be introduced to STITCH, a domain-specific language implemented atop the DLR that makes it easier to host languages such as Python and Ruby from within your C# programs. And you'll learn about metaprogramming, application scripting, and how to run DLR applications on the Silverlight platform.

Obtaining the Source Code

Source code is available for the examples shown in this book. You can download that source code from the book's catalog page on the Apress web site. Here is the URL for that page:

`http://apress.com/book/view/1430230665`

Once there, look under the book's cover image for the catalog page section entitled "Book Resources," where you'll see a link for "Source Code." Click that link to download a zip archive containing the example code for this book.

When you have the download, refer to Chapter 1. There you'll find instructions on setting up the code examples. You'll also find a description of the directory structure used in the example archive.

PART 1

■ ■ ■

DLR Fundamentals

CHAPTER 1

■ ■ ■

Introduction to DLR

DLR stands for *dynamic language runtime*. Maybe you already know something about it and the reason you picked up this book is to learn how the DLR works and how to make use of it. If you haven't heard of the DLR, you may be wondering whether it's worth your time learning it. One reason people might regard the DLR as irrelevant to their work is that they think the DLR is for implementing new languages. And since most of us write programs to solve specific problems and very few of us implement languages, learning the DLR may not seem like a good investment. That was in fact my initial misconception when I first heard of the DLR, around the time it was announced in 2007. After some study, I quickly realized the broad applicability of the DLR in many areas of my day-to-day programming work.

Because of that potential misconception, I want to highlight some areas in which the DLR shines. The point I want to get across is that the DLR is not merely for running or implementing dynamic languages. It is also very useful for application scripting, meta-programming, aspect-oriented programming (AOP), building DSLs (domain-specific languages), unit test mocking, and a lot more. Instead of just throwing out those buzz words and iterating through them with dry discussions, I figure the best way to highlight the practical usefulness of the DLR is through some examples. So that's what this chapter will do. Normally an introductory chapter like this has a Hello World example. We will have not just one, but four, plus some demonstrations.

Since most people know the DLR as a platform for building and running dynamic languages, we'll start with a Hello World example of running a dynamic language. Next we'll show a Hello World example of building a dynamic language. We'll then take that language and show how to embed it in a host application written in C#. Finally, we'll end the series of Hello World examples with a REPL (read-eval-print-loop) console for the Hello World language. It might seem strange to use the building of a programming language as a Hello World example. After all, building a programming language is no trivial task. But, as you will see, because of the rich features the DLR provides, we can do all the things mentioned with very little code.

The series of Hello World examples is about using, embedding, and building programming languages. But the DLR also does a good job of enabling application scripting. The DLR makes it very easy to add scripting capacity to your applications. Users of your application can take advantage of popular dynamic languages such as IronPython and IronRuby to extend your application with custom capabilities, automate certain tasks, or integrate your application with other systems. If you like, you can choose to create your own domain-specific language and let users script in a syntax closer to the domain of your application. And that's what later chapters in this book will show you. In Chapter 10, you'll implement a fun WPF application that uses a physics engine to detect collisions between balls. You can write IronPython code to script the movement of balls. You can also write code in the DSL that Chapter 12 will explore, to do things like stopping and starting a ball. I'll give a preview of that WPF application in this chapter.

After that, we'll see how the DLR makes it very intuitive to work with data. The technique we'll use is often referred to as **builders**. In Chapter 5, we'll explore the XML builder library we'll use to build XML data.

Finally, we'll delve into the Aspect-Oriented Programming (AOP) framework covered in Chapter 7. AOP is a programming paradigm that is very well-suited to solving the problem of cross-cutting concerns. Common cross-cutting concerns in a software system are things like transaction management, security, auditing, performance monitoring, logging, and tracing, and the like. By virtue of addressing the problem of cross-cutting concerns in an elegant manner, AOP provides tremendous value in the design and architecture of software systems. As you'll see, one nice thing about the AOP framework is that it works across dynamic and static languages, and it's also integrated with Spring.NET's AOP framework.

Even though this chapter will not get into the details of the demonstrations, I hope after seeing the examples and demonstrations, you'll feel that the benefits and applicability of DLR advocated here are more real and tangible. Without further ado, let's begin by setting up the software components needed for running the examples.

Setting Up Code Examples

If you download and unzip the file that contains this book's code examples, you'll see the following file structure:

```
ProDLR
    lib
        Antlr
        DLR
        ...
    src
        Examples
            Chapter 1
            Chapter 2
            ...
```

The Examples folder contains a subfolder for each chapter where you can find all of a chapter's code examples. Most of the code examples depend on one or more software components. The lib folder has a subfolder for each of the software components used in this book. You'll need to download those components and put the needed assembly files into the subfolders under the lib folder. The next section will describe what you need to do to download the DLR assemblies and put them into the lib\DLR folder. For the other software components, I'll describe how to set them up when we encounter them in later chapters. Throughout the book, I'll assume that the ProDLR folder is placed under C:\. If you choose to place it in a different folder, you'll need to substitute the path with your own whenever I refer to it in the book.

Software Requirements

For most of the examples in this book, you'll need the following software to follow along:

- .NET 4.0 SDK: You can download this from Microsoft's web site and follow the instructions there to install it.

- Visual Studio 2010 Express: Although you technically don't need to install this, it is highly recommended as it will make following the code examples much easier. The installation of Visual Studio 2010 Express also installs the .NET 4.0 SDK, so if you choose to install this component, you don't need to install the .NET 4.0 SDK separately.

- DLR, IronPython, and IronRuby: You can go to the DLR project web site at CodePlex to download all three in one bundle. At the time of this writing, the download page of the DLR CodePlex website provides only source code, no binaries. The next section will describe where to get the binaries and how to install them.

The DLR, IronPython, and IronRuby can run on .NET 2.0. To do so, you'll need to download different binaries from the IronPython and IronRuby websites. As we go through the installation of the DLR, IronPython, and IronRuby in the next section, I'll point out the binaries you need if you want to use .NET 2.0 as the target platform. The code examples in this book are developed to run on .NET 4.0, but Chapter 3 shows you how to target both .NET 2.0 and .NET 4.0.

Installing the DLR, IronPython, and IronRuby

Even though the files you download from the DLR CodePlex web site contain only the source code, you can get the DLR binaries from IronPython's or IronRuby's CodePlex web sites. Here are the steps you need to take to get the release bits of DLR, IronPython, and IronRuby.

1. Go to ironpython.codeplex.com/ and download IronPython 2.6.1 for .NET 4.0. That's the version I use for this book's code examples; it's an .msi file. You simply double-click it and follow the instructions to install IronPython. From now on, I'll assume that it's installed in C:\Program Files (x86)\IronPython 2.6 for .NET 4.0\. If you choose to install it in a different folder, you'll need to substitute the path with your own whenever I refer to it in the book. If you need to develop DLR-based applications that run on .NET 2.0, download IronPython 2.6.1 for .NET 2.0 SP1 instead.

2. Go to http://ironruby.codeplex.com/ and download IronRuby 1.0 for .NET 4.0 (ironruby-1.0v4.msi). That is the version of IronRuby I use in this book. Again simply double-click on it and follow the instruction to install it. I'll assume that it's installed in C:\Program Files (x86)\IronRuby 1.0v4\. If you need to develop DLR-based applications that run on .NET 2.0, download IronRuby 1.0 for .NET 2.0 SP1 instead.

3. Copy the following files from C:\Program Files (x86)\IronRuby 1.0v4\bin to C:\ProDLR\lib\DLR\release:

    - IronRuby.dll

    - IronRuby.Libraries.dll

    - Microsoft.Dynamic.dll (This and the next assembly are the DLR version 1.0 binaries).

    - Microsoft.Scripting.dll

4.   Copy the following files from C:\Program Files (x86)\IronPython 2.6 for .NET 4.0\
     to C:\ProDLR\lib\DLR\release:

   • IronPython.dll

   • IronPython.Modules.dll

To make it convenient to run the Read-Eval-Print-Loop (REPL) consoles of IronPython and
IronRuby, you might want to make sure that "C:\Program Files (x86)\IronPython 2.6 for .NET 4.0" and
"C:\Program Files (x86)\IronRuby 1.0v4\bin" are included in your Path environment variable.

Hello World Examples

Now let's get started with our four Hello World examples that run, build, and embed DLR-based
dynamic languages. Let's have some fun!

Hello World from a Dynamic Language

We'll first look at an implementation of a Hello World program in a dynamic language. IronPython is one
of the most mature DLR-based dynamic languages. There are other implementations of the Python
language, such as CPython and Jython. But those are based on their own runtimes, not on the DLR.
Figure 1-1 shows IronPython code that prints "Hello World" to IronPython's interactive console.

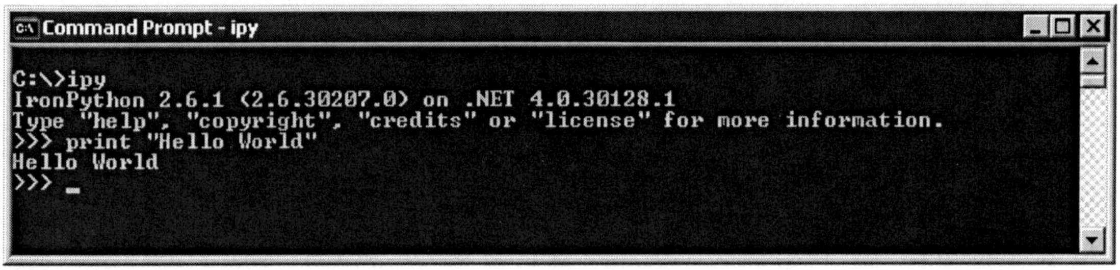

```
C:\>ipy
IronPython 2.6.1 (2.6.30207.0) on .NET 4.0.30128.1
Type "help", "copyright", "credits" or "license" for more information.
>>> print "Hello World"
Hello World
>>>
```

Figure 1-1. Hello World from IronPython

That looks fairly straightforward. Like most dynamic languages, IronPython comes with an
interactive console that reads the code you type in, evaluates that code, prints out the result of the
evaluation, and waits for the next code snippet. This is commonly called a REPL (Read-Eval-Print-Loop)
console. IronPython's REPL console is the ipy.exe executable file. If you've put the right paths in the
Windows Path environment variable as mentioned earlier, you should be able to just type ipy in the
command console to execute ipy.exe. When prompted for input by >>>, you type the code print "Hello
World", and the result of evaluating that code is printed in the next line.

Creating a "Hello" Language

Next, we'll look at implementing our own language. Yes, we'll create a whole, new language just for
"Hello World." We will implement a DLR-based language that we'll call the Hello language, and it will
print "Hello World" to the console no matter what Hello code you write. In other words, the language
accepts any input code as valid Hello code and responds to that input code by printing out "Hello

World". Because any Hello code is valid, we don't need a parser to parse the code. Nor do we need to interpret or compile any code. You can find the source code for this example is in the HelloLanguage project of the Chapter 1 solution.

Implementing a DLR-based language as simple as the Hello language means we need to implement two things: a language context and a script code. I'll explain language context and script code in more detail when we get to the discussion of the DLR Hosting API in Chapter 6. For the time being, we can understand language context as something that provides an entry point to a language's compilation capability. As for script code, just think of it as a representation of a language's compiled code for now.

Listing 1-1 shows the language context implementation for the Hello language. All of the code is boilerplate except the line in bold. We can see that a language context provides an entry point method `CompileSourceCode` that invokes the source code compilation capability of a language. The source code is represented as an instance of type `SourceUnit` and passed as an input argument to the `CompileSourceCode` method. Our implementation of the `CompileSourceCode` method simply creates an instance of `HelloScriptCode,` which represents the result of compiling the input source code, i.e., the `SourceUnit` instance.

Listing 1-2 shows the code for the `HelloScriptCode` class. `HelloScriptCode` has a method `Run,` which is supposed to know how to run Hello code. Since running Hello code means printing "Hello World" to the console, we do just that in the `Run` method and that's all. We have completed our first DLR-based language.

Listing 1-1. Hello Language Context

```
public class HelloContext : LanguageContext
{
    public HelloContext(ScriptDomainManager domainManager,
                IDictionary<string, object> options)
            : base(domainManager)
    { }

    public override ScriptCode CompileSourceCode(SourceUnit sourceUnit,
                CompilerOptions options, ErrorSink errorSink)
    {
        return new HelloScriptCode(sourceUnit);
    }
}
```

Listing 1-2. Hello Language Script Code

```
public class HelloScriptCode : ScriptCode
{
public HelloScriptCode(SourceUnit sourceUnit) : base(sourceUnit)
{}

public override object Run(Scope scope)
{
  Console.WriteLine("Hello");
  return null;
}
}
```

Embedding the Hello Language

Now that we've built a language, let's put it into use. In this example, we'll embed the Hello language in a host application written in C#. In this case, C# is said to be the host language. To achieve the goal, we need to write the C# host application, of course, and to set up proper configurations in the App.config file so the C# host application can locate the Hello language.

Listing 1-3 shows the configurations you need to put into App.config. Don't worry too much if you don't fully understand every line of the code shown here. We'll delve into it more when we discuss the DLR Hosting API in Chapter 6. Essentially, the configurations tell the DLR runtime that there is a language called Hello and that its language context is the type HelloLanguage.HelloContext we saw in the previous example.

Listing 1-3. App.config for Hosting the Hello Language

```
<configuration>
<configSections>
<section name="microsoft.scripting"
type="Microsoft.Scripting.Hosting.Configuration.Section, Microsoft.Scripting,
Version=1.0.0.0, Culture=neutral, PublicKeyToken=31bf3856ad364e35" />
</configSections>
<microsoft.scripting>
  <languages>
   <language names="Hello"
        extensions=".hello"
        displayName="Hello 1.0"
                type="HelloLanguage.HelloContext,HelloLanguage, Version=1.0.0.0,
Culture=neutral" />
   </languages>
</microsoft.scripting>
</configuration>
```

With the App.config file ready, there isn't much left to do. Listing 1-4 shows the C# code for the application that hosts the Hello language. Line 3 in Listing 1-4 reads the configuration information from App.config and creates an instance of the ScriptRuntime class. Given the information in App.config, line 4 is able to call our Hello language context behind the scenes and return an instance of ScriptEngine. The code in line 5 passes in "any text" as the input Hello code to the script engine. Line 6 calls the Execute method of ScriptSource to execute the Hello code and the words "Hello World" are printed to the console.

Listing 1-4. Method Inside Program.cs for Hosting the Hello Language

```
1)  private static void ExecuteHelloCode()
2)  {
3)      ScriptRuntime scriptRuntime = ScriptRuntime.CreateFromConfiguration();
4)      ScriptEngine engine = scriptRuntime.GetEngine("Hello");
5)      ScriptSource script = engine.CreateScriptSourceFromString("any text");
6)      script.Execute(engine.CreateScope());
7)      Console.ReadLine();
8)  }
```

Implementing REPL for the Hello Language

With very little effort, we can provide a REPL console for the Hello language like IronPython's. For this task, we'll leverage the ConsoleHost class that the DLR provides. Listing 1-5 shows how to use this class to implement the console.

Listing 1-5. REPL Console

```
class HelloConsole : ConsoleHost
{
    protected override Type Provider
    {
        get { return typeof(HelloContext); }
    }
}
```

As Listing 1-5 shows, all you need to do is override the Provider property and make it return the type HelloLanguage.HelloContext. The code is so simple because the ConsoleHost class does most of the heavy lifting, like printing the >>> prompt, reading user input, and calling HelloContext to execute that input. The REPL console in this example does not run by itself. We need the code in Listing 1-6 to run it.

Listing 1-6. Run the Hello REPL Console

```
private static void RunHelloREPL(string[] args)
{
    (new HelloConsole()).Run(args);
}
```

Figure 1-2 shows the result of running the program. As you can see, it doesn't matter what input code we type, the Hello REPL console always prints "Hello" to the screen. To exit the REPL, press Ctrl+Z.

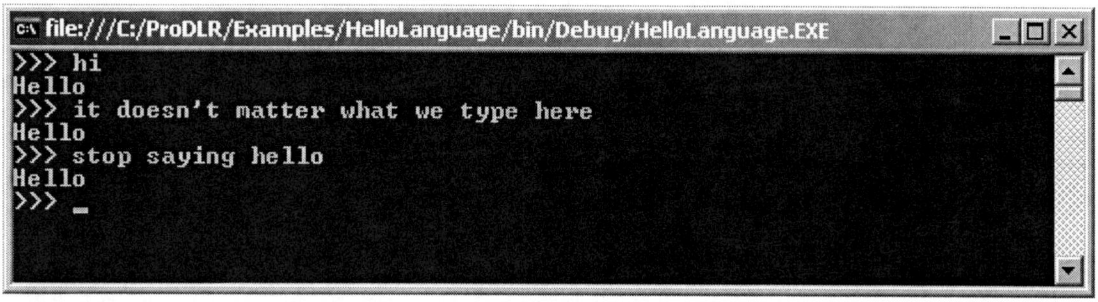

```
file:///C:/ProDLR/Examples/HelloLanguage/bin/Debug/HelloLanguage.EXE
>>> hi
Hello
>>> it doesn't matter what we type here
Hello
>>> stop saying hello
Hello
>>> _
```

Figure 1-2. Running the Hello language's REPL console

Practical Uses for the DLR

The next few subsections show some of the code examples you'll develop as you follow along in this book. The main purpose of these demonstrations is to get across the point that the DLR is more broadly applicable than for just implementing and running dynamic languages. Furthermore, I hope the demonstrations will whet your appetite and make you look forward to the later chapters where we'll explain the source code in detail. I'll indicate for each demonstration the chapter it belongs to.

Application Scripting and DSL

Figure 1-3 shows a screen capture of the WPF application we'll develop in chapter 10. The application uses the Farseer Physics Engine to detect collisions between moving balls. The Farseer Physics Engine is a project hosted on the CodePlex site. It's a 2D physics engine that is very fun to work with. It's even more fun when we introduce scripting and extensibility into the application we build. For example, we can implement a domain-specific language (DSL) with commands such as Start Ball or Stop Ball. Users of the application will be able to write some script code to control ball movements.

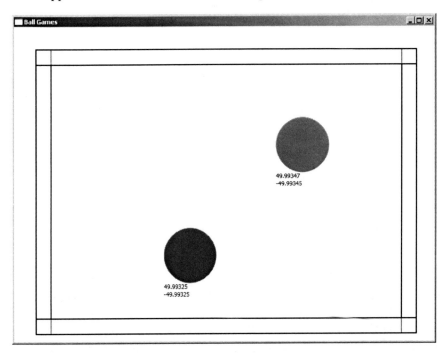

Figure 1-3. A scriptable WPF application that does collision detection

XML Builder

DLR makes it possible to design fluent APIs for working with certain kinds of data. For example, the "static" classes like XmlDocument, XmlElement, and so forth in the .NET Class Library have methods for getting an XML element or attribute by name. With the DLR, we can implement a more fluent API whose method names are directly the names of the XML elements we want to access. Listing 1-7 shows what that looks like when we use a dynamic library to build an XML snippet.

Listing 1-7. Using a Fluent API to Build an XML Snippet

```
dynamic builder = new XmlBuilder();
String xml = builder.
        Customers.b
          .Customer(firstName: "John", lastName: "Smith").b
            .Address.b
                .Street("123 Main St")
                .City("Alcatraz")
                .State("CA")
                .Zip("55555")
            .d
          .d
        .d.build();
```

The output of running the code in Listing 1-7 is shown below. As you can see in Listing 1-7, instead of calling methods that access XML elements by name, we access those names directly as if they are methods. Of course, the library works with any XML data you might want to build. I didn't implement the library in such a way that it recognizes only the Customer, Address, and other elements shown in the example. That would be cheating.

```
<Customers>
    <Customer firstName="John" lastName="Smith">
        <Address>
            <Street>123 Main St</Street>
            <City>Alcatraz</City>
            <State>CA</State>
            <Zip>55555</Zip>
        </Address>
    </Customer>
</Customers>
```

The DLR is not the only component that allows the design of fluent APIs like the one shown in the example. The Groovy language has this capability too and people have implemented many builders in Groovy for working with different kinds of data. Besides XML, the builder technique can also be applied to data sources such as file systems, registry entries, IT management, and more. For example, instead of a library that accesses files and folders in a file system by name, we can imagine a dynamic, fluent library that accesses files and folders as if their names are methods. Instead of accessing registry entries by name, we can access them as if those names are methods. You see the pattern.

Aspect-Oriented Programming

Aspect-oriented programming (AOP) is a programming paradigm for solving the problem of cross-cutting concerns, such as transaction management, auditing, security, logging, and the like. There are several techniques for implementing an AOP system. Some implementations use compile-time code weaving. Some use load-time code weaving. Some use runtime method interception. And most use a combination of these approaches. In Chapter 7, we'll see how to implement a DLR-based AOP framework that works across both static and dynamic languages. The AOP approach used in that chapter is runtime method interception. I will have more to say about the different AOP approaches when we get to Chapter 7. Here I'll just demonstrate what it looks like when we use the AOP framework to log the activities that take place in both a static object and a dynamic object.

Listing 1-8 contains two objects, customer and employee. The employee object is a typical static object that we are all familiar with. Line 7 obtains the employee object from the Spring.NET container (because our AOP framework is integrated with Spring.NET's AOP framework). The other object, customer, is a dynamic object created in line 3.

Listing 1-8. AOP-Based Logging for Both Static and Dynamic Objects

```
1)    static void Main(string[] args)
2)    {
3)        dynamic customer = new Customer("John", 5);
4)        Console.WriteLine("Customer {0} is {1} years old.\n", customer.Name, customer.Age);
5)
6)        IApplicationContext context = new XmlApplicationContext("application-config.xml");
7)        IEmployee employee = (IEmployee)context["employeeBob"];
8)        Console.WriteLine("Employee {0} is {1} years old.", employee.Name, employee.Age);
9)        Console.ReadLine();
10)   }
```

Figure 1-4 shows the result of running the program in Listing 1-8. As you can see, for both the customer and employee objects, the same AOP logging logic is applied and the console shows log statements for both objects.

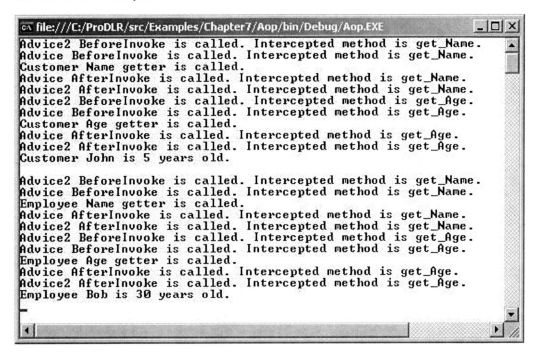

Figure 1-4. Running Listing 1-8 produces logging for both a dynamic and a static object.

Now that you've seen the Hello World examples and some practical applications of the DLR, I will introduce the DLR itself and describe what it is. Of course, the name Dynamic Language Runtime conveys a lot about what DLR is. So let's kick off the discussion by looking at each of the words that make up the name, starting with *runtime*.

Runtime

The DLR is a runtime—that's pretty obvious. A runtime is a software component that does its work at the time a program runs. Let's say you use the .NET SDK in the development of your program. The SDK comes with both runtime components and development tools. You use the development tools like the C# compiler to develop and build your application. When you ship your application to customers, you don't need to include those tools in your distribution. In contrast, you do need to include the runtime components of the SDK because your application depends on them to function properly.

So the fact that the DLR is a runtime means that if we build our applications on top of the DLR, we need to distribute it together with our applications. More specifically, it means we will need to redistribute assemblies such as Microsoft.Scripting.dll and Microsoft.Dynamic.dll, two of the assemblies that make up the DLR.

Different runtime components do different kinds of work. One major kind of work the DLR does is executing expressions, and that's something we'll explore in great length in the next chapter. For now, you can think of expressions as a kind of intermediate language like MSIL (Microsoft Intermediate Language). Expressions are to the DLR what MSIL is to the CLR (Common Language Runtime). There are many other runtimes that execute code. Just as the CLR executes MSIL code compiled from C# or VB.NET programs, the JVM (Java Virtual Machine) executes Java byte code, and IronPython runtime interprets Python code.

The DLR executes expressions by interpreting them or by compiling them into MSIL. If the DLR compiles expressions into MSIL, the MSIL code will be sent to the CLR for execution. Figure 1-5 shows this flow: The tree at the left is fed into the DLR's expression compiler. Out of the compiler comes some MSIL code, which is fed into the CLR for execution. As you can see, DLR is built on top of CLR and leverages CLR to execute the MSIL code it generates.

Figure 1-5. How the DLR executes expressions

As a runtime, the CLR provides services, such as garbage collection, runtime type checking, code access security, etc. Like the CLR, the DLR provides many services, including:

- Hosting API

- Debugging API

- Call site caching

- Expression compilation and interpretation

- Meta-object protocol for dynamic language interoperability

Besides the services listed above, because the DLR is built on top of the CLR, applications based on the DLR automatically benefit from the CLR's services. For example, .NET Application Domain and Remoting are leveraged in the DLR Hosting API to allow hosting dynamic languages in separate process or on a remote machine. The CLR's garbage collection is readily available to dynamic languages built on the DLR. If you were going to implement a language without taking advantage of the DLR, CLR, or JVM for that matter, imagine how much work you'd have to do to, for example, implement a garbage collector for your language's runtime.

While we are on the subject of runtimes and how they (i.e., the CLR and DLR) can be built on one another, let's throw IronPython into the picture. As mentioned earlier, IronPython is a runtime that interprets Python code. It is built on DLR. So when we run IronPython code, there will be three language runtimes, CLR, DLR, and IronPython, working together one on top of another.

Runtime vs. Run Time

To avoid confusion, I'd like to make clear the distinction between the word runtime and the phrase "run time." Runtime in our context is a software component. *Run time,* on the other hand, means the time when our code runs. If you say "my program throws an exception at run time," people will understand that as "your program throws an exception when it runs." However, it would be really odd if you say "my program throws an exception at runtime." The word runtime and the phrase 'run time' might appear to be interchangeable in other books or articles. The distinction we make here is only for the purpose of our discussions throughout the book.

Run Time vs. Compile Time

The terms "run time" and "compile time" (or compile-time) are often used to indicate whether something occurs when a program is executed, or when it is compiled. Run time is usually contrasted with compile-time. Run time means the time when the code runs. Compile time means the time when code is being compiled. In this section, we will compare run time and compile time by looking at the typical flow of activities of each.

Figure 1-6 shows the typical flow of compile-time activities. Basically, at compile time the compiler takes source code as input and parses it. If the code does not conform to the syntax rules of the language, the compiler stops and reports errors. If the code passes the parsing phase, the compiler typically creates an intermediate representation of the source code in the form of a tree data structure. The tree data structure is often called an AST (abstract syntax tree). The compiler uses the AST to perform code analysis, such as type checking and possibly some code optimizations. In the end, the compiler generates the output binaries. Different compilers generate different binary files. C# compiler generates .NET assemblies; Java compiler, JVM byte code; and C++ compiler, machine code.

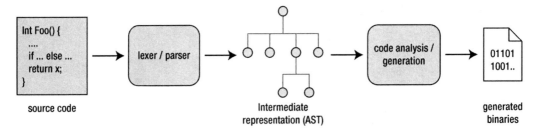

Figure 1-6. Typical flow of compile-time activities

Run time flow basically picks up where the compile-time flow left off. It takes the binaries generated as the final output of compilation and executes them. Figure 1-7 shows the typical flow of run-time activities. The flow begins with the runtime loading the binaries into memory. If the binaries are compiled from C++ code, they will contain machine code and the C++ runtime will directly execute the machine code. If the binaries are compiled from C# or VB.NET, the binaries will contain .NET IL and the CLR will at its discretion interpret the IL or JIT (just-in-time) compile the IL to machine code.

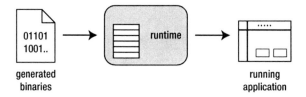

Figure 1-7. Typical flow of run-time activities

So far, I have described the flow of run-time and compile-time activities in general. Let's look at them again, this time specific to DLR-based languages and to the DLR itself. We will look at DLR-based languages first and then at the DLR itself.

A DLR-based language may or may not have a compiler. Even if it has one, you may have the choice of not using it. For example, IronPython provides a compiler you can use to compile IronPython code into IL. But depending on the situation, you might not always want to do the compilation. For example, in a scenario where you provide scripting capability and let users write IronPython code to automate or extend your application, since the IronPython code is written by users, you probably want to make it easier by not requiring them to compile their code. The code snippet below shows the IronPython code that compiles the source file sample.py into the .NET assembly file sample.dll.

```
import clr
clr.CompileModules("sample.dll", "sample.py")
```

Normally a DLR-based language like IronPython parses input source code, builds its own AST, translates that AST to DLR's AST, and invokes the DLR to interpret or compile the DLR AST. Figure 1-8 shows the flow of compiling Python code into MSIL.

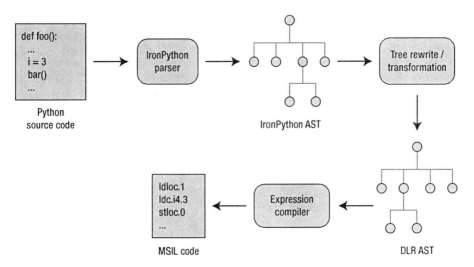

Figure 1-8. *IronPython source file compilation flow*

The DLR AST shown in the figure is nothing new, just the DLR expressions mentioned earlier. They are implemented as classes in the `System.Linq.Expressions` namespace inside the `System.Core.dll` assembly. The DLR AST in Figure 1-8 serves as input to the DLR expression compiler, which is implemented in the class `Microsoft.Scripting.Ast.LambdaCompiler`. Compiling expressions is not an easy task. Instead of doing all the work of compiling expressions by itself, `LambdaCompiler` leverages classes in the `Microsoft.Scripting.Generation` namespace to compile expressions into MSIL code. Those classes in turn use classes in the `System.Reflection.Emit` namespace, which you'll be familiar with if you've done some work at the MSIL level. The DLR, at its discretion, can also decide to interpret expressions instead of compiling them.

Dynamic vs. Static

We looked at the word runtime in the previous section. Let's look at another word that's part of DLR's name—*dynamic*. The word "dynamic" is in contrast to the word "static." In our context, we are talking about dynamic and static languages. One fundamental question we need to answer is, how do we decide which languages are dynamic languages and which are static? On the surface, it might seem that a language is dynamic if you don't need to specify types for things like function arguments and variables when you write code in that language. That is, however, not true, and a counter example is F#. F# does not require you to provide type information in your code, yet it's a static language. It enforces type rules by performing type inference and type checking at compile time.

Another criterion that might seem like a good indicator is whether the language has a compiler. As it turns out, this is true in many but not all cases. We saw a counter example of this in the previous section. There we mentioned that you can compile IronPython code into IL—and IronPython is a dynamic language.

In fact, whether a language is dynamic or static is a matter of degree. Languages that we generally regard as static, such as C# and Java, are not entirely static. I'll give an example of what I mean by that shortly. Let's explain what we mean by dynamic and static first. In the context of programming languages, *being dynamic means doing things at run time*. In contrast, being static means doing things at compile time. With that in mind, an example of C# or Java being dynamic is array bounds checking. The C# compiler by design does not check and catch the following error:

```
String[] names = new String[] {"John", "Mary"};
String name = names[10];
```

The C# compiler will give green light to the code above and we will get an array index out-of-bounds exception at run time. As you can see, the checking of array index bounds is not performed statically at compile time, but dynamically at run time.

So why doesn't the C# compiler catch the error? After all, isn't it pretty obvious that the array contains only two items? While the array index out-of- bounds error is obvious in the code snippet above, that same error (if it exists) might not be obvious in this code:

```
String[] names = GetAllNamesFromDatabase();
String name = names[10];
```

The C# compiler simply can't know how many names there are in the database unless it runs the code. The array bounds checking is a classic example of activities that even static languages would perform at run time. Moreover, there's the new "dynamic" keyword that's been added to C# 4.0. With that new feature, it becomes even clearer that there's often no black and white divide when it comes to deciding whether a language is dynamic.

If we accept that whether a language is dynamic or static is a matter of degree, here are two key factors people often use to determine that degree:

- dynamic typing
- dynamic dispatch (aka late binding)

If a language exhibits some or all of both, it's often regarded as being more dynamic. We will go over these items in the next sections. In each section, we will describe the subject in general and also specifically as it relates to the DLR.

Dynamic Typing

Both static and dynamic languages can be strongly typed. The main difference is when they do type checking. Strongly typed static languages perform type checking at compile time while strongly typed dynamic languages perform type checking at run time. It would be much clearer if we called them dynamically checked and statically checked languages. But the terms static and dynamic languages are already in wide use.

Besides that main difference, there are two other key type-related differences between static and dynamic languages: changing types of variables and changing the definition of types. Let's look at some examples.

The C# code below causes a compilation error because C#, like most static languages, does not allow you to change the type of a variable.

```
//explicit static typing. Causes compilation error.
int i = 3;
i = "hello";
```

The following C# code again causes a compilation error, even though we use the *var* keyword to declare the type of variable i. The difference between this code and the previous is that the previous code snippet explicitly tells the C# compiler that the type of variable i is int whereas this code tells the C# compiler to infer the type of variable i for us. Sure enough the C# compiler is able to do the inference and it dutifully reports back a compilation error to us.

```
//implicit static typing. Causes compilation error.
var i = 3;
i = "hello";
```

In C# 4.0, there is a new language keyword called *dynamic*. If we use that keyword to declare the type of a variable, we are telling the C# compiler that the variable's type can change. The code snippet below shows an example. The variable i is not fixed to a single type. In other words, its type is dynamic, not static, and the C# compiler won't bother doing type checking on the variable i at compile time. If we compare this example to the previous two examples, the difference should be clear. Note that all three of these code snippets are strongly typed. The first two are strongly typed and their type correctness is checked at compile time. The last code snippet is also strongly typed and its type correctness is checked at run time.

```
//dynamic typing. No compilation error. No runtime error.
dynamic i = 3;
i = "hello";
```

C# allows variables to take on different types. Dynamic languages do that too, and more. In dynamic languages, it's not only variables that can take on different types; statements like if and switch can have different types as well. The Python example below shows an if statement that returns a number in its if-branch and a string in its else-branch. The if statement resides in a function called callIf. The function is called once with the integer 6, which causes the if-branch to be executed. The function is then called with the integer 4 to cause the else-branch to be executed. If you do something like this in C#, you'll get a compilation error because the C# language requires that you return objects of the same type in both branches.

```
def callIf(n):
    if n > 5:
        return 5
    else:
        return "hello"

x = callIf(6)
print x
print type(x)

x = callIf(4)
print x
print type(x)
```

The result of running this code looks like this:

```
5
<type 'int'>
```

```
Hello
<type 'str'>
```

The other major difference between static and dynamic languages is changing a type's definition at run time. Static languages typically don't allow that. With dynamic languages like Python and Ruby, we can change a type's definition by, say, adding new methods to it. Listing 1-9 shows some Ruby code that adds new methods to a type's definition at both the class level and instance level. The example first defines a class called Customer. The Customer class has an initialize method and a callRep method. The initialize method is a special method in Ruby. It is called after an instance of the class is created to initialize the newly created instance. In this example, the Customer class has a member variable called name. The initialize method sets the member variable name to the value passed to it. The callRep method of the Customer class simply prints a message to the console indicating that the customer's representative is called.

Once the Customer class is defined, the example code in Listing 1-9 creates two customer objects: bill and bob. Here's where things get interesting. Notice that bob's callRep method is redefined to print a different message that indicates the customer has no representative assigned to him. This is an example of redefining a method at the instance level. It's quite common to be able to do that in dynamic languages, but not in static languages. Because the callRep method is redefined only for bob, bill is not affected.

Next, the code shows an example of modifying a class's definition. It does so by adding a new method called makeReferral to the Customer class. Because the new method is added to the Customer class, both bob and bill will have that method defined for them. Again, changing a class's definition at run time is quite common in dynamic languages, but not so in static languages.

Listing 1-9. Adding Methods at Class Level and Instance Level

```ruby
class Customer
  def initialize(name)
    @name = name
  end

  def callRep
    puts "#{@name}'s rep is called"
  end
end

bob = Customer.new("Bob")
bill = Customer.new("Bill")

# We can redefine a method at instance level.
def bob.callRep
  puts "#{@name} has no rep assigned"
end

bob.callRep
bill.callRep

# We can add a new method to a class.
class Customer
  def makeReferral
    puts "#{@name} makes a referral"
```

```
    end
end

bob.makeReferral
bill.makeReferral
```

To run the code in Listing 1-9, first save the code into a file called something like `Customer.rb`. Then open a command console, navigate to the folder where the file `Customer.rb` resides, and simply execute `ir Customer.rb`. In the command, "ir" refers to the REPL executable of IronRuby. And I'm assuming that "C:\Program Files (x86)\IronRuby 1.0v4\bin" is in your Path environment variable. When running the code in Listing 1-9, you should see output like the following:

```
Bob has no rep assigned
Bill's rep is called
Bob makes a referral
Bill makes a referral
```

Dynamic Dispatch

When we do coding, we generally write code that calls a method, creates a new instance of a class, applies an arithmetic operator on some operands, and so forth. A language compiler or interpreter needs to know what to do when it encounters that code. When a line of code is a method invocation, the compiler/interpreter needs to know which method of which class to invoke. The method might be overloaded and, if that's the case, the compiler/interpreter needs to resolve that and pick the right method based on the input arguments passed to the method invocation. Similarly, when the line of code is an application of an operator on some operands, the compiler/interpreter needs to know which operator it should use. The operator can be overloaded for operands of different types. If that's the case, then again some kind of resolution based on the operands' types is necessary. The resolutions we talk about here are also called method bindings or method dispatches. In static languages, the bindings are done at compile time and because compile time happens earlier than run time, the bindings are also called early bindings. In dynamic languages, the bindings are done at run time and therefore are often called late bindings. Another commonly used term that's interchangeable with late binding is dynamic dispatch. The C# code below is an example of early binding. At compile time, the C# compiler knows the type of the variable name is `String`. When we call the `ToLower` method on `name`, the compiler knows that we're calling the `ToLower` method of the `String` class. It will also check and make sure that the `String` class has a `ToLower` method that takes no input arguments and returns a `String` instance.

```
String name = "Bob";
String lowercaseName = name.ToLower();
```

The IronPython code below is an example of late binding. Basically, all of the things the C# compiler does to the previous C# code snippet are now done at run time by the IronPython runtime.

```
name = "Bob";
lowercaseName = name.ToLower();
```

You don't need to supply type information in the Python code and there is no type checking during development. But when you run the code, the IronPython runtime performs similar type checking and method binding that the C# compiler does to the C# code at compile time.

Language

The final word we haven't talked about that makes up the name of the DLR is *language*. A programming language—or a human language, for that matter—essentially consists of two parts: **syntax** and **semantics**. Syntax is the form. Semantics is the meaning of the form. For example, in English, the literal form of the sentence "Roses are red" is in the realm of syntax. Its semantics is the meaning we associate with it, the fact that roses are red.

Different programming languages define different forms of the if statement. The forms look similar, but they are not exactly the same. If you take one language's form of the if statement and use it in another language, that other language won't recognize that form and it will throw an error when it tries to parse the if statement. However, although if statements in different languages differ in their forms, they pretty much have the same semantic meaning. This is analogous to human languages. English, Chinese, and Spanish each have a syntactic form for writing down the sentence "Roses are red," and those forms all have the same meaning.

This observation of syntax and semantics leads very well to what the DLR provides. Because syntactic forms usually vary from language to language, the DLR doesn't restrict you to any specific form when you design a DLR-based language. You are totally free in defining the syntax of your language and in parsing that syntax. You define a language's syntax by specifying its grammar rules. In English, the sentence "Roses are red" is syntactically valid because it obeys the grammar rules of English. The sentence "Roses are not flowers" is also grammatically correct. But if you say it, you'll get "run time exceptions" (people frowning at you) because the sentence does not make sense semantically.

Since different if statements in different programming languages have the same semantic meaning, it's not surprising that the DLR provides a common semantics model for all DLR-based languages. That common semantics model is **DLR expressions**. When a DLR-based language maps its syntactic forms to DLR expressions, it essentially defines the semantics of those syntactic forms. DLR expressions play a pivotal role in the overall DLR architecture. It's the component that stitches together all the other core DLR components and makes the whole larger than the sum of the parts. Understanding DLR expressions is crucial in understanding how DLR works, and we will delve into them in the next chapter.

DLR expressions are a superset of LINQ expressions. In terms of implementation, LINQ expressions are the classes in the System.Linq.Expressions namespace of the System.Core.dll assembly. The DLR adds some expression classes of its own on top of LINQ expressions. Those DLR expressions are packaged in the Microsoft.Scripting.Ast namespace of the Microsoft.Dynamic.dll assembly. Throughout this book, I will use the terms DLR expressions and LINQ expressions interchangeably.

Although I just said that DLR expressions offer a common semantics model for all DLR-based languages, you can view them and use them as a syntax model if you like. That might seem confusing at first, but it's in fact not as blurry as it seems. Expressions are just objects. If we use the DLR runtime to execute them, then they have semantics and those are the semantics defined by the DLR. However, if we don't use the DLR to execute the expressions and instead interpret the expressions ourselves, those expressions are just a form of syntax up to us as to how we want to interpret them.

The LINQ query-provider mechanism is a good example of using LINQ expressions as a syntax model. Figure 1-9 shows what we mean by that statement, using LINQ to SQL as an example.

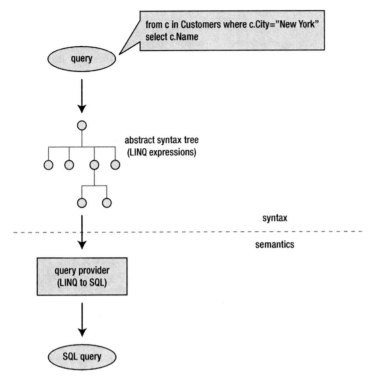

Figure 1-9. Using expressions as a syntax model

In the figure, the overall query process begins with the LINQ query at the top. The query is to retrieve the names of all customers who live in New York. It is transformed into a LINQ expression tree whose meaning is still open for interpretation. When the expression tree crosses the dashed line and reaches the LINQ to SQL query provider, it will then have the semantic meaning the query provider gives it. The query provider will interpret the expression tree according to the semantic meaning it has for the tree and the result of that is a SQL database query that can be executed to retrieve customers who live in New York.

Programming Languages in Practice

I just said that a programming language is essentially syntax plus semantics. Well, that's essentially true, but it's practically not true. Practically, using a programming language is more than just knowing the language's syntax and semantics. More often than not, you'll need a nice code editor that gives help with syntax, a debugger that allows you to step in and out of the code, libraries so that you don't need to code everything from scratch, a unit testing framework for obvious reasons, and maybe an IDE that integrates all the different pieces together in a nice and intuitive way to improve your already remarkable productivity even further. In addition to all those, you might also want to have tools for doing static code analysis, unit test coverage, performance benchmarks, and more. Table 1-1 contrasts C# with typical DLR-based languages. The table shows what you get with C# compared with what you typically need to provide if you are to implement a DLR-based language. The idea is to give you a feeling for the amount of work needed to implement a DLR-based language that has the tooling support commonly seen in a language like C#.

Table 1-1. C# versus DLR-based Languages

Facet	C#	DLR-Based Language
Compiler/interpreter C#	compiler	You are free to use your favorite software tools and components to build the language's lexer/parser. You will typically define the language's semantics by mapping the language's syntax tree to DLR expressions.
Runtime	C# uses CLR as the runtime.	Your language can use DLR, CLR as the runtime.*
Code editor	Visual Studio's code editor for C#	The DLR does not provide any feature for implementing a language's source code editor.
Debugger	Visual Studio's debugger for C#	You can leverage the DLR Debugging API.*
Libraries	.NET libraries from Microsoft and third parties are accessible to C# code.	.NET libraries from Microsoft and third parties are accessible to code written in a DLR-based language.*
Unit test framework	NUnit and others	Developers who write code in a DLR-based language can use NUnit and others as the unit test frameworks for testing their code. Most unit test frameworks are software libraries and all .NET libraries are accessible to code written in a DLR-based language.
IDE	Visual Studio	The DLR does not provide any feature for implementing an IDE or integrating into an existing IDE for your language.
Static code analysis	FxCop	The DLR does not provide any feature for implementing a static code analyzer for your language.
REPL, embedded in other languages	C# does not have a REPL console. C# can't be easily embedded in other languages.	DLR Hosting API allows dynamic languages to easily support REPL and to be embedded in other languages.*

In Table 1-1, the cells with an asterisk are the areas in which I think DLR provides the most value. As you can see, a language has a lot of aspects besides syntax and semantics. Syntax and semantics are, of course, the things that define the language. However, to become efficient and productive with a language, you need to be familiar with the various tools and libraries surrounding the language too.

Putting It Together

The previous sections describe what the DLR is by exploring the various concepts, such as runtime, language, and dynamicity. This section will introduce the DLR from a different angle. We will take a high-level look at the major components that make up the DLR. The overview of the major DLR components will serve to orient the rest of the chapters in Part 1 of this book. Figure 1-10 shows the major components that make up the DLR runtime.

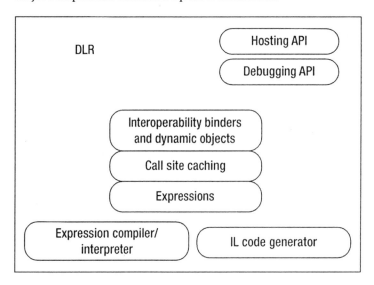

Figure 1-10. Major components of the DLR

As the figure shows, the DLR has a compiler and an interpreter. The compiler uses an IL code generator to compile DLR expressions into IL code. The interpreter interprets DLR expressions. Here's a brief description for each of the other components:

Expressions: These are the backbone of the DLR. Almost everything in the DLR centers around DLR expressions. The compiler and interpreter act on DLR expressions. The very important call site caching mechanism and the language interoperability capability that the DLR provides are based on DLR expressions. If you have some experience with LINQ, you will probably be happy to know that these are basically LINQ expressions along with some DLR extensions. It is very likely that the DLR extensions will become a part of LINQ expressions in a later version of .NET. We will explore expressions in great depth in the next chapter.

Call site caching: This is the caching mechanism that makes DLR-based applications run fast. Dynamic languages have been criticized for their performance in comparison to static languages. This is because dynamic languages perform late binding for various actions like method invocation at run time, which is traditionally several orders of magnitude slower than static languages. The call site caching component in DLR solves the problem by caching the results of late binding. The results of late binding are represented as DLR expressions. The caching mechanism is based on an optimization technique called *polymorphic inline cache* and it's implemented mainly in the CallSiteBinder class. Chapter 3 will dive deep into the details of this DLR component.

Interoperability binders and dynamic objects: This is what enables interoperability between dynamic and static languages. This component uses expressions to represent the results of late binding. It also defines a common type system that consists of twelve late-bound operations to facilitate language interoperability. Binders and dynamic objects are the two kinds of entities in DLR that contain late-binding logic. They interact in a well-established protocol in order to achieve language interoperability. Chapter 4 will cover the interoperability binders. Chapter 5 will look at dynamic objects.

Hosting API: This API allows one language to host (i.e., embed) another language. For example, with this API, we can execute Python code inside a C# application. Once we do that, we generally want to pass some objects from the C# application to the Python code and perhaps receive some objects back from the Python code. That's all possible with the DLR, thanks to the interoperability binders and dynamic objects. We will look at the Hosting API in Chapter 6. In Part 2 of this book, you'll see examples of how to use the Hosting API to allow users to script your applications.

Debugging API: This API is to help you implement a debugger for your DLR-based language. The API is still in its early stage of development and is less mature than the rest of the DLR components. This book will therefore not cover this particular topic. I would refer you to Harry Pierson's weblog at http://devhawk.net for more information on this topic.

Summary

This chapter introduces the DLR by first showing a series of four Hello World examples. It goes on to demonstrate some of the applications you'll develop over the course of this book. After the examples and demonstrations, I describe what the DLR is by explaining some fundamental concepts, such as programming languages, dynamic typing, and late binding, and we looked at the flows of compile time and run time activities. The chapter also includes a high-level discussion on programming language syntax and semantics and a partial survey of tooling support for programming languages. The chapter concludes with a brief description of the key components that make up DLR, with pointers to the chapters that will cover each of these components in more detail. The DLR has wide applicability in many areas of our day-to-day software design and development. This chapter offers a preview, and glimpse of DLR's potential. The rest of the book will dive deep and show the rest of the iceberg underneath.

CHAPTER 2

■ ■ ■

DLR Expression

DLR Expression is the backbone of the DLR. It is a separate feature that you can use without involving the rest of the DLR. If you do use it with other DLR features, there are basically two usage scenarios. One scenario involves defining a language's semantics in terms of DLR expressions. The other is defining the late binding logic of binders and dynamic objects. Don't worry if these don't make much sense to you right now. In this chapter, you will learn how to use DLR Expression by itself, while later chapter will cover the two usage scenarios. Once you get a good grasp of using DLR Expression by itself, you'll be in a good position to use DLR Expression and the other DLR features together.

DLR Expression as a Language

Let's take a look at what DLR Expression is first, before getting into the examples. **DLR Expression is much like a programming language.** It has constructs like the loop expressions, assignment expressions, and method invocation expressions you normally see in other languages. For example, a Hello World program in C# looks like this:

```
Console.Writeline("Hello World");
```

The equivalent code in DLR Expression looks like this:

```
MethodInfo method = typeof(Console).GetMethod("WriteLine", new Type[] { typeof(String) });

Expression callExpression = Expression.Call(null,
        method,
        Expression.Constant("Hello World"));
```

This code snippet uses .NET reflection to create a MethodInfo instance that represents the static WriteLine method of the Console class. The code then calls the static Call method of the Expression class to create an Expression instance. The Expression instance represents a call to the Console.WriteLine method that will print "Hello World" to the screen. The first input parameter of the Expression.Call method is the target object upon which to call the method designated by the second input parameter of Expression.Call. If the method designated by the second input parameter is a static method, there's no target object to call the method on. That's why the code snippet passes null as the first input parameter to the Expression.Call method.

So what are the differences between DLR Expression and a normal programming language, other than that the code in DLR Expression looks a ton more verbose? There are three key differences:

> **Code as data and data as code**—code expressed in DLR Expression is data that can be more easily analyzed and worked on.

A common denominator of multiple languages—Like CLR's IL instructions, DLR expressions serve as the common denominator of multiple languages.

No concrete syntax, only abstract syntax—DLR Expression defines only abstract syntax and no concrete syntax. However, it supports serialization and we can use that to serialize abstract syntax to concrete syntax or, conversely, to deserialize concrete syntax into abstract syntax.

Let's look at each of the differences in more detail in the next few sections.

Code as Data

One key difference between DLR Expression and a typical programming language is that **code in DLR Expression is data**. Code in DLR Expression exists in memory at run time as objects. In contrast, C# code exists at run time as a bunch of IL instructions. Because code in DLR Expression is data, it does not execute like the C# code does. To execute the data, we can either interpret it or we can turn it into IL code and then run it. For example, the following code turns the Hello World example above into IL code and runs it:

```
Action callDelegate = Expression.Lambda<Action>(callExpression).Compile();
callDelegate();
```

The first line in the code snippet wraps callExpression into a lambda expression and calls the Compile method to compile the lambda expression into a callable .NET delegate. This line of code essentially turns data into IL instructions. The second line in the code snippet executes the compiled code.

As you can see, instead of one line of C# code, we write a lot more code to achieve the same thing. Obviously, there has to be a reason for doing all this extra work. The reason is that once code is represented as objects in memory, it is far easier to analyze than IL instructions. Of course, if we want to execute the code, we need to turn the objects back into code by either interpreting or compiling the objects. The transformation from code to objects is based on the idea of "code as data." Likewise, the transformation from objects to code is based on the idea of "data as code." The word data here means the objects that are used to represent code. Those objects are referred to as data because we analyze them like data. The concept of "code as data" and "data as code" has been around for a long time. People often use the concept to do things like code transformation, rewriting, generation, analysis, etc. LINQ to SQL is an example of using DLR Expression to do code transformation. It transforms a tree of DLR expressions into SQL statements.

A Common Denominator like CLR

Another key differentiator between DLR Expression and a normal programming language is that **DLR Expression, like the set of IL instructions, is designed to be the common denominator of multiple languages**. IL is the common denominator of languages such as C# and VB.NET. Languages like these translate their high-level language constructs into low-level IL instructions. CLR has a runtime for executing those IL instructions, because its instructions support the high-level language constructs in those languages. DLR Expression is the common denominator of languages such as IronPython and IronRuby for the same reason. Figure 2-1 below shows the analogy between CLR IL instructions and DLR expressions in their roles of being the common denominator of multiple high-level languages.

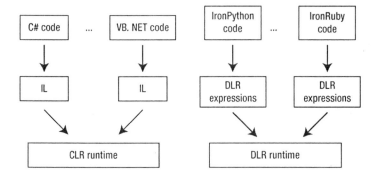

Figure 2-1. The CLR and DLR as common denominators of multiple languages

Concrete Syntax and Serialization

One more difference between DLR Expression and a normal programming language is that **DLR Expression defines only the abstract syntax and not the concrete syntax**. The concrete syntax of a language is literally what you type in a code editor when you program in that language. For example, when I write 5 + 2 in C#, I write the code in C#'s concrete syntax in a code editor. When I compile the code, the language's parser will parse the code I write in concrete syntax and represent it in memory as a tree of objects. The tree representation is called an abstract syntax tree, and it represents in abstract syntax the same code I write in concrete syntax. So what's the big deal in this distinction between concrete syntax and abstract syntax? The idea here is that multiple concrete syntax notations can be mapped to one single abstract syntax notation.

DLR Expression supports serialization. When we serialize a DLR expression tree into a file, the textual format in which we store the expression tree is one concrete syntax notation of DLR Expression. Each person is free to define his own concrete syntax for DLR Expression and implement the serialization/deserialization code.

Unlike DLR Expression, a typical programming language like C# defines one concrete syntax and one abstract syntax. So the mapping from concrete syntax to abstract syntax is one-to-one. Of course, if you like, you can come up with a custom concrete syntax for writing C# code. You would then implement a custom parser to parse that code and transform it into C#'s abstract syntax. However, I've yet to see anybody so insane. Besides, the C# abstract syntax might not be accessible to the public.

Expressions vs. Statements

So far, we've looked at DLR Expression as a programming language. In programming languages, there's a distinction between expressions and statements. The distinction between the two is very simple—expressions yield values; statements don't. This is best illustrated with some examples.

Each of the following lines of code is an expression, compound or not, in C#. To qualify as an expression, according to what we just said, the code must yield a value. In the first three lines, the value each expression yields is the number 7. The value the last expression yields is the return value of the method call. The third line is particularly interesting. It's a compound expression that consists of two assignment expressions: j = 7 and i = (j = 7). The expression j = 7 yields 7 as its value, which in turn is assigned to the variable i. If j = 7 were not an expression, there would be nothing to assign to variable i and the third line of code would cause a compilation error.

```
5 + 2
x = 7            //assignment expression
i = j = 7        //this line of code consists of two assignment expressions
someObject.Foo()     //method call expression
```

Let's now see some statements. The first line below shows that local variable declaration in C# is a statement. The second line shows that if we add semicolon to the end of an assignment expression, the result is an assignment statement. Similarly, if we add semicolon to the end of a method call expression, we get a method call statement as the result.

```
int i;  //variable declaration statement
x = 5;           //assignment statement
someObject.Foo();     //method call statement
```

The if language construct in C# is a statement, not an expression. The following code is valid in C#:

```
if (true)               //if statement
    Console.WriteLine("Hello");
```

The code below, however, is not valid C# code because the if statement yields no value that can be assigned to variable x.

```
//This code is not valid in C#
x = if (true)
    Console.WriteLine("Hello");
```

So what does all this discussion about expressions versus statements have to do with DLR Expression? Simply put, DLR Expression does not have statements. It has only expressions that yield values. That's why it's called DLR Expression, not DLR Statement. Let's look at an example and see what that means. Listing 2-1 shows an invalid C# code snippet. It's invalid because the if statement yields no value that can be assigned to variable y. The code in Listing 2-1 is similar to the code snippet we just looked at, so it shouldn't be anything new to us. Now let's look the almost equivalent code in DLR Expression in Listing 2-2. You can find the code for both Listing 2-1 and Listing 2-2 in the StatementVersusExpression.cs file of this chapter's source code project.

Listing 2-1. Invalid C# Code That Assigns an If Statement to a Variable.

```
{
  String x = "Hello";
  String y = if (true)   //This causes compilation error.
            x.ToLower();
}
```

Listing 2-2. Assigning an If Statement to a Variable in DLR Expression

```
1)   MethodInfo method = typeof(String).GetMethod("ToLower", new Type[]{});
2)   ParameterExpression x = Expression.Variable(typeof(String), "x");
3)   ParameterExpression y = Expression.Variable(typeof(String), "y");
4)   Expression blockExpression = Expression.Block(new ParameterExpression[] {x, y},
5)       Expression.Assign(x, Expression.Constant("Hello")),
```

```
6)        Expression.Assign(y,
7)            Expression.Condition(Expression.Constant(true),
8)                Expression.Call(x, method),
9)                Expression.Default(typeof(String)),
10)               typeof(String)))
11)  );
12)
13)  Func<String> blockDelegate = Expression.Lambda<Func<String>>(blockExpression).Compile();
14)  String result = blockDelegate();
15)  Console.WriteLine(result);
```

Don't be turned off by the amount of DLR Expression code that's needed to achieve what the C#
code in Listing 2-1 does. Later sections will describe DLR block expressions, conditional expressions,
and assignment expressions in more detail, with examples. For now, I'll explain the example code just
enough to illustrate the important differences between expressions in the DLR and statements in C#.

The code in Listing 2-2 has quite some interesting points. First, notice the blockExpression variable
in line 4. A DLR block expression is a container of smaller child expressions. The value of a DLR block
expression is the value of the last child expression it contains. This is the first difference from the code in
Listing 2-1. In Listing 2-1, the pair of curly braces and all the code within it make up a block statement
that yields no value.

The second difference from the code in Listing 2-1 is the assignment expression in line 6 that assigns
a conditional expression to the parameter expression y. The conditional expression is the equivalent of
the C# if statement in Listing 2-1. The parameter expression y is the equivalent of the variable y in
Listing 2-1. Unlike in C#, the if conditional construct in the DLR is an expression, not a statement. It has
a value that can be assigned to a variable.

Line 13 in Listing 2-2 compiles the whole block expression into code, a .NET delegate of type
Func<String>. That type Func<String> means the delegate takes no input arguments and returns a
String object. I didn't pick that delegate type randomly. The delegate type needs to match the type
requirements of blockExpression. In our case, blockExpression takes no input arguments and returns a
String. This echoes what I said about block expressions earlier. Remember I mentioned that a DLR block
expression has a value and that value is the value of the last child expression it contains. In our example,
the last child expression is the assignment expression that assigns the conditional expression to the
variable y expression. The value of that assignment expression is of type String and therefore the value
of the block expression is also of type String.

The result of running the code in Listing 2-2 is the text "Hello" displayed in the console. Our
discussion of expressions versus statements leads well to the next section's topic—the Expression class.

Expression Type and Kind

DLR Expression has several classes to represent different expressions, such as the block expressions,
conditional expressions, and assignment expressions we saw in the earlier sections. All those classes
derive directly or indirectly from the Expression class in the System.Linq.Expressions namespace. The
Expression class is the root base class that defines all the properties and operations common to all DLR
expressions. Because all expressions yield a value (as we discussed in the previous section), the
Expression class defines a property called Type to record the type of an expression's value. Figure 2-2
shows the key properties and methods of the Expression class this chapter covers. As the figure shows,
Type is a property in the Expression class. Its type is System.Type. So for example, if a DLR expression
represents the string literal "Hello", that expression's Type property is System.String.

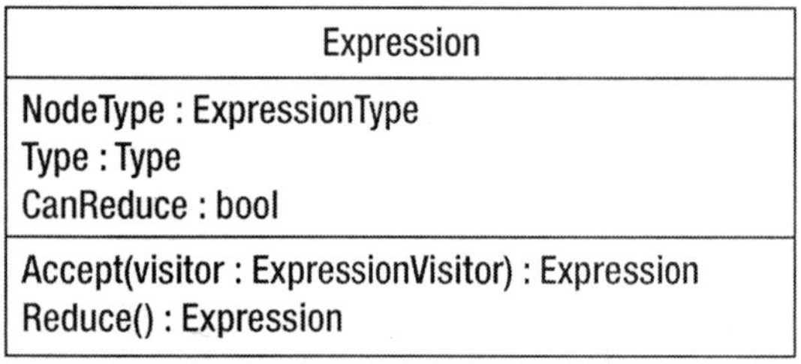

Expression
NodeType : ExpressionType Type : Type CanReduce : bool
Accept(visitor : ExpressionVisitor) : Expression Reduce() : Expression

Figure 2-2. Expression class

Besides the Type property, we'll encounter two other important properties later: NodeType and CanReduce. The CanReduce property and the Reduce method are about expression reduction, which we'll discuss later in the chapter. The Accept method is related to the Visitor design pattern we can use to change DLR expressions. We will also discuss that later, and don't worry—no prior knowledge of the Visitor design pattern is required. I'll explain the Visitor design pattern in general first, then show you how the pattern is implemented in the DLR. For now, let's look at just the NodeType property, then we'll jump right into a bunch of code examples that show how to write programs in DLR Expression.

The NodeType property gives additional information about what kind of an expression you're dealing with. For example, Table 2-1 shows some C# expressions in the first column. The equivalent DLR expressions of those C# expressions are all instances of the BinaryExpression class. Although they are all instances of BinaryExpression, they have different values for the NodeType property shown in the second column.

*Table 2-1. Binary Expressions and Their **NodeType** Properties*

C# Binary Expression	NodeType
5 + 2	ExpressionType.Add
5 – 2	ExpressionType.Subtract
5 * 2	ExpressionType.Multiply
5 / 2	ExpressionType.Divide

All of the C# expressions in Table 2-1 have one thing in common—they all have a left operand, a right operand, and an operator in the middle. In other words, if we visualize them as expression trees, they will all have the same shape shown in Figure 2-3. Because of this commonality, it's very typical in the design of abstract syntax trees to use something like DLR's BinaryExpression class to represent them all. The design approach is often called *shape-based*. Because the BinaryExpression instances all have the same shape, there needs to be a way to distinguish whether a binary expression is an addition, multiplication, subtraction, or something else. The NodeType property is there in the Expression class to carry that additional information about an expression.

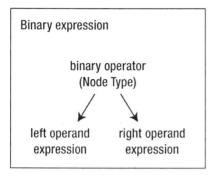

Figure 2-3. *Shape of a binary expression*

The code snippet below is an example that prints out the Type and NodeType properties of a BinaryExpression instance and two ConstantExpression instances. The two ConstantExpression instances act as the left and right operands of the binary expression. The expressions in this code example match exactly the tree shape shown in Figure 2-3. In the code snippet, the binary expression is referenced by the addExpression variable. Because the binary expression represents arithmetic addition of two integers, when the code prints out the Type property of the binary expression, the text "System.Int32" will show up on the screen. As for the two ConstantExpression instances, because they represent constant integers, when the code prints out their Type property, we will see "System.Int32" on the screen too. The NodeType property of the binary expression has the value ExpressionType.Add to indicate that the binary expression is a binary addition, not a binary multiplication or any other kind of binary expression. The NodeType property of the two ConstantExpression instances has the value ExpressionType.Constant to indicate that the expressions are constant expressions.

```
BinaryExpression addExpression = Expression.Add(
                    Expression.Constant(10),
                    Expression.Constant(20));

Console.WriteLine(addExpression.Type);
Console.WriteLine(addExpression.Left.Type);
Console.WriteLine(addExpression.Right.Type);

Console.WriteLine(addExpression.NodeType);
Console.WriteLine(addExpression.Left.NodeType);
Console.WriteLine(addExpression.Right.NodeType);
```

So far we've covered the important concepts of DLR Expression. The next few sections will introduce the various DLR expression classes, much like we'd introduce the language constructs of a programming language. You'll see examples that show how to write arithmetic, if, switch, for loop, and other DLR expressions.

Binary Expressions

Binary expressions are expressions that have a left and a right child expression, such as one that adds two integers. The expression is binary. Its left child expression is the left operand of the addition operation. Its right child expression is the right operand. Binary expressions are represented as instances of the BinaryExpression class. Listing 2-3 shows first the C# code that adds two doubles and divides the result by 3. Below the C# code is the equivalent code in DLR Expression.

In the DLR Expression part of the example, the doubles are constant expressions. The example calls `Expression.Constant` to create them. The `Expression` class provides factory methods for creating instances of built-in expression classes. The factory method for `ConstantExpression` is `Expression.Constant`. Similarly, the example calls `Expression.Add` and `Expression.Divide` to create the two binary expressions that represent the addition and division.

Listing 2-3. BinaryExamples.cs

```
public static void CSharpExample()
{
    double result = (10d + 20d) / 3d;
    Console.WriteLine(result);
}

public static void LinqExample()
{
    Expression binaryExpression = Expression.Divide(
        Expression.Add(                         //left child of division
                Expression.Constant(10d),   //left child of addition
                Expression.Constant(20d)),  //right child of addition
        Expression.Constant(3d)             //right child of division
    );

    Func<double> binaryDelegate = Expression.Lambda<Func<double>>(binaryExpression)
                                  .Compile();
    Console.WriteLine(binaryDelegate());
}
```

Both `Expression.Add` and `Expression.Divide` return an instance of `BinaryExpression`. The difference is that the `BinaryExpression` that `Expression.Add` returns has `ExpressionType.Add` as the value of its `NodeType` property whereas the `BinaryExpression` that `Expression.Divide` returns has `ExpressionType.Divide`. Tables 2-2 and 2-3 list all the different `ExpressionType` values that a binary expression's `NodeType` property can take. We have seen some of them in Table 2-1 already. Tables 2-2 and 2-3 present the complete list of all binary expressions and their `NodeType` property values. For each `ExpressionType` value in the first column of the tables, Table 2-2 and Table 2-3 show the equivalent C# binary operator in the second column. For each `ExpressionType` value, the tables don't have a column that shows the corresponding factory method in the `Expression` class for creating a binary expression for that `ExpressionType` value. I omit it because the factory method names are the same as their corresponding `ExpressionType` values. For example, in the first row of Table 2-2, the `ExpressionType` value is `Add` and the corresponding factory method is `Expression.Add`.

Table 2-2 shows the `ExpressionType` values for binary arithmetic expressions. Table 2-3 shows the `ExpressionType` values for the rest of binary expressions.

Table 2-2. *Arithmetic Binary Expressions*

NodeType property value	Example of Equivalent C# Operator
Add	5 + 2
AddAssign	x += 2
AddChecked	checked (x + 2)
AddAssignChecked	checked (x += 2)
Subtract	5 – 2
SubtractAssign	x -= 2
SubtractChecked	checked (x - 2)
SubtractAssignChecked	checked (x -= 2)
Multiply	5 * 2
MultiplyAssign	x *= 2
MultiplyChecked	checked (x * 2)
MultiplyAssignChecked	checked (x *= 2)
Divide	5 / 2
DivideAssign	x /= 2
Modulo	5 % 2
ModuloAssign	x %= 2
Power	5 ^ 2
PowerAssign	x ^= 2

Table 2-3. *Non-Arithmetic Binary Expressions*

NodeType	Example of Equivalent C# Operator
And	true & false
AndAlso	true && false
AndAssign	x &= true

NodeType	Example of Equivalent C# Operator
Or	true l false
OrElse	true ll false
OrAssign	x l= false
ExclusiveOr	true ^ false
ExclusiveOrAssign	x ^= false
LessThan	5 < 2
LessThanOrEqual	5 <= 2
GreaterThan	5 > 2
GreaterThanOrEqual	5 >= 2
Equal	5 == 2
NotEqual	5 != 2
RightShift	5 >> 2
RightShiftAssign	x >>= 2
LeftShift	5 << 2
LeftShiftAssign	x <<= 2
Assign	x = 2
ArrayIndex x[2]	
Coalesce (i	nt) x

Flow Control Expressions

This section will look at examples of if and switch flow control expressions in the DLR. Because the examples will use the expression that calls the Console.WriteLine method in several places, it helps to wrap that expression into the Print helper method shown in Listing 2-4. This way the code examples will be more succinct and easier to read.

Listing 2-4. The Print helper method in ExpressionHelper.cs

```
public class ExpressionHelper
{
    public static Expression Print(string text)
    {
        return Expression.Call(
                null,
                typeof(Console).GetMethod("WriteLine", new Type[] { typeof(String) }),
                Expression.Constant(text)
            );
    }
}
```

If-Then-Else Expressions

Listing 2-5 has two methods, CSharpExample() and LinqExample(). The code in CSharpExample() is a simple if-else statement that will print "true" to the screen when you run it. The equivalent code in DLR Expression is in LinqExample(), which calls the Expression.IfThenElse factory method to create an instance of ConditionalExpression. The conditional expression has three parts—if-test, if-true, and if-false. Each of the tree parts is an expression by itself. In this example, the if-test part is a constant expression that has true as its value. The if-true expression is a method call expression that will print "true" to the screen when executed. The if-false expression is a method call expression that will print "false" to the screen when executed.

Listing 2-5. IfExamples.cs

```
public static void CSharpExample()
{
    if (true)
        Console.WriteLine("true");
    else
        Console.WriteLine("false");
}

public static void LinqExample()
{
    Expression ifExpression = Expression.IfThenElse(
        Expression.Constant(true),
        ExpressionHelper.Print("true"),
        ExpressionHelper.Print("false")
    );

    Action ifDelegate = Expression.Lambda<Action>(ifExpression).Compile();
    ifDelegate();
}
```

Switch Expressions

Now we'll look at an example of constructing a switch expression in the DLR. As before, the code in Listing 2-6 shows the example first in C# and then in DLR Expression. The code in CSharpExample() is a simple switch statement that will print "case 1" to the screen when you run it. The equivalent code in DLR Expression is in LinqExample(), which calls the Expression.Switch factory method to create an instance of the SwitchExpression class. The switch expression in the example consists of two parts—the switch value and the two cases. The switch value is an expression. The switch cases are not; they are instances of the SwitchCase class. In this example, the switch value is a constant expression that has integer 1 as its value. The example code calls the Expression.SwitchCase factory method to create the SwitchCase instances. Each SwitchCase instance consists of two parts—the conditions and the body of the case, all of which are expressions. A switch case can have one or more conditions. In our example, the first case has one condition, the integer 1, and the second case has two conditions, the integers 2 and 3.

One important difference between the C# code and the DLR expression code is that in the latter, there is no need to have a break expression to mark the end of each case.

Listing 2-6. SwitchExamples.cs

```
public static void CSharpExample()
{
    switch (1)
    {
        case 1:
            Console.WriteLine("case 1");
            break;
        case 2:
        case 3:
            Console.WriteLine("case 2 and 3");
            break;
    }
}

public static void LinqExample()
{
    SwitchExpression switchExpression = Expression.Switch(
        Expression.Constant(1),
        new SwitchCase[] {
            Expression.SwitchCase(
                ExpressionHelper.Print("case 1"),
                Expression.Constant(1)
            ),
            Expression.SwitchCase(
                ExpressionHelper.Print("case 2 and 3"),
                Expression.Constant(2),
                Expression.Constant(3)
            )
        }
    );

    Action switchDelegate = Expression.Lambda<Action>(switchExpression).Compile();
```

```
    switchDelegate();
}
```

Scopes and Name Binding

Every language defines its own scoping rules for binding names, and so does DLR Expression. Before I explain what that means, let's look at an example. Listing 2-7 shows some C# code and the scopes it defines:

Listing 2-7. Scopes

```
namespace ExpressionExamples
{                                                  //new scope ExpressionExamples
    public class Employee
    {                                              //new scope Employee
        private double monthlySalaryRate = 1000d;

        public double calculateBonus(int performanceRating)
        {                                          //new scope calculateBonus
            return monthlySalaryRate * performanceRating;
        }                                          //end of scope calculateBonus
    }                                              //end of scope Employee

    public class FatCat
    {                                              //new scope FatCat
        private double monthlySalaryRate = 1E10;

        public double calculateBonus(int performanceRating)
        {                                          //new scope calculateBonus
            return monthlySalaryRate * 1E20;
        }                                          //end of scope calculateBonus
    }                                              //end of scope FatCat
}                                                  //end of scope ExpressionExamples
```

In the example, I purposely define the same calculateBonus method names and the same monthlySalaryRate variable names to illustrate the effect scopes have on name bindings. When the same name shows up multiple times in code, the language's compiler or interpreter needs to have rules for determining what those occurrences of the same name refer to. The rules, as it turns out, are defined in terms of scopes in most if not all languages.

In general, the way it works is very simple (we'll get to some subtle details later). First, you can't define two things with the same name in one scope. In the code above, the names Employee and FatCat have to be different because they are defined in the same scope. Second, sibling scopes are totally isolated from each other. That's why we can have the same variable names and method names in Employee and FatCat because the scopes Employee and FatCat define are siblings. Last, child scope (i.e., a scope nested within another scope) has visibility into its parent and parent's parent and so on. The scope defined by the calculateBonus method in the Employee class is a child scope of the Employee class's scope. That's why in that method, when we use the name monthlySalaryRate to calculate an employee's bonus, the C# compiler knows we are referring to the Employee class's monthlySalaryRate, not FatCat's monthlySalaryRate.

Astute readers might notice that the scopes in the code example correspond to open-close curly brace pairs one to one. What's more, the nesting of curly brace pairs and the nesting of scopes match up perfectly. That can't be just coincidence, can it? No, it isn't and in fact the essence of curly braces in C# is to define scopes for name bindings. In Listing 2-7, we saw that namespaces, classes, and methods can introduce new scopes. Besides those, in C#, the flow control statements like *while, if-then-else,* and *for* can be followed by open-close curly brace pairs and thereby introduce new scopes.

Lexical vs. Dynamic Scope

We will soon get to the discussion of DLR Expression on the subject of scopes and name binding. But first I want to show you some more examples and explain the term **lexical scope**.

Listing 2-8 shows a C# program on the left and the equivalent Python program on the right. Listing 2-9 shows a similar C# program on the left and its equivalent Python program on the right. Notice that in each program, the function addToY is called twice—once directly by the line addToY(5) and the other time indirectly by the line add4(5).

In Listing 2-8, the function add4 assigns number 4 to the outer y and then calls addToY. That does not change the fact that the name y in addToY is bound to outer y. If you run either of the two programs in Listing 2-8, you will see the numbers 7 and 9 printed on the screen.

Listing 2-8. Examples of Lexical Scopes and Name Binding with No Local Variables

```
static void addToY(int x) {                        def addToY(x):
    Console.WriteLine(x + y); //refers to outer y      print x + y   #refers to outer y
}

static void add4(int x) {                          def add4(x):
    //this y is the same as the outer y                #this y is the same as the outer y
    y = 4;                                             global y
    addToY(x);                                          y = 4
}                                                       addToY(x)

static int y = 2;    //outer y                     y = 2          #outer y
static void Main(string[] args) {
    addToY(5);                                      addToY(5)
    add4(5);                                        add4(5)
    }
```

In Listing 2-9, the function add4 assigns number 4 to a local y and then calls addToY. That again does not change the fact that the name y in addToY is bound to outer y. If you run either of the two programs in Listing 2-8, you will see the numbers 7 and 7 (because the value of outer y is never changed) printed on the screen.

Listing 2-9. Examples of Lexical Scopes and Name Binding with Local Variables

```static void addToY(int x) { Console.WriteLine(x + y); //refers to outer y } static void add4(int x) { int y = 4; //local y addToY(x); } static int y = 2; //outer y static void Main(string[] args) { addToY(5); add4(5); }```	```def addToY(x): print x + y #refers to outer y def add4(x): y = 4 #local y addToY(x) y = 2 #outer y addToY(5) add4(5)```

The point I want to emphasize with these programs is that in all four cases, (a) no matter where *addToY* is called (directly or indirectly within another function), and (b) no matter whether we change the value of a local y or the outer y before calling *addToY* within *add4*, the name y in function addToY always refers to the outer y. The point, in other words, is that the scope of addToY's name binding does not depend on where addToY is called. It depends on where addToY is defined. Since addToY is defined in the scope where the outer y is also defined, the name y in addToY always refers to the outer y. This kind of scoping rule is called lexical scoping or static scoping. The opposite of lexical scoping is dynamic scoping. With dynamic scoping, the name y in addToY might not always be bound to the outer y. The binding is more fluid, and it depends on where addToY is called. All of the languages used in this book such as DLR Expression, C#, Ruby and Python use lexical scoping. Therefore, we will not discuss dynamic scoping in more detail.

BlockExpression and Lexical Scoping

So far, we've been using C# as an example for explaining scopes and name binding. Let's see some examples in DLR Expression. Listing 2-10 shows a C# example of nested scopes. Listing 2-11 shows a similar example in DLR Expression. The C# example defines a lambda function add. The body of the add function has two blocks—i.e., the two pairs of left and right curly braces. Each block defines a scope. The outer scope declares the variable x. The inner scope declares the variable y. Because the name x is declared in the outer scope, C# does not allow us to bind that name to different object in the inner scope. That's why in the inner scope if we declare a variable of the same name x, we'll get a compilation error.

Listing 2-10. C# Example in NestedBlockExamples.cs

```
public static void BlockLexicalScopeCSharpExample()
{
    Func<int> add = () =>
    {
        int x = 2;
        {
            //int x = 1; //Compilation error. C# compiler does not allow this.
```

```
            int y = 3;
            return x + y;
        }
    };

    int result = add();
    Console.WriteLine("result is {0}", result);
}
```

DLR Expression does not impose this limitation and the code in Listing 2-11 is the proof. The DLR example, like the C# example, also has two blocks. Each block defines a scope. Unlike C#, DLR Expression allows us to declare a variable x in the outer scope (line 7) and another variable x in the inner scope (line 10). Both of these are references to the same bolded ParameterExpression instance x in line 3. However, even though they are references to the same ParameterExpression instance x, the fact that they are in different scopes has an impact on name bindings. That impact is illustrated in the example with the code Expression.Add(x, y) in line 13. The result of the addition is 3, not 5. This is because the addition expression is in the scope where the name x is bound to the inner scope's local variable x. The inner scope's local variable x is implicitly initialized with the value 0. So the result of the addition is 3.

If we don't declare the local variable x in the inner scope, the result of the addition expression will be 5. The result is 5 because the addition will add the outer scope's x and the inner scope's y. To not declare the local variable x in the inner scope, all you need to do is to replace line 10 in Listing 2-11 with the following line:

```
//result will be 5 if you use the following line of code to replace line 10 in Listing 2-11
new ParameterExpression[] { y },
```

Listing 2-11. DLR Expression Example in NestedBlockExamples.cs

```
1)    public static void BlockLexicalScopeLinqExample()
2)    {
3)        ParameterExpression x = Expression.Variable(typeof(int), "x");
4)        ParameterExpression y = Expression.Variable(typeof(int), "y");
5)
6)        Expression add = Expression.Block(
7)                new ParameterExpression[] { x },
8)                Expression.Assign(x, Expression.Constant(2)),
9)                Expression.Block(
10)                   new ParameterExpression[] {x, y}, //Unlike C#, DLR allows this.
11)                   Expression.Assign(y, Expression.Constant(3)),
12)                   Expression.Add(x, y)
13)               )
14)        //If we print out the value of x here, it will be 2.
15)           );
16)
17)
18)        int result = Expression.Lambda<Func<int>>(add).Compile()();
19)        Console.WriteLine("result is {0}", result);
20)    }
```

Notice the comment in line 14 of Listing 2-11. It says in the outer scope, if we print out the outer scope's x variable, we will see the number 2—even if the inner scope declares another variable x that's initialized to 0. Let me prove that to you in code, and then I'll summarize the key takeaways from our discussion of the DLR's BlockExpression.

Listing 2-12 shows the code that prints out the outer scope's x variable. The code in Listing 2-12 is a simplified version of the code in Listing 2-11. First, we don't need the variable y from Listing 2-11 to demonstrate the point I'm trying to make. The code in Listing 2-12 simply has a variable x in the outer scope and another variable x in the inner scope. In the inner scope, the variable x is assigned the number 1. Because the inner scope's x is bound to a different object than the outer scope's x, assigning the number 1 to the inner scope's x does not change the value of the outer scope's x. So when the code prints out the outer scope's x, the number we'll see on the screen is 2, not 1. The bolded line of code in Listing 2-12 is the line that prints out the outer scope's variable x to the screen. The bolded line of code is a call to the static Print helper method in the ExpressionHelper class. This Print helper method is slightly different from the Print helper method we saw in Listing 2-4. The Print helper method in Listing 2-4 takes a String object as the input parameter. The Print helper method here takes an Expression instance as the input parameter. Listing 2-13 shows the implementation of the Print helper method that takes an Expression instance as input.

Listing 2-12. NestedBlockExamples.cs

```
public static void OuterScopeVariableNotChangedByInnerScopeLinqExample()
{
    ParameterExpression x = Expression.Variable(typeof(int), "x");

    Expression block = Expression.Block(
            new ParameterExpression[] { x },
            Expression.Assign(x, Expression.Constant(2)),
            Expression.Block(
                new ParameterExpression[] { x },
                Expression.Assign(x, Expression.Constant(1))
            ),
            ExpressionHelper.Print(x)
        );

    Expression.Lambda<Action>(block).Compile()();
}
```

Listing 2-13. The Print Helper Method That Takes an Expression Instance as Input

```
public static Expression Print(Expression expression)
{
    return Expression.Call(null,
                typeof(Console).GetMethod("WriteLine", new Type[] { typeof(int) }),
                expression);
}
```

Here are the key takeaways from our discussions of BlockExpression:

- Even if an outer block already declares variable x, DLR BlockExpression allows an inner block of the outer block to declare variable x again. C# does not allow that.

- If an outer block and an inner block both declare variable x, those two variables are bound to different objects. Changing the value of one variable does not change the value of the other variable. This is true even when the two variables are represented by the same ParameterExpression instance.

Lambda Expressions and Closure

Lambda expressions are so called because they are based on a theory called *lambda calculus* in mathematics. Let's look at a C# example of a lambda expression and then I'll use that example to explain some concepts in lambda calculus. Although I had a lot of fun (and pain as well) with lambda calculus while taking the course "Introduction to Programming Language Theory" at Stanford, I promise I won't digress and stray into the parts of lambda calculus that aren't necessary for our discussion in this section.

Listing 2-14 shows a C# code example that creates a lambda expression. The lambda expression is the part in bold. It is an expression and therefore can be assigned to the variable add. The lambda expression takes two input parameters x and y of type int and returns a value of type int. The body of the lambda expression is { return x + y ; }. The x and y in the body of the lambda expression are bound by the input parameters x and y. Therefore, the x and y in the body of the lambda expression are said to be bound variables.

Listing 2-14. A C# Example of a Lambda Expression

```
public static void LambdaCSharpExample()
{
    Func<int, int, int> add = (x, y) => { return x + y; };
    int result = add(3, 5);
    Console.WriteLine("result is {0}", result);
}
```

Listing 2-15 shows the DLR Expression equivalent. This code calls the Expression.Lambda<T> factory method to create an instance of Expression<T>. Here T is the delegate type of the lambda expression the factory method creates. The bolded code in line 7 of Listing 2-15 is the body of the lambda expression. The x and y in line 8 are the two input parameters of the lambda expression. The x and y in the body of the lambda expression are bound by the x and y input parameters in line 8.

Listing 2-15. A DLR LambdaExpression Example

```
1)   public static void LambdaLinqExample()
2)   {
3)       ParameterExpression x = Expression.Parameter(typeof(int), "x");
4)       ParameterExpression y = Expression.Parameter(typeof(int), "y");
5)
6)       Expression<Func<int, int, int>> add = Expression
7)               .Lambda<Func<int, int, int>>(Expression.Add(x, y),
8)                                            x, y);
9)
10)      int result = add.Compile()(3, 5);
11)      Console.WriteLine("result is {0}", result);
12)  }
```

So far, the lambda expressions and bound variables we've discussed all have their roots in the lambda calculus theory. Lambda calculus also includes the opposite of bound variables, called free (or unbound) variables, and C# and DLR Expression allow free variables in lambda expressions, too. Listing 2-16 shows a C# example of a lambda expression that has free variables. The code first declares two variables x and y, then it creates a lambda expression. The body of the lambda expression is the same as the lambda expression body in Listing 2-14. However, in Listing 2-16, the lambda expression does not take any input parameters and, because of this, the variables x and y in the body of the lambda expression are said to be free variables. The free variables need to be bound before the lambda expression can be executed. Because the lexical scope in which the lambda expression is created defines the variables x and y in lines 3 and 4, the x and y in the body of the lambda expression in line 7 are bound to the variables x and y in lines 3 and 4. The lambda expression and the variables x and y in line 3 and line 4 together is called a closure.

Because the lambda expression's free variables are bound in the closure, we can execute the closure. The code in Listing 2-16 purposely executes the closure within a block that spans from line 10 to line 13. The block is redundant in the code. I wrote the code in such a way so that it's as close as possible to the almost equivalent DLR code in Listing 2-17.

Listing 2-16. A C# Example of a Lambda Expression That Has Free Variables

```
1)    public static void ClosureLexicalScopeCSharpExample()
2)    {
3)        int x = 2;
4)        int y = 1;
5)
6)        //The 'add' delegate and variables x, y form a closure.
7)        Func<int> add = () => { return x + y; };
8)
9)        int result;
10)       {
11)           //int y = 3; //C# compiler does not allow this.
12)           result = add();
13)       }
14)
15)       Console.WriteLine("result is {0}", result);
16)   }
```

Listing 2-17 shows a DLR Expression example of a lambda expression that has free variables. In Listing 2-17, the code defines a lambda expression and assigns it to the variable add in line 12. The lambda expression has two free variables, x and y, that are bound to the x and y declared in line 9. The key point here is that lexical scoping determines what the free variables x and y are bound to. The free variables x and y are bound to the x and y declared in line 9 because the x and y in line 9 are declared in the same lexical scope as the lambda expression. Because the lambda expression is defined in the outer scope, the free variables x and y are bound to the outer scope's local variables x and y. To prove that, the example deliberately invokes the closure in an inner scope where the name y is bound to the inner scope's local variable y, which has value 3. It doesn't matter where the closure is invoked. The free variables are always bound to the outer scope's local variables x and y. Therefore, the result of running the code in Listing 2-17 is 3 (i.e., 2 + 1), not 5 (i.e., 2 + 3).

Listing 2-17. A DLR Expression Example of a Lambda Expression That Has Free Variables.

```
1)   public static void ClosureLexicalScopeLinqExample()
2)   {
3)       ParameterExpression x = Expression.Variable(typeof(int), "x");
4)       ParameterExpression y = Expression.Variable(typeof(int), "y");
5)       ParameterExpression add = Expression.Variable(typeof(Func<int>), "add");
6)
7)       Expression addExpression = Expression.Block(
8)           //add is defined in the outer scope but invoked in the inner scope.
9)           new ParameterExpression[] { x, add, y },
10)          Expression.Assign(x, Expression.Constant(2)),
11)          Expression.Assign(y, Expression.Constant(1)),
12)          Expression.Assign(add, Expression.Lambda<Func<int>>(
13)                  Expression.Add(x, y))),   //x, y here are bound to outer scope's x, y
14)          Expression.Block(
15)                  new ParameterExpression[] { y },
16)                  Expression.Assign(y, Expression.Constant(3)),
17)                  Expression.Invoke(add)   //invoke add in the inner scope.
18)              )
19)          );
20)
21)      int result = Expression.Lambda<Func<int>>(addExpression).Compile()();
22)      Console.WriteLine("result is {0}", result);
23)  }
```

The GotoExpression Class

Many languages have language constructs such as for, for-each, while, and do-while for performing iterations. DLR Expression supports those, too. However, instead of providing the various high-level constructs for doing iterations, the DLR provides the GotoExpression class as a lower-level construct that those high-level constructs can base on. This section will look at GotoExpression and compare it to C#'s goto statements. The next section will show you how to use GotoExpression to achieve what C#'s while statements can do.

Listing 2-18 shows a C# example of goto statements, and Listing 2-19 shows a similar example in DLR Expression. The C# example shows that C# does not allow code that jumps from an outer scope to a label declared in an inner scope. Line 4 in Listing 2-18 tries to jump from an outer block to the InnerBlock label declared in an inner block. If you uncomment line 4, you'll get compilation error.

As this demonstrates, C# does not allow code to jump from outer scope to a label declared in an inner scope. However, C# allows jumps in the other direction: It allows code to jump from an inner scope to a label declared in an outer scope. The code in line 10 does exactly that.

Listing 2-18. GotoExamples.cs

```
1)   public static void CSharpExample()
2)   {
3)       //C# cannot do this jump
4)       //goto InnerBlock;
5)
```

```
6)        {
7)        InnerBlock:
8)            Console.WriteLine("In inner block.");
9)            //jump to outer block
10)           goto OuterBlock;
11)           Console.WriteLine("This line is unreachable");
12)       }
13)
14)   OuterBlock:
15)       Console.WriteLine("In outer block.");
16)   }
```

This limitation in C# does not exist in DLR Expression. As Listing 2-19 shows, DLR Expression allows us to jump in both directions. To jump, we need to label the target we want to jump to. So the example code in Listing 2-19 creates two instances of LabelTarget, innerBlock and outerBlock, in lines 3 and 4, to represent the two targets. In lines 12 and 17, the example calls the Expression.Label method and passes it a LabelTarget instance to mark a place in code we can jump to. To jump to a target, the example calls ExpressionGoto in lines 9 and 14. Now let's trace the execution flow of the code and see where the code jumps. In line 9, the code is to jump to the innerBlock label, which is marked in line 12. So the code execution skips line 10 and jumps to line 12. It continues to line 13 and prints out "In inner block." Then it gets to line 14. The code in line 14 is to jump to the outerBlock label, which is marked in line 17. So the code execution skips line 15 and jumps to line 17. Then it continues to line 18, prints out "In outer block" and finishes.

Listing 2-19. GotoExamples.cs

```
1)    public static void LinqExample()
2)    {
3)        LabelTarget innerBlock = Expression.Label();
4)        LabelTarget outerBlock = Expression.Label();
5)
6)        Expression<Action> lambda = Expression.Lambda<Action>(
7)            Expression.Block(
8)                //DLR can do this jump
9)                Expression.Goto(innerBlock),
10)               ExpressionHelper.Print("Unreachable"),
11)               Expression.Block(
12)                   Expression.Label(innerBlock),
13)                   ExpressionHelper.Print("In inner block."),
14)                   Expression.Goto(outerBlock),
15)                   ExpressionHelper.Print("Unreachable")
16)               ),
17)               Expression.Label(outerBlock),
18)               ExpressionHelper.Print("In outer block.")));
19)
20)       lambda.Compile()();
21)   }
```

While Loops

Now that we've introduced GotoExpression, let's see how to use it to achieve the equivalent of what while statements do in C#. First, let's see the C# example that will then be translated into the DLR Expression example. Listing 2-20 shows two C# methods. The first method, CSharpExample, has a while loop that adds the numbers 0, 1, and 2. The second method, CSharpGotoExample does the same thing except that instead of using a while loop, it uses C#'s goto statements.

Listing 2-20. C# Examples in WhileExamples.cs

```
public static void CSharpExample()
{
    int i = 0;
    while (i < 3)
        i++;

    Console.WriteLine("i is {0}", i);
}

public static void CSharpGotoExample()
{
    int i = 0;

WhileLabel:

    if (i < 3)
    {
        i++;
        goto WhileLabel;
    }

    Console.WriteLine("i is {0}", i);
}
```

As you can see, if a language already defines the if and goto constructs, the while construct is merely syntactic sugar. The syntactic sugar might let users of the language write more concise and readable code, but it doesn't let them express anything that they can't express with if and goto. Given the CSharpGotoExample method in Listing 2-20, it's pretty straightforward to translate that code into the equivalent code in DLR Expression in Listing 2-21. This code creates an instance of LabelTarget called whileLabel (line 3). It uses whileLabel to mark the target of the goto expression (line 9), then it calls the Expression.Goto factory method to create a goto expression that jumps to the target (line 13).

Notice that the code in line 12 calls the PostIncrementAssign factory method to create an expression that represents the code i++. The method PostIncrementAssign returns an instance of UnaryExpression whose NodeType property is ExpressionType.PostIncrementAssign. There are many other kinds of unary expressions for representing unary operations such as ++i, --i, -i (negation), etc. You can refer to the MSDN documentation for a comprehensive list of these unary operations.

Besides GotoExpression, another way to do looping is to use the LoopExpression class in the System.Linq.Expressions namespace. After seeing the code examples in this section, it should be straightforward to learn how to use LoopExpression by reading Microsoft's MSDN documentation. The DLR does not provide anything like a WhileExpression class for doing while loops in particular yet.

Listing 2-21. DLR Expression example in WhileExamples.cs

```
1)   public static void LinqExample()
2)   {
3)       LabelTarget whileLabel = Expression.Label();
4)       ParameterExpression i = Expression.Variable(typeof(int), "i");
5)
6)       Expression<Func<int>> lambda = Expression.Lambda<Func<int>>(
7)           Expression.Block(
8)               new ParameterExpression[] {i},
9)               Expression.Label(whileLabel),
10)              Expression.IfThen(Expression.LessThan(i, Expression.Constant(3)),
11)              Expression.Block(
12)                  Expression.PostIncrementAssign(i),
13)                  Expression.Goto(whileLabel))),
14)              i));
15)
16)      int result = lambda.Compile()();
17)      Console.WriteLine("i is {0}", result);
18)  }
```

Dynamic Expressions

So far none of our discussions about DLR Expression involves dynamic behaviors. Everything has been statically typed. Here's an example of what I mean. In the section "Expression Type and Kind," we saw the following code snippet:

```
BinaryExpression addExpression = Expression.Add(Expression.Constant(10),
                    Expression.Constant(20));
Console.WriteLine(addExpression.Type);
Console.WriteLine(addExpression.Left.Type);
Console.WriteLine(addExpression.Right.Type);
```

This code constructs a BinaryExpression object to represent the addition of two integers. The expression has two subexpressions—the left operand expression and the right operand expression. The left operand expression represents the integer constant 10 and hence its Type property is System.Int32. Similarly, the right operand expression represents the integer constant 20 and hence its Type property is also System.Int32. Adding two integers will result in another integer. Therefore, the Type property of addExpression is System.Int32. If you run the code, you'll see the text "System.Int32" printed three times on the screen.

The point I want to stress is that all three expressions know statically the type of the value they represent. So how about the dynamic C# code shown below in Listing 2-22? Is DLR Expression capable of expressing that? The answer is yes, and that's the topic of this section.

Listing 2-22. A C# Example That Contains a Late-Bound Binary Addition.

```
public static void CSharpExample()
{
    dynamic x = 5;
    dynamic y = x + 2;
```

```
        Console.WriteLine("5 + 2 = {0}", y);
    }
```

The challenge here is that when the code in the bolded line in Listing 2-22 adds x and 2, it doesn't know x's type. Well, you might think it's obvious from the code that x is an integer and has the value 5. That's true in this example. But in general, x can come to the bolded line by other means, perhaps as an input argument of the CSharpExample method. In that case, it's totally up to the caller of the CSharpExample method what the variable x will be.

Because in the bolded line we don't know the static type of x, we can't simply use BinaryExpression to represent the addition. The variable x might not be an integer. It might be some wacky object that simply knows how to add 2 to itself. In order to represent dynamic code like the bolded line in Listing 2-22, the DLR provides the DynamicExpression class. DynamicExpression works very much like what the C# compiler does when it compiles the code in Listing 2-22. So let's look at what the C# compiler does first and then use that knowledge to help us explain DynamicExpression.

When the C# compiler sees the code in Listing 2-22, it compiles it into something similar to what Listing 2-23 compiles to. The code might look baffling because it has things like *call site binder* and *call site* that I haven't explained. To fully explain those concepts requires a fair amount of background information. You'll see the detailed explanation of those concepts in Chapters 3 and 4. For now, I want to stay focused on DynamicExpression, so I'll explain those concepts just enough for our discussion.

The variable binder in Listing 2-23 knows how to do late binding for binary additions. The variable binder in our example points to an instance of the SimpleOperationBinder class, which is where the late binding logic is. Listing 2-24 shows the SimpleOperationBinder class, which returns the number 3 as the result of late binding (lines 10 to 13). So if we use an instance of SimpleOperationBinder to perform the late binding of an addition operation, no matter what the two operands of the addition are, the result will always be 3. Of course, no one would find much practical use in a binder like that. I'm using it here because it's the simplest binder I can think of for our example. The C# compiler, of course, won't compile the code in Listing 2-22 into something that uses SimpleOperationBinder. C# has a set of binder classes for performing the late binding logic it desires. We will see some examples of the C# binder classes in Chapter 4. Listing 2-23 is only a simplified illustration of what C# compiler does in compiling the dynamic code in Listing 2-22.

Once the binder is in place, to use the binder, the code in Listing 2-23 creates a call site. The call site is an instance of CallSite<T>. The generic type parameter T in this case is the delegate type Func<CallSite, object, object, object>. You can ignore it for now and be assured that it will become clear when we get to Chapters 3 and 4. The important thing to notice here is that the binder variable is passed to the CallSite<T>.Create method when the call site is created (line 6). Because of that, the call site will use the binder instance created in line 3 to do the late binding when the call site's Target method is invoked (line 9). Finally, when line 10 prints the result of the late binding, we will see the number 3 show up on the screen.

Listing 2-23. A Simplified Illustration of What C# Compiler Does with Dynamic Code (DynamicExamples.cs)

```
1)   public static void CSharpSimpleBinderExample()
     {
         CallSiteBinder binder = new SimpleOperationBinder();

         CallSite<Func<CallSite, object, object, object>> site =
             CallSite<Func<CallSite, object, object, object>>.Create(binder);

         //This will invoke the binder to do the binding.
```

```
        object sum = site.Target(site, 5, 2);
        Console.WriteLine("Sum is {0}", sum);
    }
```

Listing 2-24. SimpleOperationBinder.cs

```
1)   class SimpleOperationBinder : BinaryOperationBinder
2)   {
3)       public SimpleOperationBinder()
4)           : base(ExpressionType.Add)
5)       { }
6)
7)       public override DynamicMetaObject FallbackBinaryOperation(DynamicMetaObject target,
8)           DynamicMetaObject arg, DynamicMetaObject errorSuggestion)
9)       {
10)          return new DynamicMetaObject(
11)              Expression.Convert(Expression.Constant(3), typeof(object)),
12)              BindingRestrictions.GetExpressionRestriction(
13)                  Expression.Constant(true)));
14)      }
15)  }
```

Now that we've seen conceptually what the C# compiler does in compiling code that involves late binding, let's see how DynamicExpression is related to all that. Simply put, there are two ways to do late binding in the DLR. One is to create binders and call sites and use them like the code in Listing 2-23 shows. The other way is to create binders and instances of DynamicExpression and use them like the code in Listing 2-25 shows. Internally, when a DynamicExpression instance is compiled into IL and executed like line 11 in Listing 2-25, a call site is created and the whole late binding process will take place similarly to what the code in Listing 2-23 does. The fact that when a DynamicExpression instance is executed a call site will be created is what underlies a useful late binding technique called deferred binding. We will look at deferred binding in Chapter 4. I mention it here so that when we get to that discussion in Chapter 4, you'll associate it with what you learn in this section.

To create and use a DynamicExpression instance, you first have to have a binder. So the code in line 4 of Listing 2-25 creates an instance of the SimpleOperationBinder class we saw in Listing 2-24 to serve as the binder in this example. Then the code in line 6 calls the Dynamic factory method of the Expression class, passing it the binder object as the first input parameter. The second input parameter passed to the Dynamic factory method is the return type of the late binding operation. In our example, the late binding operation returns the number 3 as an instance of System.Object in line 11 of Listing 2-24. That's why in line 7 of Listing 2-25, the code passes typeof(object) as the second input parameter the Dynamic method. The third input parameter passed to the Dynamic method is an array of the operands of the late-bound binary operation. Lines 10 and 11 compile the DynamicExpression instance into an executable delegate, which is executed in line 13. Line 14 prints the result of the execution to the screen, which will be the number 3.

Listing 2-25. An Example of DynamicExpression in DynamicExamples.cs

```
1)   public static void LinqExample()
2)   {
3)       //prepare a call site binder
4)       CallSiteBinder binder = new SimpleOperationBinder();
```

```
5)
6)        DynamicExpression dynamicExpression = Expression.Dynamic(
7)                    binder, typeof(object),
8)                    new [] {Expression.Constant(5), Expression.Constant(2)});
9)
10)       Func<object> compiledDelegate = Expression.
11)                   Lambda<Func<object>>(dynamicExpression).Compile();
12)
13)       object result = compiledDelegate();
14)       Console.WriteLine("result is {0}", result);
15) }
```

Index Expressions

Now we'll look at an example of how to use the IndexExpression class in the System.Linq.Expressions namespace. An IndexExpression instance represents an array or property index. Listing 2-26 shows a C# example that uses an array index to change the value of an array's second element. The integer array numbers has three integers in it—7, 2, and 4. The code in Listing 2-26 changes the second element from 2 to 6. If you run the example, it will print 7, 6, 4 to the screen.

Listing 2-26. A C# Example That Uses an Array Index to Change an Array's Element

```
public static void CSharpExample()
{
    int[] numbers = { 7, 2, 4 };
    numbers[1] = 6;
    Console.WriteLine("{0}, {1}, {2}", numbers[0], numbers[1], numbers[2]);
}
```

Listing 2-27 shows the DLR Expression code equivalent to the C# code in Listing 2-26. Like the C# example in Listing 2-26, the code in Listing 2-27 also starts with the integer array numbers that has three integers in it. The code from line 5 to line 7 calls the ArrayAccess factory method of the Expression class to create an instance of the IndexExpression class. The IndexExpression instance represents index 1 of the array numbers. Then the code in lines 9 and 10 creates an assignment expression that assigns an expression representing the integer 6 to indexExpression. Because indexExpression represents index 1 of the array numbers, when the assignment expression arrayIndexExp is executed, the integer 6 will be assigned to the element whose index is 1 in the array numbers. If you run the example, it will print the same result 7, 6, 4 to the screen as the C# example in Listing 2-26 does.

Listing 2-27. A DLR Expression Example That Shows How to Use IndexExpression.

```
1)    public static void LinqExample()
2)    {
3)        int[] numbers = { 7, 2, 4 };
4)
5)        IndexExpression indexExpression = Expression.ArrayAccess(
6)            Expression.Constant(numbers),
7)            Expression.Constant(1));
8)
9)        Expression arrayIndexExp = Expression.Assign(
```

```
10)                    indexExpression, Expression.Constant(6));
11)
12)      Action arrayIndexDelegate = Expression.Lambda<Action>(arrayIndexExp).Compile();
13)      arrayIndexDelegate();
14)      Console.WriteLine("{0}, {1}, {2}", numbers[0], numbers[1], numbers[2]);
15) }
```

Expression Abstraction, Reduction and Extension

One feature of DLR Expression I like very much is **expression reduction**. The concept is simple and yet very powerful. The idea is that you can extend DLR Expression by defining your own expression classes. Since you are defining the classes, there is no way for the DLR Expression compiler/interpreter to know what they mean unless you tell it. And the way you tell it is by "reducing" your expressions to DLR expressions—the ones it already knows. In other words, the set of expression classes in System.Linq.Expressions forms the baseline. If you can define the semantic meaning of your own expression classes in terms of those baseline classes, the DLR interpreter/compiler can understand and act on your expressions.

Expression reduction provides an extension mechanism we can use to define our own custom expression classes. Not only does expression reduction make DLR Expression extensible, it also allows for different **levels of abstraction** among expression classes. This is because if X reduces to Y, you can think of X as being more abstract than Y. So if your expression classes reduce to the baseline DLR expression classes, yours are said to have a higher level of abstraction.

Let's look at an example of expression reduction. In earlier code examples, we achieve better code quality by using the ExpressionHelper.Print helper method in instead of repeating the code inside that helper method all over the place. Let's refresh ourselves a little bit about what the ExpressionHelper.Print method does. The method returns an expression that represents a call to Console.WriteLine. That's all it does. Here we'll do the same thing again, but this time we'll use expression reduction rather than the helper method. The plan is we will define a new expression class, and we will provide the logic for reducing our expression to the same expression ExpressionHelper.Print returns. Listing 2-28 shows the code for our new expression class, PrintExpression.

Listing 2-28. PrintExpression.cs

```
public class PrintExpression : Expression
{
    private String text;

    private static MethodInfo _METHOD = typeof(Console).GetMethod(
        "WriteLine", new Type[] { typeof(String) });

    public PrintExpression(String text)
    {
        this.text = text;
    }

    public String Text
    {
        get { return text; }
    }
```

53

```
    public override bool CanReduce
    {
        get { return true; }
    }

    public override Expression Reduce()
    {
        return Expression.Call(
                    null,
                    _METHOD,
                    Expression.Constant(text));
    }

    public override ExpressionType NodeType
    {
        get { return ExpressionType.Extension; }
    }

    public override Type Type
    {
        get { return _METHOD.ReturnType; }
    }

    public override string ToString()
    {
        return "print " + text;
    }
}
```

There are two basic requirements we need to meet when implementing a custom expression class. First, our class must derive directly or indirectly from System.Linq.Expressions.Expression. Second, the NodeType property of our class must return ExpressionType.Extension. Beyond those requirements, since we want our PrintExpression to be able to reduce to a MethodCallExpression, we make the CanReduce property of our class return true. The actual logic that performs the reduction is in the Reduce method. As you can see in Listing 2-28, in the Reduce method, we simply invoke the Expression.Call factory method to create and then return an instance of MethodCallExpression that represents a call to Console.WriteLine. Last but not least, don't forget to take care of the Type property. In our case, our expression's value is the same as the return value of the call to Console.WriteLine. And that value's type is _METHOD.ReturnType.

Now that we have the PrintExpression class defined, let's see how it's used. Because all the printing-related code is modularized into the ExpressionHelper.Print method, we don't need to make changes all over the place in our code. All we need is modify the ExpressionHelper.Print method to use our PrintExpression class like the code snippet below shows:

```
public class ExpressionHelper
{
    public static Expression Print(string text)
    {
        return new PrintExpression(text);
    }
}
```

That's it. Just one line of code in the method body! At run time, when the DLR Expression interpreter/compiler sees an instance of `PrintExpression`, it knows that the expression is reducible. So it calls the `Reduce` method on the expression and gets back a `MethodCallExpression` instance. The code snippet above is good, but we can make it slightly better. If you recall, DLR Expression provides factory methods for creating expressions. Our code snippet above is a factory method for creating instances of `PrintExpression`. To make our factory method look more aligned with the DLR's factory methods, let's rename the class name `ExpressionHelper` to `ExpressionEx`. Let's also change the return type of the `Print` method from `Expression` to `PrintExpression`. After those changes, our code becomes:

```
public partial class ExpressionEx
{
    public static PrintExpression Print(String text)
    {
        return new PrintExpression(text);
    }
}
```

IronPython makes a lot of use of expression reduction. If you take a look at the IronPython source code in the IronPython.Compiler.Ast namespace, you'll see classes like `ForStatement`, `ImportStatement`, `ScopeStatement`, `NameExpression` and many others. Those classes all derive directly or indirectly from `System.Linq.Expressions.Expression` and implement their specific reduction logic in the `Reduce` method.

Immutability and the Visitor Pattern

A DLR expression can have child expressions. The child expressions can in turn have their own child expressions, and so on. All together, the expressions form a tree. There is one root expression in the tree. The leaves of the tree are the terminal expressions that don't have any child expression of their own.

Every expression in the tree is immutable. Once it's created, its states are read-only and can't be changed. The only way to achieve the effect of changing the states of an expression is to create a new expression and toss out the old one. The concept I've just described is termed *immutability*.

Immutability is a very generic programming concept, and it's not specific to DLR Expression. The class `System.String` is immutable, as are many other classes that have no relation to DLR Expression. There are many nice benefits of making a class immutable. For example, instances of an immutable class are automatically thread-safe. You don't need to synchronize access to those instances from multiple threads because those instances' states are read-only and, by virtue of that, those states can't be corrupted by thread race conditions.

Because expressions are immutable and because they almost always form a tree except in trivial cases, it's not a straightforward thing to change an expression in a tree. To change an expression in a tree, you also need to change that expression's parent, and the parent's, parent and so on. Figure 2-4 shows a pictorial view of this propagation of changes. All the nodes in the tree are immutable. When we change node 1 by creating a new node, we need to assign the new node as a new child of node 2. Because node 2 is immutable, we can't simply change its children. We have to create a new node 2 and assign new node 1 as its child. We also need to assign the other unchanged child of the old node 2 to be a child of the new node 2. And because we change node 2, we have to change node 3 by creating a new node 3. We then have to assign the new node 2 as a child of new node 3. We also need to assign the other 3 unchanged children of old node 3 to be children of the new node 3.

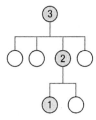

Figure 2-4. *Propagation of changes in an expression tree*

As you can see, it's a lot of work to change even a single node in a tree. When we make changes to a tree, there are mainly three things in the picture—the tree itself (i.e., the data structure), the tree traversal (i.e., walking the tree), and the actions we perform every time we encounter a node during tree traversal. Fortunately, this problem happens so often that a solution for it already exists—the Visitor design pattern. In the rest of this section, we will look at how the Visitor pattern provides an elegant solution for the problem of changing immutable trees. We will look at the pattern in general, as well as in the context of DLR Expression. As always, I will demonstrate how it works in practice with an example.

Visitor Pattern in General

Figure 2-5 shows the class diagram of the Visitor pattern in general. As the diagram shows, there are two class hierarchies in the Visitor pattern. The Element class hierarchy is the data structures and the Visitor class hierarchy is the algorithms that work on the data structures. The Client in Figure 2-5 is the glue that decides which algorithms to apply to which data structures. The spirit of the pattern is the decoupling between the data structures and the algorithms.

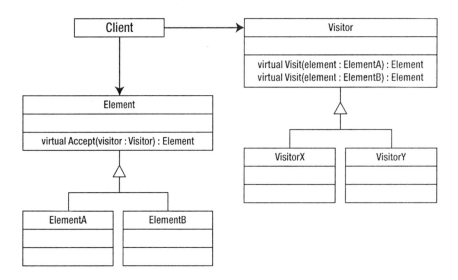

Figure 2-5. *Class diagram of the Visitor design pattern*

The Element class (which can be an interface) has an Accept method. The Accept method can be abstract in the Element class or it can have concrete implementation. Classes derived from Element can choose to override or not to override the Accept method. A typical implementation of the Accept method simply asks the visitor to visit the current element, like this:

```
virtual Element Accept(Visitor visitor)
{
    visitor.Visit(this);
}
```

From the code, it is clear that passing different visitors to the Accept method will have different results. If we need to introduce a new way of visiting the elements, we don't need to change any code in the Element class and its derivatives. We can encapsulate that new algorithm (i.e., the new way of visiting the elements) into a new subclass of the Visitor class and pass an instance of that subclass to the Accept method.

The Visitor class (it can be an interface) has one overloaded Visit method for each class derived from Element. Those overloaded Visit methods can be abstract or they can have a concrete implementation. A class derived from Visitor can choose to override those Visit methods that it wants to provide new logic for. For example, if we need VisitorX in Figure 2-5 to provide logic for visiting ElementA, then VisitorX will override only the method virtual Element Visit(ElementA element).

The previous section mentioned that when we make changes to a tree, there are mainly three things in the picture—the tree itself, the tree traversal, and the actions we perform at each node. That observation links to the Visitor pattern nicely. The tree is the data structure and is represented by the Element hierarchy in the Visitor pattern. The tree traversal plus the actions are algorithms and they are represented by the Visitor hierarchy.

Visitor Pattern in DLR Expression

DLR Expression implements a slight variation of the Visitor pattern. Figure 2-6 shows that variation in a class diagram.

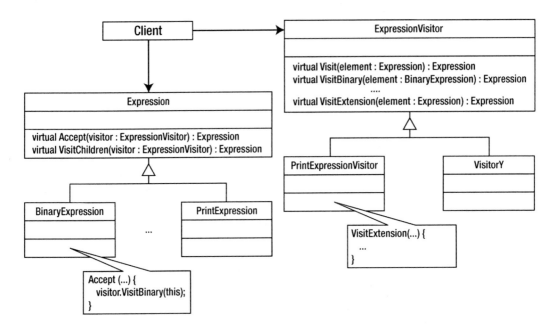

Figure 2-6. *Class diagram of the Visitor design pattern implemented in the DLR*

There is one key difference to note about the class diagram in Figure 2-6, and that's the VisitChildren method in the Expression class. The VisitChildren method is about how to visit the child expressions of the current expression. In other words, the method is about tree traversal and hence should belong to the Visitor class hierarchy. However, in DLR Expression, the method is in the Expression class hierarchy. And if you look inside the source code of the DLR, you'll see that all of the VisitChildren methods implemented in BinaryExpression, BlockExpression, and other DLR expression classes delegate the real job to methods in the ExpressionVisitor class. That appears to be unnecessarily convoluted at first glance. Why does the DLR put the VisitChildren method in the Expression class hierarchy and delegate the real job to the Visitor class hierarchy? Why not simply follow the original Visitor pattern and put the VisitChildren method in the Visitor class hierarchy in the first place? The reason is expression extension.

For the built-in DLR expression classes, the DLR knows how to traverse their child expressions. For custom extensions like the PrintExpression class we implemented, the DLR does not know how we would like to traverse the child expressions, and therefore it leaves that decision to us. The DLR defines the VisitChildren method in the Expression class so that when we define a custom expression class, we can override the VisitChildren method and implement our own logic for traversing the custom expression's child expressions. This explains why the method VisitChildren exists in the Expression class hierarchy. For the built-in DLR expression classes, DLR chooses to have a more truthful implementation of the Visitor design pattern, and hence it makes the VisitChildren method in BinaryExpression, BlockExpression, and so on delegate the real job back to methods in the ExpressionVisitor class. This choice makes total sense. The intention of the DLR Expression design is to keep the Expression class hierarchy intact while allowing developers to implement whatever tree walking and visiting behavior they fancy. Because BinaryExpression, BlockExpression, and so on delegate the real job of the VisitChildren method to ExpressionVisitor, we can override those methods when we implement a class derived from ExpressionVisitor without ever needing to change anything in the Expression class hierarchy.

If you want to look at the DLR source code to see how the built-in DLR expression classes traverse their child expressions, here's a rundown of how the VisitChildren method in BinaryExpression, BlockExpression, and so on delegates the real job back to methods in the ExpressionVisitor class. The built-in expression classes like BinaryExpression and BlockExpression all inherit the VisitChildren method implementation from the base Expression class. If you look at the VisitChildren method implemented in the Expression class, you'll see that it takes a visitor (instance of ExpressionVisitor) as the input parameter and calls the Visit method on the visitor. The visitor's Visit method will in turn call back the Accept method of the expression. As you can see, the mechanism is convoluted. The expression calls the visitor and then the visitor calls back the expression. And the convolution is not finished yet. The expression's Accept method is overridden in each Expression subclass to call some method on the visitor. For example, if the expression is an instance of BinaryExpression, its Accept method will call the VisitBinary method on the visitor. And the VisitBinary method is where the logic resides for visiting a binary expression's child expressions.

Expression Visitor Examples

Let's take a look at two examples of walking and visiting expressions. The first example is a trivial case that doesn't involve visiting child expressions. I think it's helpful to use this simpler example to lead into the second example, which involves visiting child expressions. Both examples will use the PrintExpression class we built earlier.

Listing 2-29 shows the visitor class for the PrintExpression class we saw earlier. The PrintExpression class doesn't have any child expressions. Because PrintExpression is an extension expression (i.e., its NodeType property returns ExpressionType.Extension), we override the VisitExtension method in PrintExpressionVisitor. The overridden VisitExtension method checks whether the node argument, the currently visited node, is an instance of PrintExpression. If so, the method creates a new PrintExpression instance whose text is the text of the original PrintExpression instance with "Hello" appended to the beginning.

Listing 2-29. PrintExpressionVisitor.cs

```
public class PrintExpressionVisitor : ExpressionVisitor
{
    protected override Expression VisitExtension(Expression node)
    {
        if (!(node is PrintExpression))
            return base.VisitExtension(node);

        PrintExpression printExpression = (PrintExpression) node;
        return new PrintExpression("Hello " + printExpression.Text);
    }
}
```

Listing 2-30 shows the client code that uses PrintExpressionVisitor to modify an instance of PrintExpression. The PrintExpression instance has the text "Bob" at the beginning. After the visitor visits it, the text becomes "Hello Bob", which is the text you'll see on the screen when you run the example code.

Listing 2-30. Using ExpressionVisitor to Modify a PrintExpression Instance
(ExpressionVisitorExamples.cs)

```
public static void RunExpressionVisitorExample()
{
    PrintExpressionVisitor visitor = new PrintExpressionVisitor();
    Expression bob = ExpressionEx.Print("Bob");
    Expression visitedBob = visitor.Visit(bob);
    Action visitedBobDelegate = Expression.Lambda<Action>(visitedBob).Compile();
    visitedBobDelegate();
}
```

This example shows how expression visitors work without the complexity of child expressions. In reality, that rarely happens. More often than not, we need to deal with expressions that have child expressions while we walk and visit expression trees. So let's see an example of this.

First, we need an expression class that has at least one child expression. For that, let's define a new PrintExpression2 class based on PrintExpression. Listing 2-31 shows the PrintExpression2 class. As you can see, the code is largely the same as the code of PrintExpression. The only difference is that PrintExpression stores the text to print directly as a string whereas PrintExpression2 stores a ConstantExpression that in turn stores the string text. The ConstantExpression instance is the child expression of PrintExpression2.

Because PrintExpression2 has a child expression, we override the VisitChildren method that PrintExpression2 inherits from the Expression class. In the VisitChildren method, we need to specify how we would like to visit the child expression(s). In this example, there is only one child expression and we don't need to do anything special other than having the visitor visit it. To have the visitor visit the child expression, the VisitChildren method in Listing 2-31 simply calls the Visit method on the visitor variable and passes textExpression, the child expression, as an input argument to the Visit method.

Listing 2-31. PrintExpression2.cs

```
public class PrintExpression2 : Expression
{
    private ConstantExpression textExpression;

    private static MethodInfo _METHOD = typeof(Console).GetMethod(
        "WriteLine", new Type[] { typeof(String) });

    public PrintExpression2(ConstantExpression textExpression)
    {
        this.textExpression = textExpression;
    }

    public override bool CanReduce
    {
        get { return true; }
    }

    public override Expression Reduce()
    {
        return Expression.Call(
```

```
                    null,
                    _METHOD,
                    textExpression);
    }

    public override ExpressionType NodeType
    {
        get { return ExpressionType.Extension; }
    }

    public override Type Type
    {
        get { return _METHOD.ReturnType; }
    }

    protected override Expression VisitChildren(ExpressionVisitor visitor)
    {
        return visitor.Visit(textExpression);
    }

    public override string ToString()
    {
        return "print " + textExpression.Value;
    }
}
```

Now that we have an expression that has a child expression, let's see how to visit and modify it. Listing 2-32 shows the visitor class for PrintExpression2. The visitor class overrides not only the VisitExtension method but also the VisitConstant method. This is because PrintExpression2 is an extension expression and the child of PrintExpression2 is a constant expression (i.e., an instance of ConstantExpression). Notice also that the visitor class has a state, withinPrintExpression, to track whether a constant expression it encounters is a child of a PrintExpression2 expression. There might be other constant expressions in a tree that are not children of PrintExpression2 expressions and we don't want to modify those. States like withinPrintExpression are common in detecting relationships between nodes in a tree. The relationship between a PrintExpression2 expression and its child constant expression is a tree pattern we want to match in our example. We achieve that by using the withinPrintExpression member variable of PrintExpressionVisitor2.

In Listing 2-32, the VisitConstant method uses withinPrintExpression to check whether the currently visited node is a child expression of a PrintExpression2 expression. If so, it creates a new constant expression whose text is the text of the currently visited node prefixed with "Hello ". The VisitExtension method in Listing 2-32 checks whether the currently visited node is an instance of PrintExpression2. If so, it sets withinPrintExpression to true and calls base.VisitExtension(node). The call to base.VisitExtension(node) will in turn call PrintExpression2's VisitChildren, which will call the VisitConstant method of PrintExpressionVisitor2. Finally, when all those calls return, we get back a new child constant expression whose text is prefixed with "Hello ". The new child constant expression is assigned to the variable modifiedTextExpression. Because the child constant expression has changed, the parent needs to change too. That's why the code in line 16 creates a new instance of PrintExpression2 with modifiedTextExpression as its child expression.

Listing 2-32. PrintExpressionVisitor2.cs

```
1)    public class PrintExpressionVisitor2 : ExpressionVisitor
2)    {
3)        private bool withinPrintExpression = false;
4)
5)        protected override Expression VisitExtension(Expression node)
6)        {
7)            if (!(node is PrintExpression2))
8)                return base.VisitExtension(node);
9)
10)           withinPrintExpression = true;
11)
12)           ConstantExpression modifiedTextExpression =
13) (ConstantExpression) base.VisitExtension(node);
14)
15)           //need to change the parent when the child is changed.
16)           PrintExpression2 newExpression = new
17)               PrintExpression2(modifiedTextExpression);
18)
19)           withinPrintExpression = false;
20)
21)           return newExpression;
22)       }
23)
24)       protected override Expression VisitConstant(ConstantExpression node)
25)       {
26)           if (!withinPrintExpression)
27)               return base.VisitConstant(node);
28)
29)           return Expression.Constant("Hello " + node.Value);
30)       }
31)   }
```

With this example, it should be clear why the DLR defines methods like VisitConstant, VisitBinary, and so on in the ExpressionVisitor class for the built-in expression classes. Had the DLR not done that, we would not be able to visit the constant expressions the way we do in this example without changing the ConstantExpression class. That would be a real mess.

Listing 2-33 shows the client code that uses PrintExpressionVisitor2 to visit and modify a PrintExpression2 instance. The code is largely the same as the client code we saw in the previous example (Listing 2-30). If you run the code, you will see "Hello Bob" printed to the screen.

Listing 2-33. Using ExpressionVisitor to Modify a PrintExpression2 Instance
(ExpressionVisitorExamples.cs)

```
public static void RunExpressionVisitor2Example()
{
    PrintExpressionVisitor2 visitor = new PrintExpressionVisitor2();
    Expression bob = new PrintExpression2(Expression.Constant(text));
    Expression visitedBob = visitor.Visit(bob);
```

```
    Action visitedBobDelegate = Expression.Lambda<Action>(visitedBob).Compile();
    visitedBobDelegate();
}
```

Summary

DLR Expression is the foundation that higher-level DLR features are based on. This chapter begins with a comparison between DLR Expression and a typical programming language. In that part of the chapter, I highlighted some interesting and important characteristics of DLR Expression as a programming language. Then we went through a spate of examples showing how to use the various DLR expression classes. In the last part of this chapter, we looked at the important topic of modifying immutable expression trees using the Visitor design pattern.

This chapter is not intended to be a comprehensive reference for all expression classes that the DLR defines, and so it doesn't cover all DLR expression classes. The chapter covers expression classes such as DynamicExpression and GotoExpression because (a) they are important, (b) they are harder to understand than other expression classes, and (c) they show up more frequently in the rest of the book. For the DLR expression classes not covered in this chapter, you can refer to the MSDN documentation and use what you learn in this chapter to help you figure out how to use them.

After reading this chapter, you are in a good position to explore fascinating DLR features such as binders and dynamic objects in the next three chapters. As you will see in those chapters, we will be using DLR expressions a lot.

CHAPTER 3

■■■

Late Binding and Caching

Late binding is binding that happens at run time, and it is the essence of what makes a language dynamic. When binding happens at run time as opposed to compile time, it's usually several orders of magnitude slower. And that's why the DLR has a mechanism to cache the late-binding results. The caching mechanism is as vital as air to a framework like the DLR, and it's based on an optimization technique called *polymorphic inline caching*. Although caching is not a feature you would normally use directly, it is always there working for you behind the scenes. The DLR uses what are called *binders* to do late binding. These binders have two main responsibilities—caching and language interoperability. In this chapter, we are going to look at the caching aspect of binders. The next chapter will explore their role in language interoperability.

Binders mostly concern only language implementers. As you'll see in Chapter 5, if you are implementing just some library based on the DLR's dynamic object mechanism, not a programming language, you will have little exposure to binders. When you read through this chapter and the next, it will help your understanding of binders if you put yourself in the shoes of a language implementer.

We saw binders and late binding in Chapter 2. In that chapter, when we looked at DLR expressions, the DynamicExpression class stands out among the other expression classes because of its late-binding capability. The late-binding capability of DynamicExpression actually comes from binders. That's why, when we created an instance of DynamicExpression using the Expression.Dynamic method back in Listing 2-25, we needed to pass in a binder object. How DynamicExpression uses a binder object internally will become clear after you read through this chapter.

This chapter will discuss the general concept of binding and the two flavors of it—static binding and dynamic binding. Related to the concept of binding are things like call sites, binders, rules, and call site caching, and I'll explain these terms and provide code examples. Along the way, I'll show you how to write DLR-based code that works on both .NET 2.0 and .NET 4.0. Once we are able to run DLR-based code on .NET 2.0, I'll show you how to debug into the DLR source code. Being able to do this helped me a lot in learning and understanding how the DLR works and I'm sure it will help you too.

This chapter follows nicely from the previous chapter. It will use the concepts and knowledge you learned from your study of DLR expressions. Call sites and binders are important components of the DLR, and you'll see how the infrastructure of these components builds on DLR expressions and leverages the "code as data"' concept. But first, let's begin with a look at the fundamental concept of binding.

Binding

To introduce binding, I'll start with the static method invocation we are all familiar with in C#. The idea is to use the familiarity we have with C# to provide a context for easing our way into the concepts of call sites and bindings.

In a very broad sense, binding means associating or linking one thing with another. In programming, binding is the association between names (i.e., identifiers) and the targets they refer to.

For example, in the code snippet below, the words in bold are all names. The word String is the name of a class; the words bob and lowercaseBob are variable names. The word ToLower is the name of a method.

```
String bob = "Bob";
String lowercaseBob = bob.ToLower();
```

Because binding is the association between names and the targets they refer to, it is also often called name binding. There are many approaches for determining how binding is done. We can categorize those different approaches using two aspects of binding—scope and time, as shown in Table 3-1. In terms of scope, binding can be lexical or dynamic. Lexical scoping is also called static scoping. We saw these in Chapter 2 when we looked at the DLR Expression scoping rules. To recap, scopes provide contexts for binding names. A name might refer to different objects, variables, classes, or other things when it occurs in different scopes.

If you think of scope as the spatial dimension of bindings, then the time aspect is the temporal dimension. In terms of time, binding can be early or late. As noted earlier, early binding is also called compile-time binding, because the resolution of a name to its target happens at compile time. That's when the compiler determines what a name refers to. In contrast, late binding is often called run-time binding. In this case, binding of a name to its target happens at run time. As we discussed in Chapter 1, late binding is a key characteristic of dynamic languages.

One thing I want to emphasize in Table 3-1 is that the two aspects are largely orthogonal, yet they aren't completely uncorrelated. They are orthogonal in the sense that lexical scoping rules can be applied to bind names at either compile time or run time. It doesn't matter *when* (compile time or run time) and *who* (compiler or language runtime) apply those rules. Those rules can be the same rules and the results of name bindings can be the same regardless of the when and who.

However, though the scope and time aspects are largely orthogonal, there is a little correlation between them and that is the cell marked with X in Table 3-1. If a language uses dynamic scoping rules for name binding, those rules, due to their dynamic nature, require some run-time information when they are applied to bind names. Because of that, it's not possible to design a compiler that applies those rules at compile-time. That's why the cell is marked with X—to indicate that no language falls into that category.

Table 3-1. Categorization of Binding Approaches by Scope and Time

Scope \ Time	Compile-time (early)	Run-time (late)
Lexical (static)	C#	IronPython
Dynamic X		Lisp

Call Sites and Early Binding

One concept related to binding is that of the *call site*, which refers to the location in your code that invokes a method. How the binding and the call site are related is best explained with an example. The following C# code snippet should be familiar. I used it to explain binding and I use it again to explain call sites.

```
String bob = "Bob";
String lowercaseBob = bob.ToLower();
```

What we are interested here is the method invocation in the second line of the code. This is the place (the site) that calls the method. So we say it's a **call site**.

The second line of code has a call site that calls the ToLower method of the String class. The word ToLower here is just a name. Something needs to link that name to the real ToLower method of the String class. In this case, that something is the C# compiler. This is the name binding we talked about in the previous section. In the case of a static language like C#, the compiler does the name binding. The linkage between the call site and the ToLower method is resolved at compile time and burned into the generated IL. Listing 3-1 shows what that IL code looks like. Don't be scared away by the code listing. Most people, including me, don't write code at the IL level and therefore are not familiar with IL code. The IL code shown here is not much and should be straightforward to understand. You don't need any knowledge or experience with IL to follow along.

Listing 3-1. IL Code That Shows Compile Time Name Binding

```
locals  init (
        [0] string bob,              //local variable 0 is bob.
        [1] string lowercaseBob)     //local variable 1 is lowercaseBob.
ldstr "Bob"
stloc.0  //sets local variable 0.
ldloc.0  //load local variable 0.
callvirt instance string [mscorlib] System.String::ToLower()
stloc.1  //sets local variable 1.
```

The line most important to our current discussion is the one in bold, which shows that the name ToLower in the C# code is bound to the ToLower method of the System.String class in the mscorlib.dll assembly. The binding is done at compile time and is burned into IL.

Call Sites and Late Binding

The last section showed a simple C# code snippet and its early binding behavior when compiled into IL. Now let's look at the other half of the subject—call sites and late binding. Here's a C# code snippet that has a call site and does late binding:

```
dynamic bob = "Bob";
String lowercaseBob = bob.ToLower();
```

There is only one word that's different between this code snippet and the previous one, and that's the dynamic keyword in bold. Instead of declaring the type of variable bob to be String, the code here declares the type to be dynamic. Because of that, the code is very different. The second line of the code still has a call site that calls the ToLower method. But it also has another call site that calls something that converts the result of ToLower to a String object. The conversion is necessary because the type of variable bob is dynamic and there is nothing to tell the C# compiler what the return type of the ToLower method is. The C# compiler can't even be sure that the ToLower method is defined for the variable bob.

Without knowing the type of variable bob, what does the C# compiler do in compiling the code snippet above? Since it does not know the type of variable bob, it can't simply bind the name ToLower to the ToLower method of the String class; it can only do that when it knows that the type of bob is String. So it compiles the code into something that has objects that know how to do the binding at run time. Those objects are called **binders**. Methods of those binders have the logic for carrying out the necessary late binding given the run-time type of the variable bob. Of course, for this simple code snippet, we know by looking at the code that the run-time type of variable bob is System.String. Unlike us, the binder in this case only knows at run time that the type of variable bob is System.String. When the binder gets that type information, it starts the binding by finding out whether System.String has a ToLower method that does not take any arguments. If the binder finds such a method, the binding is successful and program execution continues. Otherwise, the binding fails and an exception is thrown.

It is too abstract to just mention the binders and describe what they do at a conceptual level. So the next few sections will look at the DLR's implementations of the binders and show some code examples of how those binders perform late binding.

DLR Binders

The DLR defines several classes for representing different kinds of binders. Figure 3-1 shows the class hierarchy of the DLR binder classes. The base DLR class that represents binders is CallSiteBinder; all other binder classes derive directly or indirectly from it. The main responsibility of the CallSiteBinder class, as we will soon examine in detail, is caching late binding results. Caching is what boosts the performance of DLR-based languages and libraries. It is one of the most important features that make the DLR a practical platform for running dynamic language code.

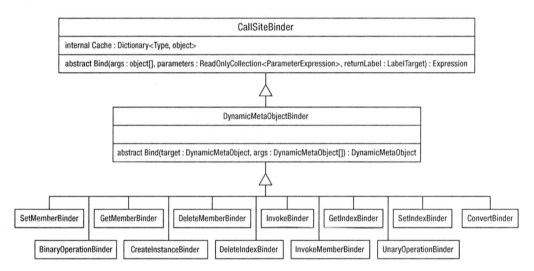

Figure 3-1. Class hierarchy of DLR binder classes

All the subclasses of CallSiteBinder shown in Figure 3-1 are designed for the purpose of language interoperability. As I mentioned earlier, DLR binders have two main responsibilities—caching and language interoperability. The class hierarchy in Figure 3-1 shows good software design on the DLR team's part, which separated those two binder responsibilities into separate classes. Because of that good design, we can use only the caching capability of DLR binders if we like, and that's what we'll do in this chapter. I will focus this discussion on the caching mechanism of DLR binders and hence on the CallSiteBinder class only. None of the code examples in this chapter will involve anything related to the subclasses of CallSiteBinder. That's what we'll cover in the next chapter. We'll take a dive deep into those subclasses and see how they enable different languages to interoperate with one another.

Set Up Code Examples

The setup of this chapter's code examples is the same as that of the other chapters, except that I want to use this chapter's examples to show you how to (a) develop DLR-based code that targets both .NET 2.0 and .NET 4.0, and (b) debug the DLR source code. I didn't call out .NET 3.5 explicitly here because if your code runs on .NET 2.0, it should be straightforward to make it run on .NET 3.5. In principle, you can apply the steps I will be showing here to the code examples of other chapters and make those code examples run on .NET 2.0.

Making a Debug Build of the DLR for .NET 2.0

Normally we write DLR-based code that targets .NET 2.0 because there's a business need for doing so. Maybe we are developing a library and we want the library to be accessible to developers who remain on the .NET 2.0 platform. Another reason for running DLR-based code on .NET 2.0 is it allows us to debug into the DLR source code. This is because in .NET 4.0, a great portion of the DLR source code is packaged into the System.Core.dll assembly. I searched the Web and there does not seem to be a debug build of that assembly. So the solution I came up with is to develop the code examples in such a way that they run on both .NET 2.0 and .NET 4.0. That way, when I need to debug into the DLR source code, I'll run the examples that target .NET 2.0 in debug mode. Here are the steps to follow if you want to set up the environment so you can debug into the DLR source code.

1. Download the DLR source code from the DLR CodePlex website. Unzip the downloaded file to a folder of your choice. I'll assume the folder you choose is C:\Codeplex-DLR-1.0.

2. Open the solution file C:\Codeplex-DLR-1.0\src\Codeplex-DLR-VSExpress.sln in Visual Studio C# 2010 Express. The solution file is for Visual Studio 2008. When you open it in Visual Studio C# 2010 Express, a wizard dialog will pop up and it will take you through the process of converting the solution file to the new Visual Studio 2010 format.

3. After the conversion is done, make sure all the projects' configuration is set to Debug. That way, when you build the solution, Visual Studio will generate debug builds of those projects. When you build the whole solution, you will get some compilation errors for the Sympl35 and sympl35cponly projects. Those projects are for an exemplary DLR-based language called Sympl. You can ignore those errors.

4. Copy the files in the C:\Codeplex-DLR-1.0\Bin\Debug folder to C:\ProDLR\lib\DLR20\debug. The files are the binaries generated by the previous step.

Developing for Both .NET 2.0 and .NET 4.0

If you follow the steps outlined in the previous section, you should be able to open this chapter's solution file C:\ProDLR\src\Examples\Chapter3\Chapter3.sln in Visual Studio C# 2010 Express and build the code examples. The solution contains two projects—CallSiteBinderExamples and CallSiteBinderExamples20. The CallSiteBinderExamples project requires .NET 4.0. The CallSiteBinderExamples20 project requires .NET 2.0. Here are the important things to note about how the projects are configured to target different .NET versions.

First, notice that the CallSiteBinderExamples project does not reference any .NET assemblies. This is because the System.Core.dll assembly is implicitly referenced by default. And because the part of the DLR used in the CallSiteBinderExamples project is already packaged into System.Core.dll, the project does not need any additional references to other .NET assemblies. On the other hand, the CallSiteBinderExamples20 references some of the assemblies you built in the previous section. Those are debug version assemblies of the DLR for .NET 2.0.

Next, notice that all the C# source files in CallSiteBinderExamples20 are links to corresponding files in CallSiteBinderExamples. This way, whenever we change a file in one project, the other project will automatically pick up the changes.

Now look at the properties of the CallSiteBinderExamples20 project. If you right-click on the CallSiteBinderExamples20 project and select Properties in the context menu, you'll see a screen that looks like Figure 3-2. To make a project target .Net 2.0 as the runtime platform, you need to set the "Target framework" dropdown option to "NET Framework 2.0," as highlighted with a red box in Figure 3-2.

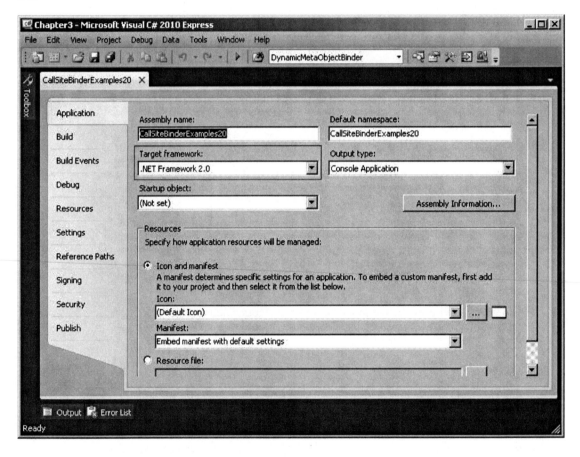

Figure 3-2. Setting the target .NET version of a project

The last thing to take note of is a conditional compilation flag. Because CallSiteBinderExamples and CallSiteBinderExamples20 share the C# source files, we need a flag to compile different parts of the code depending on the target .NET version. If you select the Build tab on the left of the screen shown in Figure 3-2, you'll see a screen that says "Conditional compilation symbols" near the top. For the CallSiteBinderExamples20 project, the conditional compilation symbol "CLR2" is defined. For the CallSiteBinderExamples project, "CLR2" is not defined.

So those are the things I did in order to make the chapter's code examples run on both .NET 2.0 and .NET 4.0. With the environment setup out of the way, let's now look at the CallSiteBinder class, the focus of this chapter.

The CallSiteBinder Class

The C# language runtime has classes that derive from CallSiteBinder. Those classes implement the run-time late binding logic C# needs. Instances of those classes are binders that know how to do late binding for operations such as method invocation. To show you the essence of binders, let's imagine that, for some reason, you want to redefine C#'s late-binding behavior so that all dynamic code like the bob.ToLower() we saw earlier will return integer 3.

Listing 3-2 shows the binder class with the needed binding logic. The class derives from CallSiteBinder and overrides CallSiteBinder's Bind method. You'll see later that, more often than not, you would derive from the class DynamicCallSiteBinder or one of its derivatives rather than CallSiteBinder when implementing your own late-binding logic. For now, let's stay the course and focus on the code example.

The Bind method is where the binding logic resides. In the DLR, the result of all late binding is an instance of the Expression class. That's why the return type of the Bind method is Expression. It's also a sign indicating that DLR Expression is the backbone of the DLR. As the requirement demands, the Bind method in Listing 3-2 returns a constant expression whose value is integer 3. It doesn't matter what is in the args array or the parameters collection. It doesn't matter whether the dynamic code is a method invocation or a property setter/getter invocation. Regardless of all of these, ConstantBinder will always return integer 3 as the binding result.

Listing 3-2. ConstantBinder.cs

```
public class ConstantBinder : CallSiteBinder
{
    public override Expression Bind(object[] args,
                ReadOnlyCollection<ParameterExpression> parameters, LabelTarget returnLabel)
    {
        return Expression.Return(
                returnLabel,
                Expression.Constant(3)
            );
    }
}
```

Although to meet the stated requirement the Bind method in ConstantBinder disregards the args and parameters arguments, it can't disregard the returnLabel argument. If you recall our discussion about GotoExpression in Chapter 2, you know returnLabel, as an instance of LabelTarget, marks a location in code that we can jump to. In this case, the returnLabel argument marks the location at which the program should continue its execution after the late binding finishes. Figure 3-3 shows a pictorial view of this.

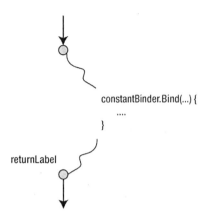

Figure 3-3. Return label and program flow

Figure 3-3 shows that somewhere during program execution, a call to constantBinder.Bind is made. Here constantBinder is an instance of the ConstantBinder class. The figure shows that after the Bind method finishes, the program is supposed to continue its execution at the location marked by returnLabel. The trick here is that program execution will not jump to the location marked by returnLabel unless we tell it to do so. That's why in Listing 3-2, the code calls the Expression.Return factory method and passes it returnLabel. That creates an instance of GotoExpression that jumps to the location marked by returnLabel. If the code does not do this jump, the Bind method, once called, will be called again and again endlessly.

DLR Call Sites

The last section showed the code for a binder that returns a constant value for all late binding operations. Earlier I explained the relation between binding and call site. Basically, a call site is a place in code that invokes an operation that needs to be bound. So, in order to use the ConstantBinder class developed in the previous section, we need a call site that invokes some late-bound operation. Because the operation is late bound, the DLR will need us to pass it a binder that knows how to do the late binding. And the binder we will use in this case is an instance of the ConstantBinder class. With this high-level understanding of all the pieces involved, let's see how they are put together in code.

Listing 3-3 shows the code that uses ConstantBinder to perform late binding. The code first creates an instance of ConstantBinder called binder. Then it creates an instance of CallSite<T> by calling CallSite<T>.Create. When calling CallSite<T>.Create, the code passes binder as the input parameter. This is how the code tells the DLR which binder to use for performing late binding. At this point, the example code has the variable site that represents the call site and the variable binder that contains the late-binding logic. The variable site knows to delegate to binder when it comes time to do late binding. And that time comes when the example code calls the Target delegate on the variable site. After the late binding is done, the Target delegate returns and the result of late binding is assigned to the variable result. If you run the code in Listing 3-3, you'll see the text "Result is 3" printed on the screen.

Listing 3-3. Program.cs

```
private static void RunConstantBinderExample()
{
    CallSiteBinder binder = new ConstantBinder();

    CallSite<Func<CallSite, object, object, int>> site =
        CallSite<Func<CallSite, object, object, int>>.Create(binder);

    //This will invoke the binder to do the binding.
    int result = site.Target(site, 5, 6);
    Console.WriteLine("Result is {0}", result);
}
```

The generic type T in CallSite<T> deserves some explanation. Recall that the main purpose of a DLR call site is to invoke some late-bound operation. The invocation of the late-bound operation is triggered by calling the Target delegate on a call site. And the type of the Target delegate is the generic type parameter T. Because Target represents some callable operation, T has to be a delegate type. Besides that, the DLR further requires the Target delegate's first parameter to be of type CallSite. In summary, the generic type parameter T can't be just any type. It has to meet the following two requirements:

- It must be a delegate type.

- The type of the delegate's first parameter must be CallSite.

In our example code, T is Func<CallSite, object, object, int>. That means the late-bound operation takes three input parameters and returns a value of type int. The types of the three parameters are CallSite, object and object respectively. Because T is the type of the Target delegate, in Listing 3-3 when the code calls Target on the variable site, the input parameters it passes to the call need to meet the method signature of the Target delegate.

Binding Restrictions and Rules

We saw in Listing 3-2 that a binding result is expressed in the form of an expression that represents the number 3. However, the example we saw there is a special case of a more generic way to represent binding results. Recall that the goal of the code in Listing 3-2 is to have a binder whose binding logic will make *all* dynamic (i.e., late binding) code return integer 3. In that requirement statement, one not so obvious condition is the bolded word "all." We can imagine a similar requirement that requires a binder that makes dynamic code to return 3 only when, say, the type of some xyz variable is System.Int32.

Having a binding result that is valid without any condition is a special case of having a binding result that is valid only under certain conditions. It is a special case because we can regard it as having a condition that always evaluates to true. This section extends the example in Listing 3-2 and handles the generic case. Listing 3-4 shows the new code example, the ConstantWithRuleBinder class. The binder class implements the binding logic that returns integer 10 only when the value of the first input parameter is greater than or equal to 5; otherwise, it returns integer 1.

The example code gets the value of the first parameter from the args array (line 8). For each input parameter, in addition to receiving its value, the Bind method also receives a representation of that parameter in the form of a ParameterExpression object. The example code gets the ParameterExpression object of the first input parameter from the parameters collection (line 9). The first input parameter's value, firstParameterValue, and its ParameterExpression object, firstParameterExpression, are used to construct the expression that represents the binding result according to the requirement we'd like to meet.

In this example, the binding result is not just expressed in the form of any expression. It is expressed in the form of a conditional expression. The conditional expression that represents the late binding result returned by a binder is called a **rule**. A rule consists of two parts—restrictions and the binding result. *The restrictions are the conditions under which the binding result is valid.* The need for restrictions has to do with something called *call site caching,* which I'll explain in the next section.

In Listing 3-4, for the case where the value of the first parameter is greater than or equal to 5, the example code calls Expression.GreaterThanOrEqual to create the restrictions (line 14). It creates the binding result similar to the example code in Listing 3-2. It calls Expression.IfThen to combine the restrictions and binding result into a rule. The rule is the final expression that the Bind method returns.

Similarly, for the case where the value of the first parameter is less than 5, the example code calls Expression.LessThan to create the restrictions (line 25). It also calls Expression.IfThen to combine the restrictions and binding result (line 24).

Listing 3-4. ConstantWithRuleBinder.cs

```
1)   public class ConstantWithRuleBinder : CallSiteBinder
2)   {
3)       public override Expression Bind(object[] args,
4)           ReadOnlyCollection<ParameterExpression> parameters, LabelTarget returnLabel)
5)       {
6)           Console.WriteLine("cache miss"); //This will be explained later in the chapter.
7)
8)           int firstParameterValue = (int) args[0];
9)           ParameterExpression firstParameterExpression = parameters.First();
10)
11)          if (firstParameterValue >= 5)
12)          {
13)              return Expression.IfThen(                    //rule
14)                      Expression.GreaterThanOrEqual(       //restrictions
15)                          firstParameterExpression,
16)                          Expression.Constant(5)),
17)                      Expression.Return(          //binding result
18)                          returnLabel,
19)                          Expression.Constant(10))
20)                  );
21)          }
22)          else
23)          {
24)              return Expression.IfThen(                    //rule
25)                      Expression.LessThan(    //restrictions
26)                          firstParameterExpression,
27)                          Expression.Constant(5)),
28)                      Expression.Return(          //binding result
29)                          returnLabel,
30)                          Expression.Constant(1))
31)                  );
32)          }
33)      }
34) }
```

Now let's see what happens when we use `ConstantWithRuleBinder` to do late binding. Listing 3-5 shows the client code that uses `ConstantWithRuleBinder`. The code creates an instance of `ConstantWithRuleBinder` called binder. It creates a call site object and assigns the call site object to the variable site, then it calls the `Target` delegate on the variable site. All of this is similar to what we saw in Listing 3-3. The main difference is that in this example the client code calls the `Target` delegate on the object site twice. The first call to the `Target` delegate has integer 8 as the value of the second input parameter. That value becomes the value of the first input parameter when it gets to the `Bind` method of the binder object. Because the value is greater than 5, the result of the late binding is 10. The second call to the `Target` delegate has integer 3 as the value of the second input parameter. Because of that, the result of the late binding is 1.

Listing 3-5. Program.cs

```
private static void RunConstantWithRuleBinderExample()
{
    CallSiteBinder binder = new ConstantWithRuleBinder();

    CallSite<Func<CallSite, int, int>> site =
      CallSite<Func<CallSite, int, int>>.Create(binder);

    int result = site.Target(site, 8);
    Console.WriteLine("Late binding result is {0}", result);

    result = site.Target(site, 3);
    Console.WriteLine("Late binding result is {0}", result);
}
```

If you run the code in Listing 3-5, you should see output like the following:

```
cache miss
Late binding result is 10
cache miss
Late binding result is 1
```

Checking Binding Rules in Debug Mode

In the previous examples, we saw how binders and call sites work together to perform late binding. Next I want to show you how the rules that represent binding results are cached. But before I get into that, I'd like to show you a useful debugging technique that helped me a lot in learning the DLR. The Visual Studio debugger comes with a tool called Text Visualizer that you can use to visualize expression trees. In this section, we'll debug into the DLR source code and use the Text Visualizer to view the binding rules returned by the code example in Listing 3-5.

If you open the ConstantWithRuleBinder.cs file in this chapter's code download, you'll see the following code snippet:

```
#if CLR2
    using Microsoft.Scripting.Ast;
#else
    using System.Linq.Expressions;
#endif
```

This code snippet uses the conditional compilation symbol CLR2 that we saw in the "Developing for Both .NET 2.0 and .NET 4.0" section. The compilation symbol is needed because when we compile the example code to run on .NET 2.0, some DLR classes used in the example code are in the Microsoft.Scripting.Ast namespace. However, those DLR classes are in the System.Linq.Expressions namespace when we compile the example code to run on .NET 4.0. The reason for the namespace difference is because in .NET 4.0, some DLR code is put into namespaces like System.Linq.Expressions and packaged into the System.Core.dll assembly.

If you run the code in Listing 3-5 from the CallSiteBinderExamples20 project in debug mode, you should be able to debug into the DLR source code. Figure 3-4 shows the screen capture of a debug session I ran. In this session, I set a break point at the line right after the call to the Bind method. The break point is in the BindCore<T> method of the CallSiteBinder class, and we have debugged into the DLR source code. The value returned by the call to the Bind method is assigned to the binding variable (the line of code is marked with a red box in Figure 3-4) and it is essentially the rule that represents the late-binding result.

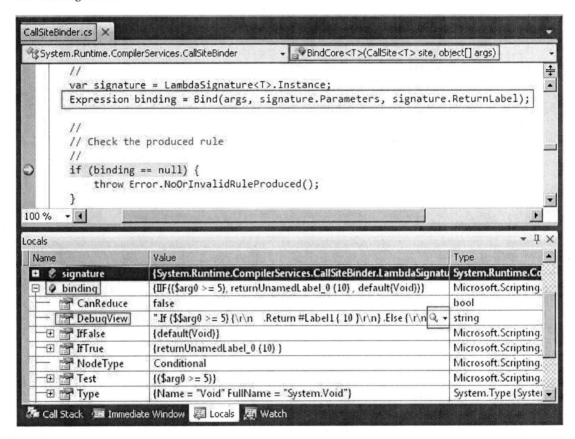

Figure 3-4. Debug view of running the code in Listing 3-5 in debug mode.

If we expand the binding variable in the bottom half of Figure 3-4 and look at its contents, we can see that under the binding variable, there is a DebugView entry. To the right of the DebugView entry, you'll see a magnifier icon with a down arrow. If you right-click on the arrow and select Text Visualizer, a dialog window pops up that will display the textual visualization of the binding rule that ConstantWithRuleBinder returns. Listing 3-6 shows the textual visualization of the binding rule when the first argument is greater than or equal to 5.

Listing 3-6. Textual Visualization When the First Argument Is Greater Than or Equal to 5

```
.If ($$arg0 >= 5) {
    .Return #Label1 { 10 }
} .Else {
    .Default(System.Void)
}
```

The rule shown in Listing 3-6 basically says "if the first argument (arg0) is greater or equal to 5, then return 10; otherwise, return some void value to indicate that a rebinding is required." The rule matches the code logic in the ConstantWithRuleBinder class. Now, if we let the debug session continue from the break point, the program execution will stop at the break point again because, in Listing 3-5, the code calls the Target delegate to do late binding again with a different input parameter. This time, the Text Visualizer displays the textual visualization of the binding rule as Listing 3-7 shows. And you can see that the rule shown in Listing 3-7 matches the code logic we have in the ConstantWithRuleBinder class for the case where the first input argument is less than 5.

Listing 3-7. Textual Visualization When the First Argument Is Less Than 5

```
.If ($$arg0 < 5) {
    .Return #Label1 { 1 }
} .Else {
    .Default(System.Void)
}
```

In summary, the code in Listing 3-5 calls the Target delegate on the call site twice, and we saw the binding rules for those two late-binding operations in Text Visualizer. When the code in Listing 3-5 calls the Target delegate for the first time, a late-binding process takes place and the rule in Listing 3-6 is produced and cached. When the code in Listing 3-5 calls the Target delegate for the second time, another late-binding process takes place because the cached rule returns a value that indicates the need for a rebinding. So the Bind method of ConstantWithRuleBinder is called again and the rule in Listing 3-7 is produced and cached. At this point, you may notice that the two rules in Listing 3-6 and Listing 3-7 can actually be combined into one single rule like this:

```
.If ($$arg0 >= 5) {
    .Return #Label1 { 10 }
} .Else {
    .Return #Label1 { 1 }
}
```

The new rule is more economic and efficient because it requires only one late-binding operation for the code in Listing 3-5. Here's why. When the code in Listing 3-5 calls the Target delegate for the first time, a late-binding process takes place. If the new rule is produced and cached as the result of the late binding, then the second time the Target delegate is called, the new rule will return integer 1 instead of a value that indicates the need for a rebinding. In order to make the binder produce the new binding rule, you need to change the implementation of ConstantWithRuleBinder in Listing 3-4 to the code in Listing 3-8, which calls the Expression.IfThenElse factory method to create a ConditionalExpression instance whose if-branch returns integer 10 and else-branch integer 1.

Listing 3-8. A More Efficient Implemenation of the Binding Logic

```
public override Expression Bind(object[] args,
    ReadOnlyCollection<ParameterExpression> parameters, LabelTarget returnLabel)
{
    Console.WriteLine("cache miss");
    ParameterExpression firstParameterExpression = parameters[0];
    int firstParameterValue = (int)args[0];

    return Expression.IfThenElse( //rule
            Expression.GreaterThanOrEqual( //restrictions
                    firstParameterExpression,
                    Expression.Constant(5)),
            Expression.Return( //binding result
                    returnLabel,
                    Expression.Constant(10)),
            Expression.Return( //binding result
                returnLabel,
                Expression.Constant(1))
        );
}
```

Before we make the code change in Listing 3-8, we see two lines of "cache miss" printed on the screen when we run the example. After the code change in Listing 3-8, when we run the example we see only one line of "cache miss." So what is "cache miss" about? That's the topic of the next section.

Caching

Late binding is expensive because it needs to make several methods calls to get the Expression instance that represents the rule, i.e., restrictions plus binding result. Then the rule needs to be interpreted or compiled into executable IL code by the DLR. The whole late-binding process usually makes the code run much slower than early-bound code. Because of that, caching the result of late binding is crucial to the success of a framework like the DLR. The previous section previewed the DLR's caching functionality but didn't explain the details. Now we'll look at this important feature of the DLR and use examples to show how the caching works.

Three Cache Levels

There is not just one cache for storing late-binding results, but three. The Target delegate we saw earlier is a cache. There's also a cache maintained in a call site, and another cache in a binder. The way they work in the late binding process is illustrated in Figure 3-5.

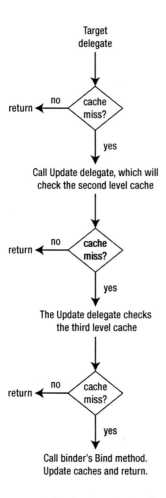

Target
delegate

no ← return   cache
miss?

yes

Call Update delegate, which will
check the second level cache

no ← return   cache
miss?

yes

The Update delegate checks
the third level cache

no ← return   cache
miss?

yes

Call binder's Bind method.
Update caches and return.

Figure 3-5. *The three cache levels and the late binding process*

When client code invokes the Target delegate on a call site for the first time to perform late binding, the DLR will first check whether there is any rule in the three caches that can serve as the result of the late binding. Because this is the first invocation of the Target delegate, the Target delegate, as a first-level (L0) cache, doesn't have anything cached yet. So the Target delegate proceeds to the second-level (L1) cache, which is the call site's cache, by calling the call site's Update delegate. The second-level cache doesn't have any rules in it because no client call has invoked the site to do late binding. The Update delegate therefore proceeds to the third and last (L2) cache, which is the binder's cache. The binder might or might not have a suitable rule in its cache for the late binding. If it does, that rule is returned to the call site and the expensive late-binding operation is avoided. The returned rule is put into the second-level cache as well as the first-level cache. On the other hand, if the binder does not have a suitable rule in its cache for the late binding, the binder's Bind method is called to do the expensive late binding. When a binder's Bind method returns a rule expression to a call site, the rule is put into level 3 and level 2 caches and is also assigned to the call site's Target delegate.

If client code performs subsequent invocations of the Target delegate on the same call site, since the Target delegate has been invoked, the rule the Target delegate caches might happen to be the right rule for the late binding. *A rule is the right rule if its restrictions evaluate to true in the late binding context.* For example, assuming the suboptimal implementation of the ConstantWithRuleBinder class shown in Listing 3-4 is used, the following line in Listing 3-5 does not pass the restrictions of the Target delegate's cached rule.

```
result = site.Target(site, 3);
```

Prior to this line of code, Listing 3-5 calls the Target delegate and passes it integer 8. Because of that, the Target delegate's cached rule has the restrictions shown in the following in bold. The restrictions test whether the first parameter of the late-binding operation is greater than or equal to 5. This is the same code you see in the suboptimal version of the ConstantWithRuleBinder class's Bind method.

```
Expression.IfThen(
    Expression.GreaterThanOrEqual(
        firstParameterExpression,
        Expression.Constant(5)),
    ... //binding result omitted
);
```

When we call the Target delegate on the same call site the second time, with integer 3 as the input parameter, that integer 3 is part of the late-binding context. The rule cached in the Target delegate has restrictions that test whether the first input parameter is greater than or equal to 5. So the cached rule is not the right rule because its restrictions evaluate to false in the late binding context. In that situation, the Target delegate invokes the call site's Update delegate and proceeds to the second-level cache.

It should be clear now how important rules and their restrictions are to the DLR's cache mechanism. Without them, the cache mechanism would be useless because there would be no information for determining whether a cached result is suitable in a late-binding context or whether an expensive call to the binder's Bind method is needed.

Late-Binding Context

The previous paragraphs mentioned the term *late-binding context*. What is it? And what's in it? A late-binding context represents the environment (i.e., the context) in which a late binding takes place. In the previous example, we saw that integer 3, the first parameter of the late-binding operation, is part of the context in which the late binding takes place. In fact, all the input parameters of a late-binding operation are in the context. Besides the input parameters, each parameter's name and type are part of the context. The order of the input parameters is also included in the context. What's more, the return type of the late-binding operation is part of the context as well. Every late-binding operation has a return type because DLR binders use DLR expressions to represent binding results and, as Chapter 2 mentioned, DLR expressions, unlike statements, always have a return type.

The information in a late-binding context can be categorized into two kinds—compile-time and run-time. For a late-binding operation, all the input parameters' types and the return type are run-time information because they are generally not known at compile time; otherwise, it would be an early-bound operation, not late bound. For compile-time information in a context, the DLR doesn't limit what you can put there. A good example of compile-time information in a late-binding context is the name of the invoked method. The C# code snippet invokes the ToLower method on the dynamic object hello. The method invocation is late bound and the C# compiler will compile the method invocation into a call site and a binder. The binder will have the method name ToLower stored in it so that when the binder needs to perform late binding, it knows the name of the method to bind. The method name ToLower is available at compile time and is a piece of information in the late-binding context.

```
dynamic hello = "Hello";
String helloInLowerCase = hello.ToLower();
```

It might seem redundant to include a parameter's type in the context when the parameter (i.e., the parameter value, the integer 3 in our example) itself is already in the context. You can simply use reflection to get the type of a parameter value. As it turns out, a parameter's type might not be the same as the type of the parameter's value. For example, a late-binding operation might expect a parameter of some base class and the type of the parameter might be a derived class.

All of the information in a late-binding context is accessible to a binder for performing late binding. When no suitable rule is in the L0, L1, or L2 caches for a late-binding operation, the call site will prepare all the information that makes up the late-binding context and passes that to the binder's Bind method, which has the following method signature:

```
public override Expression Bind(
    object[] args,                              //parameter values
    ReadOnlyCollection<ParameterExpression> parameters, //paramter names, types and order
    LabelTarget returnLabel)                    //return type and name
```

As you can see from the Bind method's signature, there is a correspondence between the pieces of run-time information in a late-binding context and the Bind method's input parameters. The second input parameter of the Bind method is of type ReadOnlyCollection<ParameterExpression>. The class ReadOnlyCollection<T> implements IList<T>. The order of the elements in ReadOnlyCollection<ParameterExpression> is the order of a late binding operation's input parameters. The Name and Type properties of the ParameterExpression class represent an input parameter's name and type in the late-binding context. The Name and Type properties of the LabelTarget class represent the return value's name and type in the late-binding context.

Table 3-2 summarizes each piece of the run-time information in a late-binding context and its corresponding input parameter in the Bind method's signature. The last column of the table uses the line result = site.Target(site, 3) in Listing 3-5 as an example and shows the value of each piece of the run-time information in the late-binding context.

Table 3-2. Late-Binding Context

Information in Context	Bind Method's Input Parameter	Example
Parameter values	object[] args	This array has integer 3 as the only element.
Parameter types, names and order	ReadOnlyCollection<ParameterExpression> parameters	This collection has only one instance of ParameterExpression whose Type property is System.Int32 and whose Name property is not explicitly set.

Information in Context	Bind Method's Input Parameter	Example
Return type and name	LabelTarget returnLabel	The LabelTarget instance's Type property is System.Int32. Its Name property is not explicitly set.

This section explains the three cache levels and how they play a part in the late binding process. Let's see some examples of these cache levels in action in the next few sections. For the purpose of demonstration, all the examples in the rest of this chapter will use the suboptimal implementation of the ConstantWithRuleBinder class shown in Listing 3-4.

L0 Cache Example

This section demonstrates how the L0 cache works. Listing 3-9 shows the client code that uses the ConstantWithRuleBinder class we saw earlier for the late-binding logic. The code is similar to the code in Listing 3-5. In this example, the code calls site.Target twice. When the code first calls site.Target, the Target delegate does not have any rule in the L0 cache. There isn't any rule in the L1 and L2 caches either. So the binder's Bind method is invoked to perform the late binding. Every time the binder's Bind method is invoked, the text "cache miss" will be printed to the screen so that we can clearly see when a cache miss happens and when a cache match is found.

After the first call to site.Target, all three caches will contain the rule returned by the binder's Bind method. Then the client code calls site.Target the second time and passes it integer 9. Because integer 9 is greater than 5, the restrictions of the rule in L0 cache evaluate to true and no expensive late binding is needed.

Listing 3-9. L0 Cache Example

```
private static void L0CachExample()
{
    CallSiteBinder binder = new ConstantWithRuleBinder();

    CallSite<Func<CallSite, int, int>> site =
        CallSite<Func<CallSite, int, int>>.Create(binder);

    //This will invoke the binder to do the binding.
    int result = site.Target(site, 8);
    Console.WriteLine("Late binding result is {0}", result);

    //This will not invoke the binder to do the binding because of L0 cache match.
    result = site.Target(site, 9);
    Console.WriteLine("Late binding result is {0}", result);
}
```

If you run the code in Listing 3-9, you'll see the following output on the screen. Notice that there is only one cache miss.

```
cache miss
Late binding result is 10
Late binding result is 10
```

L1 Cache Example

This section demonstrates how the L1 cache works. Like Listing 3-9, the client code in Listing 3-10 uses the ConstantWithRuleBinder class we saw earlier in Listing 3-4 for the late-binding logic. In this example, the code calls site.Target three times. When the code first calls site.Target, the Target delegate doesn't have any rule in the L0 cache. There isn't any rule in the L1 and L2 caches either. So the binder's Bind method is invoked to perform the late binding. So far everything is the same as in the preceding example.

After the first call to site.Target, all three caches will contain the rule returned by the binder's Bind method. To ease our discussion, let's call this rule 1. The client code calls site.Target a second time and passes it integer 3. Because integer 3 is neither greater than nor equal to 5, the restrictions of the rule the in L0 cache evaluate to false. The restrictions of the same rule in the L1 and L2 caches also evaluate to false. So the binder's Bind method is invoked to perform late binding. Let's call the rule returned this time rule 2. Rule 2 is cached together with rule 1 in the L1 and L2 caches. The L1 cache can hold up to 10 rules while the L2 cache can hold up to 128 rules per delegate type. Don't worry about the L2 cache and its cache size for now. I'll explain that in detail in the next section. The important thing to note here is that rule 1 and rule 2 are both in the L1 and L2 caches. But only rule 2 is in the L0 cache.

Because of this, when the client code calls site.Target the third time and passes it integer 9, and 9 is not less than 5, the restrictions of rule 2 in L0 cache evaluate to false. The Target delegate thus calls the Update delegate to proceed to the L1 cache. The L1 cache contains both rule 1 and rule 2. In this case, rule 1 is suitable for the late binding and therefore no call to the binder's Bind method is necessary.

Listing 3-10. L1 Cache Example

```
private static void L1CachExample()
{
    CallSiteBinder binder = new ConstantWithRuleBinder();

    CallSite<Func<CallSite, int, int>> site =
      CallSite<Func<CallSite, int, int>>.Create(binder);

    //This will invoke the binder to do the binding.
    int result = site.Target(site, 8);
    Console.WriteLine("Late binding result is {0}", result);

    //This will invoke the binder to do the binding.
    result = site.Target(site, 3);
    Console.WriteLine("Late binding result is {0}", result);

    //This will not invoke the binder to do the binding because of L1 cache match.
    result = site.Target(site, 9);
    Console.WriteLine("Late binding result is {0}", result);
}
```

If you run the code in Listing 3-10, you'll see the following output on the screen:

```
cache miss
Late binding result is 10
cache miss
Late binding result is 1
Late binding result is 10
```

L2 Cache Example

The L2 cache example in this section is a bit more complex than those in the previous sections. The reason for the complexity is that the same binder may be shared by multiple call sites. This will be easier to understand with some examples.

In the previous sections, we call the Target delegate on the same call site instance. This usually happens when you have C# code that looks like the following:

```
void Foo(dynamic name) {
    name.ToLower(); //call site is here.
}

Foo("Bob");
Foo("Rob");
```

There's only one call site instance in the Foo method. In the code snippet, the Foo method is called twice. Each time Foo is called, the same L0 and L1 caches of the one and the only call site in the Foo method are searched for a suitable rule.

Now let's see a slightly different example. If the Foo method looks like the one in the code snippet below, there will be two separate call sites, i.e., two instances of CallSite<T>. The two call sites are totally independent of each other. Each of the two call sites has its own L0 and L1 cache. Those caches are not shared across call sites.

```
void Foo(dynamic name) {
    name.ToLower(); //call site is here.
    name.ToLower(); //another call site is here.
}
```

To share cached rules across call sites, you share binders. By sharing a binder across call sites, rules in the binder's cache are shared. The code in Listing 3-11 demonstrates the sharing of an L2 cache across two call sites. The example code creates one instance of ConstantWithRuleBinder and two call sites, site1 and site2. The binder is shared between the two call sites. When the example code calls site1.Target, the binder's Bind method is invoked to do the late binding. The result of the late binding is cached in site1's L0 and L1 caches. It is also cached in the binder's L2 cache. So when site2.Target is invoked, even though site2's L0 and L1 caches don't have a suitable rule for the late binding, the binder's L2 cache has one. Therefore, the binder's Bind method is again not invoked.

Listing 3-11. L2 Cache Example

```
private static void L2CachExample()
{
    CallSiteBinder binder = new ConstantWithRuleBinder();

    CallSite<Func<CallSite, int, int>> site1 =
```

```
    CallSite<Func<CallSite, int, int>>.Create(binder);

    CallSite<Func<CallSite, int, int>> site2 =
      CallSite<Func<CallSite, int, int>>.Create(binder);

    //This will invoke the binder to do the binding.
    int result = site1.Target(site1, 8);
    Console.WriteLine("Late binding result is {0}", result);

    //This will not invoke the binder to do the binding because of L2 cache match.
    result = site2.Target(site2, 9);
    Console.WriteLine("Late binding result is {0}", result);
}
```

If you run the code in Listing 3-11, you'll see the following output on the screen. Notice that there is only one cache miss.

```
cache miss
Late binding result is 10
Late binding result is 10
```

Now, for comparison, Listing 3-12 shows the same example, except this time each site uses its own binder. The object site1 uses binder1 and site2 uses binder2.

Listing 3-12. Not Sharing the L2 Cache

```
private static void L2CachNoSharingExample()
{
    CallSiteBinder binder1 = new ConstantWithRuleBinder();
    CallSiteBinder binder2 = new ConstantWithRuleBinder();

    CallSite<Func<CallSite, int, int>> site1 =
      CallSite<Func<CallSite, int, int>>.Create(binder1);

    CallSite<Func<CallSite, int, int>> site2 =
      CallSite<Func<CallSite, int, int>>.Create(binder2);

    //This will invoke the binder to do the binding.
    int result = site1.Target(site1, 8);
    Console.WriteLine("Late binding result is {0}", result);

    //This will invoke the binder to do the binding because of no L2 cache match.
    result = site2.Target(site2, 9);
    Console.WriteLine("Late binding result is {0}", result);
}
```

If you run the code in Listing 3-12, you'll see the following output on the screen. Notice that there are two cache misses in the output.

```
cache miss
Late binding result is 10
```

```
cache miss
Late binding result is 10
```

Creating Canonical Binders

It should be clear that sharing binders across call sites is important to the performance of a DLR-based language. However, that doesn't mean a language implementer should use one binder for all call sites. The proper criterion for sharing a binder across multiple call sites is when those call sites have the same compile-time information in their late binding context. A binder shared across multiple call sites that have the same compile-time information in their late-binding context is called a *canonical binder*.

Listing 3-13 shows an example of when to use a canonical binder. The listing shows a C# code snippet that involves some late-binding operations. The code assigns a string literal to the variable x and another string literal to the variable y. Then it invokes the ToLower method on x in line 3 and on y in line 4. The two method invocations are late bound. In lines 5 and 6, the example code accesses the Length property of x and y respectively. The two property-access operations are also late bound. The question is, for the two method invocations and the two property access operations, how many binders should we use if we are implementing something like the C# compiler? Because the two method invocations are of the same kind of late-binding operations (i.e., the method invocation operation) and because they invoke the same method name ToLower (i.e., their compile-time information in their late-binding context is the same), the two method invocations should share the same canonical binder for their late binding. Similarly, because the two property-access operations are of the same kind of late-binding operations (i.e., the property get-access operation) and because they access the same property name Length (i.e., their compile-time information in their late binding context is the same), the two property-access operations should share one canonical binder for their late binding.

Listing 3-13. An Example of When to Use a Canonical Binder

```
1)    dynamic x = "foo";
2)    dynamic y = "bar";
3)    dynamic z = x.ToLower(); //call site is here.
4)    z = y.ToLower(); //another call site is here.
5)    z = x.Length;
6)    z = y.Length;
```

Summary

In this chapter, we looked at the caching mechanism of DLR binders. We saw code examples of the three cache levels in action, showing when a cache miss occurs and when a cached rule is reused. I also introduced canonical binders, and described when to share binders across multiple call sites. Along the way, I showed how to build debug versions of the DLR assemblies for .NET 2.0, how to write DLR-based code that targets both .NET 2.0 and .NET 4.0, and how to debug into the DLR source code to see the rules that represent binding results in Text Visualizer. We have covered a lot in this chapter about DLR binders and caching. The next chapter will examine how DLR binders enable language interoperability.

CHAPTER 4

■ ■ ■

Late Binding and Interoperability

DLR binders have two key responsibilities. One is the caching mechanism we looked at in the previous chapter. The other is language interoperability, and that's the main topic of this chapter. Binders alone do not language interoperability make. The key elements in the DLR that make language interoperability possible are: a *common type system* that consists of twelve operations, *binders, dynamic objects,* and an *interoperability protocol* between binders and dynamic objects. In the DLR, binders and dynamic objects work together by adhering to a mutual protocol to ensure that objects from different languages interoperate seamlessly. This chapter will cover all of the key elements in the DLR that enable language interoperability. You'll see examples that fetch dynamic objects from Ruby code and pass them to Python code. However, I won't yet show you how to implement dynamic objects from the ground up; that will be the topic of the next chapter. For this chapter, it is enough to just use dynamic objects that come from Python or Ruby code.

Binders, dynamic objects, and the interoperability protocol they participate in are crucial to a solid understanding of how the DLR works. Let's begin the journey by first looking at what language interoperability means.

Language Interoperability

There are different levels of interoperability between languages. You can view web services as one way to enable language interoperability. A web service can be written in one language while a client of the web service can be written in a different language. The two languages interoperate by sending well-defined XML payloads to each other.

For our purposes, language interoperability means the ability to take something like a class or a function written in one language and use it in another language. For example, we may take a C# class, create an instance of it, and pass the instance to IronPython. Or we could take the same C# class, pass it directly to some IronPython code, and let the IronPython code create an instance of that class. The IronPython code can call methods on the C# object, or access its member properties. Not only can we pass C# classes or objects to IronPython, we can do the same in the other direction. We can pass IronPython classes, functions, or objects to C#. Furthermore, not only do we have this interoperability between a static language like C# and a dynamic language like IronPython, we also have it between two dynamic languages. For example, we can pass IronRuby classes or objects to IronPython and vice versa.

As an example, let's define a class in IronRuby and create an instance of it in C#. Listing 4-1 shows the IronRuby class. You can find all of this chapter's code examples in the Chapter4 solution of this book's download. If you open the Chapter4 solution in Visual Studio C# 2010 Express, you'll see that it has a project called InteropBinderExamples. Because we use IronPython and IronRuby in these code examples, the InteropBinderExamples project has references to the IronPython and IronRuby assemblies, such as `IronPython.dll`, `IronPython.Modules.dll`, `IronRuby.dll`, and `IronRuby.Libraries.dll,` and it also has references to DLR assemblies, such as `Microsoft.Dynamic.dll` and `MicrosoftScripting.dll`.

Listing 4-1. The RubyProduct Class in RubyProduct.rb

```ruby
class RubyProduct
  attr_accessor :name
  attr_accessor :price

  def initialize(name, price)
    @name = name
    @price = price
  end
end
```

The code in Listing 4-1 defines a Ruby class called RubyProduct that has two member variables—name and price. The method initialize is a constructor method that gets called when new instances of the RubyProduct class are created. In this example, the constructor method takes a name and a price as input and sets them to the member variables. With RubyProduct in place, the next thing we want to do is to create an instance of it in C#. Listing 4-2 shows the code for doing that.

Listing 4-2. The Method for Creating Instances of the RubyProduct Class

```csharp
1)   class RubyExampleCode
2)   {
3)       private static dynamic productClass;
4)       private static ScriptEngine rbEngine;
5)
6)       static RubyExampleCode()
7)       {
8)           rbEngine = IronRuby.Ruby.CreateEngine();
9)           ScriptScope scope = rbEngine.ExecuteFile("RubyProduct.rb");
10)          productClass = rbEngine.Runtime.Globals.GetVariable("RubyProduct");
11)      }
12)
13)      public static dynamic CreateRubyProduct(String name, int price)
14)      {
15)          return rbEngine.Operations.CreateInstance(productClass, name, price);
16)      }
17)  }
```

The method CreateRubyProduct in Listing 4-2 creates an instance of the RubyProduct class. It does that by using the DLR's Hosting API. I won't get into the details of the DLR Hosting API for now as it's not the focus of the current discussion. I'll explain what the code does at a high level and will defer the detailed discussion of DLR's Hosting API to Chapter 6.

The static constructor of the RubyExampleCode class first creates a ScriptEngine instance for running Ruby code (line 8). The Ruby code in this example is the code in Listing 4-1 and it's in the RubyProduct.rb file. Once the Ruby code is run, an object representing the RubyProduct class is available (a class is an object in Ruby). The code in Listing 4-2 fetches that class object and assigns it to the variable productClass (line 10). The code in the CreateRubyProduct method passes productClass to some CreateInstance method to create an instance of RubyProduct. Again, don't worry too much yet if you don't feel you have a good understanding of the code. For now, it's enough to know that the CreateRubyProduct method creates an instance of RubyProduct every time it's called.

At this point, we have a Ruby class and a method that creates instances of the Ruby class in C#. Let's put them together in Listing 4-3 and see how it looks.

Listing 4-3. Client Code That Uses RubyExampleCode to Create Ruby Objects

```
static void Main(string[] args)
{
    RunRubyClassInstantiationExample();
    Console.ReadLine();
}

private static void RunRubyClassInstantiationExample()
{
    dynamic stretchString = RubyExampleCode.CreateRubyProduct("Stretch String", 7);
    Console.WriteLine("Product {0} is {1} dollars.",
            stretchString.name, stretchString.price);
}
```

The Main method in Listing 4-3 calls the RunRubyClassInstantiationExample method to run the example. This method creates an instance of the RubyProduct class by calling the static CreateRubyProduct method of the RubyExampleCode class. Once an instance of the RubyProduct class is created, the code in Listing 4-3 prints out the name and price properties of the RubyProduct instance to the console. If you run the code, you'll see output that looks like this:

```
Product Stretch String is 7 dollars.
```

The example so far shows some interoperability between C# and IronRuby. Let's crank it up a notch by throwing in a C# class and an IronPython function. What the next example will show you is the passing of both a Ruby object and a C# object to an IronPython function. The IronPython function will do some calculation with the two objects and return the result. Listing 4-4 shows the C# class, which is called CSharpProduct. Like the RubyProduct class, the CSharpProduct class has the two properties name and price. Listing 4-5 shows a Python function called addPrice that we'll use to do some calculation on both a Ruby object and a C# object. The function addPrice takes two parameters as input and adds up their price properties. The Python code is stored in the pythonExampleCode.py file.

Listing 4-4. CSharpProduct.cs.

```
public class CSharpProduct
{
    public String name { get; set; }
    public int price { get; set; }

    public CSharpProduct(String name, int price)
    {
        this.name = name;
        this.price = price;
    }
}
```

Listing 4-5. The addPrice Function in pythonExampleCode.py

```python
def addPrice(x, y):
        return x.price + y.price
```

Just as the previous example used a ScriptEngine instance to run the Ruby code, this example needs a ScriptEngine to run the Python code. Listing 4-6 shows the class PythonExampleCode that acts as a helper class for running the Python code in Listing 4-5. Like before, the code in Listing 4-6 uses DLR's Hosting API, which is the topic of Chapter 6. For now, it is enough to know that the code in Listing 4-6 uses a ScriptEngine instance to run the Python code in the pythonExampleCode.py file. After running the Python code, the addPrice method we saw in Listing 4-5 is available as an object. So the code in Listing 4-6 fetches the object that represents the addPrice Python function and assigns it to the static AddPriceDelegate variable.

Listing 4-6. PythonExampleCode.cs

```csharp
class PythonExampleCode
{
    public static Func<dynamic, dynamic, int> AddPriceDelegate;

    static PythonExampleCode()
    {
        ScriptEngine pyEngine = IronPython.Hosting.Python.CreateEngine();
        ScriptScope scope = pyEngine.ExecuteFile("pythonExampleCode.py");
        AddPriceDelegate = scope.GetVariable("addPrice");
    }
}
```

What we have so far is a C# class, a Ruby class, and a Python function. Let's put them together and have some fun. The code in Listing 4-7 passes a Ruby object (i.e., an object of a Ruby class) and a C# object (i.e., an object of a C# class) to the addPrice Python function. The example code in Listing 4-7 first creates a Ruby object and assigns it to the stretchString variable. The price of stretch string is 7 dollars. The code then creates a C# object and assigns it to the handClapper variable. The price of a hand clapper is 6 dollars. Finally, the example code passes the Ruby object and the C# object to the IronPython function. The function adds up the two prices and, sure enough, the total of stretch string and hand clapper is 13 dollars.

Listing 4-7. Passing a Ruby Object and a C# Object to a Python Function

```csharp
static void Main(string[] args)
{
    RunAddPriceExample();
    Console.ReadLine();
}

private static void RunAddPriceExample()
{
    dynamic stretchString = RubyExampleCode.CreateRubyProduct("Stretch String", 7);
```

```
    dynamic handClapper = new CSharpProduct("Hand Clapper", 6);
    int total = PythonExampleCode.AddPriceDelegate(stretchString, handClapper);
    Console.WriteLine("Total is {0}.", total);
}
```

The example does not look very complex. After all, it's just a few lines of code. Underneath the code, however, there's actually a lot happening. The DLR does great work in hiding the complexity and making the integration between languages look almost effortless. The rest of this chapter is going to take you to backstage and show you the secrets behind the curtain.

Static and Dynamic Objects

One important thing to note in the preceding example is how static objects are treated as dynamic objects. By static objects I mean objects that don't have their own late-binding logic. In contrast, dynamic objects are objects that have their own late-binding logic. In the example, instances of the CSharpProduct class are static objects while instances of the RubyProduct class are dynamic objects. A static object's class can be defined in one language while the object itself is used in another language. And the same goes for dynamic objects. A dynamic object's class can be defined in one language while the dynamic object itself is used in another language. When talking about static or dynamic objects, it helps to distinguish the *source language* in which an object's class is defined and the *target language* in which the object is being used. In the example, the source language of the RubyProduct instances is always Ruby. When the RubyProduct instances are used in C#, then C# is the target language that hosts them. Similarly when they are passed to the addPrice method of IronPython, the target language is IronPython.

Even though instances of the CSharpProduct are static objects, the example code treats them as dynamic objects by using the C# dynamic keyword. Sometimes in this book, the term "dynamic object" means a truly dynamic object like one in Python or Ruby. Sometimes, the term refers to a static object that's treated as a dynamic object. Usually the context makes it clear which case it is. When there's a chance of confusion, I'll clarify what I mean.

Because static objects don't have their own late-binding logic, when they are treated as dynamic objects, who is responsible for deciding their late-binding behavior? What actually happens is that, by default, the DLR wraps static objects with instances of the DynamicMetaObject class. This wrapping effectively turns static objects into dynamic objects. However, there is no late-binding behavior implemented in DynamicMetaObject. Instead, DynamicMetaObject delegates the job of late binding to the target language's binders. So long story short, by default, it is the target language's binders that handle the late-binding behavior of static objects.

DynamicMetaObject is the most important class in the whole discussion about dynamic objects in the next chapter. You will also run into this class a few times in this chapter, so it helps to explain at a high level what it is. *In DLR, late-binding logic can be in one of two places. It can be in binders as we have seen so far. It can also be in dynamic objects.* The late-binding logic of a dynamic object is not in the dynamic object itself. Rather, the logic is in the meta-object associated with the dynamic object. The meta-object has to be an instance of DynamicMetaObject or one of its derived classes. In other words, instances of DynamicMetaObject or its derivatives are objects that contain the late-binding logic of dynamic objects. The next chapter will show you how to implement custom late-binding logic in classes that derive from DynamicMetaObject. For now, it's enough to understand DynamicMetaObject as the base class of all classes that implement late-binding logic of dynamic objects.

Late-Binding Logic in Two Places

One question you might have is why late-binding logic resides in two places (binders and dynamic objects)? What's the difference between the late-binding logic in those places? How do you decide whether to put your custom late-binding logic in binders or in dynamic objects? The next two sections take a detailed look at these two places. After the discussion, you'll know the answers to these questions. First, let's look at the late-binding logic in binders.

Late Binding Logic in Binders

The late-binding logic in binders pertains to a target language. For example, C# implements its own set of binder classes. Those binder classes have late-binding logic that pertains to C#. Similarly, IronPython implements its own set of binder classes that have late-binding logic pertaining to IronPython. Why does each language need its own binders? Here's an example. In IronPython, you can access the __class__ field of any object to get the object's class. It doesn't matter what the object's source language is. It also doesn't matter whether the object is a static object or dynamic object. As long as we use the object in IronPython, we can expect a seamless interoperability that allows us to access the __class__ field of the object just as we can any native Python object. Clearly, if an object's source language is not Python, it won't have any clue about the Python-specific __class__ field. Even if the object happens to have a field with the name __class__, the semantics of that field might not be the same as Python's. So when we access the __class__ field of an object in some Python code, the late-binding logic pertaining to the IronPython language will kick in and perform the binding no matter whether the object is static or dynamic. If it's a static object, the IronPython language binders will be invoked anyway since the object itself does not know how to do its own late binding. If it's a dynamic object, the DLR has a mechanism that falls back to the IronPython language binders when the object does not know how to bind things like __class__. I will describe more about that fallback mechanism in a bit. First, let's look at an example that shows how the late binding logic in IronPython's binders allows us to access the __class__ field on a static .NET object.

The IronPython code snippet below adds a reference to the System.Windows.Forms.dll assembly and then creates an instance of the Form class in the System.Windows.Forms namespace. The Form class is a static .NET class and does not have a property called __class__ defined. However, the IronPython code snippet is able to access the __class__ property on the form object because, in this example, IronPython is the target language and IronPython's binders will perform the late binding when the example code tries to access the __class__ property on the form object.

```
import clr
clr.AddReference("System.Windows.Forms")
from System.Windows.Forms import Form

form = Form()
print form.__class__
```

Determining the target language of an object is not always as straightforward as this. Here's another example that's slightly more complicated. This example accesses the __class__ property on a dynamic Ruby object and a static C# object within an IronPython function. For this example, I added a new Python function in the pythonExampleCode.py file. The new function is called printClassName and it is shown in Listing 4-8. The function is very simple. It takes an input parameter and prints the parameter's __class__ attribute.

Listing 4-8. The printClassName Function in pythonExampleCode.py

```
def addPrice(x, y):
        return x.price + y.price

def printClassName(x):
        print x.__class__
```

In order to make it easy to call the printClassName function in C#, I added a new static variable called PrintClassNameDelegate in the PythonExampleCode class (which we saw earlier in this chapter). Listing 4-9 shows the code I added for this example in bold. The new static variable PrintClassNameDelegate in Listing 4-9 is a reference to the printClassName Python function shown in Listing 4-8.

Listing 4-9. PythonExampleCode.cs

```
class PythonExampleCode
{
    public static Func<dynamic, dynamic, int> AddPriceDelegate;
    public static Action<dynamic> PrintClassNameDelegate;

    static PythonExampleCode ()
    {
        ScriptEngine pyEngine = IronPython.Hosting.Python.CreateEngine();
        ScriptScope scope = pyEngine.ExecuteFile("pythonExampleCode.py");
        AddPriceDelegate = scope.GetVariable("addPrice");
        PrintClassNameDelegate = scope.GetVariable("printClassName");
    }
}
```

At this point, everything is in place and we are ready to see what the example intends to demonstrate. The code in Listing 4-10 creates a Ruby object and passes the object to the printClassName Python function. What's significant here is that the Ruby object does not have any clue about the __class__ attribute. The __class__ attribute is a Python-specific thing. When the C# code in Listing 4-10 calls the Python function and passes it the Ruby object, the target language of the Ruby object changes from C# to IronPython. The source language of the Ruby object is still Ruby, of course, and will never change. Inside the printClassName function, the target language of the Ruby object is IronPython, and thus IronPython's binders will call the shots. In this case, the Ruby object is a dynamic object. It does not know how to bind the __class__ attribute. So the binding process falls back to IronPython's binders. Because the binders have late-binding logic that pertains to the Python language, they know how to bind the __class__ attribute. So the binding is successful and the class name is printed on the screen. The key point to note about this example is that an object's target language can change from one to another.

The code in Listing 4-10 goes on to show that the Python function can work with a static object too. The example creates an instance of the CSharpProduct class and passes it to the printClassName Python function. Because the C# object is a static object, it does not know how to do any late binding. Within the printClassName Python function, the IronPython language binders are called upon to do the late binding for the C# object. And again, the binding is successful because the binders have late binding logic that pertains to the Python language, and they know how to bind the __class__ attribute.

Listing 4-10. C# Client Code That Calls a Python Function

```
private static void RunPrintClassNameExample()
{
    dynamic stretchString = RubyExampleCode.CreateRubyProduct("Stretch String", 7);
    PythonExampleCode.PrintClassNameDelegate (stretchString);

    dynamic handClapper = new CSharpProduct("Hand Clapper", 6);
    PythonExampleCode.PrintClassNameDelegate (handClapper);
}
```

If you run the example code, you'll see the following output on the screen:

```
<type 'RubyObject'>
<type 'CSharpProduct'>
```

Late-Binding Logic in Dynamic Objects

The key takeaway of the previous section is that the late-binding logic in binders pertains to a target language. In contrast, the late-binding logic in a dynamic object pertains to that object itself. The idea is that by letting the late-binding logic in a dynamic object pertain to that object itself, no matter where the dynamic object is used, its late-binding behavior is the same and will support the semantic of the dynamic object's source language. For example, instances of RubyProduct are dynamic objects and they carry their own late-binding logic with them. So they have the same late-binding behavior you'd expect a Ruby object to have, no matter if they are used by C# code, IronPython code, or some other language's code. Chapter 5 discusses late-binding logic in dynamic objects in detail. You'll see in Chapter 5 how to implement classes that derive from the DynamicMetaObject class and also how to make use of those classes. Until then, I'll focus the discussion on binders and language interoperability.

Late-Bound Actions

So far, we've talked about late-binding logic in binders and dynamic objects, but we haven't said what exactly can be bound late. The DLR defines twelve actions that can be bound by both binders and dynamic objects at run time. Let's first look at some examples of those late-bound actions, then I'll present the twelve late-bound actions and show you the DLR's binder class hierarchy that corresponds to those twelve actions.

Examples

The following line of code, extracted from Listing 4-3, shows two actions that can be bound late:

```
Console.WriteLine("Product {0} is {1} dollars.", stretchString.name, stretchString.price);
```

First, it shows that accessing a member property can be late bound. In this code, the two operations that access the name and price properties of the stretchString variable are late bound. The variable stretchString is a dynamic object created from a Ruby class. Because of that, the C# compiler does not have the static type information to bind the two operations that access stretchString's member properties at compile time.

Another not so obvious operation that is bound late in the code is **member method invocation**. Because stretchString is a dynamic object, the return values of stretchString.name and stretchString.price are also dynamic objects. When the code passes stretchString.name and stretchString.price as parameters to Console.WriteLine, the invocation of the Console.WriteLine method also becomes late bound. This is because at compile time, without knowing the actual types of all the input parameters, the C# compiler can't decide how to bind the method invocation.

If you compile the code in Listing 4-3 and disassemble the generated assembly, you can verify that indeed the stretchstring.name, stretchString.price, and Console.WriteLine in the code are late bound. Listing 4-11 shows at a conceptual level what you'll see if you disassemble the code in Listing 4-3. The code in Listing 4-11 should look familiar because it's essentially the same kind of code as in the last chapter. The difference is that in Chapter 3, the examples create their own call sites and binders and here the call sites and binders are created by the C# compiler.

Listing 4-11. A Conceptual Illustration of the Code Generated by the C# Compiler

```
if (Site4 == null)
{
    Site4 = CallSite<Action<CallSite, Type, string, object, object>>
                .Create(Binder.InvokeMember(..., "WriteLine", ...));
}

if (Site5 == null)
{
    Site5 = CallSite<Func<CallSite, object, object>>
        .Create(Binder.GetMember(..., "name", ...));
}

if (Site6 == null)
{
    Site6 = CallSite<Func<CallSite, object, object>>
                .Create(Binder.GetMember(..., "price", ...));
}

Site4.Target.Invoke(Site4, typeof(Console), "Product {0} is {1} dollars.",
    Site5.Target.Invoke(Site5, stretchString),
    Site6.Target.Invoke(Site6, stretchString));
```

Listing 4-11 includes three call sites and three binders, one binder and one call site for each of the three late-bound operations—stretchstring.name, stretchString.price, and Console.WriteLine. Before creating each call site, the code generated by the C# compiler checks whether the call site is null. If it's not null, the call site has been created already and the code will not create it again. That's why you see those if conditions in Listing 4-11. This is a good idea because if the method RunRubyClassInstantiationExample is called multiple times, the code won't create three new call sites every time the method is called. Not only that, the code in Listing 4-11 also won't create three new binders every time the RunRubyClassInstantiationExample is called. That's because the code calls the InvokeMember and GetMember methods of the Binder class to get the C# language's binders. These methods ensure that the same canonical binders are returned when the method RunRubyClassInstantiationExample is called multiple times. As you can see, the code generated by the C# compiler avoids unnecessary creation of call sites and binders. This saves memory, of course. But more importantly, because the code reuses the same call sites and binders, the caches in those call sites and binders will also be leveraged to help improve performance.

In Listing 4-11, the variable Site4 is the call site for the late binding of the Console.WriteLine method invocation. The binder passed to Site4 contains the method name "WriteLine" to be late bound. Similarly, the variable Site5 is the call site for the late binding of the stretchString.name property access. The binder passed to Site5 contains the property name "name" to be late bound. The variable Site6 is for the late binding of the stretchString.price property access.

With the three call sites and binders in place, the code in Listing 4-11 invokes the Target delegate on Site5 and Site6. The binding results of Site5.Target and Site6.Target represent the results of stretchString.name and stretchString.price. Those results are then passed to Site4.Target, which eventually prints the text on the screen.

Our discussion in this section shows that member property get–access operations and member method invocations are two kinds of operations that can be late bound. It turns out that the DLR defines in total twelve kinds operations that can be late bound, and those operations make up what's called the *Common Type System* of the DLR. Let's see what that means.

Common Type System

Most languages have their own type systems, and those type systems need to be considered if the languages are going to interoperate. For example, say we have a Java string object in a JVM and we want to bring it over to a .NET CLR runtime. There is more than one way to achieve this. One common approach is marshalling and unmarshalling objects. The idea of this approach is to serialize the Java string object to 0s and 1s, send the bits over to the CLR runtime, and then create a CLR string object by deserializing the bits. However, this approach is often cumbersome and not very efficient, mainly because we need to deal with two separate runtimes and two separate type systems. With this approach, types in one system are unrelated to types in the other system. To bridge the systems and make them interoperate, we have to do the mapping between the types. Nonetheless, it is an approach to consider when you have no control over the two languages you are trying to bridge.

So how does the DLR achieve language interoperability with regard to type systems? The DLR facilitates language interoperability by defining a common type system for DLR-based languages. This is essentially the same tactic used by the CLR, which defines the Common Type System (CTS) for static .NET languages. If two languages share the same type system, then types defined in one language will be understood by the other language without any need for mapping or translation. For example, say we have an abstract C# class. When the C# class is compiled, the fact that it is abstract is mapped to the equivalent "abstract class" construct in the Common Type System. So if we have some VB.NET code that uses the compiled C# class, the VB.NET code will know that the class is an abstract class. VB.NET code does not understand C# code directly; it knows the C# class is abstract only because the C# class has been compiled to IL (.NET Intermediate Language) based on the CTS, which VB.NET understands.

Because a common type system has to meet the needs of multiple languages so that those languages can map to it, the common type system has to be a superset of the type systems of the languages it intends to support. The challenge here is to find a superset that's sufficient and also compact. For dynamic languages, the DLR identified twelve actions/operations that together are sufficient to meet the needs of most dynamic languages. Table 4-1 summaries those twelve actions.

Table 4-1. Twelve Operations/Actions That Can Be Bound Late

Operation/Action	Description
GetMember	This action, when triggered on a dynamic object, will have the effect of getting a property of the object. You saw an example of this earlier in the chapter with stretchString.name. stretchString is a dynamic object and stretchString.name triggers the GetMember action on stretchString in order to get the name property of stretchString.
SetMember	This action sets the value of a dynamic object's property. In this table, dynamic objects mean both truly dynamic objects as well as static objects that are treated as dynamic objects. An example of the SetMember operation is stretchString.name = "stretch string," as we saw earlier.
DeleteMember	This action removes a property from a dynamic object. C# doesn't have syntax for expressing this action. In Python, an example of this action looks like this: del baz.Foo, which deletes the Foo property (attribute) from the baz object.
Invoke	This late-bound action occurs when you invoke a callable entity such as a delegate. The printClassName Python function we saw in Listing 4-8 is an example of a callable object. If we have some object foo, then the code printClassName(foo) in Python will trigger a late bound Invoke action.)
InvokeMember	This late-bound action happens when you invoke a method on a dynamic object. For example, if baz is a dynamic object, baz.Foo() will trigger a late-bound InvokeMember action.
BinaryOperation	This late-bound action will take place when you apply a binary operator on a dynamic object. For example, if baz is a dynamic object, baz + 2 will trigger a late-bound BinaryOperation action.
UnaryOperation	This late-bound action is triggered when you apply a unary operator on a dynamic object. For example, if baz is a dynamic object, ++ baz will trigger a late-bound UnaryOperation action.
GetIndex	This action returns the element at the specified index of a collection. For example, if baz is a dynamic object, baz[3] will trigger a late-bound GetIndex action.
SetIndex	This action sets the element at the specified index of a collection. For example, if baz is a dynamic object, baz[3] = "hello" will trigger a late-bound SetIndex action.

Operation/Action	Description
DeleteIndex	This action removes the element at the specified index of a collection. C# does not have syntax for expressing this action. In Python, an example of this action looks like this: del baz[3]. The Python code means deleting the fourth element from the collection baz.
CreateInstance	This late-bound action happens when you create a new instance of a class. For example, if Baz is a class, the code Baz() in Python will trigger a late-bound CreateInstance action. Currently, C# does not have syntax for triggering this late-bound action. The C# code new Baz() will create an instance of Baz in a static fashion instead of triggering a late-bound CreateInstance action.
Convert	This late-bound action will take place when you try to type cast a dynamic object. For example, if baz is a dynamic object, (String) baz will trigger a late-bound Convert action. IronPython and IronRuby don't have syntax for triggering this action.

After seeing the twelve actions that make up the DLR's common type system, let's see why this system is the key to enabling interoperability between dynamic languages. Let's begin with the familiar static language code. In the C# code snippet below, the type information of the String class is accessible to the C# code snippet regardless of which language the String class was written in. The type information is expressed in terms of the .NET Common Type System.

```
String bob = "Bob";
String lowercaseBob = bob.ToLower();
```

Now if we change that code to the following, what difference does it make in terms of type systems?

```
dynamic bob = "Bob";
dynamic lowercaseBob = bob.ToLower();
```

The most noticeable difference is that the second code snippet no longer uses the type information of the String class. Instead, it uses the DLR's common type system. In the previous case, it doesn't matter which language the String class was written in. In the latter case, it doesn't matter which language the class of the variable bob is written in. The class of the variable bob can be written in C#, VB.NET, IronPython, or some other .NET language—it doesn't matter and the example code doesn't need access to that class's type information. Instead, the example code only requires that the class of the variable bob knows how to bind and handle the method invocation when it calls the ToLower method on bob. Binding and handling method invocation is one of the twelve actions defined by DLR's common type system.

As the two examples in this section show, when we use an object, we need to know something about it. In the static case, we need to know the object's static type information. In the dynamic case, we assume that the object supports some of the twelve actions that make up the DLR's common type system.

Class Hierarchy of Binders

To recap a little, so far in this chapter you've learned two key concepts: (a) late binding logic can be implemented in binders and dynamic objects, and (b) the DLR defines twelve operations that can be late bound. Given these concepts, we can deduce that there is late-binding logic for each of the twelve operations in binders as well as in dynamic objects. I will save the explanation of the link between dynamic objects and the twelve operations for the next chapter. For now, let's see how binders and the twelve operations are related.

For each of the twelve late-bound operations in Table 4-1, the DLR defines a binder class to contain the late-binding logic for the operation. Figure 4-1 shows the class hierarchy of DLR binder classes. We have seen the class hierarchy in Chapter 3, but Chapter 3 covers only the CallSiteBinder class in the class hierarchy. This chapter will introduce you to the rest of the classes. As Figure 4-1 shows, there is a binder class for each of the twelve late-bound operations. For the SetMember late-bound operation, the corresponding binder class is SetMemberBinder. For the GetMember late-bound operation, the corresponding binder class is GetMemberBinder and so on.

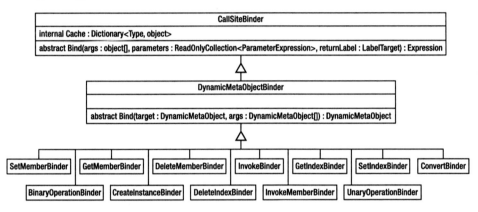

Figure 4-1. *Class hierarchy of DLR binder classes*

Each time a late-bound operation is encountered in the target language, the target language's binder class corresponding to the late-bound operation will be used. For example, in the previous section when we looked at the disassembled C# code, C# is the target language. When the C# compiler sees the code stretchString.name, it emits code that creates an instance of GetMemberBinder by calling the Binder.GetMember method as shown in Listing 4-11. The binder instance returned by the Binder.GetMember method is actually an instance of the CSharpGetMemberBinder class, which derives from GetMemberBinder. Of course, all of these C#-specific binders are the internal implementation details of C# and are well-hidden from the outside.

As you can see, the typical practice with regard to binders is that if you are implementing a new language and you want the language to interoperate with other DLR-based languages, you likely need to implement binder classes for the late-bound operations your language intends to support. When you implement your language's binder classes, you will likely do so by subclassing the twelve binder classes shown at the bottom of Figure 4-1. The binder classes you implement will contain the late-binding logic that pertains to your language. As with C#, your language does not need to be a dynamic language. It can have a mix of dynamic and static language features. Your language doesn't necessarily need to support all twelve late-bound operations by having twelve binder classes. For example, C# doesn't support the "delete member" and "delete index" late-bound operations because the C# language syntax simply doesn't allow that. It's not possible to write C# code like this:

```
String bob = "Bob";
del bob.Length;
```

The C# compiler will show a compilation error that says del is not a valid keyword. There is no language keyword in C# for deleting a member of an object. Therefore, the C# language does not need a binder class for the DeleteMember late-bound operation. Python, on the other hand, supports deleting members of an object. The code in Listing 4-12 shows an example. The code defines a class called Customer. The class has two member properties—Name and Age. After the class is defined, the code creates an instance bob of the Customer class. Then it prints the Name property of bob in line 8. The result is the text "Bob" printed on the screen. The code in line 9 deletes the Name property of bob. After that, when it prints the Name property of bob again in line 10, the IronPython runtime will throw an error because the Name property of bob has been deleted.

Listing 4-12. A Python Example That Deletes a Member of an Object

```
1)   class Customer(object):
2)       def __init__(self, name, age):
3)           self.Name = name
4)           self.Age = age
5)
6)   bob = Customer("Bob", 30)
7)
8)   print bob.Name
9)   del bob.Name
10)  print bob.Name  # This will throw an error.
```

Implement a Custom Binder Class

We've looked at the twelve late-bound actions that make up the DLR's common type system and the corresponding binder classes in DLR's binder class hierarchy. This section is going to show you how to implement a custom binder class for the GetMember late-bound action. We will use the binder class to get a member property of a Python object.

Our example will consist of a Python class, a binder class that inherits from GetMemberBinder, and some client C# code that puts everything together. The Python class is the Customer class you saw in Listing 4-12. So that part is taken care of. Here is the complete code for the Customer class and the bob object we will use in this example. The code is in the pythonExampleCode.py file.

```
class Customer(object):
    def __init__(self, name, age):
        self.Name = name
        self.Age = age

bob = Customer("Bob", 30)
```

In order to expose the bob object to C# code, we need to add the following two bolded lines of code in the PythonExampleCode class.

```
class PythonExampleCode
{
    public static Func<dynamic, dynamic, int> AddPriceDelegate;
    public static Action<dynamic> PrintClassName;
    public static dynamic Bob;

    static PythonExampleCode()
    {
        ScriptEngine pyEngine = IronPython.Hosting.Python.CreateEngine();
        ScriptScope scope = pyEngine.ExecuteFile("pythonExampleCode.py");
        AddPriceDelegate = scope.GetVariable("addPrice");
        PrintClassName = scope.GetVariable("printClassName");
        Bob = scope.GetVariable("bob");
    }
}
```

The code for our custom binder class is shown in Listing 4-13. This code is the main focus of the example. The binder class in Listing 4-13 inherits from GetMemberBinder and is called SimpleGetMemberBinder. It contains the late-binding logic that always returns the constant number 3. The constructor of SimpleGetMemberBinder takes two parameters—name and ignoreCase. The parameter name is the name of the member property to late bind. In this example, the member property to late bind will be the Name property (Python calls it attribute, but when there is no risk of confusion, I'll just call it property.). So in this example, the name parameter will be the string "Name". The ignoreCase parameter indicates whether to treat the name of the member property in a case-sensitive manner when doing late binding. As to the FallbackGetMember method in Listing 4-13, I will have more to explain about it later. For the time being, let's move on to the C# client code and see how things work together.

Listing 4-13. A Custom Binder Class for the GetMember Action

```
class SimpleGetMemberBinder : GetMemberBinder
{
    public SimpleGetMemberBinder(string name, bool ignoreCase)
        : base(name, ignoreCase)
    { }

    public override DynamicMetaObject FallbackGetMember(DynamicMetaObject target,
        DynamicMetaObject errorSuggestion)
    {
        Console.WriteLine("Doing late binding in SimpleGetMemberBinder.");

        //The binding has no restrictions. It returns a constant number.
        return errorSuggestion ?? new DynamicMetaObject(
            Expression.Convert(Expression.Constant(3), typeof(object)),
            BindingRestrictions.GetTypeRestriction(target.Expression,
                                                   target.LimitType)
        );
    }
}
```

Listing 4-14 shows the C# client code. As before, even though the code is in C#, it is not using C#'s binders. It uses the binder class in Listing 4-13 instead. You can think of this as simulating the late-binding behavior of some custom language of our own. The code in Listing 4-14 looks very similar to the code we saw in Chapter 3. It first creates an instance of SimpleGetMemberBinder and passes it the string "Name" and the Boolean value false. That tells the binder that the name of the member property to late bind is "Name" and the name of the member property should be bound in a case-sensitive manner. Next the code creates a call site. The type of the call site's Target delegate is Func<CallSite, object, object>. That means it's a delegate that takes an instance of CallSite and an instance of object as input parameters and returns an instance of object as result. The input object instance is the Python object bob. A reference to the Python object bob is available as a static member of the PythonExampleCode class. So the code in line 8 of Listing 4-14 just gets the Python object bob from the static member of the PythonExampleCode class and passes it to the Target delegate. The invocation of the Target delegate will trigger the late-binding process. After the late-binding process finishes, the result of the late binding is assigned to the variable name and printed to the screen.

Listing 4-14. C# Code That Uses SimpleGetMemberBinder for a Late-Bound GetMember Action

```
1)   private static void RunGetMemberBinderAndDynamicObjectExample()
2)   {
3)       CallSiteBinder binder = new SimpleGetMemberBinder("Name", false);
4)
5)       CallSite<Func<CallSite, object, object>> site =
6)          CallSite<Func<CallSite, object, object>>.Create(binder);
7)
8)       object name = site.Target(site, PythonExampleCode.Bob);
9)       Console.WriteLine("Customer name is {0}.", name);
10)  }
```

If you run the code in listing 4-14, you should see the following output:

```
Doing late binding in SimpleGetMemberBinder.
Customer name is Bob.
```

At this point, we've seen an implementation of a rather trivial custom binder class that always returns the number 3 as the binding result. Although the example and its implementation look trivial, there are a lot of activities going on behind the scenes between the Python object bob and our custom binder. Those activities follow a well-defined interoperability protocol, which the next section explains.

Interoperability Protocol

This section will use the example in Listing 4-14 to explain the interoperability protocol that's used between binders and dynamic objects. The whole late-binding process in Listing 4-14 begins with the call to the Target delegate of the call site. As I explained in the previous chapter, the L0, L1, and L2 caches will be checked to see if there is already a rule that's suitable for the late-binding operation. In this case, since this is the first time the call site and binder are called upon to do the late binding, there's nothing in the three caches. The details of the cache searching process are described in the previous chapter, so I'll spare those details here.

If there's a cache hit, the whole late-binding process is finished. Upon a cache miss, the Bind method that SimpleGetMemberBinder indirectly inherits from CallSiteBinder is invoked. The method's signature is shown below. The elements in the args array and the elements in the parameters collection pair up. The nth element in the parameters collection carries some information about the nth element in the args array. The first pair is special. The first element of the args array and the first element of the parameters collection represent the target object of the late-binding operation. In our example, the target object is the Python object bob. In our example, there are no more elements in the args array and the parameters collection because it is a GetMember late-bound operation. A GetMember operation does not have additional input arguments to go along with the target object.

```
public  abstract Expression Bind(object[] args, ReadOnlyCollection<ParameterExpression>
parameters, LabelTarget returnLabel);
```

The abstract Bind method defined in CallSiteBinder is implemented in DynamicMetaObjectBinder. SimpleGetMemberBinder derives from DynamicMetaObjectBinder and therefore inherits that implementation. The implementation basically takes each pair of the args array and the parameters collection and turns it into an instance of DynamicMetaObject. If you recall from the earlier discussion in this chapter, this is *a key step in enabling language interoperability*. In this step, all the objects in the args array, no matter if they are static or dynamic, will be turned into instances of DynamicMetaObject. And the defining characteristic of DynamicMetaObject instances is that they contain the late-binding logic pertaining to the objects they are associated with.

For each pair of the args array and the parameters collection, the implementation calls the static method Create of DynamicMetaObject. The Create method checks if the object from the args array is a dynamic object. In the DLR, an object is dynamic if it implements the **IDynamicMetaObjectProvider** interface, which I will explain in detail in the next chapter. In our example, the only element in the args array is a dynamic Python object. So the Create method simply gets the meta-object associated with the dynamic Python object. If the object were a static object, the Create method would wrap it up into an instance of DynamicMetaObject. If you take a look at the source code of DynamicMetaObject, you'll see that DynamicMetaObject doesn't really implement any late-binding logic. Instead, DynamicMetaObject delegates the job of late binding to the target language's binders, as I've mentioned before.

Once all the DynamicMetaObject instances are ready, the Bind method implementation in DynamicMetaObjectBinder calls the following overloaded abstract Bind method. The overloaded Bind method is defined in DynamicMetaObjectBinder and it takes the DynamicMetaObject instances as input and returns as result an instance of DynamicMetaObject.

```
public abstract DynamicMetaObject Bind(DynamicMetaObject target, DynamicMetaObject[] args);
```

As you can see, all the inputs and output of this overloaded method are of type DynamicMetaObject. From this point on in the late-binding process, the level of abstraction is elevated from objects and expressions in the original Bind method (i.e., the Bind method defined in CallSiteBinder) to instances of DynamicMetaObject. The objects and expressions in the original Bind method know nothing about language interoperability, whereas the instances of DynamicMetaObject are part of the interoperability protocol. Let's continue tracing the late-binding process and see how that protocol works.

The Bind method that takes DynamicMetaObject instances is an abstract method. Each of the twelve binder classes that inherit from DynamicMetaObjectBinder has its own implementation of that Bind method. The code in the twelve binder classes shares the same pattern. Here I'll go through the implementation of the Bind method in the GetMemberBinder class and show you that pattern. As the code excerpt from GetMemberBinder in Listing 4-15 shows, the implementation of the Bind method simply calls the BindGetMember method on the target meta-object and passes the binder itself to the call. The args input parameter of the Bind method is of no use because, as I mentioned earlier, the GetMember late-bound operation does not have any extra arguments. Even though the implementation of the Bind method is essentially just one line of code, it's one of the most important parts of the interoperability protocol. First, it shows that the binder is passing the control of late binding to the target object. If the target meta-object (i.e., the target input parameter of the Bind method) is the meta-object of a true dynamic object, such as the Python object in our example, then the line of code means the binding logic pertaining to the dynamic object will take over. This ensures that no matter which target language is using the dynamic object, the dynamic object's late-binding logic will be honored.

Listing 4-15. Excerpt from the DLR's GetMemberBinder Class

```
public sealed override DynamicMetaObject Bind(DynamicMetaObject target,
        params DynamicMetaObject[] args)
{
    //code omitted
    return target.BindGetMember(this);
}

public abstract DynamicMetaObject FallbackGetMember(DynamicMetaObject target,
DynamicMetaObject errorSuggestion);
```

Passing the binder object itself to the call of the BindGetMember is also a crucial part of the interoperability protocol. It's crucial because it allows the target meta-object to call back the binder. In the code excerpt, there's a very important abstract method called *FallbackGetMember*. This is the callback method the target meta-object will invoke if it wants to pass the late-binding control back to the binder. And that's the method the SimpleGetMemberBinder in our example overrides and implements. *The FallbackGetMember method is the method that contains the binder's late-binding logic.* In summary, this part of the interoperability protocol is that the binder calls the target meta-object's BindGetMember method, and the target meta-object at its discretion may or may not choose to call back the binder. So far so good! Now if the target meta-object does call back the binder, there are basically two cases in which that callback happens. The first is when the target meta-object utterly, completely has no clue how to perform the late binding. In this case, the target meta-object can choose to pass null as the value for the errorSuggestion parameter when it calls the FallbackGetMember method on the binder. The target meta-object can also pass a DynamicMetaObject instance that contains an Expression instance that represents an exception. In the other case, the target meta-object is able to perform a portion but not all of the late binding and it relies on the binder to finish the rest. In such case, the target meta-object will pass its partial binding result as the value for the errorSuggestion parameter when it calls back the FallbackGetMember method on the binder.

So far, this is just half of the story where the target meta-object is a true dynamic object. The other half is the case where the target meta-object is the wrapper meta-object of a static object. In this case, as I described earlier, the line of code in Listing 4-15 that calls the BindGetMember method on the input parameter target will result in a call back to the FallbackGetMember on the binder itself. This is because the BindGetMember method implemented in DynamicMetaObject simply calls the FallbackGetMember on the binder object it receives.

That's it for the interoperability protocol between binders and dynamic/static objects. I just described the interoperability protocol for GetMemberBinder. For the other eleven binder classes, the mechanism is the same. Like GetMemberBinder, each of the other eleven binder classes implements the overloaded abstract Bind method defined in DynamicMetaObjectBinder. Each binder class calls the Bind[Operation] method on the target meta-object in its implementation of the Bind method similar to what Listing 4-15 shows. Here [Operation] is the late bound operation the binder class is for. For example, the SetMemberBinder class is for the SetMember late-bound operation. The Bind method implementation in BindSetMember calls the BindSetMember method on the target meta-object. The Bind method implementation in InvokeMemberBinder calls the BindInvokeMember method on the target meta-object and so on. Like GetMemberBinder, each binder class defines an abstract Fallback[Operation] method. For example, SetMemberBinder defines an abstract FallbackSetMember method. InvokeMemberBinder defines an abstract FallbackInvokeMember method.

This description of the interoperability protocol is true only if the target language's binders choose to participate in the protocol. If you are implementing a language that does not need to interoperate with other DLR- based languages, you can derive your binder classes from just CallSiteBinder to take advantage of only the caching mechanism. This section covered a whole lot about the interoperability protocol. To help solidify your understanding of the protocol, let's see some more examples by extending the example we saw in Listing 4-14.

In Listing 4-14, the code passes a Python dynamic object to the binder. The binder is an instance of the SimpleGetMemberBinder class. Instead of a Python dynamic object, let's pass a static object to the binder and see what will happen. Listing 4-16 shows this example. The code is the same as the code in Listing 4-14, except that this time it creates an instance of the CSharpProduct class we saw earlier in this chapter. The instance is a static object and is referenced by the handClapper variable. The example code calls the Target delegate on the call site and passes it the handClapper variable.

Listing 4-16. Using an Instance of SimpleGetMemberBinder to Perform Late Binding for a Static Object

```
private static void RunGetMemberBinderAndStaticObjectExample()
{
    CallSiteBinder binder = new SimpleGetMemberBinder("name", false);

    CallSite<Func<CallSite, object, object>> site =
            CallSite<Func<CallSite, object, object>>.Create(binder);

    object handClapper = new CSharpProduct("Hand Clapper", 6);
    object name = site.Target(site, handClapper);
    Console.WriteLine("Product name is {0}.", name);
}
```

The result of running the example code is shown below. It may be a good exercise to stop reading for a moment and see if you can explain why the code prints "Product name is 3" using what you learned so far in this chapter. Read on if you are ready to see the answer. The reason it prints "Product name is 3" is because handClapper is a static object and is wrapped by a wrapper meta-object. The wrapper meta-object delegates the job of late binding to the binder. The binder in this example is an instance of our SimpleGetMemberBinder class and it returns the constant 3 as the late binding result. Therefore, the text "Product name is 3" shows on the screen.

```
Doing late binding in SimpleGetMemberBinder.
Product name is 3.
```

Obviously, in practice we would like to see "Product name is Hand Clapper" printed on the screen. The examples in this chapter and in Chapter 3 all show binder classes whose late-binding logic is as trivial as returning a constant number. That, of course, is not anywhere close to the real complexity of implementing practical classes. The examples so far leave out that complexity in order to demonstrate the key points without overwhelming you with details unnecessary to the discussion. But now that we are on the subject of implementing realistic late-binding logic, let's see how to quickly achieve that. Listing 4-17 shows the enhanced implementation of SimpleGetMemberBinder's FallbackGetMember method. Here the goal of the implementation is to provide realistic logic for binding to static .NET objects so that instead of printing "Product name is 3," the late-binding logic in our binder class will cause the product name of a CSharpProduct object to be displayed. To achieve that, you normally need to write code that uses .NET reflection to find the right member property by name. Writing such code is no easy task. Just imagine the various cases you need to consider to bind to a method of a static .NET object using .NET reflection. The method may be overloaded. If so, you need to write the code that does method-overload resolution. If the method is an extension method, you need to figure out how to handle that. Some of the method's input parameters may have default values. Some of them may need to be matched by name instead of by position. This list goes on and on. Fortunately, since much of the code that deals with .NET reflection is the same across different languages' binder classes, the DLR provides some utility classes so that we don't need to do all the hard work. One of the utility classes is DefaultBinder and that's what the code in Listing 4-17 uses to bind to static objects. Using DefaultBinder is very easy and painless. The example code in Listing 4-17 simply creates an instance of DefaultBinder and calls its GetMember method.

Listing 4-17. Using DefaultBinder to Bind to Static .NET Objects

```
public override DynamicMetaObject FallbackGetMember(DynamicMetaObject target,
    DynamicMetaObject errorSuggestion)
{
    Console.WriteLine("Doing late binding in SimpleGetMemberBinder.");

    DefaultBinder defaultBinder = new DefaultBinder();
    return defaultBinder.GetMember(this.Name, target);
}
```

Now after enhancing the binding logic in SimpleGetMemberBinder, if you run the code, you'll see the following output:

```
Doing late binding in SimpleGetMemberBinder.
Product name is Hand Clapper.
```

Summary

This chapter has gone a long way from language interoperability in general to the details of the DLR's interoperability protocol. Here is a review of the most important concepts this chapter covers.

- There are two kinds of objects—static objects and dynamic objects. Static objects can be treated as dynamic objects.

- Binders have two main responsibilities—caching and interoperability.

- There are two places in DLR where late-binding logic resides—binders and dynamic objects.

- The late-binding logic in binders pertains to a target language.

- The late-binding logic in dynamic objects pertains to those objects.

- The key elements in the DLR that makes language interoperability possible are binders, dynamic objects, the interoperability protocol between binders and dynamic objects, and a common type system that consists of twelve operations,.

As you've seen in the previous chapter and this chapter, the nice thing about the DLR's design is that the various features, such as binders, dynamic objects, and some others that we'll look at later in the book, are well-decoupled and modularized. The two key responsibilities of binders are decoupled and implemented in separate classes. Caching is the responsibility of the `CallSiteBinder` class. Language interoperability is the responsibility of the `DynamicMetaObjectBinder` class and its derivatives.

For the twelve binder classes that derive from `DynamicMetaObjectBinder`, this chapter shows examples about the `GetMemberBinder` class. Towards the end of the chapter, we saw an example that uses the `DefaultBinder` utility class to perform late binding for the `GetMember` operation on a static .NET object. Even though we discussed a lot about binders, we haven't yet covered a number of important and advanced topics about binders. For example, other than `GetMemberBinder`, this chapter does not cover in detail the other eleven derivatives of the `DynamicMetaObjectBinder` class, or topics such as deferred binding, and COM interoperability. We'll discuss those topics in Chapter 11.

CHAPTER 5

■ ■ ■

Dynamic Objects

Dynamic objects are a very important part of the DLR. So far in this book, when I've needed dynamic objects in an example, I obtained them from IronPython or IronRuby. Now I'll show you how you can implement your own custom late-binding logic in dynamic objects. Once you're in control of a dynamic object's late binding behavior, many magical things can happen. As I'll demonstrate, dynamic objects let you provide a fluent API for constructing XML documents. Moreover, the same technique can be applied to accessing files, registry entries, and so forth. In Chapter 7, we'll use dynamic objects to implement an aspect-oriented programming framework that works across both static and dynamic languages. And Chapter 8 will show you how to use dynamic objects to do meta-programming in C#, much like meta-classes work in languages like Python, Ruby and Groovy.

Expressions are the backbone of the DLR, and dynamic objects are the heart and soul. The heart and soul, of course, depend on the backbone. In the previous two chapters, you saw how we use expressions to express the late-binding logic in binders. Now you'll see how we use them to express the late-binding logic in dynamic objects. As we go through this chapter, we will not only get to know dynamic objects, we'll also put to good use what we learned about expressions in Chapter 3. Let's start with a review of what it means for an object to be dynamic, and how such an object differs from a static object.

What is a Dynamic Object?

Here, dynamic, as always, means doing things at run time. I explained run time vs. compile time as well as dynamic vs. static in Chapter 1. Now the key question is, what is it that dynamic objects do at run time? The answer is late binding. *Dynamic objects are essentially objects that know how to do their own late binding.* I already mentioned this and we saw some examples in the previous chapter. Furthermore, I also mentioned that the DLR defines twelve actions, such as InvokeMember and GetMember, that can be late bound. So, for example, if some client code calls a method on a dynamic object, the dynamic object has the logic in it that knows how to bind the method call at run time. If some client code tries to access a property on a dynamic object, the dynamic object knows how to bind the property access at run time. All of this just recaps what we discussed in the previous chapter.

If we compare a dynamic object to a static object, the difference is obvious. In C#, when you call a method on a static object, the object itself does not know how to bind the method call; the C# compiler does. The C# compiler at compile time knows the types of all the parameters that flow into the method call and uses that information to find out which method of which class to bind the method call to. If the method is overloaded, the C# compiler will perform method overload resolution. If the method is an extension method, the C# compiler will do the job of locating the right extension method.

You'll find it easier to understand the details about dynamic objects once you've seen one in action. So let's look at the C# example of a dynamic object in Listing 5-1. The dynamic object's late binding logic is trivial—always returning the constant number 3. Let's see the effects of using the dynamic object, then I'll show you how to implement its late-binding logic.

The dynamic object is an instance of a class called Customer. The customer name in this example is Bob and he is 30 years old. Because the code declares the type of the variable bob as dynamic, the variable bob is treated as a dynamic object by the C# compiler. When the code accesses the Age property of bob, the custom late binding logic of the dynamic object bob kicks in and the number 3 is returned as the result. In this example, I purposely make the late binding logic return the number 3 as the age of a customer, no matter what value the customer's Age property has so that when we print out a customer's age, it's apparent whether that age comes from the customer's Age property or from the late-binding logic. You won't see the late-binding logic in Listing 5-1. You're looking at just the tip of the iceberg now. Keep reading. Listings 5-2 and 5-3 (a little further on) fill out the example. It is in Listing 5-3 that you'll eventually see the code that returns the value 3. You can find the code for the complete example in the DynamicObjectExamples project of this chapter's code download.

Even though the Customer class implements its late-binding logic, nothing stops us from referring to a Customer object as static object. That's what the code does with the variable bill in Listing 5-1. The example creates an instance of Customer and assigns it to the variable bill. The point here is that the type of the variable bill is Customer, not dynamic. Because of that, the C# compiler will not generate IL code that has call sites and binders for any action on bill. The variable bill (I mean the object the variable bill points to, but for brevity, I'll just say the variable bill) is treated as a static object, just like any static object we see in C# code. So when the code gets the Age property of bill, there is no late binding in play and the result is that Bill is 30 years old.

Listing 5-1. Using a Dynamic Object

```
static void Main(string[] args)
{
    RunDynamicObjectAsStaticAndDynamicExample();
    Console.ReadLine();
}

private void RunDynamicObjectAsStaticAndDynamicExample()
{
    dynamic bob = new Customer("Bob", 30);
    Console.WriteLine("Bob is {0} years old.", bob.Age);

    Customer bill = new Customer("Bill", 30);
    Console.WriteLine("Bill is {0} years old.", bill.Age);
}
```

By itself, the code in Listing 5-1 will not compile. You need the code in Listings 5-2 and 5-3 to complete the example. If you've downloaded this chapter's code and want to run the whole example now, you can open the Visual Studio solution file Chapter5.sln and run the DynamicObjectExamples project in debug mode. The Main method in the Program.cs file of the DynamicObjectExamples project will call the RunDynamicObjectAsStaticAndDynamicExample method in Listing 5-1 and you should see output that looks like this:

```
Getting member Age
Bob is 3 years old.
Bill is 30 years old.
```

Listing 5-1 shows the effects of using a dynamic object as is. It also shows the effects of using a dynamic object as a static object. In previous chapters, we saw examples of static objects being treated as is and as dynamic objects. Table 5-1 summarizes all of the four cases using examples.

Table 5-1. *Dynamic and Static Objects and Their Uses*

	Used as Static Object	Used as Dynamic Object
Static object	String hello = "hello";	dynamic hello = "hello";
Dynamic object	Customer bill = new Customer("Bill", 30);	dynamic bob = new Customer("Bob", 30);

The next section will explain the DLR machinery for implementing dynamic objects and show how the Customer class we used in Listing 5-1 is implemented.

IDynamicMetaObjectProvider Interface

A dynamic object is an object that knows how to do its own late binding. Under the hood, a dynamic object does not itself carry the weight of performing late binding. Instead, it has a big brother, a meta-object, that does the heavy lifting. From a software-design perspective, the distinction between dynamic object and meta-object is nice because it decouples the late-binding logic of a dynamic object from the dynamic object itself. With that distinction, a class like Customer can still focus on the logic that's specific to the application domain without being cluttered with other responsibilities like the late-binding logic. In other words, the code in the Customer class will not be mixed with the code that implements late-binding logic.

The DLR defines an interface called **IDynamicMetaObjectProvider**. It's that interface that provides the meta-object. If a class implements the IDynamicMetaObjectProvider interface, instances of the class are dynamic objects. IDynamicMetaObjectProvider defines only the following method:

```
DynamicMetaObject GetMetaObject(Experssion parameter);
```

This is the method that returns the "big brother" of a dynamic object. When client code needs a dynamic object to do some sort of late binding, at some point in the whole late-binding process, the call site binder will call the GetMetaObject method on the dynamic object and get back a meta-object. The call site binder will then ask the meta-object to do the real work of late binding. This is the interoperability protocol described in the previous chapter. The return type of the GetMetaObject method is **DynamicMetaObject,** which is the base class of all meta-objects in the DLR. In the DLR, a meta-object must be an instance of DynamicMetaObject or of a class that directly or indirectly inherits DynamicMetaObject.

As an example, let's see an implementation of the IDynamicMetaObjectProvider interface. Listing 5-2 shows the code for the Customer class, which implements the IDynamicMetaObjectProvider interface. This effectively makes all instances of the Customer class dynamic objects. The Customer class defines a Name and an Age property. It has a constructor that takes a customer's name and age as input. The focus here is of course the GetMetaObject method. The method simply creates an instance of ConstantMetaObject and returns it. The class ConstantMetaObject is where all the late-binding logic resides. As you can see, the Customer class only has things like customer name and age that are relevant to its application domain. The binding logic is decoupled and isolated into the ConstantMetaObject class.

Listing 5-2. Customer.cs

```csharp
public class Customer : IDynamicMetaObjectProvider
{
    public Customer(String name, int age)
    {
        this.Name = name;
        this.Age = age;
    }

    public String Name { get; set; }
    public int Age { get; set; }

    #region IDynamicMetaObjectProvider Members

    public DynamicMetaObject GetMetaObject(Expression parameter)
    {
        return new ConstantMetaObject (parameter, this);
    }

    #endregion
}
```

ConstantMetaObject is the class that implements the late-binding logic and, obviously, that's where the meat as well as the complexity is. Let's see next what ConstantMetaObject looks like.

Dynamic Meta Objects

To be a class of meta-objects, ConstantMetaObject must inherit directly or indirectly from the DynamicMetaObject class. In Listing 5-3, ConstantMetaObject inherits directly from DynamicMetaObject and overrides the BindGetMember method it inherits from DynamicMetaObject. ConstantMetaObject overrides BindGetMember so it can provide its own late binding logic for the GetMember action, one of the twelve actions DLR defines in its common type system. The custom late-binding logic ConstantMetaObject provides for the GetMember action is to always return the constant number 3. This is an introductory example and the implementation is trivial. We will get to more realistic examples later when we will look at a fluent API that implements the late-binding logic for constructing XML documents.

Listing 5-3 shows the code for ConstantMetaObject. As you can see from the code listing, BindGetMember calls the ReturnConstant helper method. The ReturnConstant method calls the constructor of DynamicMetaObject and passes it two things—a DLR expression that represents the number 3 and a binding restriction that always evaluates to true. There are several important points to note about that code, in particular the use of a DynamicMetaObject instance as the return value of ReturnConstant and hence the return value of BindGetMember. At the beginning of this section, I described DynamicMetaObject as the base class that all classes of meta-objects must inherit from directly or indirectly. Now the code is showing you the use of DynamicMetaObject as the result of late binding. It turns out that DynamicMetaObject has two responsibilities. The first is to serve as the base class of the classes that *implement custom late-binding logic* of meta-objects. The second is to *carry the result of late binding*.

In the code example, the BindGetMember method being overridden is evidence of DynamicMetaObject's first responsibility. The fact that BindGetMember's return type is DynamicMetaObject is evidence of DynamicMetaObject's second responsibility. If you recall, in Chapter 3 I said that the overall result of late binding is called a rule and that a rule consists of two parts—the raw late-binding result and the conditions (i.e. restrictions) under which the raw result is valid. That's exactly why here in the ReturnConstant method you see that when DynamicMetaObject is used to carry the overall result of late binding, the code needs to pass not only the raw late-binding result (i.e., the DLR expression that represents the number 3) but also a restriction to the constructor of DynamicMetaObject.

Listing 5-3. ConstantMetaObject.cs

```
public class ConstantMetaObject   : DynamicMetaObject
{
    public ConstantMetaObject (Expression expression, object obj)
        : base(expression, BindingRestrictions.Empty, obj)
    { }

    private DynamicMetaObject ReturnConstant()
    {
        //returns constant 3
        return new DynamicMetaObject(
            Expression.Convert(Expression.Constant(3), typeof(object)),
            BindingRestrictions.GetExpressionRestriction(Expression.Constant(true)));
    }

    public override DynamicMetaObject BindGetMember(GetMemberBinder binder)
    {
        Console.WriteLine("Getting member {0}", binder.Name);
        return ReturnConstant();
    }}
```

Now you've seen the three parts that make up the introductory example—the Customer class, the ConstantMetaObject class, and the client code that puts everything together. The next few sections will look at the DynamicMetaObject class and its two responsibilities in more detail.

DynamicMetaObject and Binding Logic

Chapter 4 describes the DLR common type system and its twelve late-binding actions. For each late-binding action, a language implementer needs to implement a binder class that contains the language's custom late-binding logic for that action. As a result, there are twelve binder classes a language implementer needs to provide if the language is to support all twelve actions. Each binder class deals with only one action. The story on the dynamic object side is a little different. Like binders, a dynamic object's meta-object also needs to have its custom late-binding logic for the twelve actions. However, unlike a binder class, the class of a meta-object deals with all twelve actions. When we pick a binder to use, we know a priori which late-binding action the binder is for. The examples in the previous chapter demonstrate that. On the other hand, when we pass a dynamic object around, the same dynamic object can be used in different late-binding actions. Therefore, it makes sense for a meta-object to have late-binding logic for all twelve actions.

The class DynamicMetaObject defines twelve virtual methods that correspond to the twelve actions. Figure 5-1 shows the class diagram of DynamicMetaObject. As you can see, the names of the twelve methods all begin with Bind followed by the late binding action the method is for. I will use the notation Bind[Operation] to refer to these methods. Each Bind[Operation] method takes a binder and optionally some instances of DynamicMetaObject as input parameters. The return type of the twelve methods is also DynamicMetaObject. The twelve virtual methods are implemented in DynamicMetaObject to provide the default late-binding behaviors for dynamic objects. The default late-binding behaviors implemented in DynamicMetaObject simply fall back to the binder, the first input parameter of each method, for performing the late binding. Subclasses of DynamicMetaObject are supposed to override the twelve methods and implement their own custom binding logic.

DynamicMetaObject
Expression : Expression Restrictions : BindingRestrictions Value : object HasValue : bool LimitType : Type RuntimeType : Type
BindGetMember(binder : GetMemberBinder) : DynamicMetaObject BindSetMember(binder : SetMemberBinder, value : DynamicMetaObject) : DynamicMetaObject BindDeleteMember(binder : DeleteMemberBinder) : DynamicMetaObject BindGetIndex(binder : GetIndexBinder, indexes : DynamicMetaObject[]) : DynamicMetaObject BindSetIndex(binder : SetIndexBinder, indexes : DynamicMetaObject[], value : DynamicMetaObject) : DynamicMetaObject BindDeleteIndex(binder : DeleteIndexBinder, indexes : DynamicMetaObject[]) : DynamicMetaObject BindInvoke(binder : InvokeBinder, args : DynamicMetaObject[]) : DynamicMetaObject BindInvokeMember(binder : InvokeMemberBinder, args : DynamicMetaObject[]) : DynamicMetaObject BindBinaryOperation(binder : BinaryOperationBinder, arg : DynamicMetaObject) : DynamicMetaObject BindUnaryOperation(binder : UnaryOperationBinder) : DynamicMetaObject BindConvert(binder : ConvertBinder) : DynamicMetaObject BindCreateInstance(binder : CreateInstanceBinder, args : DynamicMetaObject[]) : DynamicMetaObject

Figure 5-1. Class diagram of the DynamicMetaObject class

A language doesn't need to have binders that support all twelve late-binding actions. Likewise, a meta-object doesn't need to have late-binding logic for all twelve actions. As you'll see in the XmlBuilder example later, the subclasses of DynamicMetaObject in that example have late-binding logic only for some of the twelve actions. If a Bind[Operation] method of DynamicMetaObject is not overridden in a subclass, the default behavior of that Bind[Operation] method is to fall back to the host language's binder and let the binder do the binding, as we saw in the previous chapter. If you recall, during the late-binding process, static objects are wrapped by instances of DynamicMetaObject and the default binding behavior of those wrapper objects is to fall back to the host language's binders.

DynamicMetaObject and Binding Result

The previous section described the DynamicMetaObject class as the ultimate base class of all classes that implement custom the late-binding logic of meta-objects. Now we will delve into DynamicMetaObject as the carrier of late-binding results.

The class diagram in Figure 5-1 shows six properties in the DynamicMetaObject class. The Expression property is the one that stores the raw binding result. The Restrictions property stores the conditions under which the raw binding result is valid. Together Expression and Restrictions make up the overall binding result. Eventually, those two properties are turned into a rule and the rule is cached in the L0, L1 and L2 caches we looked at in Chapter 3. The place where the two properties are turned into a rule is in the Bind method that DynamicMetaObjectBinder inherits from CallSiteBinder and overrides. Here is a code excerpt that shows the conversion from the two properties to a rule. You can download the DLR source code and find the complete code of the Bind method in DynamicMetaObjectBinder.cs.

```
public sealed override Expression Bind(object[] args, ReadOnlyCollection<ParameterExpression>
parameters, LabelTarget returnLabel) {

    //Skip code that does some checking.
    //Skip code that converts args and parameters into instances of DynamicMetaObject.

    DynamicMetaObject binding = Bind(target, metaArgs);

    //Skip code that does some checking.

    Expression body = binding.Expression;
    BindingRestrictions restrictions = binding.Restrictions;

    //Skip code that does some checking and processing of body and restrictions.

    if (restrictions != BindingRestrictions.Empty) {
        body = Expression.IfThen(restrictions.ToExpression(), body);
    }

    return body; //This is the rule.
}
```

Understanding the overridden Bind method in DynamicMetaObject is very important to a solid understanding of how the DLR works. The code excerpt highlights the key steps the overridden Bind method performs. First, it converts args and parameters into instances of DynamicMetaObject, as detailed in the previous chapter. Next, it calls the abstract Bind method, which subclasses of DynamicMetaObjectBinder, like GetMemberBinder and InvokeMemberBinder, implement. The overall result of the late binding is represented by an instance of DynamicMetaObject, and that instance is assigned to a variable called binding. Then the code takes the Expression and Restrictions properties of the binding variable and assigns them to the variables body and restrictions respectively. After some checking and processing of the body and restrictions variables, the code calls the static Expression.IfThen method to turn body and restrictions into a DLR expression that represents a rule. The call to Expression.IfThen basically creates a new expression that says "if the restrictions are true, then the body is the valid binding result".

Interoperability

The ConstantMetaObject class so far only provides logic that governs the late binding of the GetMember action. There are eleven other operations whose late-binding behavior we can define. Let's extend the ConstantMetaObject to cover those actions and then have some fun with it in C# and IronPython. Listing 5-4 shows the code for the extended ConstantMetaObject. As you can see, the class ConstantMetaObject overrides all of the twelve Bind[Operation] methods it inherits from DynamicMetaObject. Except for the

BindConvert method, the code in each overridden method simply calls the ReturnConstant helper method you saw you in Listing 5-3. In the interest of saving trees, Listing 5-4 shows only a couple of these methods. BindConvert is a little special because I want it to return the number 3 as an integer, not as an object. The ReturnConstant helper method returns the number 3 as an object. So the BindConvert method does not call the ReturnConstant method like the others do.

Listing 5-4. ConstantMetaObject.cs

```
public class ConstantMetaObject : DynamicMetaObject
{
    public ConstantMetaObject(Expression expression, object obj)
        : base(expression, BindingRestrictions.Empty, obj)
    { }

    public override DynamicMetaObject BindConvert(ConvertBinder binder)
    {
        Console.WriteLine("BindConvert, binder.Operation: {0}", binder.ReturnType);
        return new DynamicMetaObject(
            Expression.Constant(3, typeof(int)),
            BindingRestrictions.GetExpressionRestriction(Expression.Constant(true)));
    }

    public override DynamicMetaObject BindInvoke(InvokeBinder binder,
        DynamicMetaObject[] args)
    {
        Console.WriteLine("BindInvoke, binder.ReturnType: {0}", binder.ReturnType);
        return ReturnConstant();
    }

    public override DynamicMetaObject BindInvokeMember(
        InvokeMemberBinder binder, DynamicMetaObject[] args)
    {
        Console.WriteLine("BindInvokeMember, binder.ReturnType: {0}", binder.ReturnType);
        return ReturnConstant();
    }

    //Other Bind[Action] methods omitted.
}
```

Listing 5-5 shows the code that triggers the various late-binding actions on an instance of the Customer class. When a late-binding action is triggered, the corresponding Bind[Action] method in ConstantMetaObject will be invoked to do the late binding. From the code in Listing 5-5, you can see that the code bob.Foo(100) invokes a member method on the dynamic object bob and therefore it triggers the InvokeMember action. Similarly the code bob[100] tries to get the 100th index of the dynamic object bob and hence triggers the GetIndex action.

Listing 5-5. Triggering Late-Binding Actions in C#

```csharp
private static void RunCustomerLateBindingInCSharpExamples()
{
    dynamic bob = new Customer("Bob", 30);
    Console.WriteLine("bob.Foo(100): {0}", bob.Foo(100));        //InvokeMember
    Console.WriteLine("bob(): {0}", bob());                      //Invoke
    Console.WriteLine("bob[100]: {0}", bob[100]);               //GetIndex
    Console.WriteLine("(bob[100] = 10): {0}", (bob[100] = 10)); //SetIndex
    Console.WriteLine("(int) bob: {0}", (int)bob);             //Convert
    Console.WriteLine("(bob.Age = 40): {0}", (bob.Age = 40));   //SetMember
    Console.WriteLine("bob.Age: {0}", bob.Age);                //GetMember
    Console.WriteLine("bob + 100: {0}", bob + 100);            //BinaryOperation
    Console.WriteLine("++bob: {0}", ++bob);                    //UnaryOperation
}
```

C#, of course, is not the only language that has access to the Customer class. We can write Python code similar to the code in Listing 5-5 and expect to see the same late-binding behavior. Listing 5-6 shows the Python code that triggers the various late-binding actions on the variable bob. The variable bob comes from the C# code shown in Listing 5-7. From the code in Listing 5-6, you can see that the code bob() invokes the variable bob as a function and that triggers the Invoke action. As a result, the BindInvoke method in ConstantMetaObject is called to do the late binding. Similarly the code del bob.Age deletes the member property Age from the dynamic object bob and hence triggers the DeleteMember action.

Listing 5-6. CustomerLateBinding.py

```python
print bob()       #Invoke
print bob[100]    #GetIndex
print bob.Age     #GetMember
print bob + 100 #BinaryOperation
print ++bob       #UnaryOperation
bob[100] = 10     #SetIndex
bob.Age = 40      #SetMember
del bob.Age       #DeleteMember
del bob[100]      #DeleteIndex
```

If you compare the C# code in Listing 5-5 and the Python code in Listing 5-6, you'll notice some differences between those two listings. In Listing 5-5, we have the C# code bob.Foo(100). When the C# code runs, the BindInvokeMember method of ConstantMetaObject will be called to perform the late binding for the invocation of the Foo method on the variable bob. However, we can't write bob.Foo(100) in Listing 5-6's Python code. If we do that, we'll get an exception that says "int is not callable" because in Python, the code bob.Foo(100) will result in a late-bound GetMember action for getting the "Foo" member of the variable bob. Whatever is returned by the late-bound GetMember action will then be called like a delegate with 100 as an input argument. In our case, the late-bound GetMember action for getting the "Foo" member of the variable bob will return the number 3. The IronPython runtime will therefore try to invoke the number 3 with 100 as an input argument. Since the number 3 is not callable, we get an exception that says "int is not callable".

The C# and Python code also differ in that in the C# code, we can't trigger late-bound actions such as DeleteMember and DeleteIndex, but in Python code, we can. The reason for that is because the C# language does not have syntax for deleting a member of an object, nor does it have syntax for deleting an index of an object. This seems like a serious problem because a dynamic object can be passed around and used in different languages. The dynamic object might provide late-binding behavior for a late-bound action like DeleteMember but our ability to trigger that late-bound action depends on which language we use. Fortunately there is a solution to this problem. The solution is to use call sites and binders. We will go through the details of the solution in Chapter 12 when we discuss some more advanced topics of binders.

Another difference between Listing 5-5 and Listing 5-6 is that code like bob.Age = 40 in Python is a statement that does not yield a value. Because the code bob.Age = 40 in Python does not yield a value, we can't write code such as the print bob.Age = 40 in Listing 5-6. On the other hand, the code bob.Age = 40 in C# is an expression that yields a value. (In our case, the value it yields is the number 3.) Because of that, we can have this code Console.WriteLine("(bob.Age = 40): {0}", (bob.Age = 40)); in Listing 5-5 to print out the value.

The last difference I want to point out between Listing 5-5 and Listing 5-6 has to do with the order in which the late-bound actions are triggered. In Listing 5-5, I purposely trigger the ++ unary operation on the variable bob at the end. This is because the ++ unary operation triggered in C# has the effect of assigning the result of the unary operation to the variable bob. Because of that, after the ++ unary operation is bound and executed, the variable bob will have the value 3 and we can no longer trigger other late-binding actions on it. Compare that to the Python code in Listing 5-6 and you will see that the ++ unary operation triggered in Python does not have the effect of assigning the result of the unary operation to the variable bob.

To run the Python code in Listing 5-6, the example uses the RunCustomerLateBindingInPythonExamples method shown in Listing 5-7. The method uses the DLR Hosting API to create a script engine for running Python code. The Python code is run in something called a scope. The scope is an instance of ScriptScope and it is the execution context in which the Python code runs. As an execution context, a scope provides variable name bindings. This is the kind of name binding we talked about in Chapter 2 and is not to be confused with late binding. In this example, as the bolded line shows, the scope binds the variable name "bob" to the dynamic object referenced by the variable bob. Because the variable name is bound in the scope, the Python code in Listing 5-6 can use that variable name directly. That's as much as I have to say about the DLR Hosting API for now. The DLR Hosting API is a big topic and Chapter 6 will cover it in detail.

Listing 5-7. Triggering Late Binding Actions in IronPython

```
private static void RunCustomerLateBindingInPythonExamples()
{
    dynamic bob = new Customer("Bob", 30);
    ScriptEngine pyEngine = IronPython.Hosting.Python.CreateEngine();
    ScriptSource source = pyEngine.CreateScriptSourceFromFile("CustomerLateBinding.py");
    ScriptScope scope = pyEngine.CreateScope();
    scope.SetVariable("bob", bob);
    source.Execute(scope);
}
```

META OBJECT PROTOCOL (MOP)

There is a generic concept behind dynamic objects and meta-objects, and the connections between them. The concept is the Meta-Object Protocol, or MOP. If you ask different people what MOP is, you are very likely to get different answers. Perhaps that's because MOP as a concept is generic and some people might have a broader interpretation of its scope than others. Or it could be because there are many implementations of MOP in different programming languages and some of those implementations differ in substantial ways. One of the most well-known MOP implementations is the one in CLOS (Common Lisp Object System), which people often use as a point of reference. In this section, I'll offer my view of what MOP is and how it relates to the DLR based on the CLOS MOP.

In MOP land, there are two types of citizens: **objects** (aka base objects) and **meta-objects**. Meta-objects do things about base objects. In the DLR's MOP implementation, dynamic objects are the base objects. Instances of DynamicMetaObject and its derivatives are meta-objects. The things that meta-objects do about base objects in the DLR's MOP are the late-binding actions.

Besides base objects and meta-objects, the third important pillar of a MOP implementation is the protocol between meta-objects, which is what gives MOP its name. The MOP protocol in CLOS involves things like generic functions and methods in the Lisp language. The way generic functions and methods work is a little complicated because Lisp is a functional language and CLOS is a component that tries to add object-oriented programming support to Lisp in as elegant a way as possible. In the DLR MOP, things are simpler because it's based on the object-oriented programming system of .NET. The protocol part of the DLR MOP is pretty much the class inheritance and method overriding mechanisms provided by the object-oriented programming system of .NET.

Okay, enough of MOP and back to our main topic. DynamicMetaObject is the lowest-level class to inherit from when you want to have the most flexibility in implementing the late-binding logic of your dynamic objects. With flexibility comes complexity. Sometimes, you need the ultimate flexibility. Other times, you just want to inherit some basic late-binding behavior and do some customization based on that. For that, DLR provides two useful classes—DynamicObject and ExpandoObject. The next section will describe the DynamicObject class and then show an example that leverages DynamicObject to implement a fluent API for constructing XML documents. Through the example, you'll see that when it fits the bill, leveraging DynamicObject saves a lot of work compared with working from the ground up with DynamicMetaObject.

DynamicObject Class

DynamicObject is essentially a wrapper around the twelve methods in DynamicMetaObject. For each of those twelve methods, there is a corresponding virtual method in DynamicObject. For example, for the BindSetMember method in DynamicMetaObject, there is a method called TrySetMember in DynamicObject. I will use the notation Try[Operation] to refer to the twelve virtual methods in DynamicObject that correspond to the twelve Bind[Operation] methods in DynamicMetaObject. The key to understanding how DynamicObject works is the relation between those two sets of methods. Let's see how the two sets of methods are related.

You use DynamicObject by deriving a class from it. In the derived class, you override some or all of the twelve Try[Operation] methods defined by the DynamicObject class. In each overridden method, you implement the late-binding logic you want your dynamic object to have. For example, Listing 5-8 shows a class that inherits from DynamicObject. The class is called Employee and it overrides only the TryGetMember method. The overridden TryGetMember method has the custom binding logic for the GetMember action. Like other introductory examples in this book, the binding logic is to return the constant number 3 as the result. So inside the overridden TryGetMember method, the code assigns number 3 to the parameter result and returns true to signal that the binding is successful. The code looks much simpler than the code in ConstantMetaObject. Because ConstantMetaObject inherits from DynamicMetaObject directly, the code there needs to deal with DLR expressions and DynamicMetaObject instances. Here in the TryGetMember method, the code looks like ordinary C# code. Instead of creating a ConstantExpression instance to represent the number 3 as ConstantMetaObject does, the code in Listing 5-8 simply uses the number 3 as is.

Listing 5-8. Employee.cs

```
class Employee : DynamicObject
{
    public override bool TryGetMember(GetMemberBinder binder, out object result)
    {
        result = 3;
        return true;
    }

    public int Salary { get { return 500; } }

    public double calculateBonus(int performanceRating)
    {
        return 1000d;
    }
}
```

Listing 5-9 shows the code that uses the Employee class from Listing 5-8. The Employee class defines a Salary property, but not an Age property. When the code in Listing 5-9 accesses the Salary property of the employee variable, because of the way the late-binding logic of DynamicObject is implemented, the Salary property getter of the Employee class will be called and the number 500 will be returned. But when the code in Listing 5-9 accesses a property like Age that is not defined in the Employee class, the TryGetMember method will be called and the number 3 will be returned.

Listing 5-9. *Using the Employee Class*

```
private static void RunDynamicObjectExample()
{
    dynamic employee = new Employee();
    Console.WriteLine("Employee's salary is {0} dollars.", employee.Salary);
    Console.WriteLine("Employee is {0} years old.", employee.Age);
    Console.WriteLine("Employee's bonus is {0} dollars.", employee.calculateBonus(2));
}
```

If you run the code in Listing 5-9, you'll see output like the following:

Employee's salary is 500 dollars.
Employee is 3 years old.
Employee's bonus is 1000 dollars.

Now let's dive a little deeper and see how the late-binding logic of DynamicObject is implemented. DynamicObject implements IDynamicMetaObjectProvider. That's no different from the Customer class we saw in Listing 5-2, and it also means instances of DynamicObject are base objects that have accompanying meta-objects. Whereas the Customer class uses ConstantMetaObject to hold the real late binding logic, DynamicObject uses a private class called MetaDynamic. MetaDynamic inherits from DynamicMetaObject and overrides the Bind[Operation] methods defined in DynamicMetaObject. So far, everything is business as usual. The trick is in the overridden Bind[Operation] methods.

A Bind[Operation] method in MetaDynamic checks if the corresponding Try[Operation] method in DynamicObject is overridden. If not, it falls back to the host language's binder and let the binder do the binding. If the binder is able to do the binding, that's fine. If the binder is unable to do the binding, then whatever error the binder throws will surface up to the client code. On the other hand, if the corresponding Try[Operation] method is overridden, the Bind[Operation] method falls back to the host language's binder to see if the binder is able to do the binding. If the binder is able to do the binding, again that's fine. The binding result of the binder will be returned. In the code example in Listing 5-9, this is the case when the code tries to get the Salary property of employee. In that case, because the Salary property is defined in the Employee class, the C# language's binder is able to do the late binding for the code employee.Salary. And since the C# language's binder can do the binding, the TryGetMember method we override in the Employee class will not be invoked to do the late binding.

The following code shows the actual expression that represents the binding result of this case. The expression will be wrapped by a LambdaExpression object that will be compiled into IL and cached in L0, L1 and L2 caches. Essentially, you can view the expression below as the rule that represents the late-binding result. Here the rule has one restriction—the if condition. The restriction checks whether the dynamic object ($$arg0) is an instance of the Employee class. In our example, $$arg0 refers to the employee variable and hence is an instance of the Employee class. Since the condition is met, the if-true branch in the expression will be executed. This expression is a GotoExpression (the .Return) that contains a BlockExpression (the .Block). The BlockExpression contains a child expression that contains other child expressions and so on. Leaving all those details aside, the part in the BlockExpression that's of interest to us is the MethodCallExpression (the .Call). It contains a ConstantExpression that holds a MethodInfo object for the get_Salary method. The MethodCallExpression basically represents a call of the Salary property's get method on the Employee instance referenced by $$arg0.

```
.If (
    $$arg0 .TypeEqual DynamicObjectExamples.Employee
) {
    .Return #Label1 { .Block() {
        (System.Object)((System.Int32).Call
            .Constant<System.Reflection.MethodInfo>(Int32 get_Salary())
            .Invoke(
                $$arg0,
                .NewArray System.Object[] {}
            ))
    }}
} .Else {
    .Default(System.Void)
}
```

So far we looked at the case where the host language's binder was able to do the binding and the Try[Operation] method overridden in Employee was not invoked. Now let's see what happens when the host language's binder is unable to do the late binding. If the corresponding Try[Operation] method is overridden, and the host language's binder is unable to do the binding, the Bind[Operation] method implemented in DynamicObject will produce a rule like the following. The part of interest to us is in bold. As you can see, the bolded part is a ConditionalExpression (.If). The if-condition is a MethodCallExpression that represents a call to the TryGetMember method on the Employee instance referenced by $$arg0. And if the TryGetMember returns true, the if-true part will return $var1. What is $var1? $var1 is the *out* parameter result of TryGetMember. If you now look back at the code in TryGetMember in Listing 5-8, you will see why the method sets the result parameter to 3 and returns true.

```
.If (
    $$arg0 .TypeEqual DynamicObjectExamples.Employee
) {
    .Return #Label1 { .Block() {
        .Block(System.Object $var1) {
            .If (
                .Call ((System.Dynamic.DynamicObject)$$arg0).TryGetMember(
                    .Constant<System.Dynamic.GetMemberBinder>(...),
                    $var1)
            ) {
                $var1
            } .Else {
                .Block() {
                    .Block() {
                        .Throw .New System.MissingMemberException("Age");
                        .Default(System.Object)
                    }
                }
            }
        }
    } }
} .Else {
    .Default(System.Void)
}
```

XML Builder

The examples so far in this chapter are somewhat trivial. It's nice to use simple examples to explain concepts and occasionally look at the binding rules to see how things work under the hood. It's also important to see some practical examples and not lose sight of the forest for the trees, and that's the purpose of this section. Our practical example will implement a fluent API for building XML documents. The next few chapters will demonstrate more applications of what you learn in this chapter. You can find all of the code for this part of the chapter in the DynamicBuilder project of this chapter's code download.

Before I show you how the API is implemented, let's see first how the API makes it easy to build XML documents. Listing 5-10 shows code that uses the API to build an XML document. The XML document it builds is this:

```
<Customer>
    <Name FirstName="John" LastName="Smith">John Smith</Name>
    <Phone>555-8765</Phone>
```

```
    <Address>
        <Street>123 Main Street</Street>
        <City>Fremont</City>
        <Zip>55555</Zip>
    </Address>
</Customer>
```

As you can see, the code in the RunXmlBuilderExample method in Listing 5-10 is pretty much the same in structure as the XML file it generates. That's the selling point of the API. If you've used classes like XmlDocument, XmlElement, and friends in the .NET Class Library, you know the fluent API demonstrated in Listing 5-10 offers a more intuitive, domain-specific programming interface to XML document construction. That said, the API shown here is very limited in its capabilities and is for the purpose of illustration only. Also, the idea of the fluent API for building XML documents is not something new. Groovy, a dynamic language that runs on the Java virtual machine, has fluent APIs for building XML as well as other things.

The design of the API uses only three late binding actions—GetMember, Invoke, and InvokeMember. The design uses two special properties—b and d— to mark the beginning and the end of a block of child XML elements. For example, Street, City, and Zip are three child elements of Address because they are within the block marked by the b and d that belong to Address. Some might prefer using curly braces instead of b and d. Although that makes the syntax of the API better, the downside is you can't use the API in languages that don't support that syntax. For example, if we replace b and d with curly braces in the example, the C# compiler will report compilation errors. While developing the XML builder example, I tried to strike a balance so that the API can be used in as many languages as possible and at the same time its syntax remains reasonably fluent.

Listing 5-10. Using the Fluent API to Build an XML Document

```
static void Main(string[] args)
{
    RunXmlBuilderExample();
    Console.ReadLine();
}

private static void RunXmlBuilderExample()
{
    String xml = XmlBuilder.Create()
            .Customer.b
                .Name("FirstName", "John", "LastName", "Smith", "John Smith")
                .Phone("555-8765")
                .Address.b
                    .Street("123 Main Street")
                    .City("Fremont")
                    .Zip("55555")
                .d
            .d
            .Build();

    Console.WriteLine(xml);
}
```

Because the API uses the GetMember, Invoke, and InvokeMember actions, any language whose syntax supports those three actions can use the API. Listing 5-11 is an example of using the API in Ruby. The Ruby code is pretty self-explanatory, except perhaps for the many occurrences of to_clr_string, which are there because Ruby strings are not the same as normal .NET strings. For one thing, Ruby strings are mutable while normal .NET strings are not. Our fluent XML API expects normal .NET strings and, therefore, in the Ruby code, we use to_clr_string to convert a Ruby string to a normal .NET string. In some versions of IronRuby, the conversion might happen automatically, but I put to_clr_string in the Ruby code just to be safe. To run the Ruby code, I use the same technique as in the code in Listing 5-7. Listing 5-12 shows the C# code that uses an IronRuby script engine to run the Ruby code in Listing 5-11. I'll skip the explanation of the code in Listing 5-12 since it's the same as the explanation for the code in listing 5-7.

Listing 5-11. XmlBuilder.rb

```
xml = xmlBuilder.
 Customer.b.
     Name("FirstName".to_clr_string, "John".to_clr_string,
         "LastName".to_clr_string, "Smith".to_clr_string, "John Smith".to_clr_string).
     Phone("555-8765".to_clr_string).
     Address.b.
         Street("123 Main Street".to_clr_string).
         City("Fremont".to_clr_string).
         Zip("55555".to_clr_string).
     d.
 d.
 Build()

puts xml
```

Listing 5-12. Running the Ruby code in XmlBuilder.rb

```
private static void RunXmlBuilderInRubyExample()
{
    ScriptEngine rbEngine = IronRuby.Ruby.CreateEngine();
    ScriptSource source = rbEngine.CreateScriptSourceFromFile("XmlBuilder.rb");
    ScriptScope scope = rbEngine.CreateScope();
    scope.SetVariable("xmlBuilder", XmlBuilder.Create());
    source.Execute(scope);
}
```

You can also use the API in Python to build XML documents. Listing 5-13 shows an example. The Python code in Listing 5-13 is very close to the XML it constructs. The one annoying thing in the Python code is the backslash characters. Because white space and new line characters in Python play a role in the language's syntax, we need the backslash characters to tell the Python parser to treat those multiple lines as one logical line of code.

Listing 5-13. XmlBuilder.py.

```
xml = xmlBuilder. \
  Customer.b. \
```

```
      Name("FirstName", "John", "LastName", "Smith", "John Smith"). \
      Phone("555-8765"). \
      Address.b. \
        Street("123 Main Street"). \
        City("Fremont"). \
        Zip("55555"). \
      d. \
    d. \
  Build()

print xml
```

To run the Python code in Listing 5-13, you can use the code in Listing 5-14, which uses the DLR Hosting API to run Python code and is very similar to the code in Listing 5-12. Chapter 6 will cover the DLR Hosting API in detail.

Listing 5-14. Running the Python Code in XmlBuilder.py.

```
private static void RunXmlBuilderInPythonExample()
{
    ScriptEngine engine = IronPython.Hosting.Python.CreateEngine();
    ScriptSource source = engine.CreateScriptSourceFromFile("XmlBuilder.py");
    ScriptScope scope = engine.CreateScope();
    scope.SetVariable("xmlBuilder", XmlBuilder.Create());
    source.Execute(scope);
}
```

The implementation of the XML builder API consists of four classes—XmlBuilder, NodeBuilder, ChildNodesBuilder, and XmlBuilderHelper. Most of the real work is done in NodeBuilder and ChildNodesBuilder. The class NodeBuilder corresponds to an XML element. The class ChildNodesBuilder corresponds to a block of child elements. Listing 5-15 shows the code for NodeBuilder. An XML element has a tag name, and optionally a body, some attributes, or some child elements. Therefore, the NodeBuilder class defines the private member variables—name, body, attributes and childNodes—to represent the various parts of an XML element. Notice that the type of the childNodes member variable is ChildNodesBuilder. That's because the API implementation uses ChildNodesBuilder as a container for a list of child XML elements. Each child XML element in ChildNodesBuilder is an instance of NodeBuilder. When a ChildNodesBuilder object contains a NodeBuilder object as a child XML element, the ChildNodesBuilder object is set as the parent of the NodeBuilder object.

NodeBuilder inherits from DynamicObject. It overrides TryGetMember, TryInvoke, and TryInvokeMember. The code Phone("555-8765").Address will cause the TryGetMember method to be called because it means getting the Address member property of the NodeBuilder object that represents the Phone("555-8765") XML element. The C# code Street("123 Main Street").City("Fremont") will cause the TryInvokeMember method to be called because it means calling the City method with the string "Fremont" as the argument on the NodeBuilder object that represents the Street("123 Main Street") element.

The Python code .Phone("555-8765") in XmlBuilder.py will cause the TryInvoke method of NodeBuilder to be called. What happens is the code .Phone("555-8765") is invoked on an instance of ChildNodesBuilder. As a result, the TryGetMember method of ChildNodesBuilder will be called and the TryGetMember method will return the NodeBuilder instance that represents the Phone XML element. The NodeBuilder instance that represents the Phone XML element will be treated as a callable object by

Python. Python will call the NodeBuilder instance because the NodeBuilder instance is a delegate and the TryInvoke method of NodeBuilder will be invoked to handle the late binding.

Besides overriding TryGetMember, TryInvoke, and TryInvokeMember, NodeBuilder defines two property getters—b and d. Because of the way the late-binding logic of DynamicObject is implemented, code like Address.b will cause the property getter b, not TryGetMember, to be called.

Listing 5-15. NodeBuilder.cs

```
public class NodeBuilder : DynamicObject
{
    private string name;  //tag name of the Xml element this node builder represents
    private string body;
    private ChildNodesBuilder childNodes;
    private IDictionary<object, object> attributes;
    private ChildNodesBuilder parent;

    internal NodeBuilder(ChildNodesBuilder parentNode, string name, string body = null,
        IDictionary<object, object> attributes = null)
    {
        this.parent = parentNode;
        this.name = name;
        this.body = body;
        this.attributes = attributes;
    }

    public ChildNodesBuilder b
    {
        get
        {
            this.childNodes = new ChildNodesBuilder(parent);
            return childNodes;
        }
    }

    public ChildNodesBuilder d
    {
        get { return parent.Parent; }
    }

    public override bool TryGetMember(GetMemberBinder binder, out object result)
    {
        NodeBuilder newNode = new NodeBuilder(parent, binder.Name);
        parent.addChild(newNode);
        result = newNode;
        return true;
    }

    public override bool TryInvokeMember(InvokeMemberBinder binder,
        object[] args, out object result)
    {
        NodeBuilder newNode = XmlBuilderHelper.CreateNodeBuilder(parent, binder.Name, args);
```

126

```
            parent.addChild(newNode);
            result = newNode;
            return true;
        }

    public override bool TryInvoke(InvokeBinder binder, object[] args,
        out object result)
    {
        XmlBodyAttributes bodyAttributes = XmlBuilderHelper.ParseArgs(args);
        this.body = bodyAttributes.TagBody;
        this.attributes = bodyAttributes.Attributes;
        result = this;
        return true;
    }

    internal void Build(StringBuilder stringBuilder)
    {
        stringBuilder.AppendLine();
        stringBuilder.Append("<" + this.name);
        if (this.attributes != null)
        {
            foreach (var keyValuePair in attributes)
                stringBuilder.AppendFormat(" {0}={1}",
                        keyValuePair.Key, keyValuePair.Value);
        }

        if (body != null)
        {
            stringBuilder.AppendFormat(">{0}</{1}>", body, this.name);
            return;
        }

        if (childNodes == null)
        {
            stringBuilder.Append(" />");
            return;
        }

        stringBuilder.Append(">");
        childNodes.Build(stringBuilder);
        stringBuilder.AppendLine();
        stringBuilder.AppendLine("</" + this.name + ">");
    }
}
```

Listing 5-16 shows the code for ChildNodesBuilder, which inherits from DynamicObject. It overrides TryInvokeMember and TryGetMember. C# code like b.Street("123 Main Street") will cause the TryInvokeMember method of ChildNodesBuilder to be called. That is because the property getter b of NodeBuilder returns an instance of ChildNodesBuilder. After the property getter b of NodeBuilder returns a ChildNodesBuilder instance, the C# code b.Street("123 Main Street") calls the Street method with the string "123 Main Street" as the argument on that ChildNodesBuilder instance. Because the Street method is not defined in the ChildNodesBuilder class, the TryInvokeMember method of ChildNodesBuilder is called to handle the late binding. As for the TryGetMember of ChildNodesBuilder, it will be called, for example, when we execute Ruby code such as .Address in the XmlBuilder.rb file shown in Listing 5-11. This is because .Address is called on an instance of ChildNodesBuilder. Because the ChildNodesBuilder class does not define a property called Address, the TryGetMember method of ChildNodesBuilder is invoked to do the late binding. Let's look at the implementation of the TryGetMember and TryInvokeMember methods in Listing 5-16.

Every time TryGetMember is invoked, it means we have a new XML node to create. For example, the Ruby code .Address means we need to create a new XML node whose name is "Address". Once the new XML node is created, we need to add it to the parent XML node that contains it. As mentioned earlier, in our API design, every parent XML node uses an instance of ChildNodesBuilder to contain its child XML nodes. That's why you see that in the TryGetMember method in Listing 5-16, after creating a new instance of NodeBuilder that represents the new XML node, we add the new NodeBuilder instance as a child of the current ChildNodesBuilder instance.

Listing 5-16. ChildNodesBuilder.cs

```
public class ChildNodesBuilder : DynamicObject
{
    private List<NodeBuilder> childNodes = new List<NodeBuilder>();
    private ChildNodesBuilder parent;

    internal ChildNodesBuilder(ChildNodesBuilder parent)
    {
        this.parent = parent;
    }

    public ChildNodesBuilder d
    {
        get { return parent; }
    }

    public override bool TryGetMember(GetMemberBinder binder, out object result)
    {
        NodeBuilder newNode = new NodeBuilder(this, binder.Name);
        this.addChild(newNode);
        result = newNode;
        return true;
    }

    public override bool TryInvokeMember(InvokeMemberBinder binder,
        object[] args, out object result)
    {
        NodeBuilder newNode = XmlBuilderHelper.CreateNodeBuilder(this, binder.Name, args);
        this.addChild(newNode);
        result = newNode;
        return true;
    }

    public String Build()
```

```
    {
        StringBuilder stringBuilder = new StringBuilder();
        Build(stringBuilder);
        return stringBuilder.ToString();
    }

    internal ChildNodesBuilder Parent
    {
        get { return parent; }
    }

    internal void addChild(NodeBuilder nodeBuilder)
    {
        childNodes.Add(nodeBuilder);
    }

    internal void Build(StringBuilder stringBuilder)
    {
        foreach (var item in childNodes)
            item.Build(stringBuilder);
    }
}
```

The implementation of the TryInvokeMember method in Listing 5-16 is very similar to that of TryGetMember. When the TryInvokeMember method is invoked, it means we have a new XML node to create. For example, the C# code .Street("123 Main Street") means we need to create a new XML node whose name is "Street" and whose body is "123 Main Street". The difference between TryGetMember and TryInvokeMember is that TryInvokeMember might take input arguments that represent the attributes and body of the new XML node. In order to handle the input arguments that represent the attributes and body of an XML node, I wrote a small helper class called XmlBuilderHelper and used it in the TryInvokeMember method of ChildNodesBuilder. Listing 5-17 shows the code of the XmlBuilderHelper class.

The XmlBuilderHelper provides a helper method called ParseArgs for parsing the arguments that represent an XML node's attributes and body. The way XmlBuilderHelper parses arguments is to see first if the total number of arguments is an even number. If there is an even number of arguments, the XML node does not have a body and all of the arguments are attributes. The arguments are grouped into name-value pairs. The first argument is the name of the first attribute, the second argument the value of the first attribute, the third argument the name of the second attribute, the fourth argument the value of the second attribute, and so on. For example, the C# code .Name("FirstName", "John", "LastName", "Smith") has an even number of arguments. The first argument is "FirstName" and that will become the name of the first attribute of the XML node we create. The second argument is "John" and that will become the value of the first attribute of the XML node we create. The XML node created by the C# code .Name("FirstName", "John", "LastName", "Smith") will hence be <Name FirstName="John" LastName="Smith" />.

If there are an odd number of arguments passed to the ParseArgs method of XmlBuilderHelper, the last argument will become the body and the rest of the arguments will become the attributes of the XML node being created. So for example, the C# code .Name("FirstName", "John", "LastName", "Smith", "John Smith") has an odd number of arguments. The XML node created by that C# code will hence be <Name FirstName="John" LastName="Smith">John Smith</Name>.

Listing 5-17. XmlBuilderHelper.cs

```csharp
internal static class XmlBuilderHelper
{
    public static NodeBuilder CreateNodeBuilder(ChildNodesBuilder parent, string name,
        object[] args)
    {
        XmlBodyAttributes bodyAttributes = ParseArgs(args);
        return new NodeBuilder(parent, name, bodyAttributes.TagBody,
                bodyAttributes.Attributes);
    }

    public static XmlBodyAttributes ParseArgs(object[] args)
    {
        String newTagBody = null;
        int attrLength = args.Length;
        if ((args.Length % 2) == 1) //the element has only body
        {
            newTagBody = args[args.Length - 1].ToString();
            --attrLength;
        }

        Dictionary<object, object> attributes = (attrLength > 0) ?
                new Dictionary<object, object>() : null;

        for (int i = 0; i < attrLength; i++)
            attributes.Add(args[i], args[++i]);

        return new XmlBodyAttributes(newTagBody, attributes);
    }
}

internal class XmlBodyAttributes
{
    public String TagBody;
    public Dictionary<object, object> Attributes;

    public XmlBodyAttributes(String tagBody, Dictionary<object, object> attributes)
    {
        this.TagBody = tagBody;
        this.Attributes = attributes;
    }
}
```

Summary

This chapter focused on the IDynamicMetaObjectProvider interface and the DynamicMetaObject class. If a class implements the IDynamicMetaObjectProvider interface, then instances of the class will have associated meta-objects. Those meta-objects will be instances of DynamicMetaObject or its derivatives. If those meta-objects are instances of a class that derives from DynamicMetaObject, they can have late binding behaviors that are different from the default late-binding behaviors implemented in

DynamicMetaObject. We discussed what the default late-binding behaviors implemented in DynamicMetaObject are, and showed how to customize those default late-binding behaviors by implementing the ConstantMetaObject class. We then looked at how to trigger the various late-binding actions on instances of the ConstantMetaObject class.

Next we looked at the DynamicObject class of the DLR and explored its late-binding behaviors. Based on that understanding, we saw how to use the DynamicObject class to build a fluent API for constructing XML documents. There are many interesting ways you can use what you learned in this chapter. For example, in Chapter 8, you'll see how to leverage the DynamicObject class to implement a metaprogramming component that lets you add or remove methods and properties to or from classes or class instances at run time in C#. A static language like C# does not typically allow adding and removing methods and properties to or from classes or class instances at run time. But as you will see in Chapter 8, with DLR, that becomes possible.

CHAPTER 6

■ ■ ■

DLR Hosting API

The DLR Hosting API is a programming interface that allows one language's code to execute in another language. For ease of discussion, I'll refer to the language whose code is executed in another language as the *guest language*. The language that executes a guest language's code will be the *host language*.

The biggest source of complexity in executing a guest language's code is the need for sharing data between the host language and the guest language. For example, when we execute Python code in C#, we often want to pass some objects as input to the Python code. The objects might represent the object model of the software system we are developing. If that software system is a bank application, the objects we pass to the Python code might be customer accounts and the Python code might have functions that can operate on those customer accounts to print out monthly statements. You'll see in this chapter the mechanism used by the DLR Hosting API for sharing data between host and guest languages.

To demonstrate the value of the DLR Hosting API, we'll first take a look at how different languages host one another without the DLR Hosting API. You'll see from these examples that without the DLR Hosting API, developers need to learn each language's proprietary programming interface for hosting other languages. Given N languages, there can be as many as N x (N-1) ways for them to host one another. That's quite a heavy burden for us developers to manage even a small portion of the possible combinations. To mitigate that, DLR provides a common API for hosting languages.

In this chapter, you'll see that when you work with the DLR Hosting API, you always program to the same set of interfaces and classes defined by the API. The details specific to a guest or host language are well-encapsulated, and you don't need to concern yourself with them. And the DLR Hosting API helps not only consumers, but also producers of programming languages. If you have designed and implemented a new programming language, you can reach out to a broader audience and make your software friendlier to use by plugging your language into the DLR Hosting API. That way, users of your language can use the DLR Hosting API to host your language in C#, IronPython, or any other .NET languages.

The DLR Hosting API consists of two smaller sets of APIs, one for language consumers and the other for language producers. The part for language producers allows new languages to be plugged into the DLR Hosting API. We will focus on the language-consumer side of the DLR Hosting API here and look at the language-producer side in more detail in Chapter 9 when we go through the design and implementation of a domain-specific language called Stitch. In that chapter, you'll see how to implement the language producer side in order to plug the Stitch language into the DLR Hosting API.

Life Without the DLR Hosting API

First I want to demonstrate the key value of the DLR Hosting API by showing you what life is like without it. You'll see examples for the following scenarios related to language interoperability. Some of the examples will not use the DLR Hosting API at all. Others will use it only to a limited extent.

- Using a static language's code in another static language. We will use VB.NET code in C#.

- Using a static language's code in a dynamic language. We will use C# code in IronPython and IronRuby.

- Using a dynamic language's code in a static language. We will use IronPython and IronRuby code in C#.

- Using a dynamic language's code in another dynamic language. We will use IronPython code in IronRuby.

You'll find all of the code examples in this section in the LanguageSpecificHosting project in this chapter's code download. The examples will give you a real feel for how cumbersome it quickly gets using proprietary APIs to host other languages. After that, you'll see how the DLR Hosting API simplifies language hosting by providing a uniform and language-neutral API.

Using a Static Language's Code in Another Static Language

As the first step in our exploration, let's begin by reviewing how static languages such as C# and VB.NET interoperate. Imagine there's some VB.NET code we want to use in C# code. To do this, we need to compile the VB.NET code into a .NET assembly, then, we need to (a) reference the assembly in the C# project, and (b) add `using` statements to import the namespaces and classes defined in the VB.NET code into the C# code. For example, if the VB.NET code defines a class called `Customer` in the `Com.Xyz` namespace, to use that class in C#, the C# code needs to have a `using` statement like this:

```
using Com.Xyz;
```

Without the `using` statement, we would have to use the fully qualified class name `Com.xyz.Customer` wherever we use the `Customer` class in the C# code. As previous chapters have mentioned, language interoperability between static .NET languages such as VB.NET and C# is possible because all the static language code is compiled into the same underlying intermediate language code that shares a common type system (CTS).

Using a Static Language's Code in a Dynamic Language

Now, how about using a static language's code in a dynamic language? Let's take a look. Listing 6-1 shows what's needed for IronPython code to access C# code. The C# code, of course, needs to be compiled into a .NET assembly before it can be used by anybody. Let's assume the C# code is compiled into an assembly called Xyz.dll. Line 2 in Listing 6-1 shows that to get a hold of the C# code, the IronPython code needs to reference the Xyz.dll assembly. Referencing that assembly is equivalent to adding a reference to a VB.NET assembly in a C# project when using VB.NET code in C#. Line 3 imports the `Customer` class into the IronPython code, which is equivalent to importing namespaces and classes defined in VB.NET code into C#.

You can see that the two steps needed for IronPython code to get a hold of C# code are equivalent to those needed for C# code to get a hold of VB.NET code. However, even though the steps are by and large equivalent, they are not exactly the same. C# and IronPython each define their own ways for referencing assemblies and for importing classes.

Listing 6-1. Using C# Code in IronPython

```
import clr
clr.AddReference("xyz.dll")
from com.xyz import Customer
# ... code that uses the Customer class.
# You can use fully qualified name com.xyz.Customer too.
```

Listing 6-2 shows the IronRuby way of accessing C# (or VB.NET) code. This is again a two-step process. First we need to add a reference to the compiled assembly, Xyz.dll. Next we need to import the namespaces or classes we want to use into the IronRuby code space. As Listing 6-2 shows, IronRuby uses the require keyword for adding references to compiled .NET assemblies and the include keyword for importing a namespace. Once again, even though the two steps for using other language's code in IronRuby are equivalent, they are not exactly the same and, as IronRuby developers, we have to learn IronRuby's specific keywords to use C# code in IronRuby.

Listing 6-2. Using C# Code in IronRuby

```
require 'Xyz.dll'
include Com.Xyz
# ... code that uses the Customer class
```

Using a Dynamic Language's Code in a Static Language

We just looked at using a static language's code in a dynamic language, now we'll look at the reverse—using a dynamic language's code in a static language. One major difference between this scenario and the previous is that dynamic language code does not need to be compiled until run time. Because dynamic language code is not compiled into an assembly at compile time, we don't get a hold of the code by adding an assembly reference to our C# project. Instead, the C# code directly references the dynamic language source code, as in Listing 6-3.

The example in Listing 6-3 makes use of the DLR Hosting API only to a limited extent. It calls the CreateEngine static method of the IronPython.Hosting.Python class to create a script engine for running IronPython code. IronPython.Hosting.Python is an IronPython-specific class in the IronPython.dll assembly. In order for the code in Listing 6-3 to compile, we need to add a reference to the IronPython.dll assembly. Had we used the language-neutral DLR Hosting API to create the script engine, we wouldn't need to add the reference to the C# project. The type of the script engine instance is ScriptEngine, which is a class in the DLR Hosting API. The example in Listing 6-3 uses some features of the DLR Hosting API and some features specific to the IronPython implementation. Later in this chapter, you'll see examples that use only the DLR Hosting API.

Listing 6-3. Running IronPython Code in C#

```
private static void CSHostsIronPython()
{
    ScriptEngine engine = Python.CreateEngine();
    engine.Execute("print \"hello\"");
}
```

Listing 6-4 shows the same example but for the Ruby language. The code calls the CreateEngine static method of the IronRuby.Ruby class to get a script engine that is capable of running IronRuby code. IronRuby.Ruby is an IronRuby-specific class in the IronRuby.dll assembly.

Listing 6-4. Running IronRuby Code in C#

```
private static void CSHostsIronRuby()
{
    ScriptEngine engine = Ruby.CreateEngine();
    engine.Execute("puts \"hello\"");
}
```

Using a Dynamic Language's Code in Another Dynamic Language

Now let's look at an example in which a dynamic language hosts another dynamic language. Listing 6-5 shows how to host IronPython code in IronRuby using IronRuby's specific mechanism. The IronRuby code in Listing 6-5 calls the require method of the IronRuby module to load the Python code in helloFunc.py. The Python code in helloFunc.py defines a hello function and is shown in Listing 6-6.

The IronRuby module used in Listing 6-5 is a built-in module available to all IronRuby code. If you look at the DLR source code, you can find a class called LibraryInitializer in the IronRuby project. LibraryInitializer is derived by many generated classes that take care of loading various built-in IronRuby modules and functions. All those generated classes are placed in the Initializers.Generated.cs file under the IronRuby.Libraries project. One of those generated classes is BuiltinsLibraryInitializer. If you look into the LoadModules method of BuiltinsLibraryInitializer, you will find that one of the default modules it loads is named IronRuby. The LoadModules method of BuiltinsLibraryInitializer uses the LoadIronRuby_Class method of the same BuiltinsLibraryInitializer class to define the methods belonging to the IronRuby module. One of those methods is require and from the code in the LoadIronRuby_Class method you can see that the require method is actually backed by the Require method in the IronRubyOps class. The use of the IronRuby module in Listing 6-5 is specific to the IronRuby implementation and is not language neutral. You will see that instead of using the IronRuby module to load Python code, we can use the DLR Hosting API to load one dynamic language's code into another dynamic language.

Listing 6-5. Ruby Code Usings the hello Function Defined in helloFunc.py

```
pythonHello = IronRuby.require('Python/helloFunc.py')
pythonHello.hello
```

Listing 6-6. Python Code That Defines a hello Function.

```
def hello():
    """This function prints Hello."""
    print "Hello"
```

Overview of the DLR Hosting API

So far we've seen the various ways of hosting one language in another in different scenarios. Now I'll give you an overview of the DLR Hosting API and point out the scenarios for which the DLR Hosting API provides value—only two of the four scenarios described earlier: using a dynamic language's code in a static language and using a dynamic language's code in another dynamic language. The DLR Hosting API doesn't provide any feature for using a static language in another static language or for using static language code in a dynamic language. For those, you need to compile the static language code and add a reference to the compiled assembly file as illustrated in previous sections.

Major Classes in the API

The DLR Hosting API consists of two smaller sets of APIs, one for language consumers and the other for language providers. The classes and interfaces that make up the Hosting API are packaged into the Microsoft.Scripting.dll assembly. Some of the major classes that make up the consumer side of the DLR Hosting API are ScriptRuntime, ScriptScope, ScriptEngine, ScriptSource, and CompiledCode, all of which are in the Microsoft.Scripting.Hosting namespace. Here's a brief description of each.

ScriptRuntime: This is the class defined by the DLR Hosting API to model the runtime that dynamic code runs on. Just like C# or VB.NET code runs on the CLR runtime, dynamic code also needs a runtime. The CLR runtime can run C#, VB.NET, and other language code. Similarly, a ScriptRuntime instance can run code written in different dynamic languages.

ScriptEngine: This is what ScriptRuntime uses to run code written in different dynamic languages. At run time, for each dynamic language, there needs to be a ScriptEngine instance that knows how to execute code written in that language. A script runtime (i.e., an instance of the ScriptRuntime class) usually holds a reference to a ScriptEngine instance for each dynamic language the script runtime supports. For example, if a script runtime is capable of running IronPython and IronRuby code, the script runtime must internally hold a reference to a ScriptEngine instance that's capable of running IronPython code and a reference to another ScriptEngine instance that's capable of running IronRuby code.

ScriptScope: This is the class that allows data sharing between guest and host languages. Earlier in this chapter, I indicated that the biggest source of complexity in executing a guest language's code is the need for sharing data between the host language and the guest language. The ScriptScope class is defined to facilitate data sharing between different languages. You can think of a ScriptScope instance as a bag that holds named objects that can be passed around from one language to another. Different language code fetches a particular object from the bag by the object's name and does something useful with the fetched object.

ScriptSource: This is the class defined by the DLR Hosting API to model the source code of a DLR-based language. We can call the Compile method of ScriptSource on a ScriptSource instance to compile the source code the ScriptSource instance represents. The Compile method will return an instance of CompiledCode to represent the compiled source code.

CompiledCode: This is the class defined by the DLR Hosting API to model the compiled source code of a DLR-based language. We can call the Execute method on a CompiledCode instance to execute the compiled source code.

The documentation area of the DLR CodePlex web site has a document called dlr-spec-hosting.doc that contains a wealth of information about the consumer side of the DLR Hosting API. It divides the way you can use the Hosting API into three levels. Level One is the simplest and uses the fewest features of the Hosting API. Level Two is the middle level and Level Three, the most advanced, uses the full power of the API. Although the division seems somewhat artificial, the levels are by and large a very good measure for deciding how much of the Hosting API you'd like to use in your application. To make it easy for readers who have read or will read that document to follow along, this chapter will indicate which level of the DLR Hosting API an example uses when appropriate. As you read through this chapter, please keep in mind that the three levels are just a way to gauge how much of the Hosting API is being used. They are not reflected in any way in the Hosting API itself. There is nothing in the Hosting API that restricts you to a certain level or indicates anything about the levels. If you find yourself unsure at which level you're using the Hosting API, don't worry. It really doesn't matter much because the levels are just a conceptual categorization that does not have any concrete implementation behind it.

All the code examples for these levels are in the HostingExamples project. All Level One examples are in the LevelOneExamples.cs file. Similarly, all Level Two examples are in LevelTwoExamples.cs and Level Three examples in LevelThreeExamples.cs. One indication that the Hosting API is indeed language neutral is the assembly files referenced by the HostingExamples project. The project does not reference any of the IronPython or IronRuby assemblies. Those assemblies are not needed to compile the HostingExamples project because all the examples in the project are language neutral.

The Tale of Two APIs

Previously I mentioned that the DLR Hosting API consists of one API for language consumers and another API for language developers. The provider-side API is for language implementers to plug a new language into the DLR Hosting API so that consumers of the language can run code written in the language via the consumer side of the DLR Hosting API. We saw an example of implementing the provider-side API in Chapter 1 when we plugged in the Hello language into the DLR Hosting API by implementing a class that derives from LanguageContext and a class that derives from ScriptCode. For an API like the DLR Hosting API that allows new providers to be plugged in, it is not uncommon to see the existence of a provider API and a consumer API. For example, the Java Naming and Directory Interface (JNDI) defines a provider API called service provider interface (SPI). There are vendors who have implemented the SPI to provide naming and directory service for LDAP servers, database servers, DNS servers, and so forth. Consumers of JNDI will interact with the various naming and directory services via the consumer-side API and be kept unaware of whether the underlying provider is an LDAP server, database server, or DNS server.

The classes in the provider side and the consumer side of the DLR Hosting API have a nice correspondence. Table 6-1 shows which consumer-side class corresponds to which provider-side class. The consumer-side classes in the DLR Hosting API are really just a thin wrapper around the provider-side classes. We'll discuss only the consumer-side API now. You can find examples that implement the provider-side API in Chapters 9 and 11.

Table 6-1. Correspondence Between Provider-Side Classes and Consumer-Side Classes

Consumer-side Class	Provider-side Class
ScriptRuntime Scri	ptDomainManager
ScriptEngine LanguageContext	
CompiledCode Sc	riptCode
ScriptSource SourceUnit	
ScriptScope Scope	

The DLR Hosting API in Relation to Binders and Dynamic Objects

As part of the overview of the DLR Hosting API, I want to touch on the relation between the DLR Hosting API and language interoperability. We looked at language interoperability in the previous two chapters, where we saw that language interoperability in the DLR is made possible with binders and dynamic objects. Those two chapters and their code examples show that once the binders and dynamic objects are in place, they follow a well-established protocol in their interactions in order to enable language interoperability.

What's not really explained in those chapters is how the binders and dynamic objects come together in the first place. For example, Chapter 4 uses Python objects in C# code and explains how the Python objects interoperate with C# code. (In such scenarios, we call C# the host language and IronPython the source language). Once the C# code obtains a reference to a Python object, the C# code can call methods on the Python object and those methods can return other Python objects for the C# code to use.

But how does the C# code obtain a reference to the first Python object? The first reference doesn't need to be a reference to a Python object. It can be a reference to a Python class or a Python function. In that case, the C# code can use the Python class to create the first Python object or invoke the Python function to get back a Python object as the return value. Regardless of whether the initial item is a Python object, class, or function, the C# code needs a way to get it.

If Python were like VB.NET, the C# code would get that initial Python object, class, or function by referencing the assembly the VB.NET is compiled into. Because Python code is not compiled at compile time, instead of referencing a compiled assembly, the C# code has to reference the Python source code and be able to compile the source code at run time. That is where the DLR Hosting API comes into the picture.

You'll learn through this chapter how to use the DLR Hosting API to get a hold of, say Python objects in C# code. You can combine that knowledge with what you learned in the previous two chapters and get the whole picture of how languages interoperate.

Using Script Runtime to Execute Code

With that high-level overview of the DLR Hosting API under your belt, let's start to use the DLR Hosting API. This section will show you how to use the script runtime to execute DLR-based language code. The examples in this section will make Level One use of the DLR Hosting API and are in the LevelOneExamples.cs file. At this level, we use ScriptRuntime to execute dynamic language code stored in source files. The code can be IronPython, IronRuby, or other DLR-based language code. As long as the language implements the provider part of the Hosting API, we can use ScriptRuntime to execute its code. Let's look at some examples. Listing 6-7 shows how to use ScriptRuntime to run an IronPython source file, which is the helloFunc.py in Listing 6-6.

Listing 6-7. Using ScriptRuntime to Load and Interpret Python Code

```
1)   public static void GetPythonFunctionUsingScriptRuntime()
2)   {
3)       ScriptRuntime scriptRuntime = ScriptRuntime.CreateFromConfiguration();
4)       ScriptScope scope = scriptRuntime.ExecuteFile(@"Python\helloFunc.py");
5)       Action hello = scope.GetVariable<Action>("hello");
6)       hello();
7)       scriptRuntime.Shutdown();
8)   }
```

The code in Listing 6-7 creates a script runtime in line 3 based on the information in the App.config file. We will look at the App.config file in detail shortly. For now, let's just think of it as a black box that has in it the information needed for creating a script runtime. In Listing 6-7, the code calls the ExecuteFile method on the script runtime and passes in the name of the Python source file as the input parameter. That causes the Python code in the helloFunc.py file to be parsed and evaluated. The result of running the Python code is stored in the return value of the ExecuteFile method call.

The return value of the ExecuteFile method call is a script scope, an instance of the ScriptScope class. As described earlier in this chapter, a script scope is a container that holds objects we want to share across different languages. In this case, it is anticipated that the reason we call the ExecuteFile method is to get the result of the Python code execution. So the ExecuteFile method puts the result of executing the Python code into a script scope and returns that script scope back to the caller. Because the file helloFunc.py contains only the definition of a Python function called hello, the result of executing helloFunc.py is an instance of IronPython.Runtime.PythonFunction stored in the script scope against the name "hello". That's why line 5 in Listing 6-7 retrieves the Python function by its name "hello". Line 5 also converts the Python function of type IronPython.Runtime.PythonFunction to a .NET delegate of type Action. Because of the type conversion, line 6 can invoke the Python function like calling a normal .NET delegate.

One interesting thing to note about the ScriptScope class is that it implements the IDynamicMetaObjectProvider interface. If you've read Chapter 5, you know that means instances of ScriptScope are dynamic objects. The late binding logic for ScriptScope is implemented in such a way that we can fish out a variable as if the variable's name is a property of the scope. Listing 6-8 shows an example of this use of ScriptScope. If you compare the bolded code in Listing 6-8 to line 5 in Listing 6-7, you'll see the difference. The code in Listing 6-8 is more succinct and readable and that's the purpose of having ScriptScope implement the IDynamicMetaObjectProvider interface.

Listing 6-8. Fish Out a Variable as if the Variable's Name is a Property of the Scope

```
public static void UseScriptScopeAsDynamicObject()
{
    ScriptRuntime scriptRuntime = ScriptRuntime.CreateFromConfiguration();
    dynamic scope = scriptRuntime.ExecuteFile(@"Python\helloFunc.py");
    Action hello = scope.hello;
    hello();
    scriptRuntime.Shutdown();
}
```

Configuring the Languages You Want to Speak

In the previous section, the code examples use the CreateFromConfiguration static method of the ScriptRuntime class to create a script runtime. Behind the scenes, CreateFromConfiguration will read the configurations in the application's App.config file and use them to create the script runtime. The DLR-related configurations in an App.config file determine which dynamic languages will be supported by the script runtime. There are two ways to configure which languages will be supported by a script runtime. One way is to use App.config and the CreateFromConfiguration static method, as we've been discussing. This approach is declarative and does not require us to recompile our application should we want to support a new language in the script runtime. The other approach is to use classes such as ScriptRuntimeSetup and LanguageSetup to programmatically configure which languages will be supported in the script runtime under construction. Let's look at the two approaches in turn.

Configuring Script Runtime Declaratively

Let's start with the declarative approach for configuring which languages are supported in a script runtime. Listing 6-9 shows what the DLR-related configurations in App.config look like. App.config is .NET's mechanism for configuring an application in general. There can be different kinds of configurations in App.config for different parts of an application. For example, an App.config for a distributed application built on .NET Remoting might contain configurations related to .NET Remoting.

Each kind of configurations in an App.config file is specific to a particular aspect of the application and needs to be interpreted accordingly. The way to specify how to interpret a certain kind of configuration is by using a `<section>` element. In our case, the App.config file shown in Listing 9-6 contains information specific to the DLR Hosting API. So we have a `<section>` entry under the `<configSections>` element that specifies that the class Section in the `Microsoft.Scripting.Hosting.Configuration` namespace should be used to interpret the DLR Hosting API related configurations. The type attribute of the section element specifies the assembly-qualified name of the Section class in the `Microsoft.Scripting.Hosting.Configuration` namespace. The configurations shown in Listing 6-9 are only valid if you use the version 1.0.0.0 release bits of the Microsoft.Scripting.dll assembly. If you use a debug version of Microsoft.Scripting.dll that you build yourself, you'll have to adjust the configurations by typing in the correct assembly-qualified name of the Section class.

The configurations the `Microsoft.Scripting.Hosting.Configuration.Section` class will interpret are all lines enclosed by `<microsoft.scripting>` and `</microsoft.scripting>`. Those lines basically specify that we want the script runtime created by the `CreateFromConfiguration` static method of the ScriptRuntime class to support two languages—IronPython and IronRuby. For each language, we need to tell the DLR Hosting API the language's name, file extension, display name, and most importantly, the assembly-qualified name of a class that derives from the LanguageContext class in the `Microsoft.Scripting.Runtime` namespace. For IronPython, the class that derives from the LanguageContext class is PythonContext. For IronRuby, the class that derives from the LanguageContext class is RubyContext. LanguageContext is an important class on the provider side of the DLR Hosting API. A language implementer needs to derive a class from LanguageContext and provide language-specific behaviors in the derived class if he or she wants to plug the language into the DLR Hosting API. Again, the configurations shown in Listing 6-9 for IronPython and IronRuby are valid only if you use the release bits of IronPython 2.6.1 and IronRuby 1.0. If you use different versions or if you build the binaries yourself, you will have to adjust the configurations by typing in the correct assembly-qualified names of the PythonContext and RubyContext classes.

Listing 6-9. DLR-Related Configurations in App.config

```
<?xml version="1.0" encoding="utf-8" ?>
<configuration>
  <configSections>
    <section name="microsoft.scripting"
type="Microsoft.Scripting.Hosting.Configuration.Section,
        Microsoft.Scripting, Version=1.0.0.0, Culture=neutral,
PublicKeyToken=31bf3856ad364e35" />
  </configSections>

  <microsoft.scripting>
    <languages>
      <language names="IronPython,Python,py"
              extensions=".py"
```

```
                    displayName="IronPython 2.6.1"
                    type="IronPython.Runtime.PythonContext,IronPython, Version=2.6.10920.0,
                    Culture=neutral, PublicKeyToken=31bf3856ad364e35" />

        <language names="IronRuby;Ruby,rb"
                    extensions=".rb"
                    displayName="IronRuby 1.0"
                    type="IronRuby.Runtime.RubyContext, IronRuby, Version=1.0.0.0,
                    Culture=neutral, PublicKeyToken=31bf3856ad364e35"/>
      </languages>
    </microsoft.scripting>
</configuration>
```

Configuring Script Runtime Programmatically

After seeing the declarative approach for configuring which languages are supported in a script runtime, let's look at the programmatic approach that achieves the same thing. As a matter of fact, the declarative approach discussed in the previous section is built on top of the programmatic approach. Once you know how the programmatic approach works, you know how the declarative approach works behind the scenes.

Listing 6-10 shows a code example (in LevelThreeExamples.cs) that uses the ScriptRuntimeSetup and LanguageSetup classes to construct a script runtime. The example first creates an instance of LanguageSetup for the IronPython language. The input parameters passed to the constructor of LanguageSetup are essentially the same pieces of information we saw in the App.config file shown in Listing 6-9. Once the LanguageSetup instance is ready, we add it to an instance of ScriptRuntimeSetup and then pass the ScriptRuntimeSetup instance to the constructor of ScriptRuntime. The constructor of ScriptRuntime will use the ScriptRuntimeSetup instance we pass to it to create a script runtime that supports the IronPython language. Therefore, we can use the script runtime to execute the Python code in hello.py as the example in Listing 6-10 shows.

Listing 6-10. An Example That Creates a Script Runtime Programmatically

```
public static void RunScriptRuntimeSetupExample()
{
    LanguageSetup pythonSetup = new LanguageSetup(
        typeName: "IronPython.Runtime.PythonContext,IronPython, Version=2.6.10920.0,
Culture=neutral, PublicKeyToken=31bf3856ad364e35",
        displayName: "IronPython",
        names: new String[] { "IronPython", "Python", "py" },
        fileExtensions: new String[] { ".py" });

    ScriptRuntimeSetup setup = new ScriptRuntimeSetup();
    setup.LanguageSetups.Add(pythonSetup);
    ScriptRuntime scriptRuntime = new ScriptRuntime(setup);
    ScriptScope scope = scriptRuntime.ExecuteFile(@"Python\hello.py");
}
```

The code in Listing 6-10 shows the information for creating a LanguageSetup instance for the IronPython 2.6.1 release version. If you want to create a LanguageSetup instance for the IronRuby 1.0 release version, use the following code:

```
LanguageSetup rubySetup = new LanguageSetup(
    typeName: "IronRuby.Runtime.RubyContext, IronRuby,
        Version=1.0.0.0, Culture=neutral, PublicKeyToken=31bf3856ad364e35",
    displayName: "IronRuby",
    names: new String[]{"IronRuby", "Ruby", "rb"},
    fileExtensions: new String[]{".rb"});
```

Like Listing 6-9, the code in Listing 6-10 does not require any reference to IronPython assemblies at compile time. Another way to create a LanguageSetup instance for IronPython is to call the CreateLanguageSetup static method of the IronPython.Hosting.Python class like this:

```
LanguageSetup pythonSetup = Python.CreateLanguageSetup(new Dictionary<string, object>());
```

As you can see, using the CreateLanguageSetup static method to create a LanguageSetup instance doesn't require us to find out the assembly-qualified name of the PythonContext class. No matter which version of the IronPython.dll assembly we use, the CreateLanguageSetup static method will return the correct LanguageSetup instance for that IronPython.dll assembly. The empty dictionary object passed to the CreateLanguageSetup method in the code snippet above is supposed to contain IronPython-specific options for controlling the IronPython script engine you create with the pythonSetup variable. Similar to IronPython, IronRuby comes with the IronRuby.Ruby class that provides a static method CreateRubySetup. The CreateRubySetup method returns a LanguageSetup instance for the IronRuby.dll assembly you reference in your project. Using IronRuby.Ruby and IronPython.Hosting.Python to create LanguageSetup instances requires adding references to the IronPython.dll and IronRuby.dll assemblies at compile time. Once you get those LanguageSetup instances, you can call their TypeName property to get the assembly-qualified names of the PythonContext and RubyContext classes.

Scripting an Object Model

So far we have seen examples that use the ScriptRuntime class to execute Python code in a C# application. Those examples are simple and don't involve the host language passing data to the guest language code. The main usage scenario that the designers of the DLR have for Level One use of the Hosting API is to have the host language pass an object model to the guest language code. The idea is to let the guest language code do something useful with the object model. To show a more realistic example, Listing 6-11 demonstrates this main Level One usage scenario. In this example, I use a simple Customer class to represent the object model. In reality, the object model can be something as complex as the domain model of a banking system containing classes such as Customer, Account, BankStatement, etc.

The example in Listing 6-11 first creates an instance of the Customer class. The Customer class is implemented in C# and its code is shown in Listing 6-12. There are several ways to pass the Customer instance to the guest language code. A script runtime maintains a global script scope. The example in Listing 6-11 uses that to pass objects from a host language to a guest language. Besides using a script runtime's global script scope, we can use a language-neutral script scope or a language-specific script scope to pass objects from one language to another. You will see examples of these in later sections.

The ScriptRuntime class defines a member property called Globals whose type is ScriptScope and represents the global script scope of a ScriptRuntime instance. The example in Listing 6-11 puts the Customer instance into the script runtime's global script by calling the SetVariable method of ScriptScope. The Customer instance is associated with the name "customer" in the global script scope. Later, when we need to retrieve the Customer instance out from the global script scope, we need to get it by the name "customer".

Listing 6-11. Passing an Object Model to Guest Language Code Using the Script Runtime's Global Scope

```
public static void PassObjectModelToScript()
{
    Customer customer = new Customer("Bob", 30);
    ScriptRuntime scriptRuntime = ScriptRuntime.CreateFromConfiguration();
    scriptRuntime.Globals.SetVariable("customer", customer);
    ScriptScope scope = scriptRuntime.ExecuteFile(@"Python\simpleWpf2.py");
}
```

Listing 6-12. The Customer Class

```
public class Customer
{
    public int Age { get; set; }
    public String Name { get; set; }

    public Customer(String name, int age)
    {
        this.Name = name;
        this.Age = age;
    }

    public override string ToString()
    {
        return Name + " is " + Age + " years old.";
    }
}
```

Let's now see how the guest language code uses the Customer instance that we put into the script runtime's global scope. The guest language code in this example is the IronPython code stored in simpleWpf2.py and shown in Listing 6-13. The IronPython code basically retrieves the Customer instance from the script runtime's global scope and displays the customer's information in a WPF (Windows Presentation Foundation) application. Don't worry if you aren't familiar with WPF. My choice of WPF as the UI framework for this example is simply because I want to show something different from the console applications we've been using so far.

The key line of code in Listing 6-13 is bolded. The code import customer is how we retrieve an object associated with the name "customer" from a script runtime's global scope. After this code, the variable customer becomes available in the Python code and we simply display the customer's information by setting the result of customer.ToString() to a WPF label's Content property.

Listing 6-13. IronPython Code in simpleWpf2.py

```
import clr
import customer
clr.AddReference("PresentationFramework")
clr.AddReference("PresentationCore")

from System.Windows import (Application, Window)
from System.Windows.Controls import (Label, StackPanel)
```

```
window = Window()
window.Title = "Simple Python WPF Example"
window.Width = 400
window.Height = 300

stackPanel = StackPanel()
window.Content = stackPanel

customerLabel = Label()
customerLabel.Content = customer.ToString()
customerLabel.FontSize = 20
stackPanel.Children.Add(customerLabel)

app = Application()
app.Run(window)
```

This example passed objects from a host language to a guest language using the script runtime's global scope. Next we'll look at script scopes in more detail.

Script Scopes

There are different kinds of script scopes, but they're all instances of the ScriptScope class. ScriptScope has a property called Engine. If a script scope's Engine property is set to a particular language's script engine, the script scope is bound to that particular language and I'll refer to such script scope as engine scope. On the other hand, if a script scope's Engine property is not set to a particular language's script engine, then the script scope is said to be language neutral and I'll refer to such script scope as language-neutral scope. Why is the distinction between language-neutral scopes and engine scopes important? Let me show you some examples that demonstrate the difference between language-neutral scopes and engine scopes. After the examples, I'll explain how script scopes retrieve objects by name.

Listing 6-14 shows an example (in LevelTwoExamples.cs) that creates a script scope by calling the CreateScope method on a script runtime. The script scope created this way is language neutral. So when the code in Listing 6-14 asks the script scope whether it contains an object by the name "__doc__", the script scope will say no. If you run the code in Listing 6-14, you will see the string "scope does not contain __doc__ variable" printed on the screen.

Listing 6-14. Example of a Language-Neutral Scope

```
public static void RunLanguageNeutralScopeExample()
{
    ScriptRuntime runtime = ScriptRuntime.CreateFromConfiguration();
    ScriptScope scope = runtime.CreateScope();
    if (!scope.ContainsVariable("__doc__"))
        Console.WriteLine("scope does not contain __doc__ variable.");
}
```

Now, for comparison, let's see an example of a language-bound scope. Listing 6-15 shows such an example, which you can find in LevelTwoExamples.cs. The code in Listing 6-15 does not use the script runtime to create a script scope. Instead, it uses the script runtime to get the IronPython script engine and then calls the CreateScope method on the script engine to create a script scope bound to the

IronPython script engine. Because the script scope is bound to the IronPython script engine, when we asks the script scope whether it contains an object by the name "__doc__", the script scope will say yes.

Listing 6-15. Example of a Language-Bound Scope

```
public static void RunPythonEngineScopeExample()
{
    ScriptRuntime runtime = ScriptRuntime.CreateFromConfiguration();
    ScriptEngine pyEngine = runtime.GetEngine("python");
    ScriptScope scope = pyEngine.CreateScope();

    if (scope.ContainsVariable("__doc__"))
        Console.WriteLine("scope contains __doc__ variable.");

    String docString = scope.GetVariable("__doc__");
    Console.WriteLine("doc string is {0}", docString);
}
```

So why does a script scope behave differently depending on whether and which language's script engine it is bound to? Recall that the major responsibility of a script scope is to serve as a container that carries objects from one language to another language. When we try to retrieve an object from a script scope by name, the script scope if language-bound will use the language's binders to bind the name we request to an object in the scope. In the example in Listing 6-15, because the script scope is bound to IronPython's script engine, when we ask for "__doc__", the script scope will internally create a call site and use IronPython's GetMember binder to bind the name "__doc__". Because the Python language associates the __doc__ attribute with every object, IronPython's GetMember binder will bind the name "__doc__" to the __doc__ attribute of the script scope.

The global scope of a script runtime we looked at in the previous section is a language-neutral scope. To prove that to yourself, you can run the following code in debug mode:

```
ScriptRuntime scriptRuntime = ScriptRuntime.CreateFromConfiguration();
```

In the debugger, if you examine scriptRuntime.Globals.Engine, you'll see that the value of its LanguageContext property is an instance of the Microsoft.Scripting.Runtime.InvariantContext class. That shows that a script runtime's global scope is not bound to any particular language's script engine.

So far in this chapter, you have learned the different kinds of script scopes. Next, let's see what differences it makes when we use those different kinds of script scopes to pass objects by value or by reference from one language to another.

Value and Reference Variables

One important thing to pay attention to when using script scopes to pass objects from one language to another is whether the objects are passed by value or by reference. Passing objects from one language to another is in a way like passing objects to a method. When passing objects to a method, you need to know whether the method has any chance of mutating those objects. If the objects are passed by value to a method, the objects will not be mutated no matter what the method does with those objects inside its method scope. On the other hand, if the objects are passed by reference, they will be mutated if the method assigns new values to the objects' properties. The distinction between passing an object by value and by reference turns out to be important too in the case of script scopes. And with script scopes, the distinction between passing objects by value and by reference is slightly more complicated because there are different types of script scopes. In this section we will look at the different scopes and see the effects they have on the objects passed from one language to another.

Global Scope and Variable Passing

Let's first see an example that passes an integer and a `Customer` instance from C# code to Python code using a global scope. Listing 6-16 shows a C# example that puts a `Customer` instance and the integer 2 into the script runtime's global scope (in LevelOneExamples.cs). In the global scope, the `Customer` instance is associated with the name "customer" and the integer is associated with the name "x". Those two objects "customer" and "x" are used by the Python code in the simply2.py file, shown in Listing 6-17.

Listing 6-16. Passing a `Customer` Object and an Integer to Python Code Using a Global Scope

```
public static void PassObjectsToPythonViaGlobals()
{
    ScriptRuntime scriptRuntime = ScriptRuntime.CreateFromConfiguration();
    Customer customer = new Customer("Bob", 30);
    scriptRuntime.Globals.SetVariable("x", 2);
    scriptRuntime.Globals.SetVariable("customer", customer);

    //Changing the value of x in Python code will not change the x in Globals.
    //This is because x is a value type and also the new x in Python code
    //is not put back into Globals.
    ScriptScope resultScope = scriptRuntime.ExecuteFile(@"Python\simple2.py");

    int x = scriptRuntime.Globals.GetVariable("x");
    Console.WriteLine("x is {0}", x);
    Console.WriteLine("Bob's age is {0}", customer.Age);

    Console.WriteLine("Items in global scope: ");
    DumpScriptScope(scriptRuntime.Globals);

    Console.WriteLine("Items in the returned scope: ");
    DumpScriptScope(resultScope);
    scriptRuntime.Shutdown();
}

private static void DumpScriptScope(ScriptScope scope)
{
    foreach (var item in scope.GetItems())
        Console.WriteLine("{0} : {1}", item.Key, item.Value);
}
```

Listing 6-17. Python Code Using Instances of `Customer` and Integer in the Script Runtime's Global Scope

```
import x
import customer

print x
customer.Age = 20
```

```
x = 8
print x
```

As you can see from Listing 6-17, the Python code retrieves the "customer" and "x" objects from the script runtime's global scope, prints the value of x and then mutates the Age property of the customer as well as the value of x. The original value of x in the Python code is 2. After the mutation, the value of x becomes 8. Now here's the interesting question. What do you think the value of x and the customer's age would be in the global scope after the Python code finishes execution? To show you the answer to the question, the code in Listing 6-16 prints out the value of x and the customer's age property in the global scope after the execution of the Python code. It turns out that the value of x in the global scope is still 2 and the customer's age is changed to 20. Now if you notice, in Listing 6-16, the method ExecuteFile of ScriptRuntime returns a script scope, which is assigned to the variable resultScope. The code in Listing 6-16 calls the DumpScriptScope method to print out all the objects contained in resultScope. If you run the code in Listing 6-16, you'll see that resultScope contains an object whose name is "x" and value is 8. You will also see that resultScope contains an object whose name is "customer" and value is the same Customer instance contained in the global scope.

Because the type of x is a .NET value type, the x in the global scope is passed by value to the Python code. So when we mutate the x in Python code, we are mutating a copy of the original x in the global scope. After the Python code finishes execution, the x is not put back into the script runtime's global scope but into the new script scope returned by the ExecuteFile method. So the global scope still binds the name "x" to the original integer value 2 while the new script scope returned by the ExecuteFile method binds the name "x" to 8. In the next section you'll see an example where we use a different script scope from the global scope and the x mutated in Python code is automatically put back into the script scope by the DLR Hosting API. If the object we pass to the Python code is an object whose type is a reference type like the customer object in our example, the object is passed by reference. So when we mutate the object in the Python code, we will see those changes made to the original object in the global scope after the Python code finishes execution.

Language Neutral Scope and Variable Passing

The previous example shows what happens when using a global scope to pass variables by value and by reference. Now let's see what happens when we use a language-neutral scope to pass variables by value and by reference. Listing 6-18 shows the code example of this section (located in LevelTwoExamples.cs). The code example creates a language-neutral scope in line 6 and assigns it to the neutralScope variable. Then in lines 8 and 9, the code example puts a Customer instance and the integer 2 into the language-neutral scope. I purposely kept the code in Listing 6-18 similar to the code in Listing 6-16 so you can easily compare them. In line 11 of Listing 6-18, we create an IronPython script engine. In line 16, we use that script engine to execute the Python code stored in the simple1.py file, shown in Listing 6-19. Notice that in line 16, we tell the script engine to use the language-neutral scope when it executes the Python code. Also note that in line 16, after the execution of Python code finishes, ExecuteFile returns a script scope, which we assign to the resultScope variable. An interesting thing happens in line 19 where we compare the object identities of resultScope and neutralScope. It turns out that resultScope and neutralScope point to the same object in the managed heap. In other words, resultScope and neutralScope are one and the same. This is different from the example we saw in Listing 6-16. In Listing 6-16, the script scope returned by the ExecuteFile method of the script runtime is not the same object as the script runtime's global scope.

Now if we print out the contents of the language neutral-scope as line 23 and 24 in Listing 6-18 do, we will see that the language-neutral scope's customer variable has its Age property set to 20 and the x variable in the language-neutral scope is set to 8. This is another place where this example is different from the example in Listing 6-16. In this example, even though the variable x in the language-neutral scope has a value type and is passed to the Python code by value, in the end the variable x in the language-neutral scope is mutated by the Python code because after the Python code finishes execution, the new value of x is put back into the language-neutral scope.

Listing 6-18. Passing a Customer Object and an Integer to Python Code Using a Language-Neutral Scope

```
1)   public static void PassObjectsToPythonViaLanguageNeutralScope()
2)   {
3)       Customer customer = new Customer("Bob", 30);
4)
5)       ScriptRuntime scriptRuntime = ScriptRuntime.CreateFromConfiguration();
6)       ScriptScope neutralScope = scriptRuntime.CreateScope();
7)
8)       neutralScope.SetVariable("x", 2);
9)       neutralScope.SetVariable("customer", customer);
10)
11)      ScriptEngine scriptEngine = scriptRuntime.GetEngine("python");
12)
13)      //Changing the value of x in Python code will change the x in the neutral scope
14)      //even if x is a value type object. This is because x is put back into the
15)      //neutral scope.
16)      ScriptScope resultScope = scriptEngine.ExecuteFile(
17)                                    @"Python\simple1.py", neutralScope);
18)
19)      if (resultScope == neutralScope)
20)          Console.WriteLine("Result scope and neutral scope are the same object.");
21)
22)      Console.WriteLine("Items in the neutral scope: ");
23)      foreach (var item in neutralScope.GetItems())
24)          Console.WriteLine("{0} : {1}", item.Key, item.Value);
25)  }
```

Listing 6-19. Python Code That Uses the Customer Instance and an Integer in a Language-Neutral Scope

```
print x
customer.Age = 20

x = 8
print x
```

There is one more difference between using a global scope and using a language-neutral scope. When we use a global scope to pass objects to Python code, the Python code needs to use import statements like import customer to retrieve those objects. In contrast, when we use a language-neutral scope to pass objects to Python code, the Python code can use those objects directly with no need for the import statements, as Listing 6-19 shows.

You might notice that we discussed the effects of using a global scope and a language-neutral scope on variable passing, but I didn't say anything about engine scopes. That's because engine scope is the same as language-neutral scope with regard to variable passing.

In summary, when passing an object using a script scope, it matters whether the object's type is a value type or a reference type. It also matters whether the script scope is global or language-neutral.

Here is a summary of the important facts the code examples in Listing 6-16, Listing 6-17, Listing 6-18 and Listing 6-19 demonstrate:

- When we call the `ExecuteFile` method on a script runtime to execute guest language code, the script runtime's global scope is used to pass objects to the guest language code. The script scope returned by the `ExecuteFile` method is a different object from the global scope.

- When we call the `ExecuteFile` method on a script engine and pass in a language-neutral scope to execute guest language code, we get back a result script scope. The result script scope and the language-neutral scope are one and the same.

- If the type of an object is a reference type, it does not matter whether we use a global scope or a language-neutral scope to pass the object to the guest language code. Changes made to the object by the guest language code will be available in the script scope.

- If the type of an object is a value type and we use a global scope to pass the object to the guest language code, changes made to the object by the guest language code will not be put back into the global scope.

- If the type of an object is a value type and we use a language-neutral scope to pass the object to the guest language code, changes made to the object by the guest language code will be put back into the language-neutral scope.

Level Two Use of the DLR Hosting API

So far in this chapter, we've seen several examples relating to script scope, script runtime, and script engine. Only a few of them are making Level Two use of the DLR Hosting API. At Level Two, we can compile the source code of a DLR-based language into an instance of `CompiledCode` and execute that `CompiledCode` instance multiple times possibly in different script scopes. We can execute a `ScriptSource` instance that represents the source code of a DLR-based language without first compiling that source code. We can load assemblies into a script runtime and those assemblies will be available to all the DLR-based language code snippets that run on the script runtime. We can use a class called `ObjectOperations` to perform various operations, such as object creation and member access on an object. Don't worry if you're not clear what those Level Two uses of the DLR Hosting API are. In the next few sections, you'll see examples and detailed descriptions.

Compiling Code

If you have guest language code that you need to execute multiple times either in the same script scope or in different script scopes, it's far more efficient if you compile the guest language code once and then execute the compiled code as many times as you like. The `ScriptEngine` class provides a method called `CreateScriptSourceFromFile`, which lets you create an instance of `ScriptSource` that represents the guest language code you want to execute repeatedly. You then compile the guest language code by calling the `Compile` method on the ScriptSource instance. The `Compile` method returns an instance of `CompiledCode` that represents the compiled guest language code. With that instance of `CompiledCode`, you can call its `Execute` method to execute the compiled guest language code. The `Execute` method takes a script scope as its input parameter, which allows you to execute the compiled guest language code repeatedly in different script scopes. Listing 6-20 shows an example that compiles the Python code in simple1.py and executes the compiled code in an engine scope. The Python code in simple1.py was shown in Listing 6-19.

Listing 6-20. An Example that Executes Compiled Python Code

```
public static void RunCompiledCodeExample()
{
    ScriptEngine pyEngine = ScriptRuntime.CreateFromConfiguration().GetEngine("python");
    ScriptSource source = pyEngine.CreateScriptSourceFromFile(@"Python\simple1.py");

    ScriptScope scope = pyEngine.CreateScope();
    scope.SetVariable("x", 2);
    scope.SetVariable("customer", new Customer("Bob", 30));

    CompiledCode compiledCode = source.Compile();
    compiledCode.Execute(scope);
}
```

Listing 6-20 uses the CreateScriptSourceFromFile method of ScriptEngine to create a ScriptSource instance that represents the code in simple1.py. If the Python code we want to execute is in a string object, we can call the CreateScriptSourceFromString method of ScriptEngine and pass in the string object to create a ScriptSource instance that represents the Python code. Listing 6-21 shows such an example. The Python code in Listing 6-21 is in the pyFunc string object. The Python code defines a function that takes a number and returns true if the number is odd. The example in Listing 6-21 compiles the Python code and executes the compiled code in an engine scope. The result of the execution is fetched from the engine scope and converted to a delegate of type Func<int, bool> called IsOdd. Finally the code prints out the result of invoking IsOdd with the number 3.

Listing 6-21. Compile and Invoke a Python Function in C#

```
public static void CallPythonFunctionFromCSharpUsingCompiledCode()
{
    ScriptEngine pyEngine = ScriptRuntime.CreateFromConfiguration().GetEngine("python");
    string pyFunc = @"def isodd(n): return 1 == n % 2;";
    ScriptSource source = pyEngine.CreateScriptSourceFromString(pyFunc,
        SourceCodeKind.Statements);
    CompiledCode compiledCode = source.Compile();

    ScriptScope scope = pyEngine.CreateScope();
    compiledCode.Execute(scope);
    Func<int, bool> IsOdd = scope.GetVariable<Func<int, bool>>("isodd");
    bool result = IsOdd(3);
    Console.WriteLine("Is 3 an odd number? {0}", result);
}
```

After we create a ScriptSource instance in Listing 6-21, we don't necessarily need to call the Compile method on the ScriptSource instance in order to execute the Python code. The ScriptSource class defines an Execute method that we can call to execute the source code represented by a ScriptSource instance without compiling the source code first. The Execute method takes a script scope as input so that we can execute the source code represented by a ScriptSource instance in the script scope we want. Listing 6-22 shows an example that uses the Execute method of ScriptSource to run a Python code snippet.

Listing 6-22. Using the Execute Method of ScriptSource to Run a Python Code Snippet

```
public static void CallPythonFunctionFromCSharpUsingScriptSource()
{
    ScriptEngine pyEngine = ScriptRuntime.CreateFromConfiguration().GetEngine("python");
    string pyFunc = @"def isodd(n): return 1 == n % 2;";
    ScriptSource source = pyEngine.CreateScriptSourceFromString(pyFunc,
        SourceCodeKind.Statements);
    ScriptScope scope = pyEngine.CreateScope();
    source.Execute(scope);
    Func<int, bool> IsOdd = scope.GetVariable<Func<int, bool>>("isodd");
    bool result = IsOdd(3);
    Console.WriteLine("Is 3 an odd number? {0}", result);
}
```

Loading Assemblies into Script Runtime

Earlier in this chapter, we saw the code in simpleWpf2.py, in Listing 6-13. The code contains the following two lines in order to reference the PresentationFramework.dll and PresentationCore.dll assemblies.

```
clr.AddReference("PresentationFramework")
clr.AddReference("PresentationCore")
```

If we have many source code files that need to reference those two WPF assemblies, instead of having each file add the assembly references, we can load the assemblies into a script runtime and use the script runtime to execute the source code files. The assemblies loaded into the script runtime will be available to all the source code files and, therefore, they won't need to add the assembly references. Listing 6-23 shows how to load assemblies into a script runtime.

To load the PresentationCore.dll assembly into a script runtime, the example in Listing 6-23 calls the static Load method of the Assembly class to create an Assembly instance that represents the PresentationCore.dll assembly. The example calls the LoadAssembly method on the script runtime with the Assembly instance to load the PresentationCore.dll assembly into the script runtime. The example then repeats the same steps to load the PresentationFramework.dll assembly into the script runtime. Finally, the example uses the script runtime to execute the Python code in simpleWpf.py, which is shown in Listing 6-24. Note that in Listing 6-24, the Python code does not need to have any of the clr.AddReference("PresentationCore") and clr.AddReference("PresentationFramework") statements for adding references to PresentationCore.dll and PresentationFramework.dll.

Listing 6-23. Load WPF Assemblies into a Script Runtime

```
public static void LoadAssembliesIntoScriptRuntime()
{
    ScriptRuntime scriptRuntime = ScriptRuntime.CreateFromConfiguration();
    scriptRuntime.LoadAssembly(Assembly.Load("PresentationCore, Version=3.0.0.0,
Culture=neutral, PublicKeyToken=31bf3856ad364e35"));
    scriptRuntime.LoadAssembly(Assembly.Load("PresentationFramework, Version=3.0.0.0,
Culture=neutral, PublicKeyToken=31bf3856ad364e35"));
    ScriptScope scope = scriptRuntime.ExecuteFile(@"Python\simpleWpf.py");
}
```

Listing 6-24. simpleWpf.py

```
import clr
from System.Windows import (Application, Window)
from System.Windows.Controls import (Label, StackPanel)

window = Window()
window.Title = "Simple Python WPF Example"
window.Width = 400
window.Height = 300

stackPanel = StackPanel()
window.Content = stackPanel

helloLabel = Label()
helloLabel.Content = "Hello"
helloLabel.FontSize = 50
stackPanel.Children.Add(helloLabel)

app = Application()
app.Run(window)
```

Creating Python Class Instances Using Object Operations

The DLR Hosting API provides a class called ObjectOperations that we can use to perform various operations on an object. For example, we can use the overloaded GetMember methods of ObjectOperations to get a member property of an object. If an object is callable, we can use the overloaded Invoke methods of ObjectOperations to invoke the object. If an object is a class, we can use the CreateInstance method of ObjectOperations to create an instance of the class.

Listing 6-25 shows an example that uses the CreateInstance method of ObjectOperations to create an instance of a Python class. The Python code in Listing 6-25 is in the pyCode string object. The Python code defines a Python class called ClassA that has no attributes. The example executes the Python code, and the result is stored in the script scope against the variable name "ClassA". The example fetches that variable from the script scope and assigns it to the ClassA variable, then it shows two ways to use the ClassA variable to create an instance of the ClassA Python class. The first way uses the CreateInstance method of ObjectOperations. The code in Listing 6-25 obtains an instance of ObjectOperations for the Python language from the Operations property of the pyEngine variable, and then calls the CreateInstance method on the ObjectOperations instance to create an instance of the ClassA Python class. The second way of creating an instance of the ClassA Python class is simply invoking the ClassA variable as if it were a callable object.

Listing 6-25. Create an Instance of a Python Class in C#

```csharp
public static void CreateInstanceOfPythonClassInCSharp()
{
    ScriptEngine pyEngine = ScriptRuntime.CreateFromConfiguration().GetEngine("python");
    string pyCode = @"class ClassA(object): pass";
    ScriptSource source = pyEngine.CreateScriptSourceFromString(pyCode,
        SourceCodeKind.Statements);
    ScriptScope scope = pyEngine.CreateScope();
    source.Execute(scope);
    dynamic ClassA = scope.GetVariable("ClassA");
    object objectA1 = pyEngine.Operations.CreateInstance(ClassA);
    object objectA2 = ClassA();
}
```

Level Three Use of the DLR Hosting API

We saw a few Level Three uses of the DLR Hosting API in earlier sections. In this section, we will look at some more examples of using the DLR Hosting API at this level. We will see what a script host is and how to implement a custom script host, how to use `ObjectOperations` to get the documentation of a Python function, and how to create a script runtime in a separate .NET application domain.

Script Host

A script host in the DLR is an instance of the Microsoft.Scripting.Hosting.ScriptHost class and represents the host platform of a script runtime. Because the DLR can run not only on the usual .NET CLR runtime but also in Web environments such as the Silverlight runtime, the DLR Hosting API defines the `ScriptHost` class to abstract away the specifics of the platforms. For example, given the file path of a Python source code file, the Silverlight runtime and the usual .NET CLR runtime resolve the file path differently. The file path is an example of the platform specifics that are abstracted into the `ScriptHost` class and a related class called `PlatformAdaptationLayer`. For good software design, the DLR team isolated those platform specifics into these two classes. The rest of the DLR Hosting API is kept unaware of whether a script runtime runs on the Silverlight platform or the usual .NET CLR platform. If you're interested in knowing more about running the DLR in the Silverlight runtime, Chapter 11 has an in-depth discussion on that subject.

To show you how `ScriptHost` and `PlatformAdaptationLayer` work and how you can use them if you want to run a script runtime on a custom host platform, the example in Listings 6-26 and 6-27 shows how to implement a `ScriptHost` derived class and a `PlatformAdaptationLayer` derived class to resolve file paths differently. Listing 6-26 shows the `ScriptHost` derived class called `SimpleHostType`. The `SimpleHostType` overrides the get method of the `PlatformAdaptationLayer` property it inherits from the base class. The overridden get method returns an instance of the `SimplePlatformAdaptationLayer` class, whose code is shown in Listing 6-27.

Listing 6-26. SimpleHostType.cs

```csharp
public class SimpleHostType : ScriptHost
{
    public override Microsoft.Scripting.PlatformAdaptationLayer PlatformAdaptationLayer
```

```
{
    get
    {
        return SimplePlatformAdaptationLayer.INSTANCE;
    }
}
}
```

The implementation of SimplePlatformAdaptationLayer overrides the OpenInputFileStream method inherited from the base PlatformAdaptationLayer class. The overridden OpenInputFileStream method resolves a file path by appending "Python\" to the path and then passing the modified path the OpenInputFileStream method of the base class. The implication of this file path resolution is that if we want to run the hello.py file in the physical C:\ProDLR\src\Examples\Chapter6\HostingExamples\Python folder, we need only specify "hello.py" instead of "Python\hello.py" as the file path. Listing 6-28 shows an example of this effect.

Listing 6-27. SimplePlatformAdaptationLayer.cs

```
public class SimplePlatformAdaptationLayer : PlatformAdaptationLayer
{
    public static PlatformAdaptationLayer INSTANCE = new SimplePlatformAdaptationLayer();

    public override System.IO.Stream OpenInputFileStream(string path)
    {
        return base.OpenInputFileStream(@"Python\" + path);
    }
}
```

The code in Listing 6-28 creates an instance of ScriptRuntimeSetup and sets that instance's HostType property to typeof(SimpleHostType). Then the code uses the ScriptRuntimeSetup instance to create a script runtime. Because the script host associated with the script runtime is an instance of SimpleHostType, we specify the file path of the Python source code we want to execute on the script runtime as "hello.py" instead of "Python\hello.py". Had we not set the HostType property of the ScriptRuntimeSetup instance to typeof(SimpleHostType), the ScriptHost class would be used as the default class for creating a script host for the script runtime and we would need to specify "Python\hello.py" as the file path.

Listing 6-28. An Example That Uses the SimpleHostType Class to Resolve File Paths

```
public static void UseCustomScriptHost()
{
    ScriptRuntimeSetup setup = ScriptRuntimeSetup.ReadConfiguration();
    setup.HostType = typeof(SimpleHostType);
    ScriptRuntime scriptRuntime = new ScriptRuntime(setup);
    ScriptScope scope = scriptRuntime.ExecuteFile(@"hello.py");
}
```

Object Operations

We looked at the ObjectOperations class when we discussed the Level Two usage of the DLR Hosting API. ObjectOperations defines many methods that we can use to perform various operations on an object. Some of the methods belong to Level Two and others belong to Level Three. In this section, I will show you a Level Three use of the ObjectOperations class that obtains the documentation string of a Python function. This can be useful when you're building a tool that provides intellisense for Python functions, for example.

Listing 6-29 shows our example, in which we create a script runtime and a script engine as usual for running the Python code in helloFunc.py. We already saw the Python code in helloFunc.py earlier in this chapter. For your convenience, the Python code is displayed below with the line of code that's the focus of our current discussion in bold:

```
def hello():
    """This function prints Hello."""
    print "Hello"
```

The bolded line is the documentation string of the hello function. It is the string we want to obtain using ObjectOperations. In Listing 6-29, after the Python code is run, we fetch the object that represents the hello function from the script scope in line 6 and assign it to the helloFunction variable. In lines 8 to 10, we use the GetMemberNames method of ObjectOperations to print out all the members of the helloFunction. One of those members is the __doc__ attribute predefined by the Python language for every Python class, function, and object. The __doc__ attribute contains the documentation string of the Python hello function, and line 12 in Listing 6-29 uses the GetMember method of ObjectOperations to print the documentation string on the screen. If you run the code in Listing 6-29, you'll see the string "This function prints Hello." printed as the last line on the screen.

Listing 6-29. Printing the Documentation String of a Python Function to the Screen

```
1)   public static void GetDocStringOfPythonFunctionUsingObjectOperations()
2)   {
3)       ScriptRuntime scriptRuntime = ScriptRuntime.CreateFromConfiguration();
4)       ScriptEngine pyEngine = scriptRuntime.GetEngine("python");
5)       ScriptScope scope = pyEngine.ExecuteFile(@"Python\helloFunc.py");
6)       object helloFunction = scope.GetVariable("hello");
7)
8)       IList<String> helloFuncMembers = pyEngine.Operations.GetMemberNames(helloFunction);
9)       foreach (var item in helloFuncMembers)
10)          Console.WriteLine(item);
11)
12)      Console.WriteLine(pyEngine.Operations.GetMember(helloFunction, "__doc__"));
13)  }
```

Remote Script Runtime

A Level Three use of the DLR Hosting API is to run one or more script runtimes remotely. The script runtimes can run in a different process from the host's process or they can run in the same process but in different application domains. This section will briefly explain what an application domain is and show an example of running a script runtime in the same process as the host's but in a different application domain. The next sections will give a quick tour of .NET Remoting and show an example of running a script runtime in a process different from the host's.

A .NET application domain is like a lightweight process that creates a boundary between software components that run in a process. A process can have multiple application domains. Each application domain has its own address space for referencing objects in memory. References to objects in one address space will make no sense in another address space. Therefore, we can't pass object references in one application domain to another application domain and expect those references to point to the same objects. To share objects between two application domains, those objects need to be value objects that can be serialized in one application domain and deserialized in another. Or the objects need to be instances of classes that inherit directly or indirectly from a .NET Remoting class called MarshalByRefObject. The classes ScriptRuntime, ScriptEngine, ScriptScope, ScriptSource and CompiledCode all inherit from MarshalByRefObject. Therefore, instances of those classes can live in one application domain and be referenced in another application domain. The underlying framework that makes it possible to reference objects that live in a different application domain is .NET Remoting.

One application domain can contain multiple instances of ScriptRuntime. There are many reasons for running a script runtime in a separate application domain. For example, it's common to use the DLR to add scripting capability to an application. By providing scripting capability, you allow users of your application to extend and automate the application. Users will write code in languages such as IronPython and IronRuby and your application will run those code scripts. When your application runs code scripts written by users, you often want to protect your application from code errors or malicious attacks in those scripts. You will not want your application process to crash when a user script crashes. Sometimes you might want to run user scripts with a different security access level (SAL). For those reasons, you want to execute user scripts in a script runtime that lives in a separate application domain.

Let's see an example that runs a script runtime in a separate application domain within the same process. Listing 6-30 shows an example that creates a script runtime in a separate application domain. The example creates a new application domain by calling the static CreateDomain method of the AppDomain class in line 3. The newly created application domain is different from the application domain that runs the code in Listing 6-30. To ease the discussion, let's refer to the application domain created in line 3 as the new application domain and the application domain that runs the code in Listing 6-30 as the old application domain. In line 4, the example calls the static CreateRemote method of ScriptRuntime with the new application domain created as an input parameter. This effectively creates a remote script runtime that lives in the new application domain. The scriptRuntime variable in line 5 points not to the real remote script runtime but to a proxy of the remote script runtime. (The next section about .NET Remoting will explain more about proxies and remote objects.) When the example code calls the GetEngine method on the remote script runtime in line 6, the GetEngine method returns a script engine. The script engine is also a proxy of the real script engine object that lives in the new application domain. In the old application domain, we are able to reference the script runtime and script engine in the new application domain because the ScriptRuntime and ScriptEngine classes inherit from MarshalByRefObject.

Line 7 uses the remote script engine to execute the helloFunc.py file. The result of the execution is an object stored in the script scope against the name "hello". That object lives in the new application domain. Because of this, when we fetch that object from the script scope in line 8, we call the GetVariableHandle method on the script scope rather than the GetVariable method we saw in previous examples.

Listing 6-30. Executing Python Code in a Remote Script Runtime

```
1)   public static void CreateRemoteScriptRuntime()
2)   {
3)       AppDomain appDomain = AppDomain.CreateDomain("ScriptDomain");
```

```
4)      ScriptRuntimeSetup setup = ScriptRuntimeSetup.ReadConfiguration();
5)      ScriptRuntime scriptRuntime = ScriptRuntime.CreateRemote(appDomain, setup);
6)      ScriptEngine pyEngine = scriptRuntime.GetEngine("python");
7)      ScriptScope scope = pyEngine.ExecuteFile(@"Python\helloFunc.py");
8)      ObjectHandle helloFunction = scope.GetVariableHandle("hello");
9)      pyEngine.Operations.Invoke(helloFunction, new object[]{});
10) }
```

The rest of this chapter will dive deeper into the subject of .NET Remoting and how that relates to the DLR Hosting API. We'll start with a quick tour of .NET Remoting in general that includes nothing specific to the DLR. After that, I'll show you an example that runs a script runtime in a different process. If you are already familiar with .NET Remoting, you can skip the next section and jump directly to the example.

.NET Remoting Quick Tour

.NET Remoting is a framework that assists developers in creating applications that are distributed across application domains, processes, or physical machines. Like a number of other technologies, such as DCOM, Java RMI, and CORBA's IIOP/GIOP, the aim of .NET Remoting is to help in the development of objects or components that can be consumed remotely in an object-oriented way. Figure 6-1 shows the relationship between a .NET Remoting server and client, which might be in a different application domain within the same process, in different processes, or on different physical machines.

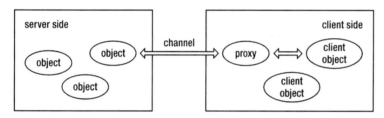

Figure 6-1. The architecture of a distributed application based on .NET Remoting

As Figure 6-1 shows, the server-side component of a .NET Remoting-based application has some objects that the client component can interact with through proxies. The proxies communicate with the server-side objects they represent through channels. The server-side objects can be remoting objects or non-remoting objects. If they are remoting objects, they can be classified into one of three kinds: client-activated, SingleCall, and Singleton, as follows:

- A client-activated object is an object that is activated at the client's request. It can hold state information between several method calls triggered by the same client on the object. A client-activated object is associated with one client only and does not allow you to share state information among several clients.

- A SingleCall object is a server-activated object. A new SingleCall object is created each time one of its methods is called by a client, and the object is destroyed when the method call is finished. Consequently, a SingleCall object holds no state information between method calls.

- A Singleton object is also server-activated object. There can be only one instance of a Singleton class. The state of a Singleton object is shared among multiple clients.

Communication channels between a .NET Remoting client and server can use network protocols such as HTTP, SMTP, and TCP. When using an HTTP channel, the request and response messages can be formatted as Simple Object Access Protocol (SOAP) messages. Besides SOAP, there are other formatting choices we can use with the HTTP transfer protocol.

The proxy object in Figure 6-1 is an instance of some type. There are a number of ways for the .NET Remoting client to get that type's information. One way is to compile the server-side code into assemblies and let the client-side project reference those assemblies. Because the assemblies contain the type information of the server-side classes, by referencing those assemblies, the .NET Remoting client is able to create proxy objects for the server-side remoting objects. Another way to make the server-side type information available to the .NET Remoting client is to use a utility program called soapsuds.exe that ships with the .NET Framework SDK.

Running Script Runtime in a Separate Process

Now let's look at an example that runs a script runtime in a different process. You can find the server-side code of this example in the ScriptServer project of this chapter's code download. The client-side code is in the ScriptClient project. The server side of the example will provide a script runtime as a remoting object and the client side will use that script runtime to execute Python code in the process that hosts the server side of the example.

A server-activated object (SAO) such as a Singleton or SingleCall object needs to have a default constructor that takes no input parameters. Because ScriptRuntime does not have a default constructor that takes no input parameters, its instances can't be server-activated objects. Therefore, if we want to use the same instance of ScriptRuntime across multiple requests from .NET remoting clients, instead of making the instance of ScriptRuntime a Singleton SAO, we need to use a factory object to act as the Singleton SAO. The factory object will provide clients access to the ScriptRuntime instance. Listing 6-31 shows a factory class called RemotingFactory. The class derives from MarshalByRefObject so that its instances can be remoting objects. RemotingFactory has only one method called GetScriptRuntime, which will return the same ScriptRuntime instance every time it's called.

Listing 6-31. RemotingFactory.cs

```
public class RemotingFactory : MarshalByRefObject
{
    private static ScriptRuntime scriptRuntime = ScriptRuntime.CreateFromConfiguration();

    public ScriptRuntime GetScriptRuntime()
    {
        return scriptRuntime;
    }
}
```

Now that we have the RemotingFactory class, we need a process to host and expose an instance of this class as a Singleton object. Listing 6-32 shows the code that, when run, creates a host process and exposes a RemotingFactory instance as a Singleton object. The code in Listing 6-32 creates a channel that uses TCP as the transport protocol and a binary formatter for formatting messages. The channel listens on port 8088. We use the static `RegisterWellKnownServiceType` method of the `RemotingConfiguration` class to register `RemotingFactory` as the type of a Singleton object whose name is "RemotingFactory". At this point, the server-side implementation of our example is done. Next, we will look at the client-side implementation.

Listing 6-32. Server Code That Hosts a RemotingFactory Instance as a Singleton Object

```
static void Main(string[] args)
{
    BinaryServerFormatterSinkProvider serverProvider =
                    new BinaryServerFormatterSinkProvider();
    serverProvider.TypeFilterLevel = TypeFilterLevel.Full;

    IDictionary props = new Hashtable();
    props["port"] = 8088;

    TcpChannel channel = new TcpChannel(props, clientSinkProvider:null,
                    serverSinkProvider:serverProvider);
    ChannelServices.RegisterChannel(channel, false);

    RemotingConfiguration.RegisterWellKnownServiceType(typeof(RemotingFactory),
        "RemotingFactory", WellKnownObjectMode.Singleton);

    Console.WriteLine("Server started. Press enter to shut down.");
    Console.ReadLine();
}
```

Listing 6-33 shows the code that implements the .NET Remoting client. The code gets a hold of the server-side Singleton object by calling the static `GetObject` method of `Activator` with "tcp://localhost:8088/RemotingFactory" as the URI of the server-side Singleton object. We use this URI because (a) the server channel uses TCP as the transport protocol, (b) the server channel listens on port 8088 of localhost, and (c) the server Singleton object is named "RemotingFactory". Once the client code gets the "RemotingFactory" Singleton object, it calls the Singleton object's `GetScriptRuntime` method to get the remote script runtime.

The remote script runtime lives in the server process. What the client code gets from calling the `GetScriptRuntime` method is a proxy of the remote script runtime. The code in Listing 6-33 calls the `GetEngine` method on the remote script runtime, which returns a script engine. The script engine is again a proxy of the real script engine object that lives in the server process. The code in Listing 6-33 uses the remote script engine to execute a Python code snippet that defines a Python function called `isodd`. The result of the execution is an object stored in the script scope against the name "hello". That object also lives in the server process. Because of that, when we fetch that object from the script scope, we call the `GetVariableHandle` method instead of the `GetVariable` method on the script scope.

Listing 6-33. The .NET Remoting Client

```
static void Main(string[] args)
{
    TcpChannel channel = new TcpChannel();
    ChannelServices.RegisterChannel(channel, false);
```

```
RemotingFactory remotingFactory = (RemotingFactory)Activator.GetObject(
            typeof(RemotingFactory), "tcp://localhost:8088/RemotingFactory");

ScriptRuntime runtime = remotingFactory.GetScriptRuntime();
ScriptEngine pyEngine = runtime.GetEngine("python");
string pyFunc = @"def isodd(n): return 1 == n % 2;";
ScriptSource source = pyEngine.CreateScriptSourceFromString(pyFunc,
    SourceCodeKind.Statements);
ScriptScope scope = pyEngine.CreateScope();
source.Execute(scope);
ObjectHandle IsOddHandle = scope.GetVariableHandle("isodd");

ObjectHandle result = pyEngine.Operations.Invoke(IsOddHandle, new object[] { 3 });
bool answer = pyEngine.Operations.Unwrap<bool>(result);
Console.WriteLine("Is 3 an odd number? {0}", answer);
Console.ReadLine();
}
```

To run the example, you need to first compile the ScriptServer and ScriptClient projects in this chapter's code download. After the compilation, you need to run ScriptServer.exe first and then ScriptClient.exe. Running ServerServer.exe causes a command console to pop up and you'll see the text "Server started. Press enter to shut down." displayed in the command console. Running ScriptClient.exe will cause another command console to pop up and display the text "Is 3 an odd number? True".

Summary

The DLR Hosting API offers a lot of value and functionality. In this chapter, we saw examples that demonstrate how cumbersome it can be to host one language in another without it. The DLR Hosting API consists of a consumer-side API and a provider-side API. We focused here on the consumer side, with many code examples that demonstrate how to use this API at different levels. We discussed in detail how the various kinds of script scopes pass value objects and reference objects around. We then introduced .NET Remoting and looked at an example that runs Python code on a script runtime that lives in a separate process. The DLR Hosting API is an interesting component that has many useful applications. In Chapter 9, we will look at a programming language called Stitch that extends the functionalities of the DLR Hosting API. In Chapter 11, you'll see how the DLR Hosting API enables DLR-based language code to be embedded in a Silverlight application.

■ ■ ■

Applying the DLR

CHAPTER 7

■ ■ ■

DLR and Aspect-Oriented Programming

Dynamic objects in the DLR provide a foundation that has many applications. In previous chapters, we've seen some practical examples that leverage this foundation and do interesting things that are either awkward or impossible in static languages. In this chapter, we are going to travel further down the path and see the fantastic application of dynamic objects in aspect-oriented programming (AOP). AOP is a programming paradigm that is very good at solving the problem of cross-cutting concerns. Common cross-cutting concerns in a software system are issues like transaction management, security, auditing, performance monitoring, logging and tracing, and so on. By virtue of addressing the problem of cross-cutting concerns in an elegant manner, AOP provides tremendous value in the design and architecture of software systems. I'll begin with an introduction of the basic AOP concepts accompanied by some simple examples, then show you how to implement an AOP framework based on dynamic objects. By the end of the chapter, you will have an AOP framework that (a) works across both static and dynamic objects and (b) is integrated with the widely adopted Spring.NET's AOP framework.

Aspect-Oriented Programming

Let's go over the important concepts of AOP now to set the stage for the rest of the chapter. After reading this section, you will know what AOP is and the problem it solves. You will also learn the meaning of terms such as pointcut, join point, and advice. If you are already familiar with these topics, you can skip this section and jump ahead.

Cross-Cutting Concerns

AOP solves the issue of cross-cutting concerns very well. This is best illustrated with an example. Listing 7-1 shows some code that logs one message at the beginning and one at the end of the Age property's get method. The real business logic of the property's get method is represented by the code comment //some business logic here. The two lines that write to the console belong to the logging concern. The code by itself might not seem to be a problem, but imagine how the code would look if we were to do this kind of logging for all property access in 20 other classes. You would quickly notice that the same code that writes messages to the console output is duplicated and scattered all over the place. That naïve approach violates the DRY (Don't Repeat Yourself) principle and creates the problem of code scattering. Furthermore, the code in listing 7-1 also illustrates the problem of code tangling because the logging code and the real business logic are enmeshed.

The code scattering and tangling are the kinds of problems AOP solves. Logging is just an example of a cross-cutting concern we commonly encounter in a software system, and it's the easiest and simplest to demonstrate. From this simple example, you can extrapolate and see that if this were an example of transaction management, the two lines of logging code would be replaced by a line of code that starts a transaction and another line of code that commits or rolls back the transaction.

Listing 7-1. Logging Messages Before and After a Property Access

```
public class Employee : IEmployee
{
    private int age;
    private String name;

    public int Age
    {
        get
        {
            Console.WriteLine("Employee Age getter is called.");
            //some business logic here.
            Console.WriteLine("End of Employee Age getter.");
            return age;
        }

        set { age = value; }
    }

    public String Name
    {
        get
        {
            Console.WriteLine("Employee Name getter is called.");
            return name;
        }

        set { name = value; }
    }
}

public interface IEmployee
{
    int Age { get; set; }
    String Name { get; set; }
}
```

Advice, Join Points, and Pointcuts

In AOP terms, the two lines of logging code we saw in the Age property's get method should be modularized into something called *advice*. Advice is the action you'd like to take to address a cross-cutting concern. The first logging statement is at the beginning of the property getter. The second logging statement is at the end of the property getter before the employee's age is returned. The beginning and the end of the property getter in this case are called *join points*. Join points are the places in code where advice can be applied. A collection of join points is called a *pointcut*. When you encapsulate pointcuts and advice into a module, you get what's called an *aspect*. Figure 7-1 shows a pictorial view of all those terms to make it easy to learn them.

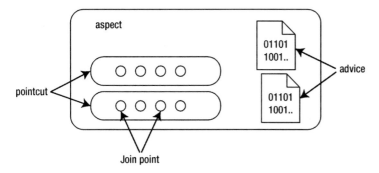

Figure 7-1. *AOP concepts and their relationships*

An Example

Now that I've introduced the concepts of AOP, let's relate the abstract concepts to concrete code. For this example, I'll use Spring.NET's AOP framework and apply it to the code in Listing 7-1. The goal here is to extract the logging statements into a piece of advice and apply that advice to the right join points. To try the example, you will need Spring.NET; I use version 1.3.0 for the examples in this chapter. Here are the steps you need to take to set up Spring.NET:

1. Go to the Spring.NET website (www.springframework.net) and download the file Spring.NET-1.3.0.zip.

2. Unzip Spring.NET-1.3.0.zip to a folder of your choice. Throughout this book, I'll assume that Spring.NET-1.3.0.zip is unzipped to C:\Spring.NET-1.3.0. If you choose to unzip the file to a different folder, you need to substitute that path with your own whenever I refer to it in the book.

3. Spring.NET consists of several components, not all of which are needed to run the code examples in this chapter. Our examples need only two components— Spring.Core.dll and Spring.Aop.dll. You need to copy the following files from C:\Spring.NET-1.3.0\Spring.NET\bin\net\2.0\release to C:\ProDLR\lib\Spring.NET\release:

    - Common.Logging.dll

    - Spring.Aop.dll, Spring.Aop.pdb and Spring.Aop.xml

    - Spring.Core.dll, Spring.Core.pdb and Spring.Core.xml

The Advice

Let's start with the advice portion of the example. Listing 7-2 shows the code for the logging advice, which is in a class called SpringBasedLoggingAdvice. The class implements the AopAlliance.Intercept.IMethodInterceptor interface. AOP Alliance is a project that defines a standard set of Java interfaces that all Java-based AOP frameworks can choose to implement. The idea is that if all

AOP frameworks implement those interfaces, we can code against those interfaces and our code will be vendor-agnostic. In the ideal situation, we can swap out a particular AOP framework and swap in another without any code change because our code depends only on the standard interfaces, not on a particular vendor's implementation. The interfaces AOP Alliance defines are Java interfaces. The developers of Spring.NET defined corresponding interfaces in .NET. IMethodInterceptor is one of those interfaces.

A class implements IMethodInterceptor if it wants to provide AOP advice by intercepting method calls. That happens to be what our example wants to do. Our example wants to intercept calls to property getters and provide some logging-related advice. So the class SpringBasedLoggingAdvice implements IMethodInterceptor, which has only an Invoke method. The implementation of the Invoke method in SpringBasedLogginAdvice is fairly straightforward. It first calls BeforeInvoke to perform the part of the advice logic that we'd like to take place before the property getter is called. In this simple example, the BeforeInvoke method simply prints a message to the console. After calling BeforeInvoke, the code in the Invoke method calls invocation.Proceed(). This will effectively call the method that is intercepted, the property getter in our case. The result of the method call is stored in the returnValue variable so that it can be returned by the Invoke method later. Before returning returnValue, the Invoke method calls AfterInvoke to perform the part of the advice logic that we'd like to take place after the property getter is called. At this point, the implementation of the Spring.NET-based advice class is done. Next, let's see how to specify the pointcut of our example.

Listing 7-2. Logging Advice Based on Spring.NET

```
public class SpringBasedLoggingAdvice : IMethodInterceptor
{
    public object Invoke(IMethodInvocation invocation)
    {
        BeforeInvoke(invocation.Method, invocation.Arguments, invocation.Target);
        object returnValue = invocation.Proceed();
        AfterInvoke(returnValue, invocation.Method,
                invocation.Arguments, invocation.Target);
        return returnValue;
    }

    private void BeforeInvoke(MethodInfo method, object[] args, object target)
    {
        Console.Out.WriteLine("Advice BeforeInvoke is called. Intercepted method is {0}.",
                method.Name);
    }

    private void AfterInvoke(object returnValue, MethodInfo method,
                object[] args, object target)
    {
        Console.Out.WriteLine("Advice AfterInvoke is called. Intercepted method is {0}.",
                method.Name);
    }
}
```

The Pointcut

Listing 7-3 shows the XML that specifies the pointcut of the example. Since this is not a chapter about Spring.NET, I won't get into too much detail about the XML file. If you want to learn more, Spring.NET has excellent online documentation you can refer to. Here, I'll only explain the XML in Listing 7-3 at a high level. A typical Spring.NET XML file consists mainly of a collection of <object> elements. In Listing 7-3, the object element whose id is getAgeCalls specifies the pointcut of our example. The pointcut is specified by the pattern expression .*Age, which matches any property or method whose name ends with Age. The object element whose id is loggingAdvice represents an instance of the SpringBasedLoggingAdvice class we saw in the previous section. The <aop:advisor> element represents something similar to an aspect. As mentioned earlier, an aspect encapsulates pointcuts and advice. That's why the <aop:advisor> element references the getAgeCalls pointcut and the loggingAdvice advice in order to indicate which pointcuts and advice it encapsulates. Finally, in order to apply the advisor to a target object, the XML defines the object element whose id is employeeBob. The object element employeeBob represents an instance of the Employee class we saw in Listing 7-1.

Listing 7-3. Application-config.xml

```xml
<?xml version="1.0" encoding="utf-8" ?>
<objects xmlns="http://www.springframework.net"
            xmlns:xsi="http://www.w3.org/2001/XMLSchema-instance"
            xmlns:aop="http://www.springframework.net/aop">

  <aop:config>

    <aop:advisor id="getAgeAdvisor" pointcut-ref="getAgeCalls"
                advice-ref="loggingAdvice"/>

  </aop:config>

  <object id="getAgeCalls"
        type="Spring.Aop.Support.SdkRegularExpressionMethodPointcut, Spring.Aop">
    <property name="patterns">
      <list>
        <value>.*Age</value>
      </list>
    </property>
  </object>

  <object id="loggingAdvice" type="Aop1.SpringBasedLoggingAdvice, Aop1"/>

  <object id="employeeBob" type="Aop1.Employee, Aop1">
    <property name="Name" value="Bob"/>
    <property name="Age" value="30"/>
  </object>

</objects>
```

A Test Run

The example so far has defined a pointcut, an advice class, and an advisor. Listing 7-4 shows the client code that demonstrates how all the pieces work together. The code first creates a Spring.NET application context from the application-config.xml file. A Spring.NET application context is basically a container of the objects defined by the <object> elements in files like application-config.xml. The objects usually have dependencies on one another. When Spring.NET creates an application context, it will make sure that the dependencies among the objects are properly wired up.

From the application context, the code in RunSimpleStaticObjectExample retrieves the object employeeBob by its object id and assigns the object to the employee variable. The last line of code calls the getter method of the Age property on the employee variable and prints the employee's age to the screen. Because the Employee class's Age property matches the pattern expression of the pointcut, the call to the Age property's getter method will be intercepted and the advice logic implemented in SpringBasedLoggingAdvice will be applied.

Listing 7-4. Example Code That Demonstrates How Advice is Applied to a Target Object.

```
private static void RunSimpleStaticObjectExample()
{
    IApplicationContext context = new XmlApplicationContext("application-config.xml");
    IEmployee employee = (IEmployee)context["employeeBob"];
    Console.WriteLine("Employee is {0} years old.", employee.Age);
}
```

The output you'll see when running the code looks like the following:

```
Advice BeforeInvoke is called. Intercepted method is get_Age.
Employee Age getter is called.
End of Employee Age getter.
Advice AfterInvoke is called. Intercepted method is get_Age.
Employee is 30 years old.
```

What happens behind the scene is that at runtime, Spring.NET creates a proxy object that wraps the employeeBob object when it sees that calls to employeeBob need to be intercepted. The employee variable actually references the proxy object, not the employeeBob object. The code employee.Age in our example therefore calls the Age property's getter method on the proxy object, and that's how method interception works. The proxy object Spring.NET creates is not just any proxy object; it is an instance of a dynamically generated class that implements the IEmployee interface. The generated class overrides the Age property's getter method. The overridden method will call the Invoke method on the advice object, and thus the logging logic is woven into the Employee class. This is called *runtime weaving* because it weaves the logic of advice into an object at runtime. There are techniques other than runtime weaving for implementing an AOP framework. For example, compile-time weaving, as its name suggests, weaves one piece of code with another at compile time. Load-time weaving does the code weaving at the time classes are loaded into a runtime such as CLR or JVM.

Of all the different techniques for implementing an AOP framework, the one of most interest to us is runtime weaving. This is because the runtime-weaving AOP and its method interception mechanism smells and tastes a lot like what dynamic objects do. Late-binding actions on dynamic objects are "intercepted" and handled by the Bind[Action] methods in DynamicMetaObject. A proxy object to a target object in AOP is like a meta-object to a base object in DLR. With this analogy between runtime-weaving

AOP and DLR dynamic objects in mind, let's take the natural next step and see how to implement a DLR-based AOP framework for dynamic objects.

AOP for Dynamic Objects

The Spring.NET aspect-oriented programming you saw in the previous section works for static .NET objects only. Now let's implement a DLR-based AOP framework that works for dynamic objects. If you open the C:\ProDLR\src\Examples\Chapter7\Chapter7.sln file in Visual Studio 2010, you can find the source code for this section in the Aop1 project. The last part of this chapter will integrate our AOP framework with the Spring.NET AOP so that the same advice objects and pointcuts can work across both static and dynamic objects.

Understanding the Framework

Before looking at how the DLR-based AOP framework is implemented, let's see how to use it and what functionalities it provides. Listing 7-5 shows the familiar Customer class I've been using in many of the examples in earlier chapters. There is not much new to say about the Customer class. What's important about this class is that (a) it implements IDynamicMetaObjectProvider and (b) it defines an Age property getter method. The meta-object class that contains the late-binding logic for Customer instances is the AopMetaObject class.

Listing 7-5. Customer.cs

```
public class Customer : IDynamicMetaObjectProvider
{
    public int Age
    {
        get
        {
            Console.WriteLine("Customer Age getter is called.");
            return 3;
        }
    }

    public DynamicMetaObject GetMetaObject(System.Linq.Expressions.Expression parameter)
    {
        return new AopMetaObject(parameter, this);
    }
}
```

As you'll see shortly, the AopMetaObject class is where aspect weaving happens. For the moment, let's write some code that uses the Customer class and see the effects. Listing 7-6 shows the client code that creates an instance of Customer and accesses its Age property.

Listing 7-6. Client Code That Demonstrates Effects of Using the Customer Class.

```
private static void RunDynamicObjectExample()
{
    dynamic customer = new Customer();
```

```
        Console.WriteLine("Customer is {0} years old.", customer.Age);
    }
```

The result of running the code in Listing 7-6 will look like the following:

Advice BeforeInvoke is called.
Customer Age getter is called.
Advice AfterInvoke is called.
Customer is 3 years old.

The two lines in bold are spit out by the advice logic in a class called SimpleLoggingAdvice. Listing 7-7 in the next section will show the code for SimpleLoggingAdvice. The point to stress here is that the advice logic you'll see in Listing 7-7 and the code in Customer's Age property are "woven" together by the AopMetaObject class. That's why when the code in Listing 7-6 accesses the Age property of the customer variable, the program first prints the result of calling SimpleLoggingAdvice's BeforeInvoke method, followed by the result of calling the Age property getter method, and finally the result of calling SimpleLoggingAdvice's AfterInvoke method.

Implementing the Framework

Now that I've shown you what using the AOP framework is like, let's see how that framework is implemented. The implementation of the AOP framework consists of two classes, SimpleLoggingAdvice and AopMetaObject. Listing 7-7 shows the SimpleLoggingAdvice class. The code in SimpleLoggingAdvice.cs is fairly simple. The only thing of importance here is the method signatures of BeforeInvoke and AfterInvoke. Both methods take no input parameters and have System.Object as the return type. To be honest, the method signatures are not practical. Usually methods like BeforeInvoke and AfterInvoke have input parameters that give them some information about the target method—i.e., the method being intercepted. If you look back at the code in Listing 7-2, you'll see that the Invoke method of IMethodInterceptor takes an instance of IMethodInvocation as an input parameter. The IMethodInvocation instance contains information about the intercepted method. Practically, the BeforeInvoke and AfterInvoke methods should take some input parameters like what IMethodInterceptor's Invoke method does. However, for this example I simplify things a bit because, as you'll see, the method signatures of BeforeInvoke and AfterInvoke will influence the implementation complexity of the AopMetaObject class. I'll tackle that complexity later and show you a more practical example when we integrate our AOP framework with Spring.NET AOP.

Listing 7-7. SimpleLoggingAdvice.cs

```
public class SimpleLoggingAdvice
{
    //For simplicity, this method does not have any input parameter.
    public void BeforeInvoke()
    {
        Console.Out.WriteLine("Advice BeforeInvoke is called.");
    }

    //For simplicity, this method does not have any input parameter.
    public void AfterInvoke()
    {
        Console.Out.WriteLine("Advice AfterInvoke is called.");
```

```
    }
}
```

The only piece of the AOP framework we haven't looked at is the AopMetaObject class. AopMetaObject is the meta-object class for the Customer class. It is also the class that weaves together the advice logic and the code in Customer's Age property. Listing 7-8 shows the implementation of AopMetaObject. To qualify as a meta-object class, AopMetaObject inherits from DynamicMetaObject. Since our example only triggers the GetMember action on instances of the Customer class, AopMetaObject overrides only the BindGetMember method. A more complete implementation of the AOP framework should also override the other Bind[Action] of DynamicMetaObject. The overridden BindGetMember method in Listing 7-8 delegates the late binding to the host language's binder by calling the BindGetMember method of DynamicMetaObject. The binder in this case is C#'s binder. When the code customer.Age in Listing 7-6 is executed, C#'s binder will ask the customer object for its meta-object. Then the C# binder will call the BindGetMember on the meta-object. The meta-object in this case is an instance of AopMetaObject and it will delegate the late binding back to the C# binder. The C# binder's binding logic will check if the Customer class has a property called Age with a getter method. If the Customer class has such a property, the C# binder will bind the GetMember action to that property. Otherwise it will return an error.

When the C# binder returns the binding result, we want to wrap the result with expressions that represent calls to both the BeforeInvoke method and the AfterInvoke method of SimpleLoggingAdvice. That's why the BindGetMember method in Listing 7-8 passes the result from the C# binder to the WeaveAspect method in line 12. The WeaveAspect method pretty much does the same thing as the Invoke method in Listing 7-2. The difference is that WeaveAspect needs to turn the code in the Invoke method we saw in Listing 7-2 into DLR expressions. Lines 25 to 28 create a DLR expression that represents a call to the BeforeInvoke method on the member variable advice declared in line 4. Line 30 assigns the late-binding result returned by the C# binder to the returnValue parameter expression. In our example, when this expression is compiled into IL, it has the effect of executing customer.Age and assigning the result to a variable. Lines 32 to 35 create a DLR expression that represents a call to the AfterInvoke method on the member variable advice. Line 37 makes returnValue the return value of the whole block expression that spans from lines 22 to 39. If you compare the block expression to the Invoke method in Listing 7-2, the similarity should be obvious. When the code in lines 25 to 28 creates the method call expression, it needs to pass in expressions that represent the input parameters to the method call. Because the BeforeInvoke method of SimpleLoggingAdvice takes no input parameters, the code in lines 25 to 28 simply passes in an empty array, i.e., the args variable, to the Expression.Call method. Similarly, because AfterInvoke takes no input parameters, the code in lines 32 to 35 also passes in the args variable to the Expression.Call method. The example in the next section will improve this and make it more practical.

Notice that in this example, for simplicity, the AOP advice is hard-coded to an instance of SimpleLoggingAdvice in line 4. In a practical situation, which advice to use should be configurable, not hard-coded. Another issue with the example is that it does not apply advice based on pointcuts. Every GetMember action handled by AopMetaObject will have the SimpleLoggingAdvice applied to it. The next section will fix those issues.

Listing 7-8. AopMetaObject.cs

```
1)   public class AopMetaObject : DynamicMetaObject
2)   {
3)       //For simplicity, which advice we use is not dependent on configuration.
4)       private SimpleLoggingAdvice advice = new SimpleLoggingAdvice();
5)
6)       public AopMetaObject(Expression expression, object obj)
```

```
7)              : base(expression, BindingRestrictions.Empty, obj)
8)          { }
9)
10)         public override DynamicMetaObject BindGetMember(GetMemberBinder binder)
11)         {
12)             return WeaveAspect(base.BindGetMember(binder));
13)         }
14)
15)         private DynamicMetaObject WeaveAspect(DynamicMetaObject originalObject)
16)         {
17)             Expression originalExpression = originalObject.Expression;
18)             var args = new Expression[0] {};
19)             ParameterExpression returnValue = Expression.Parameter(originalExpression.Type);
20)
21)             var advisedObject = new DynamicMetaObject(
22)                 Expression.Block(
23)                     new[] { returnValue },
24)                     new Expression[] {
25)                         Expression.Call(
26)                             Expression.Constant(this.advice),
27)                             typeof(SimpleLoggingAdvice).GetMethod("BeforeInvoke"),
28)                             args),
29)
30)                         Expression.Assign(returnValue, originalExpression),
31)
32)                         Expression.Call(
33)                             Expression.Constant(this.advice),
34)                             typeof(SimpleLoggingAdvice).GetMethod("AfterInvoke"),
35)                             args),
36)
37)                         returnValue
38)                     }
39)                 ),
40)                 originalObject.Restrictions
41)             );
42)
43)             return advisedObject;
44)         }
45) }
```

Integration with Spring.NET AOP

The example in the previous section cuts some corners and shows a primitive implementation of an AOP framework for dynamic objects. Let's fix those shortcuts and make the AOP framework more practical. As the first step, let's modify the example so that it reads from the application-config.xml file to find out the advice to apply, and to find out the corresponding pointcuts. If you open the C:\ProDLR\src\Examples\Chapter7\Chapter7.sln file in Visual Studio 2010, you can find the source code for this section in the Aop project.

Getting the AOP Advisors

Listing 7-9 shows the code of the helper class that reads advice and pointcuts from a configuration file. The class is called AdvisorChainFactory. It has a property called Context. Client code that uses AdvisorChainFactory is supposed to read the application-config.xml file and create a Spring.NET application context. Once that context is created, the client code should assign the application code to AdvisorChainFactory's Context property. When we get to the client code later in this section, you'll see the part of the client code that sets AdvisorChainFactory's Context property.

The GetInterceptors method of AdvisorChainFactory returns a list of AOP advice. The method takes two input parameters—method and targetType. It uses those parameters to find the matching pointcuts (line 20). For each matched pointcut, GetInterceptors puts the advice associated with the pointcut into the adviceList variable (line 21). The method parameter has information about the method that you want GetInterceptors to match against pointcuts. Similarly, the targetType parameter represents the class that you want GetInterceptors to match against pointcuts. In this case, there is only one pointcut defined in the application context, and that pointcut matches any method of any class as long as the method's name ends with "Age".

Listing 7-9. AdvisorChainFactory.cs

```
1)   class AdvisorChainFactory
2)   {
3)       private static IApplicationContext context;
4)
5)       public static IApplicationContext Context
6)       {
7)           set { context = value; }
8)       }
9)
10)      public static IList<IAdvice> GetInterceptors(MethodInfo method, Type targetType)
11)      {
12)          IList<IAdvice> adviceList = new List<IAdvice>();
13)          IDictionary advisors = context.GetObjectsOfType(typeof(IPointcutAdvisor));
14)
15)          ArrayList advisorList = new ArrayList(advisors.Values);
16)          advisorList.Sort(new OrderComparator());
17)
18)          foreach (IPointcutAdvisor advisor in advisorList)
19)          {
20)              if (advisor.Pointcut.MethodMatcher.Matches(method, targetType))
21)                  adviceList.Add(advisor.Advice);
22)          }
23)
24)          return adviceList;
25)      }
26)  }
```

Notice that GetInterceptors returns a list of IAdvice objects. Every Spring.NET advice class must implement the IAdvice interface. The fact that GetInterceptors returns a list of advice objects indicates that (a) we can have more than one advice object applied to a late-binding action and (b) the advice objects have an order (because a list contains ordered elements). As a matter of fact, Spring.NET provides a way for us to specify the order in which to apply multiple advice objects in XML configuration files. That's why we have line 16 in Listing 7-9 to sort the advisor objects according to their order. By doing the sorting, the code honors the order of advisor objects specified in a configuration file such as application-config.xml. I'll show you some examples of applying multiple advice objects in different orders using our AOP framework in a moment.

Before we move on to the rest of the AOP framework's implementation, let's take a look at the code in Listing 7-10 that tests whether the AdvisorChainFactory class works correctly. Listing 7-10 has a method called RunAdvisorChainFactoryExample that demonstrates how the GetInterceptors method of the AdvisorChainFactory class works. In RunAdvisorChainFactoryExample, the target type is the Customer class (line 20) and the method is the Age property's getter method (line 21). Given that target type and method, GetInterceptors will look for pointcuts that match them (lines 22 and 23). GetInterceptors will return the advice objects associated with the matched pointcuts. Finally, RunAdvisorChainFactoryExample prints out the class names of those advice objects. As you can see, with just a few lines of code, we can now easily find out from an application context which advice should apply to which method of which class. Notice that the init method in Listing 7-10 sets AdvisorChainFactory's Context property (line 15). This ensures that the Context property is properly set before the AdvisorChainFactory.GetInterceptors method is called.

Listing 7-10. An Example in Program.cs That Shows How RunAdvisorChainFactory Works

```
1)   class Program
2)   {
3)       private static IApplicationContext context;
4)
5)       static void Main(string[] args)
6)       {
7)           init();
8)           RunAdvisorChainFactoryExample();
9)           Console.ReadLine();
10)      }
11)
12)      private static void init()
13)      {
14)          context = new XmlApplicationContext("application-config.xml");
15)          AdvisorChainFactory.Context = context;
16)      }
17)
18)      private static void RunAdvisorChainFactoryExample()
19)      {
20)          Type targetType = typeof(Customer);
21)          MethodInfo method = targetType.GetProperty("Age").GetGetMethod();
22)          IList<IAdvice> interceptors =
23)              AdvisorChainFactory.GetInterceptors(method, targetType);
24)
25)          foreach (var interceptor in interceptors)
26)              Console.WriteLine("type of matching interceptor is {0}",
27)                  interceptor.GetType().Name);
28)      }
29) }
```

Implementing Advice

Because we are not going to hard-code the advice to use in the AopMetaObject class, we need an interface to serve as the baseline of all the advice classes our AOP framework understands. Listing 7-11 shows that baseline interface's definition. The interface is called IDynamicAdvice. Any advice class that would like to "advise" dynamic objects needs to implement IDynamicAdvice. Notice that the BeforeInvoke and AfterInvoke methods defined in IDynamicAdvice now take input parameters. BeforeInvoke takes three parameters—method, args, and target. The method parameter has information about the method being late-bound. The args parameter represents the arguments to the method being late-bound. The target parameter is the object on which the late-bound method is invoked. The AfterInvoke method takes all the three parameters that BeforeInvoke takes plus the returnValue parameter that represents the return value of the late-bound method.

Listing 7-11 also shows the modified advice class. The class is called LoggingAdvice and it implements both IDynamicAdvice and IMethodInterceptor. By implementing both of those interfaces, LoggingAdvice instances can advise both dynamic and static objects. The code in LoggingAdvice is by and large the same as the code in SpringBasedLoggingAdvice that we saw earlier.

Listing 7-11. IDynamicAdvice and LoggingAdvice.

```
interface IDynamicAdvice : IAdvice
{
    void BeforeInvoke(MethodInfo method, object[] args, object target);
    void AfterInvoke(object returnValue, MethodInfo method, object[] args, object target);
}

public class LoggingAdvice : IDynamicAdvice, IMethodInterceptor
{
    public object Invoke(IMethodInvocation invocation)
    {
        BeforeInvoke(invocation.Method, invocation.Arguments, invocation.Target);
        object returnValue = invocation.Proceed();
        AfterInvoke(returnValue, invocation.Method,
                    invocation.Arguments, invocation.Target);
        return returnValue;
    }

    #region IDynamicAdvice Members

    public void BeforeInvoke(MethodInfo method, object[] args, object target)
    {
        Console.Out.WriteLine("Advice BeforeInvoke is called. Intercepted method is {0}.",
                method.Name);
    }

    public void AfterInvoke(object returnValue, MethodInfo method,
        object[] args, object target)
    {
        Console.Out.WriteLine("Advice AfterInvoke is called. Intercepted method is {0}.",
                method.Name);
    }
```

```
        #endregion
}
```

Applying Advice

The last file we need to modify in order to complete the whole example is AopMetaObject.cs. Listing 7-12 shows the modified code.

Listing 7-12. AopMetaObject.cs

```
1)  public class AopMetaObject : DynamicMetaObject
2)  {
3)      public AopMetaObject(Expression expression, object obj)
4)          : base(expression, BindingRestrictions.Empty, obj)
5)      { }
6)
7)      public override DynamicMetaObject BindGetMember(GetMemberBinder binder)
8)      {
9)          return WeaveAspect(binder.Name, base.BindGetMember(binder));
10)     }
11)
12)     private DynamicMetaObject WeaveAspect(String name, DynamicMetaObject
13)         originalObject)
14)     {
15)         Expression originalExpression = originalObject.Expression;
16)         Type targetType = this.Value.GetType();
17)         PropertyInfo property = targetType.GetProperty(name);
18)         MethodInfo method = property.GetGetMethod();
19)
20)         Expression nullExp = Expression.Constant(null);
21)         Expression targetExp = Expression.Constant(this.Value);
22)         Expression arrayExp = Expression.Constant(new Object[] { });
23)         Expression methodExp = Expression.Constant(method);
24)
25)         IList<IAdvice> adviceList = AdvisorChainFactory
26)                         .GetInterceptors(method, targetType);
27)
28)         List<Expression> calls = new List<Expression>();
29)         List<Expression> afterCalls = new List<Expression>();
30)         foreach (var advice in adviceList)
31)         {
32)             If (!(advice is IDynamicAdvice)) continue;
33)
34)             calls.Add(Expression.Call(
35)                     Expression.Constant(advice),
36)                     typeof(IDynamicAdvice).GetMethod("BeforeInvoke"),
37)                     new Expression[] { methodExp, arrayExp, targetExp }));
38)
39)             afterCalls.Add(Expression.Call(
40)                     Expression.Constant(advice),
41)                     typeof(IDynamicAdvice).GetMethod("AfterInvoke"),
```

```
42)                              new Expression[] { nullExp, methodExp, arrayExp, targetExp }));
43)             }
44)
45)          ParameterExpression returnValue = Expression
46)                          .Parameter(originalExpression.Type);
47)          calls.Add(Expression.Assign(returnValue, originalExpression));
48)          afterCalls.Reverse();
49)          calls.AddRange(afterCalls);
50)          calls.Add(returnValue);
51)
52)          var advisedObject = new DynamicMetaObject(
53)              Expression.Block(
54)                  new[] { returnValue },
55)                  calls.ToArray()
56)              ),
57)              originalObject.Restrictions
58)          );
59)
60)          return advisedObject;
61)      }
62)  }
```

First, notice that, unlike line 4 in Listing 7-8, the code in Listing 7-12 no longer calls the constructor of an advice class. Instead, it calls the GetInterceptors method of AdvisorChainFactory in line 69 to get a list of advice objects based on pointcut matches. With this change, our example no longer hard-codes the advice objects it applies to dynamic objects. The WeaveAspect method is still the workhorse here. It's more complex than earlier because it now needs to prepare the proper expressions that satisfy the method signatures of IDynamicAdvice's BeforeInvoke and AfterInvoke. It also needs to handle not just one advice object but a list of them. Lines 16 to 23 shows the code that prepares the expressions that represent the input parameters needed for calling BeforeInvoke and AfterInvoke. Lines 30 to 43 iterate through the advice objects returned by GetInterceptors. For each advice object, the code creates a method call expression that represents a call to the advice object's BeforeInvoke method and a method call expression that represents a call to the advice object's AfterInvoke method. The expressions created in lines 20 to 23 are passed to the Expression.Call method to create the method call expressions.

After the method call expressions are created, we need to put them into a block expression like we did in Listing 7-8. The block expression that holds all the method call expressions is referenced by the calls variable in Listing 7-12. In Listing 7-8, there is only one advice object and therefore only one call expression for calling BeforeInvoke and only one call expression for calling AfterInvoke. Here we have a list of ordered advice objects. Because the advice objects have order, the call expressions we put into the block expression also need to be in order. Figure 7-2 shows how the call expressions should be ordered. In Spring.NET, we can assign a number to an advice object to denote the advice object's precedence. The lower the number is, the higher the precedence. In Figure 7-2, there are two advice objects; advice 1 has higher precedence than advice 2 and therefore it's put at the front of the advice chain in the figure. When program execution enters the advice chain, the first method that's executed is the BeforeInvoke method of advice 1. Then the BeforeInvoke method of advice 2 is executed. Then the intercepted method of the target object will be executed. In this case, the execution of the intercepted method on the target method is represented by the assignment expression created in line 47 of Listing 7-12. The execution of the program will then exit out the advice chain. On exit, the first method that's executed is the AfterInvoke method of advice 2. Then the AfterInvoke method of advice 1 is executed. That's why in line 48, all the expressions that represent calls to AfterInvoke methods are reversed before they are added to the block expression in line 49.

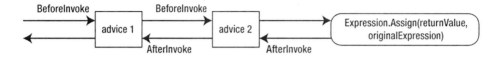

Figure 7-2. *Order of advice objects*

For the purpose of this chapter, the AOP framework implementation at this point is finished. Obviously, there are many things the framework does not support. The AopMetaObject class only overrides the BindGetMember method. A more complete implementation will override other Bind[Operation] methods and weave in the advice logic in those overridden methods. The AOP framework supports the order of advisor objects. Spring.NET provides a way for specifying the order of advice objects and our AOP framework does not account for that. Nonetheless, the AOP framework lays the groundwork for further enhancements. It also demonstrates one important scenario (i.e., the AOP programming paradigm) in which the DLR dynamic object infrastructure can be leveraged. To celebrate, let's take a break and have some fun with the AOP framework.

Cutting Across Dynamic and Static Objects

In this section, you will harvest the results of the AOP framework built in the previous sections. To use the AOP framework, I wrote a method called RunAopExample and put it in Program.cs. Listing 7-13 shows its code.

Listing 7-13. An Example in Program.cs That Uses the AOP Framework

```
1)   private static void RunAopExample()
2)   {
3)       dynamic customer = new Customer("John", 5);
4)       Console.WriteLine("Customer {0} is {1} years old.\n",
5)           customer.Name, customer.Age);
6)
7)       IEmployee employee = (IEmployee)context["employeeBob"];
8)       Console.WriteLine("Employee {0} is {1} years old.",
9)           employee.Name, employee.Age);
10)  }
```

The RunAopExample method creates a Customer instance in line 3 and fetches an IEmployee instance from the Spring.NET application context in line 7. Method calls to those two instances' property getters will be intercepted, matched against the pointcuts specified in application-config.xml, and then advised as appropriate. You'll see the following output when you run the example:

```
Customer Name getter is called.
Advice BeforeInvoke is called. Intercepted method is get_Age.
Customer Age getter is called.
Advice AfterInvoke is called. Intercepted method is get_Age.
Customer John is 5 years old.

Employee Name getter is called.
Advice BeforeInvoke is called. Intercepted method is get_Age.
```

```
Employee Age getter is called.
Advice AfterInvoke is called. Intercepted method is get_Age.
Employee Bob is 30 years old.
```

Next, let's turn it up a notch by throwing in a second advice object. By having a second advice object, we'll be able to order the two advice objects in different ways and see the effects. To make the demonstration clear, I created a new advice class by copying the LoggingAdvice class and renaming it to LoggingAdvice2. Listing 7-14 shows the code of LoggingAdvice2 with differences from LoggingAdvice in bold. As you can see, LoggingAdvice2 differs from LoggingAdvice only in the messages it prints to the console. Because the messages are different, it will be easy to see which advice object is in front of which in the advice chain later when we run the example.

Listing 7-14. LoggingAdvice2.cs

```
public class LoggingAdvice2 : IDynamicAdvice, IMethodInterceptor
{
    //Invoke method is omitted.

    public void BeforeInvoke(MethodInfo method, object[] args, object target)
    {
        Console.Out.WriteLine("Advice2 BeforeInvoke is called. Intercepted method is {0}.",
            method.Name);
    }

    public void AfterInvoke(object returnValue, MethodInfo method, object[] args,
            object target)
    {
        Console.Out.WriteLine("Advice2 AfterInvoke is called. Intercepted method is {0}.",
            method.Name);
    }
}
```

With LoggingAdvice2 in place, all that remains is to configure new advice and advisor objects in application-config.xml. Listing 7-15 shows the contents of application-config.xml after the modifications. The differences from the earlier version of application-config.xml are highlighted in bold. As you can see, a new advice object with id loggingAdvice2 and a new advisor object with id getAgeAdvisor2 are added. The object loggingAdvice2 is an instance of LoggingAdvice2. As for the getAgeAdvisor2 object, notice that its order attribute is assigned the number 2. In comparison, the order attribute of the getAgeAdvisor object is set to 5. That means in the advice chain, loggingAdvice2 will be in front of loggingAdvice. So we should expect the BeforeInvoke method of loggingAdvice2 to be called before the BeforeInvoke method of loggingAdvice when program execution enters the advice chain. When program execution exits the advice chain, we should expect the AfterInvoke method of loggingAdvice to be called first and the AfterInvoke method of loggingAdvice2 to be called second. Notice also that I changed the pointcut pattern to match not only all methods that end with Age but also the ones that end with Name.

Listing 7-15. Adding a Second Advice Object in Application-config.xml.

```xml
<?xml version="1.0" encoding="utf-8" ?>
<objects xmlns="http://www.springframework.net"
              xmlns:xsi="http://www.w3.org/2001/XMLSchema-instance"
              xmlns:aop="http://www.springframework.net/aop">

  <aop:config>
    <aop:advisor id="getAgeAdvisor" pointcut-ref="getAgeCalls"
                  advice-ref="loggingAdvice" order="5" />

    <aop:advisor id="getAgeAdvisor2" pointcut-ref="getAgeCalls"
                  advice-ref="loggingAdvice2" order="2" />
  </aop:config>

  <object id="getAgeCalls"
        type="Spring.Aop.Support.SdkRegularExpressionMethodPointcut, Spring.Aop">
    <property name="patterns">
      <list>
        <value>.*Age</value>
        <value>.*Name</value>
      </list>
    </property>
  </object>

  <object id="loggingAdvice" type="Aop.LoggingAdvice, Aop"/>
  <object id="loggingAdvice2" type="Aop.LoggingAdvice2, Aop"/>

<!-- The object employeeBob is the same as before and omitted -->
</objects>
```

If you run the example with the configuration in Listing 7-15, you'll see the following output:

```
Advice2 BeforeInvoke is called. Intercepted method is get_Name.
Advice BeforeInvoke is called. Intercepted method is get_Name.
Customer Name getter is called.
Advice AfterInvoke is called. Intercepted method is get_Name.
Advice2 AfterInvoke is called. Intercepted method is get_Name.
Advice2 BeforeInvoke is called. Intercepted method is get_Age.
Advice BeforeInvoke is called. Intercepted method is get_Age.
Customer Age getter is called.
Advice AfterInvoke is called. Intercepted method is get_Age.
Advice2 AfterInvoke is called. Intercepted method is get_Age.
Customer John is 5 years old.

Advice2 BeforeInvoke is called. Intercepted method is get_Name.
Advice BeforeInvoke is called. Intercepted method is get_Name.
Employee Name getter is called.
Advice AfterInvoke is called. Intercepted method is get_Name.
Advice2 AfterInvoke is called. Intercepted method is get_Name.
```

```
Advice2 BeforeInvoke is called. Intercepted method is get_Age.
Advice BeforeInvoke is called. Intercepted method is get_Age.
Employee Age getter is called.
Advice AfterInvoke is called. Intercepted method is get_Age.
Advice2 AfterInvoke is called. Intercepted method is get_Age.
Employee Bob is 30 years old.
```

Try changing the order attribute of getAgeAdvisor in application-config.xml from 5 to 1. Then run the example again and see what the output is.

Summary

This chapter begins with an introduction to aspect-oriented programming, explaining the basic concepts of AOP as well as terms such as join point, pointcut, advice, and aspect. We briefly touched upon three approaches for implementing an AOP framework—runtime, load-time and compile-time weaving. We talked about how Spring.NET's runtime weaving is achieved by using proxy objects. Our AOP framework and Spring.NET's AOP framework both take the runtime weaving approach. Unlike Spring.NET's AOP framework, ours leverages DLR's dynamic object infrastructure instead of using proxy objects. We went through the first iteration of our AOP framework's implementation, which works only for dynamic objects. We continued, integrating the AOP framework with Spring.NET AOP. The result is an AOP system that reads aspect-related settings from one single configuration file and works across static as well as dynamic objects.

This chapter scratches only the surface of many topics it covers. The implementation of the AOP framework leaves many things to be desired. To more fully realize the potential of the underlying iceberg whose tip we saw in this chapter, I created a project up on Google Code at http://code.google.com/p/dpier/. You are welcome to visit the project web site for updates on the development of the AOP framework.

CHAPTER 8

■ ■ ■

Metaprogramming

Metaprogramming is everywhere in the DLR. All the LINQ Expression examples you saw in Chapter 2 and all the DLR Hosting API examples you saw in Chapter 6 are metaprograms. Because metaprogramming plays such a pervasive role in the DLR, we're going to dive deeper into the subject and show you some advanced and marvelous uses of metaprogramming.

We will begin with an overview of metaprogramming. The overview will discuss what metaprogramming is and where it is used in the DLR, then we'll look at one type of metaprogramming that adds and removes methods or properties to or from a class or an instance of a class. We will illustrate the metaprogramming technique in Ruby and Python, then write some infrastructure code that enables us to use the same kind of metaprogramming technique in C# through the DLR. The infrastructure code will consist of two classes called `ClassMetaObject` and `ExpandoClass`.

We will then take a detour and build a custom LINQ query provider. The purpose of this exercise is to illustrate a typical use of DLR Expression as a metaprogramming technique. The exciting thing about the custom LINQ query provider is that we are going to gradually evolve it into a code-generation framework that utilizes the `ClassMetaObject` and `ExpandoClass` classes. At the end, we will arrive at a code-generation framework that is in spirit similar to frameworks such as the popular Ruby on Rails.

Overview of Metaprogramming

Metaprograms are programs that generate or manipulate other programs, and metaprogramming is, of course, the writing of metaprograms. Based on these definitions, you can see why the LINQ Expression examples in Chapter 2 are metaprograms. They are metaprograms because, in those examples, we construct LINQ expression trees and use those trees to generate executable IL code. The code we write to construct and compile LINQ expression trees is a metaprogram. The programs manipulated by the metaprograms consist of code represented by the LINQ expression tree. Similarly, the DLR Hosting API examples in Chapter 6 are metaprograms because those examples take Python code or Ruby code as input and manipulate the code by running it and interacting with it. The DLR Hosting API examples are metaprograms and the Python code and Ruby code are the programs manipulated by the metaprograms.

It's common to see the concept of code as data in metaprograms. In the case of the LINQ Expression examples in Chapter 2, the LINQ expression trees are data that represent code elements, such as if conditions and while loops. Once code is in the form of data (i.e., expression trees), we can write metaprograms that manipulate the code as data. In the case of the DLR Hosting API examples, the Python and Ruby code is data. Once that code is in the form of data, we can write metaprograms that manipulate the code via the DLR Hosting API.

Metaprograms can generate or manipulate programs at compile time or at runtime. An example of a metaprogram that manipulates a program at compile time is code generation. If you are a C++ programmer and you use C++ macros in your code, you are doing compile-time metaprogramming. That's because, when you compile the C++ code, the macros are processed by the preprocessor to generate code that then gets compiled together with the rest of your code by the C++ compiler. The preprocessor is the metaprogram in this case and the C++ macros in your code are the programs being manipulated by the metaprogram.

Another example of compile-time metaprogramming is a compiler. A compiler is a metaprogram that manipulates the code it compiles. All of the metaprogramming we do with the DLR happens at runtime. For example, when we use the DLR Hosting API to run Python or Ruby code, we do that at runtime. When we use an expression visitor to modify an expression tree or when we compile a lambda expression into an invocable delegate, we do that at runtime. However, that's not to say that we can't do compile-time metaprogramming with the DLR. If we use an expression visitor to modify an expression tree and use that modified tree to generate some C# code at compile time, that would be compile-time metaprogramming.

One common type of metaprogramming is the adding and removing of methods or properties to and from a class at runtime. In static languages like C#, this is in general not supported because classes are compiled at compile time and can't be modified when a program runs.

There are ways to create the illusion that a compiled C# class is modified at runtime. For example, Spring.NET AOP (Aspect Oriented Programming), a library for doing aspect-oriented programming on the .NET platform, generates proxy classes of compiled C# classes at runtime. The proxy classes add aspect-related behavior to the original C# classes and create the illusion that the original C# classes are modified to behave differently. The truth is the original C# classes are not still kept intact. They are just proxied.

■ **Note** For the sake of thoroughness, I'll point out that there is, in fact, a library that can really modify a compiled Java class as the class is being loaded by a class loader. However, that library is an exceptional case that does not invalidate my main line of discussion in this chapter.

Even though you might be able to modify a compiled Java or C# class at runtime if you are determined, doing so is generally not supported. On the other hand, many dynamic languages naturally support the addition and removal of methods and properties to and from a class at runtime. Moreover, we can also add or remove methods and properties to and from a particular instance of a class without affecting the other instances of the same class. The next part of this chapter will show you how to modify a class and its instances by adding methods or properties at runtime in Ruby, in Python, and, last but not least, in C# through the DLR.

Changing Class Definitions

Now we are going to write some metaprograms that manipulate programs by adding methods or properties to a class or to an instance of a class. We will do the same exercise three times for three different languages—first Ruby, then Python, and finally C# through DLR. Even though C# does not in general support the kind of metaprogramming we discuss in this section, you will see that with the DLR, C# as well as VB.NET developers can benefit the metaprogramming techniques that Ruby and Python developers enjoy. The metaprogramming technique we discuss in this section is the foundation that enables many marvelous applications. As you'll see later in this chapter, we will take what we build in this section to add methods and properties to a C# class or its instances and use it to facilitate runtime code generation.

Ruby

Now we'll see how to define a class in Ruby and then dynamically modify the class. The examples will show you how to add methods to a class so that all instances of the class support those methods. You can also add methods only to a specific instance. In that case, only that specific instance will support those methods and all other instances of the same class will not.

You can try out this section's Ruby code by typing it in an interactive Ruby console. Alternatively, since I have put all the code for this section in the metaExamples.rb file in the MetaExamples project of this chapter's code download, you can simply run the MetaExamples project in debug mode. The MetaExamples project is a .NET console application. The entry point Main method of the console application calls the RunRubyMetaExamples method shown in Listing 8-1 to run the Ruby code in metaExamples.rb. The RunRubyMetaExamples method uses the DLR Hosting API to run the Ruby code. We discussed the DLR Hosting API in detail in Chapter 6, so I won't duplicate that discussion here and explain the code in Listing 8-1.

Listing 8-1. C# Method That Runs the Ruby Code in metaExamples.rb

```
private static void RunRubyMetaExamples()
{
    ScriptEngine engine = IronRuby.Ruby.CreateEngine();
    engine.ExecuteFile(@"Ruby\metaExamples.rb");
}
```

To begin, let's define a Ruby class called Customer as in Listing 8-2.

Listing 8-2. Define a Ruby Class Called Customer

```
class Customer

  def initialize(name, age)
    @name = name
    @age = age
  end

  def to_s()
    @name
  end
end
```

The Customer class defines two methods: initialize and to_s. The initialize method will be called by the Ruby runtime when an instance of the Customer class is created. The initialize method takes two input parameters and stores them in two class member variables, @name and @age. In Ruby, the naming convention requires the name of a class member variable begin with @. The to_s method of the Customer class will be called when a Customer instance is converted to a string object, for example, when we print a Customer instance to the console.

With the Customer class defined, let's create a couple of instances of it and see how they work. Listing 8-3 shows this part of the example's code.

Listing 8-3. Create Instances of the Customer Class

```
bob = Customer.new("Bob", 26)
mary = Customer.new("Mary", 30)

puts bob
puts mary
```

In Listing 8-3, we create two instances of Customer. In Ruby, a class is an object. The name of a class is a constant that points to the class object. To create an instance of a Ruby class, you call the new method on the name of the class, as the code Customer.new("Bob", 26) in Listing 8-3 shows. Because the name of the class is a reference to the class object, what you are effectively doing is calling the new method on the class object, which causes the initialize method of that class to be called. After two instances of Customer are created, we print those two instances to the screen by calling the puts method. The method puts is Ruby's built-in method for printing objects to the screen. Internally, puts calls the to_s method of the Customer class to print out the names of Bob and Mary, our two Customer instances.

To demonstrate the metaprogramming capability Ruby provides, let's suppose we want to modify the Customer class so that we can set Bob and Mary as each other's spouse. To achieve this, we simply use line 2 to add a spouse attribute accessor to the Customer class. The code in line 2 will add two accessor methods, spouse and spouse=, to the Customer class. A class member variable in a Ruby class is by default private and not accessible to the world outside of the class. In order to make the @spouse class member variable accessible to the world outside of the Customer class, we need the code in line 2 that adds the spouse and spouse= accessor methods to the Customer class. With those accessor methods, we can set Mary as Bob's spouse, as line 12 shows. When line 12 assigns the variable mary to the spouse attribute of bob, the spouse= method of bob will be invoked. The spouse= method in Listing 8-4 is implemented in such a way that if Mary is Bob's spouse, then Bob is also set as Mary's spouse. Notice that the code in Listing 8-4 is executed after Listings 8-3 and 8-2. That means even after instances of the Customer class are created in Listing 8-3, we can still modify the class and the instances will just pick up the new spouse and spouse= accessor methods we added. Because the spouse and spouse= accessor methods are added to the Customer class, all the instances of the Customer class will support those two accessor methods.

Listing 8-4. Modify the Customer Class in Ruby

```
1)   class Customer
2)     attr_accessor :spouse
3)
4)     def spouse=(spouse)
5)       if @spouse != spouse
6)         @spouse = spouse
7)         spouse.spouse = self
8)       end
9)     end
10) end
11)
12) bob.spouse = mary
13)
14) puts "Bob's spouse is " + bob.spouse.to_s
15) puts "Mary's spouse is " + mary.spouse.to_s
```

Listing 8-4 shows how to add methods to a class so that all instances of the class will support those methods. Listing 8-5 shows how to add a method to a particular Customer instance, not to the Customer class. The code in adds a calculate_late_fee method to customer Bob and a different calculate_late_fee method to customer Mary. Bob's late fee is 200 while Mary's is 100. Because the calculate_late_fee method is associated with a particular instance, we can have one implementation of the method for Bob that returns 200 and another for Mary that returns 100.

Listing 8-5. Add Methods at the Instance Level

```
def bob.calculate_late_fee()
    200
end

def mary.calculate_late_fee()
    100
end

puts "Bob's late fee is " + bob.calculate_late_fee.to_s
puts "Mary's late fee is " + mary.calculate_late_fee.to_s
```

Python

We just saw how to add methods to a class as well as to an instance of a class in Ruby. Now we'll look at the same example in the Python language. You can run this section's Python code listings in sequence by typing them in a Python interactive console. Alternatively, because I have put all the Python code for this section in the metaExamples.py file in the MetaExamples project of this chapter's code download, you can run the MetaExamples project's entry point Main method. This calls the RunPythonMetaExamples method in MetaExamples' Program.cs file to execute the Python code in metaExamples.py.

As in the previous example, our first step is to define the Customer class in Python, as Listing 8-6 shows. The code in Listing 8-6 defines the Customer class as a subclass of the object class. The Customer class contains two methods: __init__ and __str__. The method __init__ is the constructor that will be called when new instances of the Customer class are created. The method __str__ will be called when we convert a Customer instance to a string representation. Methods of a class must take an explicit self argument that represents the instance on which the methods are invoked. That's why both __init__ and __str__ have self as an input parameter. The input parameter does not have to be named self. This is just a naming convention that most Python programmers follow. You can think of the self parameter as sort of Python's equivalent of the this variable in C#. The body of the __init__ method assigns the name and age of a customer to the name and age attributes of the self parameter. Attributes in a Python class like the ones in our example are like class member variables in a C# class. But unlike class member variables in C#, attributes in a Python class don't need to be explicitly declared. That's why you don't see the name and age attributes declared anywhere in Listing 8-6, yet the __init__ method can assign the name and age of a customer to the name and age attributes of the self parameter.

Listing 8-6. Define the Customer Class in Python

```
class Customer(object):
  def __init__(self, name, age):
    self.name = name
    self.age = age
```

```
def __str__(self):
    return self.name
```

If we now create instances of the Python Customer class, as Listing 8-7 shows, we can print the string representations of those instances and expect to see the names Bob and Mary show up on the screen.

Listing 8-7. Create Instances of the Customer Class in Python

```
bob = Customer("Bob", 26)
mary = Customer("Mary", 30)

print bob
print mary
```

Now here's the part where we add the method for setting a customer's spouse to the Customer class. Listing 8-8 shows how to do that in Python. To add a method to an already defined class in Python, we first define a Python function by itself. In Listing 8-8, we define the set_spouse function alone in lines 1 to 3. The body of the function ensures that if Bob is Mary's spouse, then Mary is also Bob's spouse. After the set_spouse function is defined, we add it to the Customer class as the set_spouse method of the Customer class in line 5. Because the set_spouse method is added to the Customer class, all instances of the Customer class will support that method. In line 7, we test our modification to the Customer class by calling the set_spouse method on the variable bob. When we do this, the set_spouse function is called with the self parameter set to the variable bob. As a matter fact, we can replace line 7 in Listing 8-8 with this equivalent code set_spouse(bob, mary) and everything will work the same. Lines 9 and 10 print out Bob's spouse and Mary's spouse to show that the testing we do in line 7 works correctly.

Listing 8-8. Modify the Customer Class in Python

```
1)   def set_spouse(self, spouse):
2)       self.spouse = spouse
3)       spouse.spouse = self
4)
5)   Customer.set_spouse = set_spouse
6)
7)   bob.set_spouse(mary)
8)
9)   print "Bob's spouse is " + str(bob.spouse)
10)  print "Mary's spouse is " + str(mary.spouse)
```

Next we will add methods to individual Customer instances. To do so in Python, we make use of a standard Python module called types. Before we can use that module, we need to do a few things so that the IronPython runtime will be able to locate the module. First, the types module is not included as part of the DLR source code. In order to run the code in Listing 8-9, you need to download IronPython from http://ironpython.codeplex.com and install it. I downloaded IronPython 2.6.1 for .NET 4.0 and installed it in C:\Program Files (x86)\IronPython 2.6 for .NET 4.0. If you install it in a different folder, you'll need to modify the path in line 2 of Listing 8-9 accordingly. The installation of IronPython places the standard Python types module in C:\Program Files (x86)\IronPython 2.6 for .NET 4.0\Lib. That's the path we need to add to Python's system path so that the IronPython runtime knows to look there for modules we want to import. So in line 2 of Listing 8-9, we add the path to Python's system path. In line 3 we import the types module. Without installing IronPython and without the code in line 2, importing the types module in line 3 would fail.

After the types module is successfully imported, the rest of the code is pretty similar to the Ruby example we saw earlier. We first define a function called bob_late_fee in lines 5 and 6. Then we call the MethodType function of the types module to associate the bob_late_fee function with the variable bob. Similarly for the variable mary, we define a function called mary_late_fee and use the MethodType function of the types module to associate the mary_late_fee function with the variable mary. If you run the code in Listing 8-9, you should see on the screen that Bob's late fee is 200 and Mary's late fee is 100. This shows that in Python, as in Ruby, we can add a method to a particular instance without affecting other instances of the same class.

Listing 8-9. Add Methods to Instances of the Customer Class in Python

```
1)   import sys
2)   sys.path.append(r'C:\Program Files (x86)\IronPython 2.6 for .NET 4.0\Lib')
3)   import types
4)
5)   def bob_late_fee(self):
6)       return 200
7)
8)   bob.calculate_late_fee = types.MethodType(bob_late_fee, bob)
9)
10)  def mary_late_fee(self):
11)      return 100
12)
13)  mary.calculate_late_fee = types.MethodType(mary_late_fee, mary)
14)
15)  print "Bob's late fee is " + str(bob.calculate_late_fee())
16)  print "Mary's late fee is " + str(mary.calculate_late_fee())
```

DLR

So far you've seen how to add methods to a class as well as to an instance of a class in both Ruby and Python. Many other dynamic languages, such as Groovy, also provide the means for modifying a class's or an object's behavior at runtime. With the advent of the DLR, the good news is we don't have to code in a dynamic language like Ruby or Python to benefit from the metaprogramming capabilities those languages provide. With a little bit of work, we can define a class in C# and be able to add methods to the class and also to instances of the class. Let's see how that is done.

In this section, we will define two main classes: ClassMetaObject and ExpandoClass. The purpose of ClassMetaObject is to hold the methods we add to individual objects, and the purpose of ExpandoClass is to hold the methods we add to a class. As an example of how you can use these methods, we will define a Customer class that derives from ClassMetaObject. When we create an instance of the Customer class and add methods to that instance, those methods will be stored in an instance of ClassMetaObject. When we add methods to the Customer class, those methods will be stored in an instance of ExpandoClass.

The Customer class code is shown in Listing 8-10. As you can see, the C# Customer class mimics the Ruby and Python Customer classes we saw in the previous sections. The C# Customer class defines a constructor that takes the name and age of a customer. The ToString method is overridden to return the name of a customer. One important thing to note about the C# Customer class is that it derives from ClassMetaObject so that instances of the Customer class can be associated with new properties and methods. Furthermore, the Customer class contains a private static member variable _class that points to an instance of ExpandoClass. This is so that new properties and methods can be added to the Customer class. I made the member variable _class a static variable because I want all instances of the Customer class to share one single ExpandoClass instance that holds all the properties and methods we add to the Customer class. We will look at how ClassMetaObject and ExpandoClass are implemented in a minute. First, however, I'd like to repeat the Ruby and Python examples we saw in the previous sections and show how the same example works in C# using the Customer class.

Listing 8-10. Define the Customer Class in C#

```
public class Customer : ClassMetaObject
{
    private static ExpandoClass _class = new ExpandoClass();

    public static dynamic CLASS
    {
        get { return _class; }
    }

    private string name;
    private int age;

    public Customer(string name, int age)
    {
        this.name = name;
        this.age = age;
    }

    public override string ToString()
    {
        return this.name;
    }

    protected override ExpandoClass Class
    {
        get { return _class; }
    }
}
```

Like the Ruby and Python examples in the previous sections, the code in Listing 8-11 creates two instances of the Customer class. After the two Customer instances are created, we want to define a method for setting a customer's spouse and a method for retrieving a customer's spouse. The method we define for setting a customer's spouse is the SetSpouse delegate in Listing 8-11. The delegate takes two input parameters that represent the two parties in a marital relationship. The method body of the SetSpouse delegate enforces the rule that if Bob is Mary's spouse, then Mary must also be Bob's spouse. Notice that the two input parameters of SetSpouse are of the type dynamic. Within the method body of the SetSpouse delegate, the code accesses the Spouse property of the input parameter self. The Spouse property is not defined originally in the C# Customer class. But that's okay because we add the Spouse property to the Customer class in line 16. In line 17, we add the SetSpouse delegate as the SetSpouse method to the Customer class. As you can see from lines 16 and 17, to add a property or method to the Customer class, we add it to the customerClass variable, which is obtained from the static CLASS property of the Customer class. Recall from the code in Listing 8-10 that the static CLASS property of the Customer class returns the single ExpandoClass instance that's shared among all Customer instances and that's meant to store all new properties and methods added to the Customer class.

After adding the Spouse property and the SetSpouse method to the Customer class, we call the SetSpouse method on the variable bob in line 18, just as we did in the previous Ruby and Python examples. When we print out Bob's spouse and Mary's spouse in lines 20 and 21, we can verify that things do work as expected and that we have dutifully officiated at the matrimony. And just as what happens to newlyweds who simply go on a honeymoon and forget to pay their wedding expenses on time, Bob and Mary incurred late fees on their credit card accounts. To reflect that irresponsibility on the part of Bob and Mary, the code in lines 23 and 24 assigns one anonymous delegate as the CalculateLateFee method to the variable bob and another anonymous delegate as the CalculateLateFee method to the variable mary. When you print out Bob's and Mary's late fees, sure enough you will see that Bob has a late fee of 200 and Mary has a late fee of 100 dollars.

Listing 8-11. An Example of Adding Methods at the Class and Instance Levels in C#

```
1)   private static void RunMetaLibExample()
2)   {
3)       dynamic customerClass = Customer.CLASS;
4)       dynamic bob = new Customer("Bob", 26);
5)       dynamic mary = new Customer("Mary", 30);
6)
7)       Action<dynamic, dynamic> SetSpouse = (self, spouse) =>
8)       {
9)           if (self.Spouse != spouse)
10)          {
11)              self.Spouse = spouse;
12)              spouse.Spouse = self;
13)          }
14)      };
15)
16)      customerClass.Spouse = null;
17)      customerClass.SetSpouse = SetSpouse;
18)      bob.SetSpouse(bob, mary);
19)
20)      Console.WriteLine("Bob's spouse is {0}.", bob.Spouse);
21)      Console.WriteLine("Mary's spouse is {0}.", mary.Spouse);
22)
23)      bob.CalculateLateFee = (Func<int>) (() => { return 200; });
24)      mary.CalculateLateFee = (Func<int>)(() => { return 100; });
25)
26)      Console.WriteLine("Bob's late fee is {0}.", bob.CalculateLateFee());
27)      Console.WriteLine("Mary's late fee is {0}.", mary.CalculateLateFee());
28) }
```

Let's see how ClassMetaObject and ExpandoClass are implemented. Listing 8-12 shows the ClassMetaObject code. ClassMetaObject derives from the System.Dynamic.DynamicObject class that the DLR provides. We discussed DynamicObject in Chapter 5.

Basically, the class DynamicObject defines some methods that you can override in a derived class to define the late-binding behavior of the derived class's instances. Here in ClassMetaObject we override the TryGetMember and TrySetMember methods inherited from DynamicObject. The TryGetMember method of

ClassMetaObject will be called when we try to access a property or call a method on an instance of ClassMetaObject or a class that derives from ClassMetaObject.

For example, in Listing 8-11, when the code bob.Spouse is executed, because the Spouse property is not defined in the C# Customer class, the TryGetMember method that the Customer class inherits from ClassMetaObject will be called to perform the late binding of the Spouse property. The logic of the TryGetMember method implemented in ClassMetaObject first checks if the requested property or method is available at the instance level by looking up the property or method name in the items dictionary. The items dictionary is a private member variable in ClassMetaObject that holds dynamic properties and methods at the instance level. If the requested property or method is not found at the instance level, the TryGetMember method in ClassMetaObject proceeds to perform the class-level lookup by calling the TryGetMember method on the Class property.

As Listing 8-12 shows, the Class property is a reference to an ExpandoClass instance. The job of the Class property is to hold the dynamic properties and methods at the class level. Because every subclass of ClassMetaObject will have its own class-level dynamic properties and methods, I make the Class property an abstract property. Every subclass of ClassMetaObject should implement the abstract Class property by returning its own ExpandoClass instance in the Class property's get method. That's what the Customer class does, and you can see that if you take a look at how the Class property is implemented in the Customer class in Listing 8-10.

The TrySetMember in ClassMetaObject is implemented a little differently from the TryGetMember. The code in the TrySetMember sets a property or method at the instance level by putting an entry in the items dictionary. Unlike the TryGetMember method, the code does not bother with setting properties and methods at the class level. This is because the TrySetMember method is called when code like self.Spouse = spouse in Listing 8-11 is executed. As you can see, when such code is executed, we want to set the Spouse property of the instance referenced by self. In other words, we want to set the Spouse property at the instance level. If the client code wants to set a property at the class level, then instead of doing something like self.Spouse = spouse, the client code should set the property by using code like the customerClass.Spouse = null in Listing 8-11. This code will cause the TrySetMember method of ExpandoClass, which you will see in a minute, to be called.

In summary, an important point to keep in mind when using the ClassMetaObject and ExpandoClass classes is that when setting a dynamic property or method at the instance level, you need to set it to an instance of ClassMetaObject. If you want to set a dynamic property or method at the class level, you need to set it to an instance of ExpandoClass. However, you can retrieve an instance-level or class-level dynamic property or method by getting it from a ClassMetaObject instance.

Listing 8-12. The ClassMetaObject Class

```
public abstract class ClassMetaObject : DynamicObject
{
    protected abstract ExpandoClass Class
    {
        get;
    }

    private Dictionary<string, object> items = new Dictionary<string, object>();

    public override bool TryGetMember(
        GetMemberBinder binder, out object result)
    {
        if (items.TryGetValue(binder.Name, out result))
            return true;
```

```
        else
            return Class.TryGetMember(binder, out result);
    }

    public override bool TrySetMember(
        SetMemberBinder binder, object value)
    {
        items[binder.Name] = value;
        return true;
    }
}
```

The ExpandoClass code is similar to that of ClassMetaObject, only simpler. Listing 8-13 shows how the ExpandoClass class is implemented. Like ClassMetaObject, ExpandoClass also derives from DynamicObject and overrides the TryGetMember and TrySetMember methods. ExpandoClass defines a private member variable called items to hold class-level dynamic properties and methods.

Listing 8-13. The ExpandoClass Class

```
public class ExpandoClass : DynamicObject
{
    Dictionary<string, object> items = new Dictionary<string, object>();

    public override bool TryGetMember(
        GetMemberBinder binder, out object result)
    {
        return items.TryGetValue(binder.Name, out result);
    }

    public override bool TrySetMember(
        SetMemberBinder binder, object value)
    {
        items[binder.Name] = value;
        return true;
    }
}
```

To illustrate how ExpandoClass works in concert with ClassMetaObject, I'll trace how the SetSpouse method is added to the Customer class and then later invoked on a Customer instance. Recall the following code snippet in Listing 8-11:

```
customerClass.SetSpouse = SetSpouse;
bob.SetSpouse(bob, mary);
```

In the code snippet, when we assign the SetSpouse delegate to the SetSpouse member of customerClass, because customerClass is an instance of ExpandoClass, the TrySetMember method of ExpandoClass will be invoked and the SetSpouse method will be added to the C# Customer class at the class level. When we call the SetSpouse method on bob, because bob is an instance of ClassMetaObject, the TryGetMember method of ClassMetaObject will be invoked. The TryGetMember method of ClassMetaObject will not find a method by the name SetSpouse because the SetSpouse method was added to bob at the instance level. So the TryGetMember method of ClassMetaObject will proceed to call the `TryGetMember` method of `ExpandoClass` and the `SetSpouse` method we added to the C# `Customer` class will be retrieved and eventually called.

LINQ Query Provider

So far in this chapter, I have shown how we can add methods to a class and to a particular instance of a class dynamically, completely in C# without any use of a dynamic language such as Ruby or Python. Now we are going to take a detour and look at another kind of metaprogramming technique that is made possible by the DLR. The metaprogramming technique I'll show you is based on DLR Expression, and I will demonstrate it by implementing a custom LINQ query provider. The exciting thing about doing this is that we are going to gradually evolve the custom LINQ query provider into a code-generation framework that utilizes the `ClassMetaObject` and `ExpandoClass` classes we built in the previous section. At the end, we'll arrive at a code-generation framework that is in spirit similar to frameworks such as the popular Ruby on Rails.

Understanding the End Goal

In this section we'll build a LINQ query provider. However, our true goal is to understand not the LINQ query provider itself, but rather the DLR Expression metaprogramming the LINQ query provider is based on. As you'll see, DLR Expression allows us to represent code as data. The data is in the form of expression trees that we can easily manipulate using the Visitor design pattern we looked at in Chapter 2. We saw many examples of DLR Expression in Chapter 2. The code here will be similar, except that this time our DLR Expression example is framed in the context of LINQ query providers.

LINQ is a component of the .NET Framework that allows writing code like the following to query a data source:

```
IEnumerable<Customer> selectedCustomers =
              from c in customers
              where c.FirstName.Equals("Bob") select c;
```

In the code snippet, the variable `customers` is the data source from which we want to select customers whose first name is Bob. The variable `customers` might represent data in database, information in XML files, or a collection of objects in memory. As far as the query is concerned, it doesn't matter whether the underlying data store is a database or an XML file. As long as there is a LINQ query provider that knows how to take our LINQ query and fetch the right data from the underlying data store, our LINQ query will run just fine.

From this little explanation of LINQ, you can see that the two major players in LINQ are queries and query providers. Queries are decoupled from the actual data store. The only link between queries and the actual store is a query provider. A query provider knows how to take queries and execute them against a particular data store. In this section, the custom query provider we will implement is one that executes queries against a collection of in-memory objects.

Implementing the Query Class

The implementation of the custom query provider consists of three main classes: `Query<T>`, `QueryProvider<T>`, and `QueryExpressionVisitor<T>`. The `Query<T>` class represents the queries that will be processed by our custom query provider as DLR expression trees. The `QueryProvider<T>` class implements the logic of our custom query provider. `QueryProvider<T>` is the class that contains the logic for executing instances of the `Query<T>` class. When a `QueryProvider<T>` instance executes instances of the `Query<T>` class, it uses instances of the `QueryExpressionVisitor<T>` class to manipulate the DLR expression trees of the Query<T> instances. We will now go over the code of the three classes, Query<T>, QueryProvider<T>, and QueryExpressionVisitor<T>. You will see as an example a typical use of DLR Expression as a metaprogramming technique.

Listing 8-14 shows the Query<T> class. To be a class that represents LINQ queries, Query<T> must implement the IQueryable<T> interface. Of the property accessors and interface methods we must implement in order to implement the IQueryable<T> interface, the two most important ones are the Expression property get accessor and the Provider property get accessor. As mentioned previously, the Query<T> class represents queries as DLR expression trees. The Expression property is the evidence of that. The property holds a DLR expression that can have child expressions. Those child expressions can have child expressions, and so on. All together, the expressions form an expression tree that represents a query. As to the Provider property, it's there in Query<T> to decouple queries from the actual data store. It is the link between queries and the actual store.

Listing 8-14. The Query<T> Class

```
public class Query<T> : IQueryable<T>
{
    private IQueryProvider provider;
    private Expression expression;

    public Query(IQueryProvider provider)
    {
        this.provider = provider;
        this.expression = Expression.Constant(this);
    }

    public Query(IQueryProvider provider, Expression expression)
    {
        if (!typeof(IQueryable<T>).IsAssignableFrom(expression.Type))
            throw new ArgumentException("expression");

        this.provider = provider;
        this.expression = expression;
    }

    Expression IQueryable.Expression
    {
        get { return expression; }
    }

    Type IQueryable.ElementType
    {
        get { return typeof(T); }
    }

    IQueryProvider IQueryable.Provider
    {
        get { return provider; }
    }

    public IEnumerator<T> GetEnumerator()
```

```
    {
        return ((IEnumerable<T>)provider.Execute(expression)).GetEnumerator();
    }

    IEnumerator IEnumerable.GetEnumerator()
    {
        return ((IEnumerable)provider.Execute(expression)).GetEnumerator();
    }
}
```

Implementing the QueryProvider Class

Listing 8-15 shows the QueryProvider<T> class. To be a class that represents LINQ query providers, QueryProvider<T> must implement the IQueryProvider interface. The constructor of QueryProvider<T> takes a list of objects as input and assigns that list to the class member variable records. This variable represents the data store our custom query provider works against. I chose to use a list of objects as the data store for the sake of simplicity without losing any generality. Had I chosen a database as the data store, we would need to go through the extra work of setting up a database.

The IQueryProvider interface defines four methods and we implement all of them in QueryProvider<T>. The four methods are the two CreateQuery methods and the two Execute methods. Our implementation of the generic version of the CreateQuery method simply creates an instance of Query<T> and returns it. The non-generic version of the CreateQuery method is implemented to throw a NotImplementedException because the method is not needed in our example. The generic version of the Execute method delegates its work to the non-generic version of the Execute method, which is where the interesting things happen. The non-generic version of the Execute method takes an expression tree that represents a LINQ query as input and executes that query against the data store records. The expression tree that represents a LINQ query can be very complex and can contain expressions that represent where clauses, order-by clauses, group-by clauses, and so on. A practical implementation of the Execute method would need to be able to handle most of those different clauses. For the purpose of our example, it's enough to just handle the where clauses. In fact, all I want the query provider to be able to handle is the following query:

```
Query<Customer> customers = new Query<Customer>(provider);
from c in customers where c.FirstName.Equals("Bob") select c;
```

The variable provider in the query is an instance of QueryProvider<T>. The query uses the Customer class that we haven't introduced yet. But, basically, the query invokes our custom query provider to fetch customers whose first name is Bob. The query is constructed using the keywords from, in, where, and select that the C# language provides. Those keywords are just syntactic sugar over a set of underlying methods defined in the System.Linq.Queryable class. When the C# compiler sees those keywords, it translates them into calls to the underlying methods in System.Linq.Queryable. If we don't use the syntactic sugar, we can equivalently express our query with the following code:

```
Query<Customer> customers = new Query<Customer>(provider);
Queryable.Where<Customer>(customers, c => c.FirstName.Equals(firstName));
```

The return value of Queryable's Where<T> method is IQueryable<T>. The first input parameter of the Where<T> method is also of type IQueryable<T>. What the Where<T> does internally is very simple. It constructs a MethodCallExpression instance that represents a call to the Where<T> method. The MethodCallExpression instance has two input arguments that are made child expressions of the MethodCallExpression instance. The two input arguments are expressions that represent the first and second input parameters of the Where<T> method. After constructing the MethodCallExpression instance, the Where<T> method creates a new instance of Query<T>. Then it sets the new Query<T> instance's Expression property to the MethodCallExpression instance. Once you understand how our query is represented as a MethodCallExpression instance, it should be easy to understand why the non-generic version of the Execute method is implemented the way it is in Listing 8-15.

In the Execute method, we first check if the input expression that represents the query to execute is a MethodCallExpression. If so, we further check if the MethodCallExpression represents a call to the Where<T> method of the Queryable class. If that's not the case, then the query is outside the scope of what we want our custom query provider to support and therefore we throw a NotSupportedException. If the input expression parameter of the Execute method does represent a call to the Where<T> method of the Queryable class, we use an expression visitor to visit the MethodCallExpression and its descendant expressions. The expression visitor is an instance of QueryExpressionVisitor<T>, whose code is shown Listing 8-16. The expression visitor's job is to retrieve the lambda function that makes up the where clause of our query. In our query, that lambda function is c => c.FirstName.Equals(firstName) and it is stored as a descendant expression under the MethodCallExpression. Once the visitor retrieves the expression representing the lambda function, in line 39 of Listing 8-15 we get that expression from the visitor's Predicate property and use the expression to find matching objects in the class member variable records. Because the LINQ component of the .NET Framework comes with a LINQ query provider called LINQ to Objects for executing LINQ queries against IEnumerable<T> collections such as the class member variable records, line 39 simply uses the LINQ to Objects query provider to find the matching objects. This might strike you as a little absurd because we could have used the LINQ to Objects query provider directly without building a custom query provider that uses the LINQ to Objects provider internally. That's true, except that if we had used the LINQ to Objects query provider directly, I wouldn't be able to use our custom query provider as a typical example of how DLR Expression is used as a metaprogramming technique. Besides, you can think of this use of the LINQ to Objects provider as simplification of a more practical case where we would have more complex logic for querying the data store. Next, let's take a look at how to implement the QueryExpressionVisitor<T> class to retrieve the expression that represents the lambda function in a where clause.

Listing 8-15. The QueryProvider<T> Class

```
1)    public class QueryProvider<T> : IQueryProvider
2)    {
3)        private IList<T> records;
4)
5)        public QueryProvider(IList<T> records)
6)        {
7)            this. records = records;
8)        }
9)
10)       public IQueryable<T> CreateQuery<T>(Expression expression)
11)       {
12)           if (expression == null)
13)               return new Query<T>(this);
14)           else
15)               return new Query<T>(this, expression);
16)       }
17)
18)       public IQueryable CreateQuery(Expression expression)
19)       {
```

```
20)            throw new NotImplementedException();
21)        }
22)
23)        public TResult Execute<TResult>(Expression expression)
24)        {
25)            return (TResult)this.Execute(expression);
26)        }
27)
28)        public object Execute(Expression expression)
29)        {
30)            if (!(expression is MethodCallExpression))
31)                throw new NotSupportedException("The expression needs to be a
    MethodCallExpression");
32)
33)            MethodCallExpression methodCallExpression = (MethodCallExpression) expression;
34)            if (methodCallExpression.Method.DeclaringType == typeof(Queryable)
35)                && methodCallExpression.Method.Name == "Where")
36)            {
37)                QueryExpressionVisitor<T> visitor = new QueryExpressionVisitor<T>();
38)                visitor.Visit(methodCallExpression);
39)                return records.Where<T>(visitor.Predicate);
40)            }
41)            else
42)                throw new NotSupportedException(
43)                        "The expression needs to be a call to the Where method of
    Queryable");
44)        }
45) }
```

Implementing QueryExpressionVisitor

To qualify as a DLR expression visitor class, a class must derive from
System.Linq.Expressions.ExpressionVisitor. The class ExpressionVisitor defines methods for
different expression classes. A subclass of ExpressionVisitor will inherit those methods and override the
ones that it wants to provide custom logic for.

In the case of our example, QueryExpressionVisitor<T> overrides the VisitMethodCall method it
inherits from ExpressionVisitor. The overridden VisitMethodCall method will be called for every
MethodCallExpression node in the expression tree being traversed. Because the lambda expression we
want QueryExpressionVisitor<T> to retrieve is a child expression of a MethodCallExpression, we override
the VisitMethodCall method in QueryExpressionVisitor<T>. In the overridden VisitMethodCall
method, we check whether the method call expression node being visited represents a method call to
the Where<T> method of the Queryable class. If so, we proceed to get the second argument of the method
call expression because that second argument is the expression that represents the lambda function in a
where clause.

One little thing to be mindful of is that the lambda expression we want to retrieve might be wrapped
by unary expressions whose node type is ExpressionType.Quote. The reason for quoting a lambda
expression is so that when the quoted expression is compiled, it will compile into an expression instead
of a lambda function, as would be the case without the quoting. Because of the possible quoting of the
lambda expression, the code in Listing 8-16 uses a method called GetPastQuotes to get past the unary
expressions to the lambda expression we are interested in. When we get a hold of the lambda expression,

we assign it to the Predicate field of QueryExpressionVisitor<T> so that we can use it in the Execute method of QueryProvider<T>.

Listing 8-16. The QueryExpressionVisitor<T> Class

```
internal class QueryExpressionVisitor<T> : ExpressionVisitor
{
    public Func<T, bool> Predicate;

    internal QueryExpressionVisitor()
    { }

    protected override Expression VisitMethodCall(MethodCallExpression m)
    {
        if (m.Method.DeclaringType == typeof(Queryable) && m.Method.Name == "Where")
        {
            //The second argument of the method call expression is a lambda expression that serves
            //as the predicate for the 'Where' clause.
            LambdaExpression lambda = (LambdaExpression)GetPastQuotes(m.Arguments[1]);
            Predicate = (Func<T, bool>) lambda.Compile();
        }

        return base.VisitMethodCall(m);
    }

    private Expression GetPastQuotes(Expression expression)
    {
        while (expression.NodeType == ExpressionType.Quote)
            expression = ((UnaryExpression) expression).Operand;

        return expression;
    }
}
```

This section uses the implementation of a custom query provider to demonstrate the use of DLR Expression as a metaprogramming technique. We saw that queries written in code end up being represented by DLR expressions. This is the concept of code as data in action. The code in this case is the query code from c in customers where c.FirstName.Equals("Bob") select c; and the data is the MethodCallExpression and its descendant expressions that represent the query code. We also saw how the DLR expressions are interpreted and executed by a query provider. This is the concept of data as code in action. The data in this case is the DLR expressions and that data is used as code by our custom query provider. The code we write to interpret and execute DLR expressions is a metaprogram. The program that the metaprogram acts on is the code represented by the DLR expressions.

Data Access

Now that we have gone through the implementation of a custom query provider, I am going to show you three ways of using that query provider, as well as the pros and cons of each approach. At the end of this part of the chapter, you will arrive at a primitive code-generation prototype that is in spirit similar to frameworks like Ruby on Rails.

Before we start to look at the three different ways of using our custom query provider, there is some preparation work to do. First, let's define a Customer class like the one in Listing 8-17. The Customer class is straightforward. We will use it as the type of the objects we query.

Listing 8-17. The Customer Class for Trying Out Our Custom Query Provider

```
public class Customer
{
    public string FirstName { get; set; }
    public string LastName { get; set; }

    public override string ToString()
    {
        return FirstName + " " + LastName;
    }
}
```

Next we need some instances of the Customer class to serve as the data source of our LINQ queries. For that, let's create the DataStore class shown in Listing 8-18. The code in Listing 8-18 is pretty simple. It creates a list of Customer instances and uses that list to create an instance of QueryProvider<Customer> whenever the static GetQueryProvider method is called.

Listing 8-18. The DataStore Class That Contains the Data We Will Query Against

```
public class DataStore
{
    private static IList<Customer> customers = new List<Customer>(new Customer[] {
                        new Customer {FirstName="Bob", LastName="Smith"},
                        new Customer {FirstName="John", LastName="Smith"},
                        new Customer {FirstName="Bill", LastName="Jones"},
                        new Customer {FirstName="Mary", LastName="Jones"},
                        new Customer {FirstName="Bob", LastName="Jones"}});

    public static IQueryProvider GetCustomerQueryProvider()
    {
        return new QueryProvider<Customer>(customers);
    }
}
```

We have now completed the preparation work and we are ready to see the three ways to use our custom query provider. The first approach does not involve any late binding and therefore will be familiar to those who have worked with LINQ queries before. Let's take a look.

Static Data Access

Because this approach to using our custom query provider does not involve any late binding, I'll refer to it as the static data access approach. In the architecture of a software system, it is not uncommon to have a layer that handles data access. The responsibility of the data access layer is to (a) handle the interactions with data stores such as a database, and (b) decouple the rest of the software system from the specifics of the data stores. For the purpose of our example, let's imagine that we are building the data access layer of a software system. The data access layer will interact with our custom query provider. We want the data access layer to abstract away the fact that we are using a LINQ query provider so that if we ever need to swap out the LINQ query provider and replace it with, say, an object-relational mapping component like NHibernate, the rest of the software system can stay the same.

To achieve the data-access abstraction we want, we can define the interface ICustomerDao shown in Listing 8-19. The interface defines the signature of the FindByFirstName and FindByLastName methods and does not dictate what data store we should use in implementing the interface. We might have a concrete implementation of the ICustomerDao interface that uses a database as the backing data store. We might have another concrete implementation of the ICustomerDao interface that uses in-memory objects as the backing data store. Because the rest of our software system works with the data-store-agnostic ICustomerDao interface, we can swap out one concrete implementation and swap in another and the rest of our software system won't be affected.

Listing 8-19. The ICustomerDao Interface

```
public interface ICustomerDao
{
    IEnumerable<Customer> FindByFirstName(string firstName);
    IEnumerable<Customer> FindByLastName(string lastName);
}
```

Listing 8-20 shows the CustomerDao class that implements the ICustomerDao interface by using a LINQ query provider internally. As you can see, the implementation of the FindByFirstName method uses the from, where, in, and select C# language syntactic sugar to construct and return an instance of IQueryable<Customer> as an instance of IEnumerable<Customer>. This is okay because IQueryable<T> derives from the IEnumerable<T> interface. The implementation of the FindByLastName method is similar to that of the FindByFirstName method.

Listing 8-20. The CustomerDao Class

```
public class CustomerDao : ICustomerDao
{
    private IQueryProvider provider;

    public CustomerDao(IQueryProvider provider)
    {
        this.provider = provider;
    }

    public IEnumerable<Customer> FindByFirstName(string firstName)
    {
        return from c in provider.CreateQuery<Customer>(null)
                where c.FirstName.Equals(firstName)
            select c;
    }

    public IEnumerable<Customer> FindByLastName(string lastName)
    {
```

```
            return from c in provider.CreateQuery<Customer>(null)
                    where c.LastName.Equals(lastName)
                    select c;
    }
}
```

The code in the `CustomerDao` class does not run by itself. Listing 8-21 shows an example that creates an instance of `CustomerDao` and calls the `FindByFirstName` and `FindByLastName` methods on the instance. The example is pretty self-explanatory. One thing to note is that when `FindByFirstName` or `FindByLastName` returns an `IQueryable<Customer>` type cast as an `IEnumerable<Customer>` instance, the LINQ query represented by the `IEnumerable<Customer>` instance is not executed yet. The LINQ query is executed when the code in Listing 8-21 starts iterating through the `IEnumerable<Customer>` instance. This is because when that happens, the `GetEnumerator` method of the `Query` class will be called. If you look at the code in the `GetEnumerator` method of the `Query` class, you will see that there the LINQ query is executed by a query provider.

Listing 8-21. An Example of Using the CustomerDao Class

```
private static void RunCustomerDaoExample()
{
    CustomerDao customerDao = new CustomerDao(DataStore.GetCustomerQueryProvider());
    IEnumerable<Customer> customers = customerDao.FindByFirstName("Bob");

    foreach (var item in customers)
        Console.WriteLine(item);

    customers = customerDao.FindByLastName("Jones");

    foreach (var item in customers)
        Console.WriteLine(item);
}
```

Even though the `ICustomerDao` interface and the `CustomerDao` class provide a nice abstraction of the underlying data access details to the rest of our software system, one downside of this approach is the amount of boilerplate code we need to write. For each property, such as `FirstName` in the `Customer` class, we need to define a method like `FindByFirstName` method in `ICustomerDao` and implement that method in `CustomerDao`. It would be nice if we could freely define properties like `FirstName` and `LastName` in `Customer` and the rest of the data access code, such as the `FindByFirstName` and `FindByLastName` methods, would just be there automatically. Well, that's what our next approach is going to do.

Dynamic Data Access

Let's look at the second approach for using our custom query provider in the data access layer. In this approach, we will leverage the metaprogramming facilities made possible by DLR Expression and dynamic objects so that methods like `FindByFirstName` and `FindByLastName` don't need to be manually coded. Because the approach we are going to look at uses the late-binding capability of the DLR, I'll refer to it as the dynamic data access approach. Listing 8-22 shows the data access layer class, `DynamicDao<T>`, that has the logic for responding to invocations of the `FindByFirstName` and `FindByLastName` methods, without us needing to write those methods manually. The idea of the dynamic data access approach is that we don't define and implement methods like `FindbyFirstName` and `FindByLastName` in

DynamicDao<T>. Instead we make DynamicDao<T> a subclass of DynamicObject. So when the methods FindbyFirstName and FindByLastName are invoked on an instance of DynamicDao<T>, the TryInvokeMember method of DynamicDao<T> will be invoked to handle the late binding of those method invocations. In the body of the TryInvokeMember method, we implement the late-binding logic in such a way that if the method invoked is FindByFirstName or FindByLastName, we return an IQueryable<Customer> instance. The IQueryable<Customer> instance when executed will return only customers whose first name (or last name) matches the queried first name (or last name).

In Listing 8-22, the code in the TryInvokeMember method first gets the invoked method name from the Name property of the binder parameter. If the invoked method is FindByFirstName, the Name property of the binder parameter will be the string "FindByFirstName". So we strip out "FindBy" and obtain the property name "FirstName". If the invoked method is FindByFirstName, we want the TryInvokeMember method to return as the result an IQueryable<Customer> instance equivalent to the IQueryable<Customer> instance returned by the FindByFirstName method of the CustomerDao class we saw in the previous section. The bulk of the code in the TryInvokeMember method is to construct a DLR expression that represents the predicate lambda function to use in the where clause of the query object we aim to construct. The predicate lambda function expressed in C# code will look something like this:

```
(T x) => x.[propertyName].Equals(arg);
```

In this C# code, if the TryInvokeMember function is invoked to find customers whose first name is "Bob", then T will be the type Customer, [propertyName] will be FirstName and arg will be "Bob". The predicate lambda function in C# maps very nicely to the predicate expression we try to construct in Listing 8-22. The x.[propertyName] part in the C# lambda function above is a property member access and it maps to the Expression.MakeMemberAccess method call in line 18. In the body of the C# lambda function, the call to the Equals method maps to the Expression.Call method call in line 17. The whole C# lambda function maps to the Expression.Lambda method call in line 16. The C# lambda function has one input parameter x, which maps to the parameter variable created in line 14.

Once the predicate expression is constructed, we pass it as the input parameter to the Where<T> method call in line 26 so that the query we return as the late-binding result will have a where clause with the desired predicate for matching customers.

Listing 8-22. The DynamicDao<T> Class

```
1)   public class DynamicDao<T> : DynamicObject
2)   {
3)       private IQueryProvider provider;
4)
5)       public DynamicDao(IQueryProvider provider)
6)       {
7)           this.provider = provider;
8)       }
9)
10)      public override bool TryInvokeMember(InvokeMemberBinder binder, object[] args,
11)          out object result)
12)      {
13)          String propertyName = binder.Name.Substring(6); //6 is the length of 'FindBy'
14)          ParameterExpression parameter = Expression.Parameter(typeof(T));
15)          PropertyInfo propertyInfo = typeof(T).GetProperty(propertyName);
16)          Expression<Func<T, bool>> predicate = Expression.Lambda<Func<T, bool>>(
17)              Expression.Call(
```

```
18)                    Expression.MakeMemberAccess(
19)                        parameter,
20)                        propertyInfo),
21)                    propertyInfo.PropertyType.GetMethod("Equals", new Type[]
    {typeof(object)}),
22)                    Expression.Constant(args[0])),
23)                parameter);
24)
25)        Query<T> query = new Query<T>(provider);
26)        result = query.Where<T>(predicate);
27)        return true;
28)    }
29) }
```

Listing 8-23 shows an example that creates an instance of DynamicDao<Customer> and calls the FindByFirstName and FindByLastName methods on the instance. You can run the code and verify that everything works as expected.

Listing 8-23. An Example of Using the DynamicDao<T> Class

```
private static void RunDynamicDaoExample()
{
    dynamic customerDao = new DynamicDao<Customer>(DataStore.GetCustomerQueryProvider());
    IEnumerable<Customer> customers = customerDao.FindByFirstName("Bob");

    foreach (var item in customers)
        Console.WriteLine(item);

    customers = customerDao.FindByLastName("Jones");

    foreach (var item in customers)
        Console.WriteLine(item);
}
```

The dynamic data access approach shown in this section frees us from having to define and implement methods like FindByFirstName and FindByLastName for each property in the Customer class. However, the code in the TryInvokeMember method of DynamicDao<T> looks pretty ad hoc to me. The code works for our simple example, but in practical cases, we could have different kinds of methods than the "FindBy" methods we want to bind late. If we handle those practical cases the way we do in DynamicDao<T>, we will have to parse those different kinds of method names and use those names to guide the program's execution path. We would need to refactor the code in DynamicDao<T> substantially so that we don't put all the late-binding logic in the TryInvokeMember method. Essentially, the problem with DynamicDao<T> as it is implemented is the lack of a well-structured mechanism for routing a method invocation to the right late-binding logic. One way to amend the issue is to refactor the code in DynamicDao<T>. Another way is to leverage the ClassMetaObject and ExpandoClass classes we built earlier in this chapter. The next section shows how to do that.

Generated Data Access

We will now show the third approach for using our custom query provider in the data access layer. In this approach, we will leverage the metaprogramming features of the ClassMetaObject and ExpandoClass classes we built earlier so that we have a well-structured mechanism for routing a method invocation to the right late-binding logic. The idea of this approach is to generate methods like FindByFirstName and FindByLastName at runtime and add those methods to a data access layer class. With this approach, we no longer need to parse method names and use those names to pick the right late-binding logic, as we did in the DynamicDao<T> class. Because the approach demonstrated in this section is based on the concept of code generation, I will refer to it as the generated data access approach.

Listing 8-24 shows the class GeneratedDao<T> to which we will add the FindByFirstName and FindByLastName methods. The code in Listing 8-24 might look complicated at first, but it's actually quite simple once you understand the code structure. First, the class GeneratedDao<T> derives from ClassMetaObject. That means we can add new methods to GeneratedDao<T> at the class level or instance level. New methods added to GeneratedDao<T> at the class level are added to the static _class variable. Our goal is to add a "FindBy" method for each property in type T to GeneratedDao<T> at the class level. To achieve that, in Listing 8-24 we define the AddMethods method that loops through all the properties of T and calls the AddMethodForProperty method for each property. AddMethodForProperty calls the CreateNewMethodExpression method to get an expression that represents the new method to be added for a property. Using FindByFirstName as an example, the expression returned by CreateNewMethodExpression when compiled will be equivalent to the following C# code:

```
Func<String, IEnumerable<Customer>> FindByFirstName =
    (firstName) =>
    {
        IQueryable<Customer> query = provider.CreateQuery<Customer>(null);
        return query.Where(c => c.FirstName.Equals(firstName));
    };
```

The equivalent C# code is the same as the FindByFirstName method we saw in CustomerDao. Here we are just implementing the same method in terms of DLR expressions. The CreateNewMethodExpression method internally calls the GetWhereMethodInfo method to get a System.Reflection.MethodInfo instance for the Where method of the Queryable class. CreateNewMethodExpression calls the CreatePredicateExpression to get the expression that represents the predicate (the c => c.FirstName.Equals(firstName) in the above code snippet) in the query's where clause. Once AddMethodForProperty gets the lambda expression returned by the CreateNewMethodExpression method, it constructs an expression that adds the lambda expression as a new method to _class by calling the TrySetMember method on _class.

Listing 8-24. The GeneratedDao<T> Class

```
public class GeneratedDao<T> : ClassMetaObject
{
    private static ExpandoClass _class = new ExpandoClass();

    protected override ExpandoClass Class
    {
        get { return _class; }
    }

    private IQueryProvider provider;
    private MethodInfo whereMethod = null;

    public GeneratedDao(IQueryProvider provider)
```

```
        {
            this.provider = provider;
            AddMethods();
        }

        private void AddMethods()
        {
            PropertyInfo[] properties = typeof(T).GetProperties();
            foreach (PropertyInfo propertyInfo in properties)
                AddMethodForProperty(propertyInfo);
        }

        private void AddMethodForProperty(PropertyInfo propertyInfo)
        {
            LambdaExpression newMethod = CreateNewMethodExpression(propertyInfo);

            SetMemberBinder binder = new SimpleSetMemberBinder("FindBy" + propertyInfo.Name,
    false);
            Expression addMethodExpression = Expression.Call(
                Expression.Constant(_class),
                _class.GetType().GetMethod("TrySetMember"),
                Expression.Constant(binder), newMethod
            );

            Func<bool> func = Expression.Lambda<Func<bool>>(addMethodExpression).Compile();
            func();
        }

        private Expression<Func<T, bool>> CreatePredicateExpression(
            PropertyInfo propertyInfo, ParameterExpression argExpression)
        {
            //predicate = (T x) =>
            //{
            //    x.propertyName.Equals(arg);
            //}

            ParameterExpression parameter = Expression.Parameter(typeof(T));
            return Expression.Lambda<Func<T, bool>>(
                Expression.Call(
                    Expression.MakeMemberAccess(
                        parameter,
                        propertyInfo),
                    propertyInfo.PropertyType.GetMethod("Equals", new Type[] { typeof(object) }),
                    argExpression),
                parameter);
        }

        private MethodInfo GetWhereMethodInfo()
        {
            if (whereMethod != null)
                return whereMethod;
```

```
        MethodInfo[] allMethods = typeof(Queryable).GetMethods(
        BindingFlags.Public | BindingFlags.Static);
        foreach (var method in allMethods)
        {
            if (method.Name.Equals("Where"))
            {
                ParameterInfo[] parameters = method.GetParameters();
                Type[] genericTypes = parameters[1].ParameterType.GetGenericArguments();
                if (genericTypes[0].GetGenericArguments().Length == 2)
                    whereMethod = method;
            }
        }

        whereMethod = whereMethod.MakeGenericMethod(new Type[] { typeof(T) });
        return whereMethod;
    }

    private LambdaExpression CreateNewMethodExpression(PropertyInfo propertyInfo)
    {
        ParameterExpression argExpression = Expression.Parameter(propertyInfo.PropertyType);
        Expression<Func<T, bool>> predicate = CreatePredicateExpression(propertyInfo,
argExpression);

        //provider.CreateQuery<Customer>(null);
        Expression queryExpression = Expression.Call(
            Expression.Constant(provider), "CreateQuery",
            new Type[] { typeof(T) }, Expression.Constant(null, typeof(Expression)));

        //query.Where(c => c.FirstName.Equals(firstName));
        Expression body = Expression.Call(null,
            GetWhereMethodInfo(), queryExpression,
            predicate);

        return Expression.Lambda(body, argExpression);
    }
}
```

To try out the GeneratedDao<T> class, you can run the code in Listing 8-25. This code creates an instance of GeneratedDao<Customer> and calls the FindByFirstName and FindByLastName methods on the instance.

Listing 8-25. An Example of Using the GeneratedDao<T> Class

```
private static void RunGeneratedDaoExample()
{
    dynamic customerDao = new GeneratedDao<Customer>(DataStore.GetCustomerQueryProvider());

    IEnumerable<Customer> customers = customerDao.FindByFirstName("Bob");
    foreach (var item in customers)
        Console.WriteLine(item);
```

```
    customers = customerDao.FindByLastName("Jones");
    foreach (var item in customers)
        Console.WriteLine(item);
}
```

Summary

This chapter gives an overview of metaprogramming and then shows some exciting ways you can use metaprogramming in your .NET applications. Thanks to the DLR, your applications don't need to use dynamic languages in order to benefit from the metaprogramming techniques traditionally available only in dynamic languages. In particular, this chapter implements two classes, `ClassMetaObject` and `ExpandoClass`, that serve as the foundation of other marvelous applications of metaprogramming. As an example of the wonderful things you can do with `ClassMetaObject` and `ExpandoClass`, we use those classes in building a code-generation framework that is in spirit similar to frameworks such as the popular Ruby on Rails. Because the code-generation framework is just an example, it omits a lot of details and shows only the concept. Though I can't promise, I have plans in my mind to continue the development of the code-generation example shown in this chapter, and to experiment with model-driven development and domain-specific language development with it. You are welcome to head over the dpier project web site at `http://code.google.com/p/dpier/` and check out the progress.

■ ■ ■

## CHAPTER 9

Stitch — A DSL for Hosting Languages

Back in Chapter 6, we looked at the DLR Hosting API. In that chapter, we saw that the Hosting API provides a uniform way for a host language like C# to embed languages like IronPython and IronRuby. Although the Hosting API provides a good layer of abstraction between host and hosted languages, there's still room for pushing the level of abstraction even higher—and that's the topic of this chapter. We'll go through the design and implementation of a domain specific language (DSL) called Stitch that I developed for language hosting. Using Stitch, we can host not just DLR-based languages but also languages like Windows PowerShell—uniformly and declaratively. The set of languages Stitch is capable of hosting is extensible. Moreover, the runtime of the Stitch language provides execution modes for running code sequentially or in parallel.

The Stitch language is so named because it is built to make it easy and painless to stitch together other languages. It's a DSL, not a general purpose language, because it is designed to solve only the issues encountered in language hosting and nothing else.

The Need for Stitch

In Chapter 6, we saw examples like the one in Listing 9-1 that use the DLR Hosting API to host IronPython code in C#. The nice thing about these examples is that if we change the language we're hosting from IronPython to IronRuby, we don't need to code against a different hosting API. Our code will still use the `ScriptRuntime` class to get an instance of `ScriptEngine`. It will still use an instance of the `ScriptScope` to pass information to the IronRuby code.

Listing 9-1. Uusing the DLR Hosting API to Host IronPython Code

```
ScriptEngine engine = ScriptRuntime.CreateFromConfiguration().GetEngine("python");
ScriptSource source = engine.CreateScriptSourceFromFile(@"Python\simple1.py");

ScriptScope scope = engine.CreateScope();
scope.SetVariable("x", 2);
scope.SetVariable("y", 3);

CompiledCode compiledCode = source.Compile();
compiledCode.Execute(scope);
```

Although the DLR Hosting API provides a language-agnostic API for hosting multiple languages, there are some issues in the Listing 9-1 code, as the following list describes.

The DLR Hosting API is imperative: It's very imperative because the code we write instructs how to run IronRuby or IronPython code by creating instances of `ScriptRuntime` and `ScriptEngine`, calling methods on those instances, fishing out objects from script scopes, and so on and so forth. Instead of doing all of this, it would be nice if we could be declarative and avoid having to tell the Hosting API *how* to execute IronPython or IronRuby code every step of the way.

The DLR Hosting API is platform-dependent: The code examples we saw in Chapter 6 can run only on .NET using the DLR runtime. The Hosting API can't be used to run the same Python, Ruby or other dynamic language scripts on a different platform, such as the JVM. It would be nice if we could write the code once and run it on different platforms.

The DLR Hosting API serves only DLR-based languages: It can't host languages such as PowerShell, Ant, Maven, etc. Developers still need to know how to use PowerShell from IronPython or how to use IronPython from PowerShell, or how to use PowerShell from Ruby or vice versa. We don't want to learn the different ways of using one language within another. We want a generic approach that works for all scenarios.

The DLR Hosting API provides no high level support for parallel execution of scripts: We can use Parallel Extensions. But it would be nice if there were a higher level of abstraction for hosting languages.

The design goal of the Stitch DSL is to address these four issues. Let's see the solution Stitch provides.

Syntax of the Stitch Language

Let's look at the Stitch language syntax now and see how it addresses the four issues we just mentioned. When I started out designing Stitch's syntax, I wrote down something like this:

```
<Python>
… Python code…

<Ruby>
… Ruby code…
```

The syntax prototype uses `<Python>` to introduce a block of Python code and `<Ruby>` a block of Ruby code. With the syntax prototype, you can stitch together multiple pieces of Python code and Ruby code in any order you like. The syntax is declarative because it does not specify *how* to run the Python or Ruby code. It only indicates which block is Python code and which block is Ruby code. With this syntax prototype, how to run the Python and Ruby code becomes the job of the Stitch language runtime, not the job of developers who write Stitch code.

The syntax prototype is not only declarative, it's also platform-independent. It's not tied to anything .NET or DLR-specific. If we implement a Stitch runtime that runs on the Java virtual machine, then any Stitch code we write can also run on the Java virtual machine.

To run code written in languages that are not DLR-based, such as PowerShell, I extended the syntax prototype to something like the following:

```
<Python>
… Python code…
```

```
<Ruby>
… Ruby code…

<PowerShell>
… PowerShell code…
```

So far, everything seems pretty simple. The devil, of course, is in the details. The different language code snippets we stitch together are not islands. To do interesting things, they often need to send information to each other like this:

```
<Python>
x = 5
z = 3

<Ruby>
y = x + 2
```

This syntax prototype conveys the idea that the variables x and z defined in the Python code are accessible to the Ruby code that follows. The syntax looks good except for a couple of issues. First, the Ruby code has a dependency on the Python code because it uses the variable x from the Python code. The dependency is not very explicit. To find the dependency, we have to scan through all the lines of code and analyze them. Another issue with the syntax prototype is that the variable z in the Python is accessible to but not used in the Ruby code. This is not desirable because the Ruby code might unknowingly define a variable by the same name z and accidentally change the value of the Python variable z. To solve those two issues, I changed the syntax prototype to something like this:

```
<Python()>
x = 5
z = 3
<return(x, z)>

<Ruby(x)>
y = x + 2
<return()>
```

This syntax prototype basically says that the Python code takes no input parameters and returns x and z as results. The Ruby code takes x as an input parameter and returns no results. With this syntax, the variable z defined in the Python code will not be accessible to the Ruby code because the Ruby code does not declare z to be its input parameter. The syntax also makes the dependency between the Ruby code and Python code explicit. To find the dependency, we only need to see which variables the Python code returns and which input parameters the Ruby code requires. Once the dependencies between different language code snippets are explicit, the Stitch language runtime can easily tell which code snippets can run in parallel. For example, if the Ruby code did not require the variable x as an input parameter, the Stitch runtime would detect no dependency between the Ruby code and the Python code and it would therefore run the two code snippets in parallel.

At this point, the design of Stitch's syntax solves all of the four issues I set out to address. One last thing I want to do is to make the syntax look as natural as possible to developers who write Stitch code. To that end, I changed the syntax to something like this:

```
<foo () Python>
x = 5
```

```
<return(x)>

<bar () include baz.py>
<return(y)>
```

Instead of `<Python()>`, the new syntax uses `<foo () Python>`. The word `foo` is a unique identifier we attribute to a language code snippet. The language name Python is moved from before the input parameter list to after the list. This change makes the syntax look more like a C# method definition. In Stitch terms, a language code block is called a *function*. In the previous code example, there are two functions—`foo` and `bar`. The `foo` function is a Python code block that takes no input parameters and returns the variable x as the result. The `bar` function is a Python code block that takes no input parameters and returns the variable y as the result. Another change is the new `include` syntax keyword for including code from a file. In the example above, the `include` keyword will include the code in the file baz.py. The Stitch code example declares that the code in baz.py takes no input parameters and returns the variable y as result. When using the `include` keyword, we don't need to specify which language the included code is written in because the file extension of baz.py already indicates that the language is Python.

That's all for the syntax of the Stitch language. Next I'll explain how to set up the software components required for running the code examples in this chapter. After that, we'll look at four examples of Stitch code that demonstrate the core features of the Stitch language.

Requirements for the Example

To follow along with the code examples in this chapter, you'll need to install some software. You'll also need to understand how I've organized the code for this chapter in the example download for this book.

Software Requirements

To follow along this chapter's code examples, you'll need to download and install Windows PowerShell and the C# runtime of ANTLR. Here's what to do:

1. Download and install PowerShell. The version I use is 1.0. Instructions for downloading are available from: www.microsoft.com/windowsserver2003/technologies/management/power shell/download.mspx.

2. Download the C# runtime of ANTLR from www.antlr.org/download/CSharp. The file I downloaded is DOT-NET-runtime-3.1.3.zip. Unzip the file into C:\ProDLR\lib\Antlr.

After completing these steps, you should have the following two assemblies on your hard disk:

- C:\ProDLR\lib\Antlr\bin\net-2.0\Antlr3.Runtime.dll

- C:\Program Files\Reference Assemblies\Microsoft\WindowsPowerShell\v1.0\System.Management.Automatio n.dll

These will be the only assemblies you need for the examples in this chapter.

Organization of the Code

The code for this chapter is organized into four projects:

The Eclipse Stitch project—this project has only a file called Stitch.g. The file defines the grammar of the Stitch language. I wrote the grammar definitions in the ANTLR grammar language and used ANTLR to generate the lexer and parser (in C# code) for Stitch. ANTLR is a popular software component for defining language grammars and for generating lexers and parsers. The lexer and parser generated by the grammar file are put into the C# Stitch project.

The C# Stitch project—this project has the implementation of the Stitch language's runtime as well as Stitch's language plug-in framework.

The PowerShellStitchPlugin project—this project implements the Stitch language plug-in for the PowerShell language.

The StitchDemoApplication project—this project is the client program that hooks up the PowerShell plug-in with the Stitch language runtime. The project contains the test Stitch scripts you saw earlier in this chapter.

In the sections that follow, we will begin to explore the Stitch language implementation by first looking at some examples of how Stitch is used. Then we'll look at the language grammar. After that, we'll examine the language plug-in framework and the core Stitch language runtime.

Stitch in Use

Now that you've set up the required software components for this chapter, let's run some examples to get a feel for Stitch's language features. We are going to look at four examples. In this chapter's Visual Studio solution, you'll find the code for all four examples in the Scripts folder of the StitchDemoApplication project. The first example, testScript1.st, demonstrates the declarative aspect of the Stitch language. The second example, testScript2.st, shows that Stitch is capable of hosting non-DLR based languages. The third example, testScript3.st, shows that Stitch scripts can be hosted within other Stitch scripts. The fourth example, testScript4.st, hosts several Python scripts and executes them both sequentially and in parallel. Let's begin.

Being Declarative

Stitch is a declarative language, not an imperative one. When writing Stitch code, you express *what* you want to get done, not *how* you want it to get done. Listing 9-2 shows the code for our first Stitch example, which demonstrates the declarative nature of the Stitch language. The code consists of three Stitch functions—arithmetic, addition, and calculation. The arithmetic function is a Python code block that defines the myadd Python function. The addition function includes the add3.py script file. If you open add3.py, you'll see that it has only one line of Python code that defines a function called add3: def add3(x): return x + 3. The calculation function takes the myadd and add3 functions as input and uses them to do some simple calculations. As you can see, the code in Listing 9-2 is declarative, exactly what I want to demonstrate.

Listing 9-2. A Stitch Script Showing Stitch's Declarative Nature

```
1)   <arithmetic () Python>
2)   def myadd(x, y): return x + y
3)   <return(myadd)>
4)
5)   <addition () include Scripts\\add3.py>
6)   <return(add3)>
```

```
7)
8)   <calculation (myadd, add3) Ruby>
9)   puts myadd.call(5, 2)
10)  puts add3.call(2)
11)  <return()>
```

To run the code in Listing 9-2, you can use the C# code in Listing 9-3, which you'll find in the Program.cs file of the StitchDemoApplication project. The C# code creates an instance of the StitchScriptEngine class and tells the Stitch script engine that we want to run the Stitch code in the sequential mode. Later in this chapter, we'll see the different modes for executing Stitch code and how they are implemented. In Listing 9-3, the code passes a PowerShellPlugin instance to the constructor of StitchScriptEngine so that the Stitch script knows how to stitch PowerShell code with other language code blocks. Later in the chapter we'll see the plug-in framework of the Stitch language and how you can use it to add support for new languages into Stitch. When you run the code in Listing 9-3, you'll see two numbers, 7 and 5, printed on the screen.

Listing 9-3. The C# Program That Runs the Stitch Code in testScript1.st

```
private static void RunTestScript1()
{
    StitchScriptEngine engine = new StitchScriptEngine(
        ExecutionMode.Sequential, new ILanguagePlugin[] { new PowerShellPlugin() });

    engine.RunScriptFile(@"Scripts\testScript1.st");
}
```

Hosting DLR- and Non-DLR-Based Languages

Unlike the DLR Hosting API, the Stitch language allows you to host both DLR and non-DLR-based languages. The code in Listing 9-4 shows a Stitch example that hosts a PowerShell code block and a Python code block. The PowerShell code block is the function called getServiceA. It contains one line of PowerShell code that returns all Windows services whose name begins with "A". The Python code block is the printServiceA function, which takes the Windows services returned by the getServiceA function and prints the names of those Windows services to the screen.

As in the previous example, we will use some C# code to run the Stitch script in Listing 9-4. Since the C# code is almost the same as the code in Listing 9-3, I won't show it here, but you can find it in the RunTestScript2 method inside the Program.cs file of the StitchDemoApplication project. When you run the code, you'll see the names of the Windows services that are installed on your machine whose name begins with "A".

Listing 9-4. Stitching Together a PowerShell Script and a Python Script

```
<getServiceA () PowerShell>
get-service A*
<return(serviceAList)>

<printServiceA (serviceAList) Python>
for item in serviceAList:
  print item.Members["ServiceName"].Value
<return()>
```

Hosting Stitch Itself

When we stitch pieces of cloth into larger pieces, it seems perfectly natural that we can further stitch those larger pieces into even larger pieces. The Stitch language allows us to stitch code just as we'd stitch pieces of cloth. The code in Listing 9-5 shows a Stitch example that stitches the two Stitch scripts, testScript1.st and testScript2.st, from the previous two sections.

To run the code in Listing 9-5, you can use the C# code in the RunTestScript3 method inside the Program.cs file of the StitchDemoApplication project. When you run the code, you'll see the combined results of the previous two examples printed on the screen.

Listing 9-5. Hosting Two Stitch Scripts in a Larger Stitch Script

```
<addition () include Scripts\\testScript1.st>
<return()>

<addition () include Scripts\\testScript2.st>
<return()>
```

Executing in Parallel

The Stitch language runtime provides execution modes for running Stitch code in either a sequential manner or in parallel. Later in this chapter, you will see that the implementation of the Stitch language runtime uses .NET Parallel Extension to run Stitch code in parallel. For now, let's just see an example that shows the parallel execution feature of Stitch in action. The code in Listing 9-6 has three Stitch functions—task1, task2, and task3. Each of the functions consists of a block of Python code that prints a message to the screen and calls Thread.SpinWait to simulate some busy work. The three Stitch functions don't have any dependency among them and therefore are perfectly ideal for parallel execution.

Listing 9-6. Three Python Scripts with no Dependency among Themselves

```
<task1 () Python>
import clr
from System.Threading import Thread
print "Task1 runs on thread id " + Thread.CurrentThread.ManagedThreadId.ToString()
Thread.SpinWait(1000000000)
<return()>

<task2 () Python>
import clr
from System.Threading import Thread
print "Task2 runs on thread id " + Thread.CurrentThread.ManagedThreadId.ToString()
Thread.SpinWait(1000000000)
<return()>

<task3 () Python>
import clr
from System.Threading import Thread
print "Task3 runs on thread id " + Thread.CurrentThread.ManagedThreadId.ToString()
Thread.SpinWait(1000000000)
<return()>
```

The C# code in Listing 9-7 runs the Stitch script in Listing 9-6 twice, first in a sequential manner and then in a parallel manner. To run a Stitch script sequentially, you specify the execution mode to be ExecutionMode.Sequential when you create the StitchScriptEngine instance. To run a Stitch script in parallel, you specify the execution mode to be either ExecutionMode.ParallelNoWait or ExecutionModel.ParallelWaitAll. If you specify ExecutionMode.ParallelNoWait, the thread executing the RunTestScript4 method will continue to run without waiting for the three Stitch functions in Listing 9-6 to finish. On the other hand, if you specify ExecutionMode.ParallelWaitAll, the thread executing the RunTestScript4 method will be suspended until all three of the Stitch functions complete. We will see the implementation details of the three execution modes later in the chapter. If you run the code in Listing 9-7 on a multi-core CPU machine, you'll see that in the first run of testScript4.st, all of the three Stitch functions task1, task2, and task3 run on the same thread (the same thread id is printed on the screen). The second run of the Stitch script is much faster as the three Stitch functions run on different threads (different thread ids are printed on the screen).

Listing 9-7. Using the Stitch Runtime to Run Stitch Code Sequentially and in Parallel

```csharp
private static void RunTestScript4()
{
    StitchScriptEngine engine = new StitchScriptEngine(
            ExecutionMode.Sequential, new ILanguagePlugin[] { new PowerShellPlugin() });

    Stopwatch stopwatch = Stopwatch.StartNew();
    engine.RunScriptFile(@"Scripts\testScript4.st");
    stopwatch.Stop();

    Console.WriteLine("Sequential runner takes {0} milliseconds.",
        stopwatch.ElapsedMilliseconds);

    engine = new StitchScriptEngine(
            ExecutionMode.ParallelWaitAll, new ILanguagePlugin[] { new PowerShellPlugin() });

    stopwatch = Stopwatch.StartNew();
    engine.RunScriptFile(@"Scripts\testScript4.st");
    stopwatch.Stop();

    Console.WriteLine("Parallel runner takes {0} milliseconds.",
        stopwatch.ElapsedMilliseconds);
}
```

Stitch Language Grammar

We saw the Stitch language syntax in the "Syntax of the Stitch Language" section. Now we are going to formally define the grammar of the Stitch syntax and use the grammar to generate the lexer and parser for the Stitch language. Because I wrote the grammar in the ANTLR grammar language and used Eclipse as the IDE for writing the grammar, if you want to follow along this part of the Stitch language implementation, you'll need to set up some software components. ANTLR is a popular lexer/parser generator and more. There are many lexer/parser generators out there and people often prefer certain ones over others. Because of that and also because I want to keep this chapter's focus on the DLR Hosting API, I won't dive too deeply into how ANTLR works. A fair coverage of a lexer/parser generator can easily grow into several chapters and that's really beyond the scope of what I'm aiming to cover here.

If you want, you can completely skip all the ANTLR-related parts and simply take the generated lexer/parser C# code as given. For those who would like to follow this chapter's code from the very beginning, I'll describe the software components you need to install.

Setting Up Eclipse and ANTLR

I used the following software components to develop the ANTLR-based grammar for the Stitch language.

- Java Development Kit (JDK) 6.

- Eclipse 3.6.0.

- ANTLR 3.2

- ANTLR IDE 2.1.0

You should already have Java and Eclipse installed, or know how to get them. Here are the steps to follow to install the two ANTLR components:

1. Download the complete ANTLR 3.2 jar file (antlr-3.2.jar) from www.antlr.org and place it in the C:\antlr-3.2\lib folder. If you put it in a different folder, you'll need to substitute the file path with your own when I refer to C:\antlr-3.2.

2. Install ANTLR IDE 2.1.0 and its prerequisites. You can download it from the ANTLR IDE project web site at http://antlrv3ide.sourceforge.net/. According to the download page of the web site, ANTLR IDE 2.1.0 requires GEF 3.6.0 or above, Zest 1.2.0 or above, and Dynamic Language Toolkit (DLTK) Core 2.0.0.

After you've downloaded and installed all of these components, you need to set them up properly by configuring the Eclipse IDE to use the ANTLR 3.2 jar file. To do so, launch Eclipse and select Window->Preferences in the menu. In the Preferences dialog that pops up, expand the ANTLR node in the tree on the left and select the Builder node under the ANTLR node. In the right panel, click the Add... button and you'll see a dialog like the one in Figure 9-1. All of the fields in the second dialog will be blank at this point, because you haven't told Eclipse about the ANTLR 3.2 jar file you want to use. In the second dialog, click the Directory... button and another dialog will pop up. Select C:\antlr-3.2 as the folder and click OK. At this point, you should see something that what's shown in Figure 9-1.

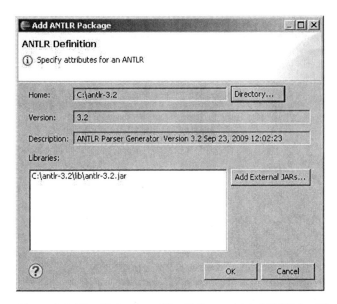

Figure 9-1. The dialog for telling Eclipse which ANTLR.jar file to use

Once you've told Eclipse which ANTLR jar file to use, you can write ANTLR-based language grammars. For the Stitch language, I created a Java project called Stitch in Eclipse, then I converted the project into an ANTLR project. To do that, right-click on the Stitch project in Eclipse and select Configure->Convert to ANTLR Project… in the context menu. With the Stitch project in place, the next step is to create a grammar file.

Defining the Grammar

To create a grammar file, right-click on the src folder in the Stitch project and select New->Other… in the context menu. A dialog will pop up. This is the wizard for creating a new file in Eclipse. The first step is to select the type of file you want to create, in this case an ANTLR combined grammar file as shown in Figure 9-2.

Figure 9-2. The Eclipse new-file creation wizard

Click Next and select CSharp2 as the language. This causes ANTLR to generate the lexer/parser code in C# later. Name the grammar file Stitch.g. Once Stitch.g is created, open it in the Eclipse IDE and paste the contents of C:\ProDLR\src\Examples\Chapter9\Eclipse\Stitch\src\Stitch.g into the Stitch.g file you just created. The code you pasted is the ANTLR-based grammar that defines the syntax of the Stitch language. Listing 9-8 shows an abbreviated version of this code. A detailed explanation of the grammar is beyond the scope of this chapter, so I'll only explain the code briefly.

Stitch.g contains what is known as a context-free grammar. Context-free grammars are mathematically well-defined and explored, with the same level of expressiveness as the pushdown automata. If you want to learn more about the theoretical foundation of context-free grammars and pushdown automata, you can refer to books about automata theory or compiler construction. To learn more about ANTLR in particular, I recommend the books written by Terence Parr, the creator of ANTLR.

Listing 9-8. The Grammar Definition of the Stitch DSL

```
1)   grammar Stitch;
2)
3)   options {
4)     language = CSharp2;
5)   }
6)
7)   @header {
8)   using System.Collections.Generic;
9)   using Stitch.Ast;
```

```
10)  }
11)
12)  @namespace { Stitch }
13)
14)  //program rule
15)  //func rule
16)  //parameters rule
17)  //funcCode
18)  //include
19)  //CODEBLOCK : '>' .* '<';
20)
21)  ... other rules omitted ...
```

Before we look more closely at the code in Listing 9-8, let's briefly go over what a context-free grammar is made up of. It consists of production rules, each of which has a left-hand side and a right-hand side. In ANTLR's notation, a rule's left-hand side and right-hand side are separated by a colon and therefore look like this:

```
A : B C
```

In this example, A is the left-hand side of a production rule and it's called a non-terminal. B C is the right-hand side, and B or C can be non-terminals or terminals. The difference between terminals and non-terminals is that terminals don't show up on the left-hand side of a production rule. Besides terminals and non-terminals, ANTLR allows us to have some C# code in a production rule. The C# code needs to be placed in curly braces, like this:

```
A : {…} B {…} C {…}
```

That's the one-minute introduction to context-free grammars and some of ANTLR's notations. There are many details that I omitted. I'll explain some of the details as we go over the code in Listing 9-8.

In Listing 9-8, line 1 declares the name of our grammar. Line 4 tells ANTLR to generate the lexer and parser code in C#. Lines 7 through 10 declare a @header block, which is the place where we can add extra C# using statements that the generated C# parser code will need. Everything in the @header block will show up in the generated parser code before the generated C# parser class. Line 12 tells ANTLR that we want the generated C# parser class to be in the Stitch namespace.

The real grammar of the Stitch language begins at line 14 and continues to the end of the file. The grammar basically consists of eight production rules. Listing 9-8 does not show the complete definition of each rule. We will see the complete definition of the program rule in the next few paragraphs. Because the rule definitions all follow the same pattern, after the program rule is explained in detail, I will go over the other rules only briefly.

The complete definition of the program rule in Stitch.g is like this:

```
program returns [IList<IFunction> result]
    : { result = new List<IFunction>(); }
    (func { $result.Add($func.result); } )*
    ;
```

If we strip out the C# code and some extra stuff (i.e. the returns declaration after program) that's mixed into the rule, the rule becomes this:

```
program  : (func)* ;
```

This much simpler form of the program rule basically says that the program non-terminal is made up of zero or more func (the asterisk means zero or more) non-terminals. Here the program non-terminal represents a Stitch script and the func non-terminal represents a Stitch function. We saw earlier in the "Stitch in Use" section that a Stitch script is made up of zero or more Stitch functions. So this rule is in line with the Stitch syntax we saw earlier.

Now let's look at the C# code and the returns declaration in the program rule. Both are in the production rule to serve the purpose of creating an abstract syntax tree (AST) from source code parsing. The C# code will obtain the result of the func rule and put it in an IList instance. If a Stitch script is made up of three Stitch functions, during source code parsing, the func rule will be applied three times and the IList instance that holds the results of the func rule will have three elements in it. We haven't explained the func rule yet but suffice it to say that the func rule returns an IFunction instance as the result. The IFunction interface is one of the Stitch AST classes defined in the C# Stitch project. Given the program rule, what happens when ANTLR generates the parser code is that ANTLR will generate a method whose name is also program in the generated C# parser class. The return type of the program method will be IList<IFunction>.

The program non-terminal is defined in terms of the func non-terminal. The func non-terminal is in turn defined in terms of some terminals and non-terminals. The non-terminals are defined in terms of other terminals or non-terminals and so on. If we strip out the C# code and the returns declaration that are mixed into each rule, like we did to the program rule, we get the simpler form of the rules as Table 9-1 shows.

Table 9-1. *The Simpler Form of the Production Rules That Define the Syntax of the Stitch DSL.*

Rule name	Rule definition
program rule	program : (func)* ;
func rule	func : '<' IDENT '(' parameters? ')' funcCode 'return(' parameters? ')>';
parameters rule	parameters : IDENT (',' IDENT)*;
funcCode rule	funcCode: (include I IDENT) CODEBLOCK;
include rule	include : 'include' FILEPATH;
CODEBLOCK rule	CODEBLOCK : '>' .* '<';
FILEPATH rule	FILEPATH : (LETTER I DIGIT) (LETTER I DIGIT I '.' I '\\' I '/')* '.' (LETTER I DIGIT)+;
IDENT rule	IDENT : LETTER (LETTER I DIGIT)*;

Test-Driving the Grammar

There are two ways to test drive the grammar defined in the last section. One way is to use the nice GUI feature that ANTLR IDE 2.1.0 provides. The other is to write some C# code that exercises the generated lexer and parser files. We will look at both approaches.

Figure 9-3 shows you how the GUI for testing a grammar looks in Eclipse. To try out the GUI feature, you need to first make Stitch.g the active file in the Eclipse IDE. Once Stitch.g is the active file, you'll see three tabs at the bottom of the code editor. The Grammar tab is for writing the grammar we saw in Listing 9-8. The Interpreter tab is for testing the grammar. After you select the Interpreter tab, you'll see a list of all parser and lexer rules defined in Stitch.g in the upper left area. The screen capture in Figure 9-3 shows that the rule "program" is selected. There are two panes that take up most of the screen in Figure 9-3. The upper pane shows the test script I typed in for testing the grammar. You can save the test script by pressing the Save icon in the upper right corner. To run the test script, you press the Run icon close to the Save icon. When you run a test script, you'll see the result as a tree in the lower pane. You can examine the tree to see if the grammar you defined parses the test script as expected.

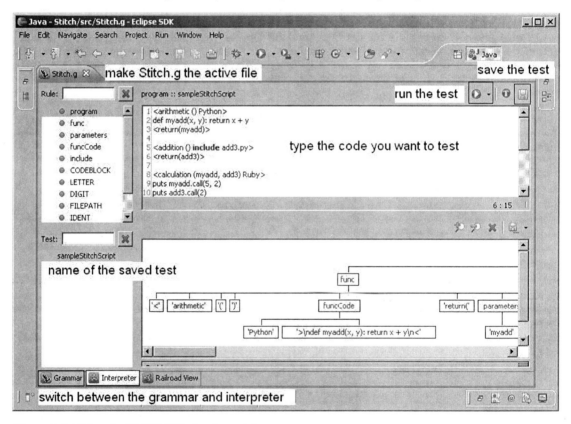

Figure 9-3. Using the ANTLR IDE plug-in to debug a grammar

Another way to test a grammar is to write some code that exercises the generated lexer and parser code. Listing 9-9 shows the C# code that test-drives the StitchParser class and the StitchLexer class generated from Stitch.g. You'll find the code in Listing 9-9 in Program.cs of the StitchDemoApplication project.

This code example uses the file testScript1.st as the test script. The code in line 3 opens testScript1.st as a file stream. The file stream is passed to the lexer object in line 4. The code in line 5 creates a token stream out of the lexer object. The token stream is passed to a parser object in line 6. And in line 7, the code calls the program method on the parser object. The program method represents the grammar rule program defined in Stitch.g. The program method returns a list of IFunction objects because in Stitch.g, the program rule is specified to return a list of IFunction objects as the result.

Listing 9-9. A C# Example That Excercises the Generated Lexer and Parser Code

```
1)   static void RunParserExample()
2)   {
3)       ICharStream input = new ANTLRFileStream(@"Scripts\testScript1.st");
4)       StitchLexer lexer = new StitchLexer(input);
5)       ITokenStream tokenStream = new CommonTokenStream(lexer);
6)       StitchParser parser = new StitchParser(tokenStream);
7)       IList<IFunction> functions = parser.program();
8)       Console.WriteLine("There are {0} scripts in the source file.", functions.Count);
9)   }
```

It's good to test-drive a grammar using the two techniques illustrated in this section and make sure that the grammar works as expected. Normally I use the GUI approach when I experiment with the grammar under creation. Once the grammar is stable, I use the C# approach to write unit tests that I can run to quickly and automatically check the correctness of the grammar.

Lexer and parser alone are not enough for executing Stitch code. The program method of the StitchParser class returns a list of IFunction objects. Each IFunction object represents a block of script code written in Python, Ruby, or some other language. We need to take those IFunction objects and figure out how to execute them. In the next section, we'll look at the Stitch runtime, which does exactly that.

The Stitch Runtime

The Stitch runtime is the component that executes Stitch code. This section and the next will give an overview of how the Stitch runtime performs its job. Subsequent sections will dive deeper into the details. Figure 9-4 shows the Stitch runtime (the Stitch box in the middle) in relation to the components it interacts with. The Stitch runtime interacts with two kinds of components—client applications and language plug-ins. For language plug-ins, the Stitch runtime provides two interfaces that serve as the contract for interactions. The two interfaces are ILanguagePlugin and IScript. If you want to extend the Stitch runtime by adding support for a new language, you need to implement those two interfaces. We will look at how to implement a Stitch language plug-in for Windows PowerShell later in the chapter.

Besides language plug-ins, the Stitch runtime interacts with client applications. A client application uses the Stitch runtime to run Stitch code, in one of two ways. One way is to use the StitchScriptEngine class in the C# Stitch project directly. The other way is to use the StitchScriptEngine indirectly via the DLR Hosting API. The Stitch runtime provides the StitchContext class and the StitchScriptCode class to support invoking the StitchScriptEngine via the DLR Hosting API.

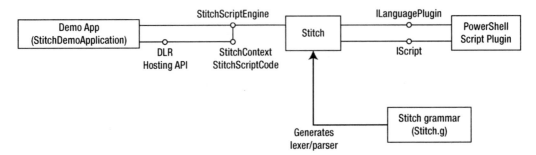

Figure 9-4. The Script runtime in relation to the components it interacts with.

Overview of the Runtime

I'd like to give an overview of the Stitch runtime first. If you take the Stitch rectangle in Figure 9-4 and enlarge it, you'll see the subparts that make up the Stitch runtime and how they work together, as shown in Figure 9-5. Figure 9-5 shows the flow of activities that take place when the Stitch runtime executes a Stitch script file. To execute Stitch code, the Stitch runtime uses a lexer to translate textual Stitch source code into a stream of tokens. The tokens are fed into a parser that turns the tokens into an abstract syntax tree, which is made up of instances of the classes in the `Stitch.Ast` namespace. We saw the lexer and parser in action when we looked at the code in Listing 9-9. The most interesting part of the abstract syntax tree is the list of `IFunction` objects returned by `StitchParser`'s program method. The Stitch runtime uses a function execution coordinator to coordinate the execution of the list of `IFunction` objects. The Stitch runtime provides both a parallel coordinator and a sequential coordinator that you can use to coordinate the execution of Stitch functions.

At a very high level, a coordinator takes as input a list of `IFunction` objects and a registry of the languages supported by the Stitch runtime. For the Stitch runtime to support a language like PowerShell, you need to register the language's plug-in with the runtime. We will look at the language plug-in mechanism of Stitch in a later section. For now, let's focus on the overall flow of executing a Stitch script. Once a coordinator has the inputs it needs, it creates a script runner for each `IFunction` object. A script runner, as its name suggests, runs a block of script code. It does so by calling the `Execute` method of an `IScript` instance, which encapsulates the actual logic for executing a function. We will begin our exploration of the Stitch runtime by first looking at the script engine in the next section.

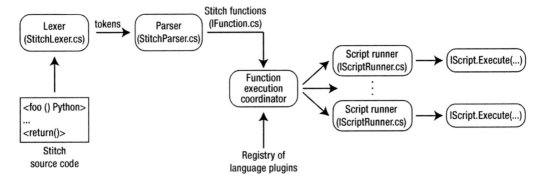

Figure 9-5. The flow of activities that take place when the Stitch runtime executes a Stitch script.

The Script Engine

We saw earlier how StitchScriptEngine is used to execute Stitch code. Using StitchScriptEngine to execute Stitch code is a two-step process. First you call StitchScriptEngine's constructor to create an instance of the class. Then you call either the RunScriptFile method or the RunScriptCode method to execute the Stitch code. When you call the StitchScriptEngine constructor, you need to pass in an execution mode and a collection of language plug-ins. The execution mode tells the Stitch runtime whether you want to execute Stitch code sequentially or in parallel. The collection of language plug-ins represents the languages you want to plug into the Stitch runtime. Listing 9-10 shows the code of the StitchScriptEngine's constructor. The important thing to note about the code in Listing 9-10 is that, depending on the execution mode, the StitchScriptEngine constructor will create either an instance of ParallelFunctionExecutionCoordinator or an instance of SequentialFunctionExecutionCoordinator. We will see an explanation of those coordinator classes in a minute.

Listing 9-10. The Constructor of the StitchScriptEngine Class

```
public StitchScriptEngine(ExecutionMode executionOption,
    ICollection<ILanguagePlugin> plugins)
{
    switch (executionOption)
    {
        case ExecutionMode.ParallelNoWait:
            this.coordinator = new ParallelFunctionExecutionCoordinator(false);
            break;
        case ExecutionMode.ParallelWaitAll:
            this.coordinator = new ParallelFunctionExecutionCoordinator(true);
            break;
        case ExecutionMode.Sequential:
            this.coordinator = new SequentialFunctionExecutionCoordinator();
            break;
    }

    … language plugin related code omitted …
}
```

StitchScriptEngine provides one method called RunScriptFile for executing Stitch code in a file and another method called RunScriptCode for executing Stitch code as a string. The implementations of the two methods are similar. Listing 9-11 shows the code inside the RunScriptCode method. This code is almost the same as the code in Listing 9-9. The only difference is that the RunScriptCode method takes the list of IFunction objects returned by the parser and passes it to the RunScripts method of a function execution coordinator, which is the topic of the next couple of sections.

Listing 9-11. The RunScriptCode Method in StitchScriptEngine.cs.

```
public void RunScriptCode(String code)
{
    ICharStream input = new ANTLRStringStream(code);
    StitchLexer lexer = new StitchLexer(input);
    ITokenStream tokenStream = new CommonTokenStream(lexer);
    StitchParser parser = new StitchParser(tokenStream);
    IList<IFunction> functions = parser.program();
```

```
    coordinator.RunScripts(functions, registry);
}
```

Function Execution Coordinator

A Stitch script can have multiple Stitch functions. Some functions might depend on the output of other functions. Because of the dependencies among functions, the Stitch runtime uses a coordinator to manage the execution of functions. (This coordinator is illustrated in Figure 9-5.) The concept of function execution coordinators is defined as the IFunctionExecutionCoordinator interface in the C# Stitch project. Listing 9-12 shows the interface definition. The interface has only one method called RunScripts that takes as input a list of IFunction objects and a registry of languages supported by the Stitch runtime.

Listing 9-12. The IFunctionExecutionCoordinator Interface

```
interface IFunctionExecutionCoordinator
{
    void RunScripts(IList<IFunction> functions, ILanguageRegistry registry);
}
```

The C# Stitch project has two classes that implement the IFunctionExecutionCoordinator interface. Those two classes are ParallelFunctionExecutionCoordinator and SequentialFunctionExecutionCoordinator. ParallelFunctionExecutionCoordinator is used when we run Stitch code in parallel (i.e., when the execution mode is ExecutionMode.ParallelWaitAll or ExecutionMode.ParallelNoWait). SequentialFunctionExecutionCoordinator is used when we run Stitch code sequentially (i.e, when the execution mode is ExecutionMode.Sequential). When implementing the C# Stitch project, I thought about opening up the coordinator-related stuff so that new coordination logic could be plugged into the Stitch language runtime. For the sake of simplicity, I decided to leave that feature out of this chapter. The feature will be implemented in the dPier open source project at http://code.google.com/p/dpier/. In this section, we are going to look at only the ParallelFunctionExecutionCoordinator class. The implementation in the SequentialFunctionExecutionCoordinator class is much simpler and less interesting than ParallelFunctionExecutionCoordinator.

Listing 9-13 shows the RunScripts method implemented in ParallelFunctionExecutionCoordinator. The RunScripts method takes two parameters—functions and registry—as input. It calls the CreateScriptRunners method in the same class. The CreateScriptRunners method returns a ParallelScriptRunner instance for each IFunction object in the functions parameter. The idea of creating script runners here is that the coordinator class will concern only the coordination of executing multiple functions. It will not concern how each individual function is executed. The execution of a single, individual function is handled by a script runner, not by the coordinator. That's why the code in Listing 9-13 calls the CreateScriptRunners method to create a parallel script runner for each IFunction object. Once the script runners are created, the code in Listing 9-13 calls the Run method on those script runners to start the execution of Stitch functions.

Listing 9-13. The RunScripts Method in ParallelFunctionExecutionCoordinator.cs.

```
public void RunScripts(IList<IFunction> functions, ILanguageRegistry registry)
{
    IList<ParallelScriptRunner> scriptRunners =
            this.CreateScriptRunners(functions, registry);
```

```
    foreach (var scriptRunner in scriptRunners)
        scriptRunner.Run();

    … code omitted …
}
```

Creating script runners for running Stitch functions in parallel requires some work. A parallel script runner can be created for running Python code, Ruby code, or another language's code. So, following good software design principles, the language-specific part (the part specific to how Python, Ruby, and other languages execute their code) of running a Stitch function is separated from the ParallelScriptRunner class and abstracted into the IScript interface. The IScript interface will be implemented by language plug-ins, which we'll see in a later section. With the IScript interface and Stitch's plug-in mechanism, we can use one single ParallelScriptRunner class to run different language code in parallel. ParallelScriptRunner keeps a reference to an IScript instance in its script field and delegates the execution of a Stitch function to that IScript instance.

When creating a parallel script runner for a Stitch function, we need to get an IScript instance that knows how to execute the language-specific code in a Stitch function. Listing 9-14 shows how to achieve that. Listing 9-14 shows the code in the CreateScriptRunners method of ParallelFunctionExecutionCoordinator. In line 10, the code calls the CreateScript method on the registry parameter to get an IScript instance that knows how to execute the language-specific code in a function.

Other than delegating the job of executing a Stitch function to an IScript instance, another main responsibility of the ParallelScriptRunner class is to keep track of a Stitch function's dependencies. If a Stitch function A depends on the return values of Stitch functions B and C, the parallel script runner for function A will keep in its prerequisites field a reference to each of B's and C's parallel script runners. That's why the code in line 26 calls the AddPrerequisite method on the scriptRunner object to track a Stitch function's dependencies.

Listing 9-14. The CreateScriptRunners Method in ParallelFunctionExecutionCoordinator.cs.

```
1)    private IList<ParallelScriptRunner> CreateScriptRunners(
2)                      IList<Ast.IFunction> functions, ILanguageRegistry registry)
3)    {
4)        IDictionary<String, ParallelScriptRunner> returnValueToRunnerDict =
5)                        new Dictionary<String, ParallelScriptRunner>();
6)        IList<ParallelScriptRunner> scriptRunners = new List<ParallelScriptRunner>();
7)
8)        foreach (var function in functions)
9)        {
10)           IScript script = registry.CreateScript(function);
11)           ParallelScriptRunner scriptRunner = new ParallelScriptRunner(
12)                         script, function.InputParameters);
13)           scriptRunners.Add(scriptRunner);
14)           foreach (var returnValue in function.ReturnValues)
15)           {
16)               returnValueToRunnerDict.Add(returnValue, scriptRunner);
17)           }
18)       }
19)
20)       for (int i = 0; i < functions.Count; i++)
21)       {
```

```
22)            ParallelScriptRunner scriptRunner = scriptRunners[i];
23)            foreach (var item in functions[i].InputParameters)
24)            {
25)                if (returnValueToRunnerDict.ContainsKey(item))
26)                    scriptRunner.AddPrerequisite(returnValueToRunnerDict [item]);
27)            }
28)        }
29)
30)        return scriptRunners;
31) }
```

Parallel Extensions for .NET

Because the parallel script runner we'll look at in the next section leverages the .NET Task Parallel Library (TPL) to do parallel programming, we will take a little detour and introduce the parts of TPL that are needed for our later discussion. TPL is a library within a larger component called Parallel Extensions. Before Parallel Extensions was released, I used to write code to deal with .NET thread pools. Thread pools in .NET are not friendly at all to developers. In those dark days, I lost a lot of brain cells, only to end up with code that was a headache to maintain. I can say from experience that TPL makes multithreaded programming much easier than thread pools do. Even though with TPL, writing parallel programs is simpler, it is still a very difficult thing to do correctly. That's why I'm attempting to make it easier to run scripts in parallel by implementing the Stitch language.

Listing 9-15 shows the TPL example we will look at in this section. The example creates in total eight TPL tasks. A TPL task is a unit of work that runs on a single thread. Multiple tasks can run on different threads in parallel if those tasks can be parallelized. One scenario in which two tasks can't be parallelized is when one task depends on the other. The eight TPL tasks in Listing 9-15 illustrate how task dependency affects parallel execution of tasks. In Listing 9-15, task1, task2, and task3 don't depend on anyone else. We create those tasks by calling the static Task.Factory.StartNew method and passing in a delegate that represents the actions we want the task to perform. Because we use the StartNew method to create those tasks, the tasks will start running after they are created.

task4 depends on task1. When we create task4, we use the static Task.Factory.ContinueWhenAll method. The first parameter to the ContinueWhenAll method is an array of tasks that task4 depends on. The second parameter is the delegate that represents the actions we want task4 to perform. Because we use the ContinueWhenAll method to create task4, task4 won't start executing until task1 is done. Similarly, task5 depends on task2; task6 on task4; task 7 on task2, task4 and task5; and finally task8 on task3 and task5. Every time you run the code in Listing 9-15, you will likely see "task 1", "task 2", "task 3", and so on printed on the screen in different order. One thing you can count on is that "task 4" will never be printed before "task 1" because task4 won't start to run until task1 is done.

Listing 9-15. Tasks That Have Dependencies among Them

```
private static void RunTaskDependencyExample()
{
    Task task1 = Task.Factory.StartNew(() => { Console.WriteLine("task 1"); });
    Task task2 = Task.Factory.StartNew(() => { Console.WriteLine("task 2"); });
    Task task3 = Task.Factory.StartNew(() => { Console.WriteLine("task 3"); });

    Task task4 = Task.Factory.ContinueWhenAll(new[] {task1},
        tasks => { Console.WriteLine("task 4"); });
    Task task5 = Task.Factory.ContinueWhenAll(new[] { task2 },
        tasks => { Console.WriteLine("task 5"); });
```

```
    Task task6 = Task.Factory.ContinueWhenAll(new[] { task4 },
        tasks => { Console.WriteLine("task 6"); });
    Task task7 = Task.Factory.ContinueWhenAll(new[] { task2, task4, task5 },
        tasks => { Console.WriteLine("task 7"); });
    Task task8 = Task.Factory.ContinueWhenAll(new[] { task3, task5 },
        tasks => { Console.WriteLine("task 8"); });
}
```

Script Runner

We will now use what we discussed about the Task Parallel Library to explain how the parallel script runner is implemented. A script runner is an object that knows how to run a script. As mentioned earlier, a script runner does not execute a Python script or Ruby script directly. Instead, it delegates that job to an IScript instance so that the script runner can remain language neutral. The concept of script runner is defined as the IScriptRunner interface in the C# Stitch project. Listing 9-16 shows the interface definition of IScriptRunner.

Listing 9-16. The Interface Definition of IScriptRunner

```
interface IScriptRunner
{
    void Run();
}
```

The IScriptRunner interface does not look very interesting. It has only a Run method that takes no input and returns no result. Let's see how the IScriptRunner interface is implemented by the ParallelScriptRunner class. The other class that implements the IScriptRunner interface is SequentialScriptRunner. SequentialScriptRunner is used by SequentialFunctionExecutionCoordinator whereas ParallelScriptRunner is used by ParallelFunctionExecutionCoordinator. Since the code in SequentialScriptRunner is relatively simple and straightforward, I will skip its explanation.

Listing 9-17 shows the StartTask method in the ParallelScriptRunner class. If a script runner does not have any prerequisites (line 6), then it can run immediately without waiting for other script runners to finish. So the code in line 8 calls the Task.Factory.StartNew method to start a new task immediately. The new task will run the lambda delegate that's passed to the TaskFactory.StartNew method call. The code in line 10 creates a dictionary object to hold the variables that are required by the language-specific code as input. Because the script runner does not have any prerequisites, the language-specific code does not require any input variables. That's why the dictionary object created in line 10 is an empty dictionary. The role the dictionary object plays is analogous to the role a ScriptScope instance plays in the DLR Hosting API. I chose to use a dictionary object as the carrier of the variables required by language-specific code because the Stitch language needs to support not only DLR-based languages but also non-DLR-based ones. So instead of using the DLR-specific ScriptScope class, I use IDictionary<String, Object>.

If a script runner has prerequisites, we need to run those prerequisites and wait for them to finish before we can kick off the script runner. The code in lines 19 and 20 loops through a script runner's prerequisites and starts them running. For each prerequisite, the code puts its task object (an instance of Task<IDictionary<String, Object>>) in the taskList variable. Then in line 22, the code calls the Task.Factory.ContinueWhenAll method to create a task object that will start to run only when all the tasks in taskList are finished. The task created in line 22 will run the lambda delegate defined in Listing 9-17 from line 23 to line 37. The lambda delegate prepares a dictionary object to hold the input variables needed by the language-specific code. This time, because the script runner has prerequisites, the dictionary object can't be empty. It needs to contain the results of the prerequisites' tasks. The code

231

from line 25 to line 34 puts the results of the prerequisites' tasks into a dictionary object. Then, in line 36, the code calls the Execute method on the script variable, passing it the dictionary object to kick off the execution of language-specific code.

Listing 9-17. The StartTask Method in ParallelScriptRunner.cs

```
1)   Task<IDictionary<String, Object>> StartTask()
2)   {
3)       if (task != null)
4)           return task;
5)
6)       if (prerequisites.Count == 0)
7)       {
8)           task = Task.Factory.StartNew<IDictionary<String, Object>>(() =>
9)           {
10)              IDictionary<String, object> scope = new Dictionary<String, object>();
11)              return this.script.Execute(scope);
12)          });
13)
14)          return task;
15)      }
16)
17)      List<Task<IDictionary<String, Object>>> taskList =
18)                          new List<Task<IDictionary<string, object>>>();
19)      foreach (var prerequisite in prerequisites)
20)          taskList.Add(prerequisite.StartTask());
21)
22)      task = Task.Factory.ContinueWhenAll(taskList.ToArray(),
23)              (tasks) =>
24)              {
25)                  IDictionary<String, object> scope = new Dictionary<String, object>();
26)                  foreach (var prerequisiteTask in tasks)
27)                  {
28)                      foreach (var item in prerequisiteTask.Result)
29)                      {
30)                          if (!scope.ContainsKey(item.Key) &&
31)                          this.inputParameters.Contains(item.Key))
32)                              scope.Add(item);
33)                      }
34)                  }
35)
36)                  return this.script.Execute(scope);
37)              });
38)
39)      return task;
40)  }
```

So far, we have looked at the function execution coordinator and script runner of the Stitch runtime. We saw how the coordinator coordinates and the runner runs. I mentioned that it's the IScript interface, not the IScriptRunner interface, that actually runs a Stitch function's language-specific code. The Stitch runtime comes with a built-in class DlrScript that implements the IScript interface for all DLR-based languages. For non-DLR-based languages like PowerShell, we can extend the Stitch runtime to support them by implementing the IScript interface and another interface called ILanguagePlugin. The two interfaces, IScript and ILanguagePlugin, make up the contract between the Stitch runtime and language plug-ins. Let's see the built-in DlrScript class in the next section. After that, we'll look at how the language plug-in mechanism works using the PowerShell plug-in as an example.

Running DLR-based Language Code

The IScript interface is meant to be implemented for each language that can be plugged into the Stitch runtime. Listing 9-18 shows the interface definition of IScript.

Listing 9-18. The IScript Interface

```
public interface IScript
{
    IDictionary<String, object> Execute(IDictionary<String, object> scope);
}
```

It turns out that for DLR-based languages like IronPython and IronRuby, because the DLR Hosting API provides a uniform way for executing those languages' code, we only need one implementation of the IScript interface for plugging all those languages into the Stitch runtime. The Stitch runtime comes with a built-in class, DlrScript, that implements the IScript interface for all DLR-based languages. Listing 9-19 shows the Execute method in DlrScript.

The Execute method takes a dictionary object as input. As explained in the previous section, the dictionary object carries the variables that are required by the language-specific code. The code in Listing 9-19 first creates an instance of ScriptScope and then copies the variables in the dictionary object to the ScriptScope object. Once the ScriptScope instance is ready, the Execute method uses the DLR Hosting API to get a ScriptEngine instance. The Execute method then uses the ScriptEngine instance to run the DLR-based language code. The results of this are in the ScriptScope instance the Execute method created earlier. Those results are copied into a dictionary object and returned to the caller of the Execute method.

Creating a new instance of ScriptScope in the Execute method means that we are not sharing a single ScriptScope object among the execution of multiple Stitch functions. This is important because Stitch functions can run in parallel and the ScriptScope class is not thread safe. We would have a lot of locking and thread synchronization to worry about if we shared a ScriptScope object in the concurrent execution of multiple Stitch functions.

One important thing to note about the code in Listing 9-19 is that the copying of variables from the dictionary object to the ScriptScope object is a shallow copying, meaning that the copying only copies object references and doesn't create new instances of those variables. That means even though the ScriptScope object is not shared among multiple Stitch functions, the variables contained in the ScriptScope object might be shared. And that seems to put us back to the thread synchronization issue we wanted to avoid. The reason I didn't implement a deep copying of the variables in the dictionary is because I expect the variables to be read-only. The design of the Stitch language adopts the functional programming paradigm and requires that if we intend to run Stitch functions in parallel, those Stitch functions should only produce new results and not alter their input variables. If all Stitch functions in a Stitch script don't alter their input variables, those variables are read-only and therefore are safe to be shared among multiple threads.

Listing 9-19. The Execute Method in DlrScript.cs

```
public IDictionary<String, object> Execute(IDictionary<String, object> dictionary)
{
    ScriptScope scope = runtime.CreateScope();
    foreach (var item in dictionary)
        scope.SetVariable(item.Key, item.Value);

    ScriptEngine engine;
    lock (runtime)
    {
        engine = runtime.GetEngine(lang);
    }
    ScriptSource source = engine.CreateScriptSourceFromString(code,
        SourceCodeKind.Statements);
    source.Execute(scope);
    IDictionary<String, object> result = new Dictionary<String, object>();
    foreach (var item in scope.GetItems())
            result.Add(item.Key, item.Value);

    return result;
}
```

Language Plug-In

The last section shows the built-in support for executing DLR-based languages in the Stitch runtime. The Stitch runtime can be extended to support non-DLR-based languages if we provide Stitch plug-ins for those languages. The next few of sections will show how to develop a Stitch plug-in for the PowerShell language and how the plug-in mechanism works.

Develop a Stitch Plug-In for PowerShell

Developing a Stitch plug-in means implementing two interfaces: ILanguagePlugin and IScript. In this section, we are going to look at the implementation of those two interfaces for the PowerShell language. The implementation of the IScript interface will contain the logic for running PowerShell code. The implementation of the ILanguagePlugin will contain some information about the PowerShell language needed by the Stitch runtime. You can find those implementations in the PowerShellStitchPlugin project in this chapter's code download.

   We have seen the IScript interface in the previous section. Listing 9-20 shows the code of the PowerShellScript class that implements the IScript interface for the PowerShell language. The logic for running PowerShell code is in the Execute method. I won't go into the details of how PowerShell works. For our purpose, it's enough to know that PowerShell uses something called a pipeline to execute PowerShell commands (i.e., PowerShell code) in a Runspace instance. The Runspace instance provides an execution context for the pipeline. The Execute method shown in Listing 9-20 creates a Runspace instance and a pipeline, puts PowerShell code as commands into the pipeline, and calls the pipeline's Invoke method to execute PowerShell code. The results returned by Invoke are the results of running PowerShell code. Those results are put into a dictionary object and returned to the caller of the Execute method. The code in the Execute method is for demonstration purposes. It does not use the Execute method's input parameter to set the input of the pipeline. That means the PowerShell code we write or include in a Stitch script can't take any input variables.

Listing 9-20. The PowerShellScript *Class That Implements the* IScript *Interface for the PowerShell Language*

```
class PowerShellScript : IScript
{
    private string code;
    private string returnValue;

    public PowerShellScript(string code, string returnValue)
    {
        this.code = code;
        this.returnValue = returnValue;
    }

    public IDictionary<String, object> Execute(IDictionary<String, object> scope)
    {
        Runspace runspace = RunspaceFactory.CreateRunspace();
        runspace.Open();
        Pipeline pipeline = runspace.CreatePipeline();
        pipeline.Commands.AddScript(code);
        Collection<PSObject> results = pipeline.Invoke();
        runspace.Close();
        IDictionary<String, object> result = new Dictionary<String, object>();
        result.Add(returnValue, results);
        return result;
    }
}
```

The other interface we need to implement for supporting PowerShell in the Stitch runtime is ILanguagePlugin. Listing 9-21 shows the interface definition of ILanguagePlugin, which defines a FileExtensions property for returning the file extensions of a language as a list of String objects. It also defines a LanguageNames property for returning the names of a language. When a language plug-in is hooked up (i.e., registered) with the Stitch runtime, the Stitch runtime will record the file extensions and language names so that the runtime can look up the right language plug-in by file extension or language name later.

Listing 9-21. The ILanguagePlugin *Interface*

```
public interface ILanguagePlugin
{
    IList<string> FileExtensions { get; }
    IList<string> LanguageNames { get; }
    IScript CreateScript(Ast.IFunction function);
}
```

For example, say we have the following Stitch code:

```
<getServiceA () PowerShell>
get-service A*
<return(serviceAList)>
```

The language name in this case is "PowerShell." When the Stitch runtime executes the code, it parses it into an IFunction instance. The IFunction instance has a String property called LanguageName, whose value in this case is "PowerShell". The Stitch runtime queries a registry that contains information about language plug-ins. The registry keeps one dictionary that maps a language name to the corresponding ILanguagePlugin instance and another dictionary that maps a language's file extension to the corresponding ILanguagePlugin instance. The registry is an instance of the ILanguageRegistry interface, which is shown in Listing 9-22. The ILanguageRegistry interface defines a Register method for registering new language plug-ins and a CreateScript method that creates an IScript object for an IFunction object. The Stitch runtime queries a registry by calling the registry's CreateScript method and passing it an IFunction object. The CreateScript method of ILanguageRegistry, in our example, will get the "PowerShell" language name from the IFunction object and use that name to look up the corresponding language plug-in. The CreateScript method of ILanguageRegistry will then call the CreateScript method of ILanguagePlugin on the looked-up language plug-in. The IScript object returned by the CreateScript method of ILanguagePlugin will eventually be wrapped with either a parallel script runner or a sequential script runner so that the PowerShell code can run in parallel or in sequence with other Stitch functions.

Listing 9-22. The ILanguageRegistry Interface

```
interface ILanguageRegistry
{
    IScript CreateScript(Ast.IFunction function);
    void Register(ILanguagePlugin plugin);
}
```

Now that we've seen the ILanguagePlugin interface, let's see the PowerShellPlugin class that implements the ILanguagePlugin interface for the PowerShell language in Listing 9-23. The implementation is fairly straightforward. For ILanguagePlugin's FileExtensions property, the code simply returns ".sp". For the LanguageNames property, the code returns "PowerShell". The implementation of ILanguagePlugin's CreateScript method in Listing 9-23 simply creates and returns an instance of the PowerShellScript class we saw in Listing 9-20.

Listing 9-23. The PowerShellPlugin Class That Implements the ILanguagePlugin Interface for the PowerShell Language

```
public class PowerShellPlugin : ILanguagePlugin
{
    private IList<string> fileExtensions = new List<string>(new string[] { ".ps" });
    private IList<string> languageNames = new List<string>(new string[] { "PowerShell" });

    public IList<string> FileExtensions
    {
        get { return fileExtensions; }
    }

    public IList<string> LanguageNames
    {
        get { return languageNames; }
    }

    public IScript CreateScript(IFunction function)
```

```
    {
        String returnValue = null;
        if (function.ReturnValues.Count > 0)
            returnValue = function.ReturnValues[0];

        return new PowerShellScript(function.Code, returnValue);
    }
}
```

Configuring a Plug-In

Now that we have the PowerShell plug-in in hand, we need to register it with the Stitch runtime in order to use it. There are two ways to achieve this. One way is to pass an instance of `PowerShellPlugin` to the constructor of `StitchScriptEngine` as in the following code snippet:

```
StitchScriptEngine engine = new StitchScriptEngine(
    ExecutionMode.Sequential, new ILanguagePlugin[] { new PowerShellPlugin() });
```

The other way to register a language plug-in with the Stitch runtime is by configuration. Listing 9-24 shows what the configuration looks like in the App.config file. The configuration is based on the fact that Stitch is integrated with the DLR Hosting API. Because of this, we have the code from lines 5 through 8 to let the DLR Hosting API know about the Stitch language. And the code from lines 11 to 16 are the way the DLR Hosting API provides for passing custom information in the form of key-value pairs to a DLR Hosting API-enabled language. In this case, the custom information passed to the Stitch language runtime is two key-value pairs. The first pair has "plugin" as the key and the assembly-qualified type name of the `PowerShellPlugin` class as the value. This key-value pair will cause the `PowerShellPlugin` to be registered with the Stitch runtime. The second key-value pair has "executionMode" as the key and "ParallelNoWait" as the value. This key-value pair declares which execution mode we want the Stitch runtime to operate in.

Listing 9-24. Configuration That Registers the PowerShell Plug-in with the Stitch Runtime

```
1)  <microsoft.scripting>
2)    <languages>
3)       ...
4)
5)      <language names="Stitch"
6)               extensions=".st"
7)               displayName="Stitch 1.0"
8)               type="Stitch.StitchContext, Stitch, Version=1.0.0.0, Culture=neutral"
    />
9)
10)   </languages>
11)   <options>
12)     <set option="plugin" language="Stitch"
13)          value="PowerShellStitchPlugin.PowerShellPlugin,
14)                    PowerShellStitchPlugin, Version=1.0.0.0, Culture=neutral" />
15)     <set option="executionMode" language="Stitch" value="ParallelNoWait" />
16)   </options>
17) </microsoft.scripting>
```

Summary

In this chapter, we started with a list of abstractions that could be built on top the DLR Hosting API to make language hosting more declarative and less tied to the underlying .NET and DLR platform. We then went through the uses and implementations of the Stitch domain specific language that provide those abstractions. The Stitch language is declarative and platform-independent, and it can run both DLR-based and non-DLR based-language code in sequence or in parallel. We looked at the design and grammar definition of Stitch's syntax, and at the key components, such as the function execution coordinator and script runner, in the Stitch runtime. Finally, we saw how to implement a Stitch plug-in for the PowerShell language, and how to register the plug-in with the Stitch runtime.

There are many features and improvements that could be added to the Stitch language as presented in this chapter. For example, we could implement language plug-ins for running Ant, Maven, or other language scripts. The Stitch language can make the execution modes extensible and allow language scripts to run in different ways. I created the dpier project up on Google Code at http://code.google.com/p/dpier/ for the continuous development of the Stitch language. You can visit the project web site to get the latest updates and give feedback.

CHAPTER 10

■ ■ ■

Application Scripting

One of the most common uses of the DLR and dynamic languages is in the area of application scripting. Application scripting allows users to control an application's behavior by writing scripts. For example, users might write scripts to automate routine tasks. They might use scripts to add new features or to customize existing functionalities. They might write scripts that integrate an application with other applications. The usage scenarios are many and the benefits are real. In this chapter, we will look at this important use of the DLR and dynamic languages. Specifically, we will develop a fun application that has balls bouncing around, and we will open up part of the application for users to customize. The way we open up the application is by exposing its object model for users to script. Users or third-party vendors can write custom IronPython code to script the object model. Our application will use the DLR Hosting API to load and run those custom IronPython scripts.

Ball World

The application we will build in this chapter is called Ball World. You can find the complete source code in the BallWorld project of this chapter's code download. Figure 10-1 shows a snapshot of what Ball World looks like when it runs.

The Ball World application is a simple, standalone program that simulates a world of balls with different colors and sizes. The world is two-dimensional and is bounded by four invisible walls. The world has an initial state that determines what balls are in the world and specifies the colors, sizes, speed, and positions of the balls. It is the initial state that we will open up for users and third-party vendors to script. Unlike the world we live in, the world of balls does not have gravity that constantly pulls the balls downward. A ball in our simulated world moves in a straight line until it hits one of the four bounding walls or another ball. When a ball hits any of the four walls, it bounces back. When two balls collide, they assert a force on each other and hence change each other's direction of movement. The mass of a ball is proportional to its size. So when a big ball collides with a smaller ball, the bigger one will have a less dramatic change in its direction of movement than the smaller one.

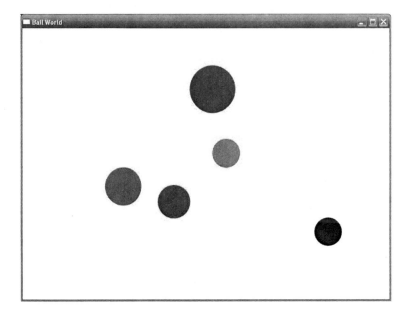

Figure 10-1. The Ball World Application

Ball World is a WPF (Windows Presentation Foundation) application. Don't worry if you have little or no experience with WPF. The focus of this chapter is on application scripting, and WPF just happens to be the underlying framework our example application is built on. We will stay focused on application scripting and will only get into the specifics of the WPF part of the Ball World application as necessary.

Besides WPF, the other component the Ball World application is built on is an open source project called Farseer Physics. Farseer Physics is a library that provides many cool features people normally need when they develop game applications that need to simulate the physical world. In our case, we will use only a very limited subset of the features Farseer Physics provides for detecting the collisions between two balls or between a ball and a wall. You don't need to have any prior experience with Farseer Physics or in game development. This chapter will not have too detailed a discussion on those subjects. Our focus is on application scripting and I chose to use the Farseer Physics library only to make Ball World more fun to play with.

Software Requirements

To run the Ball World application you need the compiled binaries of the Farseer Physics library. Here are the steps for setting up the Farseer Physics library for Ball World.

1. Download the Farseer Physics source code from the CodePlex web site at http://farseerphysics.codeplex.com/. The version of Farseer Physics I used for developing the Ball World application is 2.1.3. The later version 3.0 is different from version 2.1.3 in substantial ways and is not backward-compatible. Be sure to download version 2.1.3 to follow along this chapter's code examples. For each version of Farseer Physics, there are different packages you can download for different runtime environments. Because our runtime

environment is WPF, you should download the package called Farseer Physics 2.1.3 Class Library. I will assume that you unzip the downloaded package into the folder C:\Farseer Physics 2.1.3 Class Library. If you use a different folder, you'll need to adjust the rest of the setup steps in this section accordingly.

2. Open the FarseerPhysics.csproj file in Visual Studio C# 2010 Express. Because this file is for an older version of Visual Studio, you'll be prompted to convert it to a format that Visual Studio C# 2010 Express understands. Simply go through that conversion wizard and have the FarseerPhysics.csproj file converted. After the conversion is done, you'll see a project called FarseerPhysics in the Solution Explorer of Visual Studio.

3. Build the FarseerPhysics project. The compiled binaries will be placed in C:\Farseer Physics 2.1.3 Class Library\bin\Debug. Copy all the files in that folder to C:\ProDLR\lib\FaseerPhysics\Debug and you are done.

Application Architecture

As mentioned earlier, Ball World is a WPF application. In the world of WPF, there is a popular pattern called MVVM (Model-View-ViewModel) for architecturing applications. A detailed discussion of the MVVM pattern is beyond the scope of this chapter and might not be of interest to readers who don't base their application's user interface on WPF. I'll cover MVVM just enough here so you know how the Ball World application is structured in the context of the MVVM pattern.

MVVM is a design pattern for structuring the user interface layer of an application. If you've built UI applications, you are most likely familiar with the MVC (Model-View-Controller) pattern used in many non-WPF UI applications. The MVVM pattern is similar. For WPF applications, people use MVVM instead of the more traditional MVC design pattern because MVVM takes advantage of capabilities such as data binding that WPF provides. As its name suggests, the MVVM pattern basically consists of three parts: model, view, and viewmodel. Model is made up of classes that represent the objects of the application's domain. View defines the look and feel of the application. ViewModel is the part that uses WPF data binding to bridge the view and the model. If you compare MVVM to the MVC pattern, you'll see the similarities. The MVC pattern also consists of three parts: model, view, and controller. The model part of MVVM corresponds to the model part of MVC. The view part of MVVM corresponds to the view part of MVC. And the viewmodel part of MVVM corresponds to the controller part of MVC.

For our Ball World application, I adopted the MVVM pattern but simplified things by combining the model and viewmodel into a single object model. This is okay for a simple application like Ball World. For a more complex application, the general practice would be to implement the full MVVM pattern. The single object model we have for Ball World contains classes that represent balls and the world of balls. It is the model that the view (i.e., the UI) will reflect. It is also the model that users of our application will script against. Let's begin our exploration of the Ball World application's implementation by looking at the object model.

Application Object Model

At the core of the Ball World application is an object model that includes classes for representing balls and the world of balls. Of those classes, the BallWorldViewModel class shown in Listing 10-1 is the most important to our discussion. The BallWorldViewModel class models the world of balls. Because of that, it has a private member variable called balls for containing the balls in a ball world. Each ball is an instance of the BallViewModel class. The Balls property in the BallWorldViewModel class is defined so that code outside of that class can access the balls contained in the private member variable balls. Notice that the type of the private member variable balls is ObservableCollection<BallViewModel>. The class ObservableCollection is WPF-specific and it's there to assist data binding. As you'll see later when we get to the view part of the Ball World application, the XAML code we write to define the look and feel of Ball World will use WPF data binding to bind a UI element to the Balls property of BallWorldViewModel. The way WPF data binding works is that it needs some kind of notification for updating the UI element every time the Balls property is changed. The need for notification is met by using the ObservableCollection class in Listing 10-1. Besides the Balls property and the balls member variable, other important things about the BallWorldViewModel class are the private physicsEngine member variable, the AddBall method, and the RunInitScript method. The private physicsEngine member variable is an instance of BallWorldPhysicsEngine, which we will talk about in "The Physics Engine" section later when we discuss the use of the Farseer Physics library in our application. For now, let's focus the discussion on AddBall and RunInitScript.

AddBall and RunInitScript are the methods in our application that enable application scripting. Rather than hard-coding the balls we'd like to put into a ball world, we externalize that part of the application logic into a Python script file called InitScript.py. Users can customize the Ball World application by writing their Python code in the InitScript.py file to define the balls and their colors, positions, and speed in a ball world. The RunInitScript method uses the DLR Hosting API (discussed in Chapter 6) to load the InitScript.py file. RunInitScript runs the Python code in a script scope where the variable name "world" is bound to the BallWorldViewModel instance that represents the ball world. Because the BallWorldViewModel instance that represents the ball world is in the script scope, as you will see in the next section, the Python code of InitScript.py can add balls to the ball world by calling the AddBall method on the BallWorldViewModel instance. AddBall creates an instance of BallViewModel to represent the new ball to be added to the ball world. Then it adds the new BallViewModel instance to two places. First, it adds the new BallViewModel instance to the private balls member variable so that the new ball will show up in the user interface. When this occurs, thanks to the ObservableCollection class, a property-change notification is triggered and the WPF data binding takes care of showing the new ball in the user interface automatically.

The second place where the AddBall method adds the new BallViewModel instance is the physics engine, represented by the physicsEngine member variable of the BallWorldViewModel class. This is so the physics engine knows about the new ball and can detect the collisions when the new ball collides with other balls. You'll see more code and explanations about the physics engine and collision detection in "The Physics Engine" section later in the chapter.

Listing 10-1. BallWorldViewModel.cs

```
public class BallWorldViewModel
{
    private BallWorldPhysicsEngine physicsEngine = new BallWorldPhysicsEngine();
    private ObservableCollection<BallViewModel> balls;

    public BallWorldViewModel()
    {
        balls = new ObservableCollection<BallViewModel>();
        BorderViewModel border = new BorderViewModel(
                    720f, 520f, 60, new Vector2(400f, 300f));
        physicsEngine.AddBorder(border);
        physicsEngine.Start();
        RunInitScript();
    }
```

```
    public ObservableCollection<BallViewModel> Balls
    {
        get { return balls; }
    }

    public void AddBall(Color color, float radius,
        float x, float y, float speedx, float speedy)
    {
        BallViewModel ball = new BallViewModel(color, radius,
            new Vector2D(x, y), new Vector2D(speedx, speedy));
        balls.Add(ball);
        physicsEngine.AddBall(ball);
    }

    private void RunInitScript()
    {
        ScriptRuntime scriptRuntime = ScriptRuntime.CreateFromConfiguration();
        scriptRuntime.Globals.SetVariable("world", this);
        ScriptScope scope = scriptRuntime.ExecuteFile(@"Script\InitScript.py");
    }
}
```

I'll spare you the details of the BallViewModel class since it has nothing related to the DLR, nor to application scripting. If you want to see how the BallViewModel class is implemented, you can find its code in this chapter's code download.

One last thing to note about the code in Listing 10-1 is the use of the DLR Hosting API in the RunInitScript method. In RunInitScript we call the static CreateFromConfiguration method of the ScriptRuntime class. As we discussed in Chapter 6, behind the scenes, CreateFromConfiguration reads the configurations in the application's App.config file and uses them to create the script runtime. The DLR-related configurations in an App.config file determine which dynamic languages will be supported by the script runtime that CreateFromConfiguration creates. For the script runtime to support IronPython, we need to put the code in Listing 10-2 into the App.config file of the BallWorld project. Chapter 6 has a detailed explanation of the DLR-related configurations in an App.config file. If you are unfamiliar with the code in Listing 10-2, refer to Chapter 6 for more information.

Listing 10-2. App.config

```
<?xml version="1.0" encoding="utf-8" ?>
<configuration>
  <configSections>
    <section name="microsoft.scripting"
        type="Microsoft.Scripting.Hosting.Configuration.Section, Microsoft.Scripting,
        Version=1.0.0.0, Culture=neutral" />
  </configSections>
  <microsoft.scripting>
    <languages>
      <language names="IronPython,Python,py"
                extensions=".py"
                displayName="IronPython 2.6.1"
                type="IronPython.Runtime.PythonContext,IronPython,
                    Version=2.6.10920.0, Culture=neutral" />
```

```
    </languages>
  </microsoft.scripting>
</configuration>
```

Application Scripting

Now let's see how to script the Ball World application by writing some Python code in the InitScript.py file, which, as you saw in the previous section, is loaded and executed by the Ball World application. The script code in InitScript.py controls the initial state of the ball world. Users can modify the Python code in InitScript.py to create a ball world that has a custom initial state without recompiling the Ball World application. Listing 10-3 shows a sample InitScript.py file. If you unzip this chapter's code download, you can find the InitScript.py file in the Chapter10\BallWorld\Script folder. When you open the chapter's Visual Studio solution in Visual Studio C# 2010 Express and compile the source code, the Ball World application's executable file—BallWorld.exe—will be generated in the Chapter10\BallWorld\bin\Debug folder and the InitScript.py file will be copied over to the Chapter10\BallWorld\bin\Debug\Script folder. Run BallWorld.exe to launch the Ball World application. When you want to change the initial state of the Ball World application without recompiling the Ball World source code, change the InitScript.py file in the Chapter10\BallWorld\bin\Debug\Script folder, not the InitScript.py file in the Chapter10\BallWorld\Script folder. The InitScript.py file in the Chapter10\BallWorld\bin\Debug\Script folder will be refreshed with the contents you put in the InitScript.py file in the Chapter10\BallWorld\Script folder when you recompile the chapter's source code.

The Python code in Listing 10-3 is fairly straightforward. First we have the line import clr because we are going to use some .NET assemblies. The line import world brings the object associated with the name "world" in the script runtime's global scope into the scope of the Python script. The script runtime has the name "world" in its global scope bound to a BallWorldViewModel instance that represents the ball world because we established that binding in the RunInitScript method of the BallWorldViewModel class. As you can see in Listing 10-3, once the variable world is in the scope of the Python script, we can define the initial state of a ball world by calling the AddBall method on the variable world. When we call the AddBall method, we specify the color, size, initial x-axis position, initial y-axis position, initial x-axis speed, and initial y-axis speed of the new ball we are creating. The coordinate system of our Ball World application has an x-axis going from left to right and a y-axis going from top to bottom. The (0, 0) origin of the coordinate system is at the very top-left corner of our application's UI. So the line world.AddBall(Colors.Blue, 50, 250, 200, -50, 50); creates a ball whose color is blue, size is 50, initial x-axis position 250, initial y-axis position 200, initial x-axis speed –50 (meaning that the ball will move to the left in the x-axis direction), and initial y-axis speed 50.

Because we use color constants like Blue, Red, and Green defined in the System.Windows.Media.Colors class to specify the color of a ball, we need to bring the Colors class into the scope of the Python script. To do so, we first use the line clr.AddReference("PresentationCore") to create a reference to the PresentationCore.dll WPF assembly because the System.Windows.Media.Colors class is packaged into that WPF assembly. Then we use the line from System.Windows.Media import (Colors) to bring the Colors class into the scope of the Python script.

Listing 10-3. A Sample InitScript.py file

```
import clr
import world
clr.AddReference("PresentationCore")
from System.Windows.Media import (Colors)
```

```
world.AddBall(Colors.Blue, 50, 250, 200, -50, 50);
world.AddBall(Colors.Red, 30, 200, 400, 50, 50);
world.AddBall(Colors.Black, 30, 100, 400, 20, 40);
world.AddBall(Colors.Green, 40, 250, 300, -30, 50);
world.AddBall(Colors.Purple, 35, 320, 270, 40, -40);
```

There are many ways to enable scripting for an application. Loading and executing script files like the Ball World application does is one way. Another way to enable scripting for the Ball World application might be to have a text box in the user interface where users can type in the script code. There could be a button by the text box that users can click to execute the script code. The Ball World application could be easily extended to support languages other than IronPython that users could write their script code in. We could open up more of the application's behaviors for users to script by exposing more methods and objects in the application's object model. Those additional methods and objects would be like the AddBall method of the BallWorldViewModel class that users can script in their Python code. No matter which way we use to enable scripting for the Ball World application, no matter which languages we support for users to write their script code in, and no matter which parts of our application we open up for scripting, the basic scripting mechanism of using the DLR Hosting API to execute dynamic language code as demonstrated in Listing 10-2 and Listing 10-3 remains the same.

Besides allowing users to change the behavior of a certain part of an application, the basic scripting mechanism demonstrated in this chapter can also be used as a plug-in infrastructure for an application. Users can use the plug-in infrastructure to extend an application by plugging in new functionalities. For example, say we are developing an image-processing application and we want to allow the image files to be saved in different file formats. Not only do we want to support the set of file formats we are aware of, we also want to allow users to plug in support for a file format that is beyond our reach. For this scenario, we could build our application in such a way that it loads a user script file containing the logic for saving the object model representing an image in our application to the user's specific file format.

If you have experience in building a plug-in infrastructure or in enabling scripting for an application using a static language like C#, you can tell how the approach demonstrated in this chapter is different. With a static language, you would need to define some classes or interfaces as the contract between your plug-in (or scripting) infrastructure and users' extensions (or scripts). When users implement their extensions to be plugged into your application, their code would need to reference the .NET assembly that contains the contract classes or interfaces in order for their code to compile. Using the DLR Hosting API to build a plug-in infrastructure or to enable application scripting, on the other hand, does not require a .NET assembly shared between you, the application creator, and people who wish to extend your application by providing plug-ins or scripts. Even though no shared .NET assembly is required to serve as the programming contract between you and people who extend your application, that doesn't mean there is no programming contract at all. In the case of the Ball World application, the contract is that the variable by the name world is accessible to script code and that the script code can invoke a method called AddBall on the variable world. The contract between the Ball World application and the InitScript.py file is checked and enforced at runtime. The contract packaged in a .NET assembly and referenced by people who extend your application is checked and enforced at compile time. A major benefit of delaying to runtime the checking and enforcement of the contract between you and users who extend your application is that users can just type in their code and have the code executed while your application is up and running. There is no need to reference contract assemblies, no need to compile code, no need to deploy the compiled code, and no need to restart the application for it to load the new version of a user's compiled code.

So far in this chapter, we have looked at how the Ball World application uses the DLR Hosting API to enable application scripting. The next section will cover the physics engine that detects ball collisions in the Ball World application. After that, we will look at the XAML code that defines the user interface of the Ball World application. The physics engine and the XAML code are not really related to application scripting. Because of that, I will go through those two components of the Ball World application only briefly and skip the details.

The Physics Engine

The Ball World application uses the Farseer Physics engine to simulate the movements of balls in a physical world. Farseer Physics is a library that provides a ton of cool features, but we're using only the collision detection feature to detect collisions between two balls or between a ball and a wall. When such a collision happens, the Farseer Physics library triggers an event that we can subscribe to and handle.

In order for the Farseer Physics engine to detect object collisions, we need to describe the walls and balls in our simulated world to the engine first. The way collision detection works in Farseer Physics version 2.1.3 is that for every object like a ball or a wall, we need to create two things in the engine: a body and the body's geometries. The body represents the object in the engine and the geometries define the object's shape. The physics engine uses objects' shapes to detect collisions among objects.

In the Ball World application, I centralized all use of the Farseer Physics engine into a class called BallWorldPhysicsEngine. Listing 10-4 shows that class's code. The three important methods of the BallWorldPhysicsEngine class are: AddBall, AddBorder, and OnCollision. The AddBall method adds a body and its geometry in the physics engine for a ball. The AddBorder method adds a body that represents the border of a ball world. The body's shape is defined by four geometries, one for each wall of the ball world. The OnCollsion method is the event handler for the OnCollision event that the Farseer Physics library triggers when two objects collide. In Listing 10-4, the OnCollision method is registered to the OnCollision event of a ball's geometry by the bolded line in the AddBall method.

The Farseer Physics engine simulates a physical world by constantly calculating the positions of bodies. The engine runs in a loop and calculates the positions of bodies in each iteration of the loop. Every time a body's position takes on a new value as determined by the physics engine's calculation, we need to be informed so we can update the Position property of the corresponding BallViewModel instance accordingly. That's why in Listing 10-4 the code in the AddBall method registers an event handler for the Updated event of the body that represents a ball in the physics engine. The physics engine will trigger the Updated event when a body's position takes on a new value, and our event handler will be called with the new position value. Inside the event handler, we update the Position property of the BallViewModel instance that corresponds to the body whose Updated event was triggered.

Listing 10-4. BallWorldPhysicsEngine.cs

```
public class BallWorldPhysicsEngine
{
    private PhysicsEngineLoop physicsEngineLoop;
    private PhysicsEngine physicsEngine;
    private PhysicsSimulator physicsSimulator;

    public BallWorldPhysicsEngine()
    {
        physicsEngineLoop = new PhysicsEngineLoop();
        physicsEngineLoop.IsRunningChanged += IsRunningChangedEventHandler;

        physicsEngine = new PhysicsEngine(new Vector2(0f, 0f));
        physicsSimulator = physicsEngine.PhysicsSimulator;
        physicsEngine.SetLoop(physicsEngineLoop);
    }
```

```
public void Start()
{
    physicsEngineLoop.Start();
}

public void AddBorder(BorderViewModel border)
{
    //use the body factory to create the physics body
    Body borderBody = BodyFactory.Instance.CreateRectangleBody(
            physicsSimulator, border.Width, border.Height, 50);
    borderBody.IsStatic = true;
    borderBody.Position = border.Position;

    //left border geometry
    Vector2 geometryOffset = new Vector2(
            -(border.Width * .5f - border.BorderWidth * .5f), 0);
    CreateBorderGeom(borderBody, border.BorderWidth, border.Height, geometryOffset);

    //right border geometry
    geometryOffset = new Vector2(border.Width * .5f - border.BorderWidth * .5f, 0);
    CreateBorderGeom(borderBody, border.BorderWidth, border.Height, geometryOffset);

    //top border geometry
    geometryOffset = new Vector2(0, -(border.Height * .5f - border.BorderWidth * .5f));
    CreateBorderGeom(borderBody, border.Width, border.BorderWidth, geometryOffset);

    //bottom border geometry
    geometryOffset = new Vector2(0, border.Height * .5f - border.BorderWidth * .5f);
    CreateBorderGeom(borderBody, border.Width, border.BorderWidth, geometryOffset);
}

private void CreateBorderGeom(
    Body borderBody, float width, float height, Vector2 geometryOffset)
{
    Geom geom = GeomFactory.Instance.CreateRectangleGeom(
        physicsSimulator, borderBody, width, height, geometryOffset, 0);
    geom.RestitutionCoefficient = 1f;
    geom.FrictionCoefficient = 0f;
    geom.CollisionGroup = 100;
}

public void AddBall(BallViewModel ball)
{
    float bodyMass = ball.Radius;
    Body body = BodyFactory.Instance.CreateCircleBody(ball.Radius, bodyMass);
    body.Position = ball.Position.Vector;
    body.LinearVelocity = ball.Velocity.Vector;

    BodyModelHelper<BallViewModel> helper = new BodyModelHelper<BallViewModel>(
        ball, body,
        (UpdateEventHandler<BallViewModel>) delegate(
                    BallViewModel ball1, Vector2 position, float rotation)
```

247

```
    {
        ball1.Position = new Vector2D(position.X, position.Y);
        ball1.Velocity = new Vector2D(body.LinearVelocity.X, body.LinearVelocity.Y);
    });

    body.Updated += delegate { helper.Update();  };

    Geom geom = GeomFactory.Instance.CreateCircleGeom(body, ball.Radius, 60, 25);
    geom.FrictionCoefficient = 0f;
    geom.RestitutionCoefficient = 1f;
    geom.OnCollision += OnCollision;

    physicsEngine.AddBody(body);
    physicsEngine.AddGeom(geom);
}

private bool OnCollision(Geom geom1, Geom geom2, ContactList contactList)
{
    float geom1Speed = geom1.Body.LinearVelocity.Length();
    float geom2Speed = geom2.Body.LinearVelocity.Length();

    if (geom1Speed > 80)
    {
        float factor = 50 / geom1Speed;
        geom1.Body.LinearVelocity.X = geom1.Body.LinearVelocity.X * factor;
        geom1.Body.LinearVelocity.Y = geom1.Body.LinearVelocity.Y * factor;
    }

    if (geom2Speed > 80)
    {
        float factor = 50 / geom2Speed;
        geom2.Body.LinearVelocity.X = geom2.Body.LinearVelocity.Y * factor;
        geom2.Body.LinearVelocity.Y = geom2.Body.LinearVelocity.Y * factor;
    }

    return true;
}

//other code omitted.
}
```

User Interface

The only major component of the Ball World application we haven't looked at is the part that defines the application's user interface. Because Ball World is a WPF application, its user interface is defined declaratively in XAML. For a simple application like Ball World, there is not much code we need to write to define its user interface, so I put all of the XAML code in a single file called MainView.xaml, as shown in Listing 10-5. The code mainly consists of two WPF data templates. In WPF, a data template defines the look and feel of instances of a certain class. In our example, one of the WPF data templates defines the look and feel of instances of the BallViewModel class. In other words, the data template defines what a ball looks like in our application user interface. The other data template defines the look and feel of instances of the `BallWorldViewModel` class. The two data templates use WPF data binding to bind UI elements to properties of the `BallViewModel` and `BallWorldViewModel` classes. For example, the data template for the `BallViewModel` class uses an `Ellipse` instance to represent a ball. The `Ellipse` instance's color is determined by its `Fill` property, which is bound by the data template to the `Color` property of the `BallViewModel` class.

Listing 10-5. MainView.xaml

```xaml
<Window x:Class="BallGames.MainView"
    xmlns="http://schemas.microsoft.com/winfx/2006/xaml/presentation"
    xmlns:x="http://schemas.microsoft.com/winfx/2006/xaml"
    xmlns:local="clr-namespace:BallGames.ViewModel"
    Title="Ball World" Width="800" Height="600">
    <Window.Resources>
        <local:ColorConverter x:Key="colorConverter" />

        <DataTemplate DataType="{x:Type local:BallViewModel}">
            <StackPanel>
                <Ellipse Fill="{Binding Color, Converter={StaticResource colorConverter}}"
                        Width="{Binding Diameter}" Height="{Binding Diameter}" />
            </StackPanel>
        </DataTemplate>

        <DataTemplate DataType="{x:Type local:BallWorldViewModel}">
            <ItemsControl ItemsSource="{Binding Path=Balls}">
                <ItemsControl.ItemsPanel>
                    <ItemsPanelTemplate>
                        <Canvas />
                    </ItemsPanelTemplate>
                </ItemsControl.ItemsPanel>
                <ItemsControl.ItemContainerStyle>
                    <Style>
                        <Setter Property="Canvas.Left"
                                Value="{Binding Path=NormalPosition.X}" />
                        <Setter Property="Canvas.Top"
                                Value="{Binding Path=NormalPosition.Y}" />
                    </Style>
                </ItemsControl.ItemContainerStyle>
            </ItemsControl>
        </DataTemplate>

    </Window.Resources>

    <Canvas x:Name="ballWorldCanvas">
        <ContentControl x:Name="content" />
    </Canvas>
</Window>
```

Toward the bottom of Listing 10-5 is a `<Canvas>` element that serves as the overall container for the rest of the Ball World application's UI elements. The `<Canvas>` element has only a `<ContentControl>` as the child element it contains. In the code-behind file of MainView.xaml, we set the `<ContentControl>`

element's Content property to an instance of BallWorldViewModel as the bolded line in Listing 10-6 shows. The data template for the BallWorldViewModel class is used to render the instance of BallWorldViewModel we assign to the <ContentControl> element's Content property and we end up with the <Canvas> element containing the rest of the Ball World application's UI elements.

Listing 10-6. The Code-Behind File of MainView.xaml, MainView.xaml.cs

```
public partial class MainView : Window
{
    public MainView()
    {
        InitializeComponent();
        BallWorldViewModel viewModel = new BallWorldViewModel();
        content.Content = viewModel;
    }
}
```

Summary

This chapter looks at using the DLR and dynamic languages for application scripting—a very powerful and quite common use of the DLR. The same concepts that enable application scripting can also be used to build a plug-in infrastructure that allows users and third-party vendors to extend an application with plug-ins. To add some fun to the topic under discussion, we used a WPF application that simulates a physical world of balls to demonstrate how the DLR helps enable application scripting.

■ ■ ■

## CHAPTER 11

DLR in Silverlight

There are many platforms we can run DLR-based applications on. So far, our discussions and code examples have focused exclusively on using the DLR in desktop applications. In this chapter, instead of having code examples running on the .NET platform, we will look at examples that run on the Silverlight platform.

Silverlight is a client-side Web platform Microsoft developed for running Rich Internet Applications (RIAs). The Silverlight runtime runs as a plug-in in a Web browser. When you run a Silverlight application, that application runs on the Silverlight runtime. In this chapter, we'll develop many Silverlight applications that make use of the DLR. We will run those applications on the Silverlight runtime within the context of a Web browser.

Besides Silverlight, Microsoft has other Web platforms, such as ASP.NET Web Forms, ASP.NET MVC, and ASP.NET AJAX. Unlike Silverlight, which performs most of its processing in the client-side browser, the various ASP.NET platforms are server-side frameworks that perform most of their processing in the Web server. There are some projects that aim to facilitate the usage of DLR-based languages in the various ASP.NET frameworks. For example, ASP.NET Dynamic Language Support is a subproject that allows developers to write IronPython or IronRuby code in ASP.NET Web pages. The project is hosted at `http://aspnet.codeplex.com`. There is a project called IronRubyMvc, which facilitates the use of IronRuby in ASP.NET MVC applications. You can find the project at `http://github.com/jschementi/ironrubymvc`. We will not cover how to use DLR in the context of the various ASP.NET frameworks because, personally, I don't see a clear roadmap from Microsoft for supporting the DLR and dynamic languages on the ASP.NET frameworks. Readers interested in applying the DLR to ASP.NET applications can go to the ASP.NET Dynamic Language Support and IronRubyMvc web sites to find out more. In this chapter, we will focus on leveraging the DLR in client-side Web development based on Silverlight.

Different Client Side Web Scripting Approaches

There are a few ways to use dynamic languages in Silverlight applications. One way is to use dynamic languages like class libraries. With this approach, we access the dynamic languages via the DLR Hosting API. A later section in this chapter will demonstrate this approach. Another way to use dynamic languages in Silverlight applications is to use a utility program called Chiron.exe and some Silverlight application project templates. This is the first approach released by Microsoft to provide a Web scripting experience that allows people to script in Python and Ruby like they do in JavaScript. However, this approach fell somewhat out of fashion when the newer "just text" approach became available, so we'll cover only the "just text" approach.

The "just text" approach, as its name suggests, allows developers to build a Silverlight application by running code as text, without the trouble of compiling and packaging the code. Normally when developing a Silverlight application, we have to compile code and package deliverables into specific file types, such as XAP or slvx files either manually or by using tools. Every time we make some changes, we need to repeat the compilation and packaging steps if we want to manually test those changes. With the "just text" approach, changing and manually testing a Silverlight application that uses the DLR is much simplified. All we need to do is make the changes to a Web page and reload that Web page in the browser. You'll see many examples that take advantage of this approach later in this chapter. If you want to learn more about the "just text" approach after reading this chapter, one excellent document to read is *Back to "Just Text" with Silverlight,* which you can download at www.ironpython.net/browser/spec.v2.html.

Apache HTTP Server Configurations

To use the "just text" approach for hosting DLR-based language code in Silverlight, you need a web server and a browser that supports Silverlight. For this chapter's examples, I used Apache HTTP Server 2.2.16 as the web server and Google Chrome as the browser. You can use other web servers, such as Microsoft IIS, and other browsers such as FireFox or Internet Explorer to follow along.

I'll start by showing you how to set up the Apache HTTP Server for running the examples. The first thing to do, of course, is to download and install it. Once you have it installed, you need to configure a virtual host for the examples. To do so, you need to add the following line in C:\WINDOWS\system32\drivers\etc\hosts:

```
127.0.0.1        ProDLR
```

Next, open the file C:\Program Files\Apache Software Foundation\Apache2.2\conf\httpd.conf in a text editor and add the following line at the end of the file:

```
Include conf/virtual-hosts.conf
```

Last, create the file C:\Program Files\Apache Software Foundation\Apache2.2\conf\virtual-hosts.conf. Open the file in a text editor. Copy and paste the code in Listing 11-1 into the file.

Listing 11-1. virtual-hosts.conf

```
<Directory "C:\ProDLR\src\Examples\Chapter11">
    Order allow,deny
    Allow from all
</Directory>

# Use name-based virtual hosting.
NameVirtualHost 127.0.0.1:80

<VirtualHost 127.0.0.1:80>
    ServerName ProDLR
    DocumentRoot "C:\ProDLR\src\Examples\Chapter11"
    CustomLog logs/ProDLR.access.log combined
    ErrorLog logs/ProDLR.error.log
</VirtualHost>
```

The code in Listing 11-1 sets up a virtual host that will host the web site for this chapter's examples. The web site's name is ProDLR, which means the web site's URI is http://ProDLR. The physical folder that stores the web site's files is C:\ProDLR\src\Examples\Chapter11. If the folder has a file called xyz.html, you can view the file in the browser if you point the browser to http://ProDLR/xyz.html. The <Directory...> entry in Listing 11-1 is to grant necessary permissions for browsers to access the files in

C:\ProDLR\src\Examples\Chapter11. Without the ‹Directory…› entry, you'll get an error message that says you don't have permission to access the files when you later run the code examples.

After making these changes, remember to restart the Apache HTTP Server. You can verify that the Apache HTTP Server is set up properly by loading the page http://ProDLR/index.html. You should see a page that says your Apache HTTP Server is all set. Now that the Apache HTTP Server installed and the virtual host configured, we'll look at some examples of the "just text" approach for running DLR-based language code in Silverlight applications.

Using the Hosted Gestalt Components

The "just text" approach is made possible by a few software components, the product of a project called *Gestalt* whose home page is http://visitmix.com/labs/gestalt/. You can use the Gestalt components in two ways. Because the Gestalt components are hosted on http://gestalt.ironpython.net and http://gestalt.ironruby.net, the easiest way to use Gestalt is to use those hosted components. The other way to use the Gestalt components is to download them and host them ourselves. This requires more work but allows for more flexibility. In this section, we will look at how to use the hosted Gestalt components. The next section will show you how to download and host those components yourself and discuss what benefits that brings you.

Listing 11-2 shows an example that uses the Gestalt components hosted on http://gestalt.ironpython.net to run Python code in a Silverlight application. In Listing 11-2, line 3 embeds the dlr-latest.js JavaScript file from http://gestalt.ironpython.net into the HTML page. When executed, the JavaScript code in dlr-latest.js will create a Silverlight control in the HTML page. A Silverlight control created directly in an HTML page typically looks like this:

```
<html>
<body>
...
  <object data="data:application/x-silverlight-2," type="application/x-silverlight-2"
       width="100%" height="100%">
    <param name="source" value="xyz.xap"/>
    <param name="onError" value="onSilverlightError" />
    <param name="autoUpgrade" value="true" />
    ...other code omitted...
  </object>
</body>
</html>
```

As you can see, a Silverlight control in the code snippet above is created and embedded in the HTML page using an ‹object› tag. Within the object tag, there are several ‹param› tags we can use to affect the created Silverlight control. The most important ‹param› tag is the one whose name attribute is source. The source parameter declares the Silverlight application that will run inside the Silverlight control. The Silverlight control created by dlr-latest.js has a source parameter set to dlr.xap. The file dlr.xap is a Silverlight application that is capable of executing DLR-based language code embedded in HTML pages. Currently you don't see the file dlr.xap anywhere in the code example because that file is hosted on the Gestalt web site. I will show you the contents of dlr.xap in the next section when we download the Gestalt components and host them ourselves.

In Listing 11-2, there is a second ‹script› block from line 10 to line 12. The script block contains Python code that uses the HTML DOM API to change the innerHTML property of the HTML element whose id is greeting. The Python code is passed to the dlr.xap Silverlight application for interpretation.

Internally, dlr.xap uses the DLR Hosting API to execute the Python code. Listing 11-3 shows the same example for the Ruby language.

Listing 11-2. PythonHtmlDomHostedGestalt.htm

```
1)   <html>
2)   <head>
3)     <script src="http://gestalt.ironpython.net/dlr-latest.js"
4)             type="text/javascript">
5)     </script>
6)   </head>
7)
8)   <body>
9)     <h1 id="greeting"></h1>
10)    <script type="text/python">
11)      document.greeting.innerHTML = "Hello!!!"
12)    </script>
13)  </body>
14)  </html>
```

Listing 11-3. RubyHtmlDomHostedGestalt.htm

```
<html>
<head>
  <script src="http://gestalt.ironruby.net/dlr-latest.js"
          type="text/javascript">
  </script>
</head>

<body>
  <h1 id="greeting"></h1>
  <script type="text/ruby">
    document.greeting.innerHTML = "Hello World from Ruby in Silverlight!"
  </script>
</body>
</html>
```

Hosting the Gestalt Components

In the previous section we used the hosted Gestalt components to run Python and Ruby code in a Silverlight application. Although using the hosted Gestalt components makes it almost effortless to start embedding Python and Ruby code in HTML pages, there are times when you would not want your Silverlight application to rely on a network connection to the Gestalt web sites or on the Gestalt web sites themselves. In such situations, you'd want to download the Gestalt components and host them yourself. This section will show you how to do so.

First you need to download the Gestalt components, which you can do at http://visitmix.com/labs/gestalt/downloads/. The file I downloaded is Gestalt-1.0.zip. Once you download the file, unzip it to C:\Gestalt1.0, then copy the folder C:\Gestalt1.0\dlr and place it in C:\ProDLR\src\Examples\Chapter11. You should now have in your file system the C:\ProDLR\src\Examples\Chapter11\dlr folder that contains the following files: dlr.js, dlr.xap, gestaltmedia.js, IronPython.slvx, IronRuby.slvx, and Microsoft.Scripting.slvx. As you can see, the dlr.js and dlr.xap files mentioned in the previous section's examples are now sitting in your local file system. Let's see some examples that use those local files instead of the ones hosted on the Gestalt web sites. Then we will dissect the file dlr.xap to see how the Gestalt components work together to allow DLR-based language code to be embedded in HTML pages.

Listing 11-4 shows basically the same example as Listing 11-2. The only difference between the two is that in Listing 11-4, instead of pulling the dlr-latest.js file from http://gestalt.ironpython.net, we use the file dlr.js in the dlr folder. Here the dlr folder is a path relative to the HTML file's location. Our example is in C:\ProDLR\src\Examples\Chapter11\PythonHtmlDomLocalGestalt.htm. So to path of the file C:\ProDLR\src\Examples\Chapter11\dlr\dlr.js relative to PythonHtmlDomLocalGestalt.htm is /dlr/dlr.js. Listing 11-5 shows the same example for the Ruby language.

Listing 11-4. PythonHtmlDomLocalGestalt.htm

```
<html>
<head>
  <script src="/dlr/dlr.js" type="text/javascript"></script>
</head>

<body>
  <h1 id="greeting"></h1>
  <script type="text/python">
    document.greeting.innerHTML = "Hello World from Python in Silverlight!"
  </script>
</body>
</html>
```

Listing 11-5. RubyHtmlDomLocalGestalt.htm

```
<html>
<head>
  <script src="/dlr/dlr.js" type="text/javascript"></script>
</head>

<body>
  <h1 id="message"></h1>
  <script type="text/ruby">
    document.message.innerHTML = "Hello World from Ruby in Silverlight!"
  </script>
</body>
</html>
```

Dissecting the Gestalt Components

The Gestalt components we downloaded in the previous section are placed in the C:\ProDLR\src\Examples\Chapter11\dlr folder. Let's go through those components and see how they enable DLR-based language code to be embedded in HTML pages.

The file dlr.js in C:\ProDLR\src\Examples\Chapter11\dlr has JavaScript code that when embedded in an HTML page will create a Silverlight control. The Silverlight control's source parameter, as I mentioned earlier, is set to the dlr.xap file in C:\ProDLR\src\Examples\Chapter11\dlr. A xap file is in fact a zip file. If you rename dlr.xap to dlr.zip and open it, you will see that dlr.zip has two files:

AppManifest.xaml and languages.config. The dlr.xap file is a Silverlight application and AppManifest.xaml specifies the entry point assembly and entry point type of the Silverlight application. The languages.config file configures which languages are supported in the dlr.xap Silverlight application.

The entry point type of a Silverlight application must be a type that is in the entry point assembly and that derives from System.Windows.Application. If you open AppManifest.xaml, you'll see that the entry point assembly of dlr.xap is Microsoft.Scripting.Silverlight.dll and the entry point type is the class Microsoft.Scripting.Silverlight.DynamicApplication.

An instance of the entry point type Microsoft.Scripting.Silverlight.DynamicApplication represents a running Silverlight application that is capable of interpreting DLR-based language code. When an example HTML page of this chapter is loaded in the browser, the Silverlight control created by dlr.js will load the dlr.xap Silverlight application and an instance of the entry point type Microsoft.Scripting.Silverlight.DynamicApplication will be created. The source code for building the Microsoft.Scripting.Silverlight.dll assembly is part of the DLR source code you can download from the DLR Codeplex web site. If you open the C:\Codeple-DLR-1.0\Src\Codeplex-DLR-VSExpress.sln file, you'll see that the Visual Studio solution contains a project called Microsoft.Scripting.Silverlight. That is the project that contains the source code for building Microsoft.Scripting.Silverlight.dll. Building the assembly is not as straightforward as clicking a button in Visual Studio; we'll see how to build the assembly later. For now, let's take a look at some important code snippets in the Microsoft.Scripting.Silverlight project to see how the whole "just text" works end to end.

The entry point type of the dlr.xap is Microsoft.Scripting.Silverlight.DynamicApplication and you can find its code in the file DynamicApplication.cs of the Microsoft.Scripting.Silverlight project. The class DynamicApplication registers an event handler for the Startup event that it inherits from the System.Windows.Application base class. The event handler is the method DynamicApplication_Startup in DynamicApplication.cs and it will be invoked when the dlr.xap Silverlight application is executed in a browser. One fact about Silverlight applications is that they have access to the document object model (DOM) of the HTML page that hosts them. The DOM of an HTML page provides access to all of the HTML tags and their attributes as objects. The code in the DynamicApplication_Startup method uses the DOM of the HTML page that hosts the dlr.xap Silverlight application to scan for all the <script> tags in the HTML page. If you take a look at the code in the DynamicApplication_Startup method, you'll see that it creates an instance of a class called DynamicScriptTags and then calls the FetchScriptTags method on that instance. The FetchScriptTags method uses the HTML DOM to scan for the <script> tags that contain DLR-based language code. For each <script> tag that contains DLR-based language code, the code in FetchScriptTags will create an instance of DynamicScriptTags.ScriptCode and put that instance in a list. A DynamicScriptTags.ScriptCode instance can represent either DLR-based language code inlined in a <script> tag or DLR-based language code included from an external file via a <script> tag.

The DynamicApplication_Startup method will then create an instance of the DynamicEngine class and call the Run method of DynamicScriptTags with the DynamicEngine instance. The Run method uses the DLR Hosting API to execute the DLR-based language code snippets stored as DynamicScriptTags.ScriptCode instances. One thing to note about the Run method is that it calls the CreateScope method of DynamicEngine to get a script scope that's shared by all the DynamicScriptTags.ScriptCode instances that represent code snippets inlined in a <script> tag. A later section will show an example HTML page that has two <script> tags, one containing inline Ruby code and the other containing inline Python code. You'll see that the two inlined code snippets are executed in the same script scope. If a DynamicScriptTags.ScriptCode instance represents code that is included from an external file via a <script> tag, the Run method will call the CreateScope method to create a new script scope for executing the external file's code.

The CreateScope method of DynamicEngine is of particular interest because it's where the intrinsic objects available to all DLR-based language code are injected into a script scope. This should look natural if you've read about how the DLR Hosting API works in Chapter 6. The intrinsic objects made available by the "just text" approach to all DLR-based language code are the following:

- A variable named *document* that represents the host HTML document. The type of the variable is System.Windows.Browser.HtmlDocument.

- A variable named *window* that represents the host HTML window. The type of the variable is System.Windows.Browser.HtmlWindow.

- A variable named *me* and another variable named *xaml*. Both of the variables represent the root visual element of the associated XAML code if any. The two variables point to the same object. The type of the two variables is System.Windows.UIElement.

Don't worry if you don't quite understand the intrinsic variables. There will be code examples later in the chapter to show how to use those intrinsic variables.

Scripting HTML

So far, we have seen examples that use Ruby or Python code to manipulate the DOM of the host HTML page by changing the inner text of an HTML element. Now let's look at some examples that use Ruby or Python code as event handlers for HTML events.

Listing 11-6 defines a Ruby function called onclick_event_handler. The function is registered as the event handler for the onclick event of an HTML button. When the HTML button is clicked, onclick_event_handler will be invoked and the inner text of the HTML element whose id is message will be set to "Hello!!!" Notice that the intrinsic variable document is used in the Ruby code. The intrinsic variable document represents the host HTML page, and the example Ruby code uses it to get a hold of HTML elements, such as the button whose id is click_me and the element whose id is message.

Note that in Listing 11-6, there are two <script> tags that contain inlined Ruby code. Because the two code snippets are inlined in the <script> tags, they will execute in the same script scope. That is important for the example to work. Because the two code snippets execute in the same script scope, the Ruby function onclick_event_handler is available and visible in the other <script> tag that registers the Ruby function as the event handler for the HTML button's onclick event. Listing 11-7 shows the same example for the Python language.

Listing 11-6. RubyHtmlEvent1.htm

```
<html>
<head>
  <script src="/dlr/dlr.js" type="text/javascript"></script>
</head>

<body>
  <h1 id="message"></h1>
  <script type="text/ruby">
      def onclick_event_handler(sender, event)
          document.message.innerHTML = "Hello!!!"
      end
  </script>

  <input id="click_me" type="button" value="click me" />
  <script type="text/ruby">
      document.click_me.attach_event('onclick',
          System::EventHandler.new(method(:onclick_event_handler))
```

```
      )
  </script>
</body>
</html>
```

Listing 11-7. PythonHtmlEvent1.htm

```
<html>
<head>
        <script src="/dlr/dlr.js" type="text/javascript"></script>
</head>

<body>
  <h1 id="message"></h1>
  <script type="text/python">
  def onclick_event_handler(sender, event):
    document.message.innerHTML = "Hello!!!"

  </script>

  <input id="click_me" type="button" value="click me" />
  <script type="text/python">
  import System
  document.click_me.AttachEvent('onclick', System.EventHandler(onclick_event_handler))
  </script>
</body>
</html>
```

To emphasize the fact that inlined DLR language code snippets are executed in the same script scope, Listing 11-8 shows an example that purposely defines a global Ruby variable called $message in one <script> tag and uses the variable in another <script> tag. Because the Ruby code in the two <script> tags are inlined, the $message variable defined in one <script> tag is available and visible in the other <script> tag. Listing 11-9 shows the same example for Python.

Listing 11-8. RubyHtmlEvent2.htm

```
<html>
<head>
        <script src="/dlr/dlr.js" type="text/javascript"></script>
</head>

<body>
  <h1 id="message"></h1>
  <script type="text/ruby">
        def onclick_event_handler(sender, event)
            document.message.innerHTML = $message
        end
  </script>

  <input id="click_me" type="button" value="click me" />
  <script type="text/ruby">
```

```
        $message = "Hello!!!"

        document.click_me.attach_event('onclick',
            System::EventHandler.new(method(:onclick_event_handler))
        )
    </script>
</body>
</html>
```

Listing 11-9. PythonHtmlEvent2.htm

```
<html>
<head>
        <script src="/dlr/dlr.js" type="text/javascript"></script>
</head>

<body>
  <h1 id="message"></h1>
  <script type="text/python">
  def onclick_event_handler(sender, event):
    document.message.innerHTML = message

  </script>

  <input id="click_me" type="button" value="click me" />
  <script type="text/python">
  import System
  message = "Hello!!!"
  document.click_me.AttachEvent('onclick', System.EventHandler(onclick_event_handler))
  </script>
</body>
</html>
```

The previous examples in this section show how to define a function and register it as an event handler for an HTML element's event. If you like, you can define the function and register it in one go, as Listing 11-10 shows. The example in Listing 11-10 defines an anonymous Ruby function that serves as the event handler for an HTML button's onclick event.

Listing 11-10. RubyHtmlEvent3.htm

```
<html>
<head>
        <script src="/dlr/dlr.js" type="text/javascript"></script>
</head>

<body>
  <h1 id="message"></h1>
  <script type="text/ruby">
        $message = "Hello!!!"
  </script>
```

```
    <input id="click_me" type="button" value="click me" />
    <script type="text/ruby">
        document.click_me.onclick do
            document.message.innerHTML = $message
        end
    </script>
</body>
</html>
```

We can define the function in Ruby and register the Ruby function with an HTML button's event in Python. Listing 11-11 mixes Ruby code and Python code in one HTML page. Both the Ruby code and Python code are inlined in a <script> tag and hence executed in the same script scope. Therefore, the Ruby function is available and visible in the Python code.

Listing 11-11. PythonRubyHtmlEvent.htm

```
<html>
<head>
        <script src="/dlr/dlr.js" type="text/javascript"></script>
</head>

<body>
  <h1 id="message"></h1>
  <script type="text/ruby">
        def onclick_event_handler(sender, event)
            document.message.innerHTML = "Hello!!!"
        end
  </script>

  <input id="click_me" type="button" value="click me" />
  <script type="text/python">
  import System
  document.click_me.AttachEvent('onclick', System.EventHandler(onclick_event_handler))
  </script>
</body>
</html>
```

Scripting XAML

With the "just text" approach, not only can we script the HTML DOM in DLR-based languages, we can also work with UI markups expressed in XAML. XAML is a .NET object serialization format that can serialize .NET objects into XML and vice versa. Listing 11-12 shows an example that displays a green rectangle in the browser. The rectangle is expressed in XAML by the <Rectangle> tag within the <Canvas> tag. At runtime, the XML tags will be parsed and deserialized into .NET objects that represent a canvas and a rectangle.

Listing 11-12. RectangleXaml.htm

```
<html>
<head>
  <script src="/dlr/dlr.js" type="text/javascript"></script>
```

```
      </head>

      <body>
        <script type="application/xml+xaml" width="150" height="150">
          <Canvas xmlns="http://schemas.microsoft.com/winfx/2006/xaml/presentation"
                  xmlns:x="http://schemas.microsoft.com/winfx/2006/xaml"
                  Width="150" Height="150">
            <Rectangle Width="50" Height="50" Canvas.Left="20" Canvas.Top="20" Fill="Green" />
          </Canvas>
        </script>
      </body>
      </html>
```

The example in Listing 11-12 contains only a XAML code snippet and does not employ any Ruby or Python code to script the XAML UI elements. The next example, shown in Listing 11-13, demonstrates how to script the XAML rectangle element and change the rectangle's color from green to red.

The first important thing to note about the code in Listing 11-13 is that the code id="rect" is added in line 9. The id attribute uniquely identifies the XAML code from line 10 to line 16. In line 19, we refer to the XAML code by its unique id. This effectively associates the Python code from line 20 to line 23 with the XAML code and makes the intrinsic variable me in line 23 refer to the root UI visual element of the XAML code. Because the code in line 14 gives the XAML rectangle a unique name as its identifier, in line 23 we are able to refer to the XAML rectangle as me.rectangle. In line 23 we create a new instance of the SolidColorBrush class that has the red color and assign the SolidColorBrush instance to the Fill property of me.rectangle to change the XAML rectangle color to red. Because we use the SolidColorBrush class and the Colors class in line 23, we need to import them from the System.Windows.Media namespace in line 21.

Listing 11-13. PythonXamlEvent1.htm

```
1)    <html>
2)    <head>
3)      <script src="/dlr/dlr.js" type="text/javascript"></script>
4)    </head>
5)
6)    <body>
7)      <h1 id="message"></h1>
8)
9)      <script id="rect" type="application/xml+xaml" width="150" height="150">
10)       <Canvas xmlns="http://schemas.microsoft.com/winfx/2006/xaml/presentation"
11)               xmlns:x="http://schemas.microsoft.com/winfx/2006/xaml"
12)         Width="150" Height="150">
13)
14)         <Rectangle x:Name="rectangle" Width="50" Height="50"
15)                 Canvas.Left="20" Canvas.Top="20" Fill="Green" />
16)       </Canvas>
17)     </script>
18)
19)     <script class="rect" type="text/python">
20)     import clr
21)     from System.Windows.Media import (SolidColorBrush, Colors)
22)
```

```
23)    me.rectangle.Fill = SolidColorBrush(Colors.Red)
24)    </script>
25)  </body>
26)  </html>
```

The code in Listing 11-14 shows one more example of manipulating XAML elements in Python code. What's new in this example is how to register a Python function as an event handler for a XAML button's Click event. This is analogous to the example that registers a Ruby or Python function as an event handler for an HTML button's onclick event. The code in Listing 11-14 is largely the same as that in Listing 11-13. One difference is that Listing 11-14 has a <Button> tag in the XAML UI markup. The unique name of the <Button> tag is clickMeButton and we refer to it as me.clickMeButton in the embedded Python code. The <script> tag that contains the Python code defines a Python function called onclick_event_handler and registers the Python function to the me.clickMeButton.Click event. One caveat about the code in Listing 11-14 is that while you might think you can register the event handler like the following, you can't:

```
<script id="rect" type="application/xml+xaml" width="150" height="150">
  <Canvas ...>
    <Rectangle ... />
    <Button x:Name="clickMeButton" Click="onclick_event_handler" .../>
  </Canvas>
</script>
```

Registering a Python or Ruby function as the event handler in XAML markup is not yet supported by the "just text" approach.

Listing 11-14. PythonXamlEvent2.htm

```
<html>
<head>
  <script src="/dlr/dlr.js" type="text/javascript"></script>
</head>

<body>
  <h1 id="message"></h1>

  <script id="rect" type="application/xml+xaml" width="150" height="150">
    <Canvas xmlns="http://schemas.microsoft.com/winfx/2006/xaml/presentation"
            xmlns:x="http://schemas.microsoft.com/winfx/2006/xaml"
            Width="150" Height="150">

      <Rectangle x:Name="rectangle" Width="50" Height="50"
                 Canvas.Left="20" Canvas.Top="20" Fill="Green" />
      <Button x:Name="clickMeButton" Width="70" Height="20"
                 Canvas.Left="20" Canvas.Top="90" Content="Click Me" />
    </Canvas>
  </script>

  <script class="rect" type="text/python">
  import clr
  from System.Windows.Media import (SolidColorBrush, Colors)
```

```
    def onclick_event_handler(sender, event):
        me.rectangle.Fill = SolidColorBrush(Colors.Red)

    me.clickMeButton.Click += onclick_event_handler
    </script>
</body>
</html>
```

DLR Settings

Earlier in this chapter, I mentioned that the dlr.js file contains JavaScript code that when embedded in an HTML page creates a Silverlight control. Because we need to be able to create Silverlight controls with different behaviors and capabilities, the dlr.js file provides some settings we can configure when we embed the file in a host HTML page. In this section, we will look at a setting that causes a language console to show up in the host HTML page. The language console will take the code you enter, evaluate it, and display the evaluation results, much like the ir.exe command console of IronRuby and the ipy.exe command console of IronPython.

The JavaScript code in dlr.js essentially defines an object called DLR. The object DLR has some properties and functions defined for it. Examples of the properties are path, settings, and autoAdd. Examples of the functions are createSilverlightObject, getSettings and defaultSettings. The settings property of the DLR object can point to an object that can have properties such as width, height, console, and id. The console property is the one that controls whether a language console will show up in the host HTML page. This section will only cover the console property. A later section will cover the path property of the DLR object. You can refer to *Back to "Just Text" with Silverlight* for details on the settings you're interested in.

Listing 11-15 shows an example that displays a language console in the host HTML page by setting the console property to true. If you run the example by pointing your browser to http://prodlr/PythonConsole.htm, you'll see a language console at the bottom of the web page where you can type in Python code after the console prompt and press the Enter key to have the Python code evaluated. Note that when assigning values to the DLR object's properties, we have to do so before the dlr.js file is included in the HTML page. Listing 11-16 shows the same example for the Ruby language.

Listing 11-15. PythonConsole.htm

```
<html>
<head>
  <script type="text/javascript">
    window.DLR = {}
    DLR.settings = {console: true}
  </script>

  <script src="/dlr/dlr.js" type="text/javascript"></script>
</head>

<body>
  <script type="text/python"></script>
</body>
</html>
```

Listing 11-16. RubyConsole.htm

```html
<html>
<head>
  <script type="text/javascript">
    window.DLR = {}
    DLR.settings = {console: true}
  </script>

  <script src="/dlr/dlr.js" type="text/javascript"></script>
</head>

<body>
  <script type="text/ruby"></script>
</body>
</html>
```

Speak Your Own Language in Silverlight

So far in this chapter, you've seen how to use the Gestalt project to host IronPython and IronRuby code in Silverlight. You've seen examples that use the Gestalt components hosted on `http://gestalt.ironruby.net` and `http://gestalt.ironpython.net`. You've also seen how to download the Gestalt code and host the Gestalt components yourself. It's nice to leverage the Gestalt components in a Silverlight application. However, if you ever need to host your custom language code in Silverlight or if you want to target different DLR versions for your Silverlight application, you'll need to build your own Gestalt-like components. The rest of this chapter will show you how to do that, from the ground up.

First, we will build a new custom language—the Hello language you saw in Chapter 1. To host the custom language in Silverlight, we need to implement the provider side of the DLR Hosting API for the language. Second, we will host the Hello language in Silverlight without using Microsoft.Scripting.Silverlight.dll or any Gestalt-like components. In this exercise, you'll see that hosting a custom language in Silverlight is really no different from using a class library. Finally, we will create our custom Gestalt-like components and use them to host the Hello language in a Silverlight application. To follow these examples, you need to install some software components. You also need to build the Microsoft.Scripting.Silverlight project in the DLR source code. Let's go through those steps for setting up the development environment we need for this chapter's examples.

Software Requirements

Here are the software components you need in order to try out the examples in the rest of this chapter.

- You need to have Visual Web Developer 2010 Express installed.

- You need to have the Silverlight 4 Toolkit April 2010 Release and Silverlight 4 Tools for Visual Studio 2010 installed. The easiest way to install these components is to install Microsoft Web Platform Installer 2.0. Once it's installed, you can use it to download and install both components. Alternatively, you can go to the respective web sites for Silverlight 4 Toolkit April 2010 Release and Silverlight 4 Tools for Visual Studio 2010 to download and install them.

After installing these software components, some people expressed in various discussion forums that they got an error message saying that Silverlight Developer Runtime is not installed. If you happen to run into that issue, you can fix it by downloading the Silverlight Developer Runtime at `http://go.microsoft.com/fwlink/?LinkID=188039` and installing it.

Build DLR for Silverlight

Before we start coding, there's one last bit of preparation work that needs to be done—building the DLR source code with Silverlight as the target platform. This is necessary because we will be building Silverlight applications and the DLR assemblies we've been using so far are for.NET applications. The challenge here is that if you open the C:\Codeplex-DLR-1.0\Src\Codeplex-DLR-VSExpress.sln and try to build the Microsoft.Scripting.Silverlight project, you will get a bunch of compilation errors. Fortunately, a workaround was posted on the DLR Codeplex discussion forum and it works like a charm. Here's how to build the DLR source code for Silverlight.

1. Open the Visual Studio command prompt. The command prompt seems to be installed as part of the installation of Visual Studio C++ 2010 Express.

2. In the command prompt, navigate to the C:\Codeplex-DLR-1.0\Src folder and execute the following command:

```
msbuild
Hosts\SilverLight\Microsoft.Scripting.SilverLight\Microsoft.Scripting.Silverlight.csproj
/p:Configuration="Silverlight 4 Debug" /p:SilverlightPath="C:\Program Files\Microsoft
Silverlight\4.0.50826.0"
```

In the command, the version of Silverlight I used in 4.0.50826.0. If you want to use a different version, adjust the command accordingly. After executing the command, the Microsoft.Scripting.Silverlight project and its dependencies should all be built successfully. The assemblies generated by the build process are in the C:\Codeplex-DLR-1.0\Src\Hosts\SilverLight\Bin\Debug folder.

3. Copy the files in C:\Codeplex-DLR-1.0\Src\Hosts\SilverLight\Bin\Debug to C:\ProDLR\lib\SilverlightDLR\debug.

You now have the DLR binaries needed for building Silverlight applications. You'll reference those binaries in the Silverlight projects you build in the rest of this chapter.

The Hello Language

Our goal now is to implement the provider side of the DLR Hosting API for the Hello language. You can find all the code presented in this section in the HelloConsole solution of this chapter's code download. If you want to start from scratch, you can fire up Visual Web Developer 2010 Express and create a new project. The project is a C# Silverlight class library. I named the project HelloLanguage and the solution HelloConsole. You will be prompted to select a version of Silverlight as the target version for the new project. For this example, I selected Silverlight 4. The project needs to reference the Microsoft.Dynamic.dll and Microsoft.Scripting.dll assemblies located in C:\ProDLR\lib\SilverlightDLR\debug. Those are the assemblies you built in the previous section.

Hello is a language that accepts any code as valid input and returns the string "Hello!!!" as the result of evaluating the code. To plug the Hello language into the DLR Hosting API, we need to implement the provider side of the DLR Hosting API for the language. For our simple Hello language, that means we need to implement a class that derives from LanguageContext and a class that derives from ScriptCode.

The class that derives from LanguageContext is called HelloContext and is shown in Listing 11-17. LanguageContext is a class meant to be subclassed by a language implementer. The subclass is supposed to provide functionalities such as returning the script engine and compiling and interpreting the source code of the custom language. In Listing 11-17, HelloContext provides the functionality of compiling Hello language code by overriding the CompileSourceCode method it inherits from LanguageContext. The CompileSourceCode method in Listing 11-17 simply creates an instance of HelloScriptCode and returns it. Listing 11-18 shows the code of the HelloScriptCode class.

Listing 11-17. The HelloContext Class

```
public class HelloContext : LanguageContext
{
    public HelloContext(ScriptDomainManager domainManager,
        IDictionary<string, object> options)
        : base(domainManager)
    { }

    public override ScriptCode CompileSourceCode(SourceUnit sourceUnit,
        CompilerOptions options, ErrorSink errorSink)
    {
        return new HelloScriptCode(sourceUnit);
    }
}
```

Listing 11-18. The HelloScriptCode Class

```
public class HelloScriptCode : ScriptCode
{
    public HelloScriptCode(SourceUnit sourceUnit)
        : base(sourceUnit)
    { }

    public override object Run(Scope scope)
    {
        return "Hello!!!";
    }
}
```

Now that we have the Hello language plugged into the DLR Hosting API, the next step is to create a Silverlight application that makes use of the Hello language. There is more than one way to host a custom language in a Silverlight application. No matter which approach we take, the basic requirement—that the custom language be plugged into the DLR Hosting API—remains the same. In the rest of this chapter, we will look at two different approaches for hosting the Hello language in Silverlight applications. One uses the compiled Hello language assembly HelloLanguage.dll as a typical .NET class library. The other is the "just text" approach.

Hello Console in Silverlight

In this section, we will create a Silverlight application that hosts the Hello language by using the DLR Hosting API and the HelloLanguage.dll assembly directly. The Silverlight application will not use the Microsoft.Scripting.Silverlight.dll assembly, nor will it use of any of the Gestalt-like files.

To begin, first create a new C# Silverlight application project. If you don't have the HelloConsole solution you created in the previous section open, you need to open it. Once you are in the HelloConsole solution, you can select File   New Project… to create this section's new project. In the New Project wizard, expand the Visual C# node on the left and select the Silverlight subnode underneath the Visual C# node, as the screen capture in Figure 11-1 shows. Notice that the selected project template in the middle of the wizard dialog is Silverlight Application.

Figure 11-1. *Creating a new Silverlight application project for hosting the Hello language in a Silverlight application*

Once you hit OK, the next step in the New Project wizard is the configuration of the Web project that will host the new Silverlight application. Figure 11-2 shows the selections you should make in this step.

Figure 11-2. Configuring the Web project that will be used to host the new Silverlight application

After you click the OK button, you'll see two new projects added to the HelloConsole solution. The new project HelloConsole is the Silverlight application. The other new project, HelloConsole.Web, is the Web project that will host the HelloConsole Silverlight application. The HelloConsole.Web project as generated is fine for our purpose and we don't need to make any changes to it. For the HelloConsole project, you need to add to it references to the following:

- Microsoft.Dynamic.dll and Microsoft.Scripting.dll in C:\ProDLR\lib\SilverlightDLR\debug

- Microsoft.CSharp.dll

- The HelloLanguage project in the same solution

Next, open the file MainPage.xaml and replace its contents with the code in Listing 11-19, which declares the UI of our Silverlight application in XAML. The UI is a UserControl that uses a StackPanel to lay out its child element, a TextBox. The TextBox is the Hello console in which users can type in Hello code and see the result of evaluating that code. The name of the TextBox is helloConsole.

Listing 11-19. MainPage.xaml

```
<UserControl x:Class="HelloConsole.MainPage"
    xmlns="http://schemas.microsoft.com/winfx/2006/xaml/presentation"
    xmlns:x="http://schemas.microsoft.com/winfx/2006/xaml"
    xmlns:d="http://schemas.microsoft.com/expression/blend/2008"
    xmlns:mc="http://schemas.openxmlformats.org/markup-compatibility/2006"
    mc:Ignorable="d"
    d:DesignHeight="300" d:DesignWidth="400">
```

```
    <StackPanel>
        <TextBox x:Name="helloConsole" KeyUp="TextBox_KeyUp"
                    Height="200" Margin="10"
                    TextWrapping="NoWrap" AcceptsReturn="True"
                    VerticalScrollBarVisibility="Visible" Text=">>>" />
    </StackPanel>
</UserControl>
```

The UI declarations shown in Listing 11-19 are associated with a code-behind file called MainPage.cs. The helloConsole textbox specifies an event handler for the KeyUp event of TextBox. The event handler is a C# method and its code is in MainPage.cs. Listing 11-20 shows the code in MainPage.cs. The class MainPage declares a member variable scriptEngine in line 3. The scriptEngine variable is initialized in the constructor. The initialization of the scriptEngine variable should look familiar if you have read Chapter 6. Basically, the code creates an instance of LanguageSetup that contains the setup information of the Hello language. Then it puts the LanguageSetup instance into a ScriptRuntimeSetup instance and uses the ScriptRuntimeSetup instance to create a script runtime. After the script runtime is created, the code obtains a reference to the Hello language's script engine by calling the GetEngine method on the script runtime in line 19.

The scriptEngine member variable is used in the TextBox_KeyUp method to evaluate the Hello code users type in the UI. The Hello code we want to evaluate is whatever users type after the >>> console prompt and before the Enter key is pressed. So TextBox_KeyUp checks first if the currently released key is the Enter key. If yes, then line 27 extracts the text the user typed after the last >>> console prompt. In line 28, we use scriptEngine to execute the extracted Hello code and store the execution result in a variable. In line 29 we display the execution result in the helloConsole textbox and print out a new >>> console prompt.

Listing 11-20. MainPage.cs

```
1)  public partial class MainPage : UserControl
2)  {
3)      private ScriptEngine scriptEngine;
4)
5)      public MainPage()
6)      {
7)          InitializeComponent();
8)
9)          LanguageSetup langSetup = new LanguageSetup(
10)             typeName: "HelloLanguage.HelloContext,HelloLanguage,
11)                 Version=1.0.0.0, Culture=neutral",
12)             displayName: "Hello",
13)             names: new String[] { "Hello" },
14)             fileExtensions: new String[] { ".hello" });
15)
16)         ScriptRuntimeSetup setup = new ScriptRuntimeSetup();
17)         setup.LanguageSetups.Add(langSetup);
18)         ScriptRuntime scriptRuntime = new ScriptRuntime(setup);
19)         scriptEngine = scriptRuntime.GetEngine("Hello");
20)     }
21)
22)     private void TextBox_KeyUp(object sender, KeyEventArgs e)
23)     {
```

```
24)            if (e.Key == Key.Enter)
25)            {
26)                int index = helloConsole.Text.LastIndexOf(">>>");
27)                String code = helloConsole.Text.Substring(index + 3);
28)                String result = scriptEngine.Execute(code);
29)                helloConsole.Text += result + "\n>>>";
30)                helloConsole.SelectionStart = helloConsole.Text.Length;
31)            }
32)        }
33) }
```

If you run the Silverlight application, you'll see a textbox with the >>> console prompt showing up in the browser. If you type some dummy characters and press enter, you'll see something that looks like Figure 11-3.

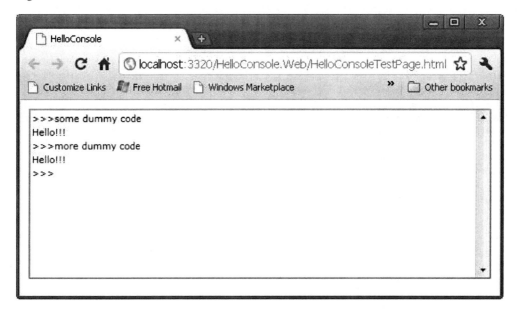

Figure 11-3. *The Silverlight application running in the browser*

Gestalt-like Hello Console on Silverlight

In the previous section we developed a Silverlight application that displays a console for the Hello language. The Silverlight application does not depend on the Microsoft.Scripting.Silverlight.dll assembly and does not use any of the Gestalt-like components. Now let's take the "just text" approach and use the Microsoft.Scripting.Silverlight.dll assembly to host the Hello language console in a Silverlight application. I will walk you through the steps you need to take to build your own Gestalt-like components that support your custom language. The example we'll build requires creating the following:

- dlr.xap

- Microsoft.Scripting.slvx

- HelloLanguage.slvx

- the test HTML page

We need to create dlr.xap because (a) we want to support only the Hello language in our Silverlight application and (b) we want to target Silverlight 4.0 as the runtime for running the Silverlight application. For those two reasons we can't use the dlr.xap downloaded from the Gestalt web site.

To create our own dlr.xap, we will copy all files except Microsoft.Scripting.slvx, IronPython.slvx and IronRuby.slvx in C:\ProDLR\src\Examples\Chapter11\dlr to C:\ProDLR\src\Examples\Chapter11\hellodlr. Rename the file dlr.xap in C:\ProDLR\src\Examples\Chapter11\hellodlr to dlr.zip. There are two files in dlr.zip: AppManifest.xaml and languages.config. Open AppManifest.xaml and replace the file's contents with the following:

```
<Deployment xmlns="http://schemas.microsoft.com/client/2007/deployment"
        xmlns:x="http://schemas.microsoft.com/winfx/2006/xaml"
  RuntimeVersion="4.0.50826.0"
EntryPointAssembly="Microsoft.Scripting.Silverlight"
EntryPointType="Microsoft.Scripting.Silverlight.DynamicApplication"
ExternalCallersFromCrossDomain="ScriptableOnly">
  <Deployment.Parts>
  </Deployment.Parts>
  <Deployment.ExternalParts>
    <ExtensionPart Source="Microsoft.Scripting.slvx" />
  </Deployment.ExternalParts>
</Deployment>
```

As you can see, in AppManifest.xaml, we specify that the Silverlight runtime we want to target for our Silverlight application is version 4.0.50826.0. If you use a different version of Silverlight, you'll need to adjust the code you put into AppManifest.xaml accordingly. Next you need to modify the languages.config file. Open languages.config in a text editor and replace its contents with the following:

```
<Languages>
  <Language
    names="Hello"
    languageContext="HelloLanguage.HelloContext"
    extensions=".hello"
    assemblies="HelloLanguage.dll"
    external="HelloLanguage.slvx"
  />
</Languages>
```

Note that in the languages.config file, we configure our Silverlight application to support only the Hello language. We also specify that the binaries of the Hello language will be packaged into the HelloLanguage.slvx file. Let's perform the packaging and create the HelloLanguage.slvx file.

To create HelloLanguage.slvx, you need to build the Chapter11 Visual Studio solution if you haven't done so. Then you need to zip up HelloLanguage.dll in C:\ProDLR\src\Examples\Chapter11\HelloConsole\HelloLanguage\Bin\Debug. Name the zip file

HelloLanguage.slvx and place it in C:\ProDLR\src\Examples\Chapter11\hellodlr. That's it for the HelloLanguage.slvx file.

The last file we need to create is Microsoft.Scripting.slvx. We can't use the Microsoft.Scripting.slvx file downloaded from the Gestalt web site because we want to use the version of DLR assemblies we built ourselves in our Silverlight application. To create Microsoft.Scripting.slvx, you need to zip up the three files Microsoft.Scripting.dll, Microsoft.Scripting.Silverlight.dll, and Microsoft.Dynamic.dll in C:\ProDLR\lib\SilverlightDLR\debug. Name the zip file Microsoft.Scripting.slvx and place it in C:\ProDLR\src\Examples\Chapter11\hellodlr.

At this point, our Silverlight application is complete and we are ready to take it for a test drive. To try out the Silverlight application, open a Web browser and navigate to http://prodlr/HelloConsole.htm. Your browser will look like Figure 11-4. At the bottom of the Web page there is a console for the Hello language. If you type in any code and press the Enter key, the code you type in will be evaluated and the text "Hello!!!" will be printed out as the result of the code evaluation.

Figure 11-4. Hello language console powered by a Gestalt-like Silverlight application

Listing 11-21 shows the HelloConsole.htm code. It's pretty much the same as the examples we saw earlier that display a Python or Ruby console in the browser. One thing to note about the code in Listing 11-21 is that it sets the path property of the DLR object to "/hellodlr". This is necessary because the default value of the DLR object's path property is "/dlr". However, because all the Gestalt-like files that make up our Silverlight application are placed in the hellodlr folder, we need to overwrite the default value of the DLR object's path and set it to "/hellodlr".

Listing 11-21. HelloConsole.htm

```html
<html>
  <head>
    <script type="text/javascript">
      window.DLR = {}
      DLR.path = "/hellodlr"
      DLR.settings = {console: true}
    </script>

    <script src="/hellodlr/dlr.js" type="text/javascript"></script>
  </head>

  <body>
    <script type="text/Hello">
        dummy code
    </script>
  </body>
</html>
```

Summary

This chapter begins with an overview of different software projects and components that facilitate the use of DLR-based languages in various server-side and client-side Web environments. We then focused on the "just text" approach for hosting DLR-based language code in HTML pages. First, we looked at several examples that demonstrate the integration between the HTML DOM, XAML code snippets, and IronPython and IronRuby code. Some examples show how to use the HTML DOM in IronPython and IronRuby code to modify an HTML page. Others show how to register an IronRuby or IronPython function as the event handler for a XAML or HTML element's event.

Next, we developed a trivial language and used it in a Silverlight application without using any Gestalt-like components. Then we took the "just text" approach for hosting our custom language in a Silverlight application. We walked through the steps of creating HelloLanguage.slvx and our custom dlr.xap and Microsoft.Scripting.slvx. The "just text" approach as well as all of this chapter's examples are fundamentally based on the DLR Hosting API. We saw some excellent applications of the DLR Hosting API in earlier chapters of this book, and this chapter shows you one more excellent application of the DLR Hosting API.

CHAPTER 12

■ ■ ■

Dynamic Languages on JVM

So far, we've been discussing the DLR and its applications. In this chapter, we will look at the framework in the Java world that's equivalent to the DLR. We will see how that Java framework facilitates running dynamic language code on the Java virtual machine, how to host dynamic languages in a Java program, and what kind of language interoperability the framework supports. When appropriate, we'll compare the Java framework and the DLR. If you have a need to write Java programs that use dynamic languages, this chapter will help you quickly get up to speed by leveraging what you've learned so far.

Quick Comparisons

You'll find that support for dynamic languages in the .NET and Java worlds corresponds to each other quite nicely. Before we compare each feature area in more detail, it's helpful to have an overall view of how the .NET and Java platforms stack up against each in their support for dynamic languages. To that end, Table 12-1 shows some quick comparisons. The first column shows dynamic language support on the .NET platform, the second shows the corresponding support on the Java platform.

Table 12-1. Support for Dynamic Languages on .NET and Java

.NET	Java
IronPython is an implementation of the Python language that runs on .NET CLR.	Jython is an implementation of the Python language that runs on the JVM.
IronRuby is an implementation of the Ruby language that runs on .NET CLR.	JRuby is an implementation of the Ruby language that runs on the JVM.
DLR Hosting API	Java Specification Request (JSR) 223 Scripting for the Java Platform is the equivalent API of the DLR Hosting API in the Java world. The JSR 223 API allows hosting dynamic languages in a Java program.
DLR binders, dynamic objects	On the Java side, the closest thing to DLR binders and dynamic objects is JSR 292: Supporting Dynamically Typed Languages on the Java Platform.

In Table 12-1 you can see that the equivalent of the DLR Hosting API on the Java side is the JSR 223 API. Table 12-2 compares the two APIs.

Table 12-2. Comparison of DLR Hosting API and JSR 223.

DLR Hosting API	JSR 223 Scripting for the Java Platform
ScriptRuntime class	ScriptEngineManager class
ScriptEngine class	ScriptEngine class
App.config. DLR Hosting API uses the App.config file to discover script engines that are available in a deployment environment.	META-INF/services/javax.script.ScriptEngineFactory. JSR 223 uses the javax.script.ScriptEngineFactory file to discover script engines that are available in a deployment environment.
ScriptScope class	ScriptContext class
CompiledCode class	CompiledScript class
ScriptSource class	N/A. JSR 223 does not define a class that's equivalent to DLR Host API's ScriptSource class.
Silverlight. DLR Hosting API makes it possible to run dynamic language code not only in a standalone application but also in Silverlight applications.	Servlet container. Using JSR 223, one can host dynamic language code in not only standalone Java applications but also in a Servlet container.

This chapter is organized into two parts. The first part will look at some well-known dynamic language implementations that run on the JVM and also how to host those languages in Java programs using JSR 223. The second part will develop a simple programming language that deals with logic operations. We will see how to provide a JSR 223 implementation for the simple language so that it can be hosted in Java programs. You will find that almost all of the discussions in this chapter correspond nicely to our earlier discussions on DLR.

Python and Ruby on JVM

Many dynamic language implementations use the JVM as their runtime. That means those implementations will turn their code into Java bytecode at run time and have the JVM execute the bytecode. This is analogous to what happens on the .NET side. Like the JVM executing Java bytecode, the .NET CLR executes Intermediate Language (IL) instructions. Language implementations such as IronPython and IronRuby run on the CLR by eventually translating their code into IL code and having the CLR execute the IL code.

In this part of the chapter, we will look at Jython and JRuby, two dynamic language implementations that run on the JVM. You'll see how those language implementations provide interoperability with Java code, as well as how to use the Java equivalent of the DLR Hosting API to host Python and Ruby code in Java programs. You'll find the code for this in the JavaHostingExamples project. In order to run the code, you need the following software components installed:

- JDK 6 or above. The version I used for developing the code examples is JDK 1.6.0 update 14.

- Eclipse IDE. The version I used is Eclipse 3.6.

- Jython. I downloaded version 2.5.1 and installed it in C:\jython2.5.1. After the installation, you need to copy C:\jython2.5.1\jython.jar to C:\ProDLR\src\Examples\Chapter12\JavaScripting\lib\Jython

- JRuby. I downloaded version 1.5.1 and installed it in C:\jruby-1.5.1. After the installation, you need to copy C:\jruby-1.5.1\lib\jruby.jar to C:\ProDLR\src\Examples\Chapter12\JavaScripting\lib\JRuby\1.5.1.

- Normally you would need to download the script engines that implement the JSR 223 API for the languages we want to host in a Java program. However, in this case, we don't need to bother because the files jruby.jar and jython.jar already contain the script engines. If you use a dynamic language implementation that doesn't include a JSR 223 script engine in its binaries, you can go to https://scripting.dev.java.net/ and see if a JSR 223 script engine that implements the JSR 223 API is available for the language.

Hosting Python Code in Java Programs

Jython is to JVM as IronPython is to CLR. IronPython is an implementation of the Python language that runs on the CLR. Similarly, Jython is an implementation of the Python language that runs on the JVM. One key benefit of targeting the CLR or JVM as the runtime is the ability to leverage the enormous assets of readily available .NET or Java libraries. IronPython gives Python developers access to .NET libraries while Jython gives them access to Java libraries. Earlier we saw examples of Python code that uses classes written in C#. Now we'll look at some examples of Python code that run on JVM and uses classes written in Java.

Listing 12-1 shows an example that uses the JSR 223 API to host Python code in a Java program. If you recall in Chapter 6 how we used the DLR Hosting API to host Python code in a C# program, you'll understand the code in Listing 12-1 right away. With the DLR Hosting API, we create an instance of ScriptRuntime and use it to get an instance of ScriptEngine for executing Python code. Here in Listing 12-1 we create an instance of javax.script.ScriptEngineManager and use it to get an instance of javax.script.ScriptEngine. To get an instance of javax.script.ScriptEngine that's capable of running Python code, the code in Listing 12-1 calls the getEngineByName method on the ScriptEngineManager instance and passes the string "jython" as the argument. In Chapter 6, to get an instance of Microsoft.Scripting.Hosting.ScriptEngine that's capable of running Python code, we call the GetEngine method on a ScriptRuntime instance and pass the string "python" as the argument.

To show the interoperability between Jython and the Java language, the example in Listing 12-1 creates an instance of a Java class called Product whose code is shown in Listing 12-2. The Product class has two fields: name and price. For each field, the Product class provides getter and setter methods for getting and setting the field's value. Once the Product instance is created, the example in Listing 12-1 calls the put method on the ScriptEngine instance to put the Product instance into the script engine's variable bindings. In this case, the Product instance is bound to the name handClapper. This step is equivalent to calling the SetVariable method on a Microsoft.Scripting.Hosting.ScriptEngine instance. With the DLR Hosting API, we call the SetVariable method on a Microsoft.Scripting.Hosting.ScriptEngine instance to bind an object to a name. Once an object is bound to a name, the Python code can retrieve the object by that name and that's what the Python code in Listing 12-1 does. The code is the string "print handClapper.getName()" passed to the eval method of

ScriptEngine. This step is equivalent to calling the Execute method on a
Microsoft.Scripting.Hosting.ScriptEngine instance.

Listing 12-1. A Java Program That Uses the JSR 223 API to Host Python Code

```
private static void printProductNameInPython()
throws ScriptException, NoSuchMethodException, IOException {
    ScriptEngineManager manager = new ScriptEngineManager();
    ScriptEngine engine = manager.getEngineByName("jython");
    Product handClapper = new Product("Hand Clapper", 6);
    engine.put("handClapper", handClapper);
    engine.eval("print handClapper.getName()");
}
```

Listing 12-2. A Java Class Whose Instance Will be Passed to Python Code

```
public class Product {
    private String name;
    private int price;

    public Product(String name, int price) {
        this.name = name;
        this.price = price;
    }

    public String getName() {
        return name;
    }

    public void setName(String name) {
        this.name = name;
    }

    public int getPrice() {
        return price;
    }

    public void setPrice(int price) {
        this.price = price;
    }
}
```

As you can see, each line of code in Listing 12-1 has a counterpart in the DLR Hosting API. The
concept of passing Java objects to Python code is also the same as that in the DLR Hosting API. The
example in Listing 12-1 prints the name of a product in Python code. The next example in Listing 12-3
also prints the name of a product in Python code. The difference here is that the Python code is used as
an invocable function in the Java program. The code in Listing 12-3 is largely the same as the code in
Listing 12-1 except for lines 6 and 7. In Listing 12-3 at line 6, instead of evaluating Python code as a
string, the example code reads the Python code from the file printProductName.py in the
src/main/resources folder. This is analogous to calling the ExecuteFile of DLR Hosting API's

ScriptEngine class to execute Python code in a file. If you open the file printProductName.py, you'll see that it defines a Python function like this:

```
def printProductName(x):
  print x.getName()
```

In line 7 of Listing 12-3, the code casts the type of the engine variable to Invocable and calls the invokeFunction method on the type-casted variable. The purpose of this line of code is to invoke the printProductName function defined in printProductName.py. As you can see, the syntax here for invoking a Python function in Java is not as seamless and intuitive as the syntax we get with the DLR Hosting API. Using the DLR Hosting API, we refer to a Python function as a .NET delegate and we directly invoke the .NET delegate to execute it. Here in Listing 12-3, we have to invoke the Python function by its name, instead of calling it directly as if it were a Java method.

Listing 12-3. A Java program That Uses the JSR 223 API to Invoke a Python Function

```
1)   private static void printProductNameByInvokingPythonFunction()
2)   throws ScriptException, NoSuchMethodException, IOException {
3)       ScriptEngineManager manager = new ScriptEngineManager();
4)       ScriptEngine engine = manager.getEngineByName("jython");
5)       Product handClapper = new Product("Hand Clapper", 6);
6)       engine.eval(new FileReader(new File("src/main/resources/printProductName.py")));
7)       ((Invocable) engine).invokeFunction("printProductName", handClapper);
8)   }
```

Hosting Ruby Code in Java Programs

The previous examples show how to host Python code in Java programs. Let's see how to do the same thing for Ruby code. The example code in Listing 12-4 uses some Ruby code to calculate the total price of two products. The Ruby code is placed in the calculateTotal.rb file in the src/main/resources folder, and it looks like this:

```
def calculateTotal(x, y)
  return x.getPrice() + y.getPrice()
end
```

The Ruby code defines a function called calculateTotal that takes two input parameters. The calculateTotal function calls the getPrice method on the two input parameters and returns the sum of the two prices. The code in Listing 12-4 is very similar to the code in Listing 12-3. In Listing 12-4, we get a script engine that knows how to evaluate Ruby code by calling the getEngineByExtension method of ScriptEngineManager. We create two instances of the Java Product class and pass them to the Ruby calculateTotal function. In order to call the Ruby calculateTotal function, we need to cast the type of the engine variable to Invocable and then we invoke the Ruby function by its name.

Listing 12-4. A Java Program That Uses the JSR 223 API to Host Ruby Code

```
private static void calculateProductTotalInRuby() throws ScriptException,
NoSuchMethodException, IOException {
    ScriptEngineManager manager = new ScriptEngineManager();
    ScriptEngine engine = manager.getEngineByExtension("rb");
    Product handClapper = new Product("Hand Clapper", 6);
```

```
    Product stretchString = new Product("Stretch String", 8);
    engine.eval(new FileReader(new File("src/main/resources/calculateTotal.rb")));
    Long total = (Long) ((Invocable) engine).invokeFunction("calculateTotal", handClapper,
stretchString);
    System.out.println("Total is: " + total);
}
```

As we saw in the examples, the JSR 223 API is the equivalent API of the DLR Hosting API. Like the DLR Hosting API, the JSR 223 API defines a uniform API for hosting different dynamic languages. Before JSR 223, Scripting for the Java Platform, (and its predecessor, the Bean Scripting Framework, or BSF), many languages were already communicating with Java. Some languages would take textual code as input from a Java program and return the evaluation result back. Others would keep references to objects in a Java program, invoke methods on those objects, or create new instances of a Java class. Because each language would communicate with Java in its own way, developers would have to learn the script engine's proprietary programming interface every time they wanted to use a script engine in their Java programs.

To solve this problem, JSR 223 defines a contract that all script engines conforming to the specification must honor. The contract consists of a set of Java interfaces and classes, as well as a mechanism for packaging and deploying a script engine. The DLR Hosting API is also designed to solve the same problem that JSR 223 addresses. When you work with script engines conforming to JSR 223 or the DLR Hosting API, you'll always program to the same set of interfaces defined by the specification. The details specific to the script engine are well encapsulated, and you'll never need to concern yourself with them.

JSR 223 and the DLR Hosting API help not only consumers, but also producers of script engines. If you have designed and implemented a programming language, you can reach out to a broader audience and make your software friendlier to use by wrapping it with a layer that implements the JSR 223 interfaces or one that supports the DLR Hosting API.

Overview of the BoolScript Example

In the rest of this chapter, we'll play the role of a script-engine producer. The examples so far show how to use JSR 223 script engines that others have implemented. In the rest of this chapter, you will learn how to implement a JSR 223 script engine for a custom language of your own. Before we look at the JSR 223 interfaces and an implementation of them, I'd like to point out that though the name of the JSR contains the word scripting, that's not to say you're limited on the languages that can be integrated with Java the JSR 223 way. You can take any language you fancy and wrap it with a layer that conforms to the contract laid out in JSR 223. The language can be object-oriented, functional, or in any other programming paradigm. The rest of this chapter will implement a simple language and then wrap it with a layer that supports the JSR 223 API. Because the language is simple, we can stay focused on the topic of JSR 223 without the details of a complex language overwhelming us.

Don't worry whether you have prior experience constructing a programming language of your own. This article is not about programming languages; it's about JSR 223's contract between programming languages and Java.

Figure 12-1 shows all the parties in our example and how they relate to each other. The example defines a simple language that I affectionately call BoolScript. I will refer to the program that compiles and executes BoolScript code as the BoolScript engine. Besides compiling and executing BoolScript code, to qualify as a JSR 223 script engine, the BoolScript engine also implements the contract defined in the JSR 223 specification. As depicted in Figure 12-1, all the BoolScript engine's code is packaged into a single jar file called boolscript.jar.

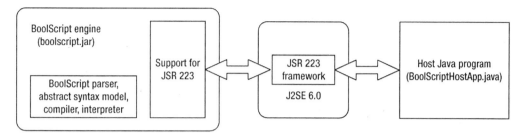

Figure 12-1. *Overview of the BoolScript example*

JSR 223 is a specification in and of itself. Beginning with version 6.0, the Java Standard Edition (J2SE) includes a JSR 223 framework that implements the JSR 223 specification, and that's the middle box in Figure 12-1. In addition to BoolScript.jar and J2SE's JSR 223 framework, the third component, shown on the right, is a Java program that uses the BoolScript engine. The program hosts the BoolScript engine, and its code is in BoolScriptHostApp.java. Notice that a host Java program always interacts with a script engine indirectly via a JSR 223 framework.

To run the example, you need Java SE 6.0 or above. You'll also need the ANTLR runtime component because I used ANTLR to develop the lexer and parser of BoolScript. You can download the Java runtime of ANTLR at www.antlr.org/download.html. The file I downloaded is antlr-runtime-3.2.jar. Put the jar file in the C:\ProDLR\src\Examples\Chapter12\JavaScripting\lib\Antlr\3.2 folder.

Once you have the software components installed, you're all set to run this part of the chapter's code example, which is divided into the following two Eclipse projects:

- BoolScript contains the source code of the BoolScript engine.

- BoolScriptDemo contains the source code of the host Java program.

The BoolScript project is already compiled and packaged into a jar file called boolscript.jar, which goes in C:\ProDLR\src\Examples\Chapter12\JavaScripting\lib\BoolScript and is referenced by the BoolScriptDemo project.

To run the example, you need only compile the host Java program in BoolScriptHostApp.java and run the generated Java .class file. You need to include the two files antlr-runtime-3.2.jar and boolscript.jar in the Java classpath when running the host Java program. After running the example, you'll see output like this:

```
Bool Script Engine
Mozilla Rhino
answer of boolean expression is: false
answer of boolean expression is: false
answer of boolean expression is: true
answer of boolean expression is: false
answer of boolean expression is: true
```

BoolScript Language

Before we delve into the details of JSR 223, let's quickly go over the BoolScript language. BoolScript is so simple that all you can do with it is evaluate Boolean expressions. Here's what code written in BoolScript looks like:

```
(True | False) & True
(True & x) | y
```

As you can see, BoolScript supports two operators: & (logic AND) and | (logic OR). Besides operators, it supports three operands: True, False, and variables whose values might be either True or False. That's it for BoolScript.

You'll find the ANTLR grammar file that defines the syntax of BoolScript in C:\ProDLR\src\Examples\Chapter12\JavaScripting\BoolScript\src\main\resources\BoolScript.g

Listing 12-5 shows the simplified version of BoolScript's syntax grammar, which essentially defines that a BoolScript program is zero or more expressions. Each expression is terminated by a semicolon, and a program is terminated by the EOF (end of file) token. The grammar goes on and defines an expression as a term followed by either "& or "|", followed by another term. A term is defined as a variable identifier (the IDENT token), an expression enclosed by left and right parentheses, and the keyword "True" or the keyword "False". During development time, the grammar file BoolScript.g is used to generate the lexer and parser Java code that knows how to parse BoolScript code at runtime. The generated lexer and parser Java code is in the BoolScriptLexer.java and BoolScriptParser.java files of the BoolScript Eclipse project.

Listing 12-5. Simplified Version of the BoolScript Syntax Grammar

```
program : (expression ';')* EOF ;
expression : term ('&' term | '|' term)*;
term : IDENT
    | '(' expression ')'
    | 'True'
    | 'False';

fragment LETTER : ('a'..'z' | 'A'..'Z') ;
fragment DIGIT : '0'..'9';
IDENT : LETTER (LETTER | DIGIT)*;
```

Script Engine Factory

To see what a JSR 223 framework does between a host Java program and a script engine, let's assume you want to use a script engine in your Java program. First, you'll need to create an instance of the script engine. Second, you'll need to pass textual code to the engine and have the engine evaluate it. Alternatively, you might want the engine to compile the code and save the compiled code for later execution. Let's walk through these steps, bearing in mind that whatever we do, we want to use the script engine only through the JSR 223 framework.

To check whether a script engine is available for a certain language in your deployment environment, you first create an instance of javax.script.ScriptEngineManager and then use it to query the existence of a script engine. You can query the existence of a script engine by its name, its mime types, or file extensions. If we store BoolScript code in *.bool files, the file extension in our case would be bool. The code below queries the existence of the BoolScript engine by file extension:

```
ScriptEngineManager engineMgr = new ScriptEngineManager();
ScriptEngine bsEngine = engineMgr.getEngineByExtension("bool");
```

The BoolScript project specifies the file extensions of BoolScript source files in BoolScriptEngineFactory. The class implements the methods getExtensions, getMimeTypes, and getNames of the javax.script.ScriptEngineFactory interface. And it is in those methods that I declared the name, mime types, and file extensions of the BoolScript language. Listing 12-6 shows the code of the BoolScriptEngineFactory class. As you can see, the name of the BoolScript engine is declared to be "Bool Script Engine" and the version is 1.0.0. The name of the BoolScript language is declared to be "Bool Script Language". The mime type of BoolScript language source code is declared to be "code/bool".

Listing 12-6. BoolScriptEngineFactory Class

```java
public class BoolScriptEngineFactory implements ScriptEngineFactory {

        public String getEngineName() {
                return "Bool Script Engine";
        }

        public String getEngineVersion() {
                return "1.0.0";
        }

        public String getLanguageName() {
                return "Bool Script Language";
        }

        public String getLanguageVersion() {
                return "1.0.0";
        }

        public ScriptEngine getScriptEngine() {
                return new BoolScriptEngine();
        }

        @Override
        public List<String> getNames() {
                ArrayList<String> extList = new ArrayList<String>();
                extList.add("bool script");
                return extList;
        }

        @Override
        public List<String> getExtensions() {
                ArrayList<String> extList = new ArrayList<String>();
                extList.add("bool");
                return extList;
        }

        @Override
        public List<String> getMimeTypes() {
                ArrayList<String> extList = new ArrayList<String>();
                extList.add("code/bool");
                return extList;
        }
```

```
        //Other methods omitted.
}
```

Script Engine Discovery Mechanism

Both the DLR Hosting API and JSR 223 allow us to create a script engine in a language-specific way or in a language- agnostic way. For example, with the DLR Hosting API, we can create a Python script engine in a language-specific way like this:

```
ScriptEngine engine = Python.CreateEngine();
```

We can achieve the same thing in a language-agnostic way like this:

```
ScriptRuntime scriptRuntime = ScriptRuntime.CreateFromConfiguration();
ScriptEngine scriptEngine = scriptRuntime.GetEngine("python");
```

Chapter 6 already covers those two different ways of creating a Python script engine in the DLR Hosting API, so I'll save the explanations here and go straight to showing you the language-specific and - agnostic ways of creating a script engine in JSR 223. We can create a BoolScript script engine in a language-specific way by invoking the BoolScriptEngine constructor like this:

```
ScriptEngine bsEngine = new BoolScriptEngine();
```

We can achieve the same thing in a language-agnostic way like this:

```
ScriptEngineManager manager = new ScriptEngineManager();
ScriptEngine engine = manager.getEngineByExtension("bool");
```

You might wonder, why bother using ScriptEngineManager to create an instance of BoolScriptEngine when we can create it ourselves simply by invoking the constructor of BoolScriptEngine. Well, you can certainly do that. In fact, I did that a few times for the purpose of quick testing when I developed the example code. Creating a script engine directly might be okay for testing a script engine, but for a real usage scenario, it violates the principle that a host Java program should always interact with a script engine indirectly via a JSR 223 framework. It defeats JSR 223's purpose of information hiding. JSR 223 achieves information hiding by using the Factory Method design pattern to decouple script engine creation from a host Java program. Another problem with directly instantiating a script engine's instance is that it bypasses any initializations that ScriptEngineManager might perform on a newly created script engine instance. Are there initializations like that? Read on.

Given the string bool, how does ScriptEngineManager find BoolScriptEngine and create an instance of it? The answer is something called the script engine discovery mechanism in JSR 223. This is the mechanism by which ScriptEngineManager finds the BoolScriptEngine class. In the following discussion of this mechanism, you'll see what initializations ScriptEngineManager does to a script engine and why.

According to the script engine discovery mechanism, a script engine provider needs to package all the classes that implement a script engine plus one extra file in a jar file. The extra file must have the name javax.script.ScriptEngineFactory. The jar file must have the folder META-INF/services, and the file javax.script.ScriptEngineFactory must reside in that folder. If you look at boolscript.jar's contents, you'll see this file and folder structure.

The content of the file META-INF/services/javax.script.ScriptEngineFactory must contain the full names of the classes that implement ScriptEngineFactory in the script engine. In our example, we have only one such class, and the file META-INF/services/javax.script.ScriptEngineFactory looks like this:

```
net.sf.model4lang.boolscript.engine.BoolScriptEngineFactory
```

After a script engine provider packages his or her script engine in a jar file and releases it, users install the script engine by putting the jar file in the Java classpath. Figure 12-2 shows the events that take place when a host Java program asks the JSR 223 framework for a script engine.

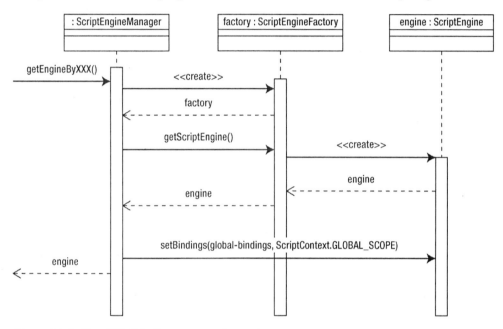

Figure 12-2. *How JSR 223 discovers a script engine*

When asked to find a particular script engine by name, mime types, or file extensions, a ScriptEngineManager will go over the list of ScriptEngineFactory classes (i.e., classes that implement the ScriptEngineFactory interface) that it finds in the classpath. If it finds a match, it will create an instance of the engine factory and use the engine factory to create an instance of the script engine. A script engine factory creates a script engine in its getScriptEngine method. It is the script engine provider's responsibility to implement the method. If you look at BoolScriptEngineFactory, you'll see that our implementation for getScriptEngine looks like this:

```
 public ScriptEngine getScriptEngine()
{
    return new BoolScriptEngine();
}
```

The method is very simple. It just creates an instance of our script engine and returns it to ScriptEngineManager (or whoever the caller is). What's interesting is after ScriptEngineManager receives the script engine instance, and before it returns the engine instance back to the client Java program, it initializes the engine instance by calling the engine's setBindings method. This brings us to one of the core concepts of JSR 223: variable bindings. After I explain the concepts and constructs of bindings, scope, and context, you will know what the setBindings call does to a script engine.

Bindings, Scope, and Context

Recall that the BoolScript language allows you to write code like this:

```
(True & x) | y
```

But it doesn't have any language construct for you to assign values to the variables x and y. I could have designed the language to accept code like this:

```
x = True
y = False
(True & x) | y
```

But I purposely left out the assignment operator = and require that BoolScript code must execute in a context where the values of the variables are defined. This means that when a host Java program passes textual code to the BoolScript engine for evaluation, it also needs to pass a context to the script engine, or at least tell the script engine which context to use. The idea of using a context to pass objects between a host Java program and the hosted script code is the same as the ScriptScope class in the DLR Hosting API. The ScriptContext class defined in JSR 223 is equivalent to the ScriptScope class in the DLR Hosting API.

You can think of a script context as a bag that contains data you want to pass back and forth between a host Java program and a script engine. The construct that JSR 223 defines to model a script context is the interface javax.script.ScriptContext. A bag would be messy if we put a lot of things in it without some type of organization. So to be neat and tidy, a script context (i.e., an instance of ScriptContext) partitions data it holds into scopes. The construct that JSR 223 defines to model the concept of scope is the interface javax.script.Bindings. Figure 12-3 illustrates context, its scopes, and data stored therein.

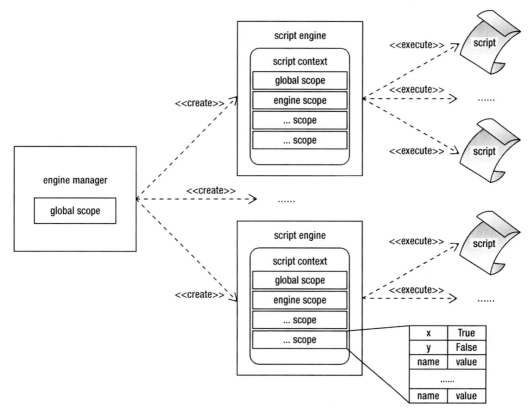

Figure 12-3. *Context and scope in script engine managers and script engines*

There are several important things to note in Figure 12-3:

- A script engine contains a script context.

- A script engine manager (i.e., an instance of ScriptEngineManager) can be used to create multiple script engines.

- A script engine manager contains a scope called global scope, but it does not contain a context.

- Each scope is basically just a collection of name-value pairs. Figure 12-3 shows that one of the scopes contains a slot whose name is x and a slot whose name is y. A scope is an instance of javas.script.Bindings.

- The context in a script engine contains a global scope, an engine scope, and zero or more other scopes.

- A script engine can be used to evaluate multiple scripts (i.e., separated code snippets written in the script language).

What do we mean by the global scope and the engine scope in Figure 12-3 and why do we need them? A global scope is a scope shared by multiple script engines. If you want some piece of data to be accessible across multiple script engines, a global scope is the place to put the data. Note that a global scope is not global to all script engines. It's only global to the script engines created by the script engine manager in which the global scope resides.

An engine scope is a scope shared by multiple scripts. If you want some piece of data to be accessible across multiple scripts, an engine scope is the place to put the data. For example, say we have two scripts like this:

```
(True & x) | y      //Script A

(True & x)          //Script B
```

If we want to share the same value for x across the two scripts, we can put that value in the engine scope held by the script engine we will use to evaluate the two scripts. And suppose we want to keep the value of y to only Script A. To do that, we can create a scope, remembering that this scope is visible only to Script A, and put the value of y in it.

As an example, Listing 12-7 shows the interpretBoolCodeExample method in BoolScriptHostApp.java. The method evaluates the BoolScript code x & y; True | y; using the variable bindings that exist in the script engine's scope.

Listing 12-7. Evaluating BoolScript Code in a Script Engine's Scope

```java
private static void interpretBoolCodeExample() {
        ScriptEngineManager scriptManager = new ScriptEngineManager();
        List<Boolean> boolAnswers = null;
        ScriptEngine bsEngine = scriptManager.getEngineByExtension("bool");

        try
        {
                bsEngine.put("x", new Boolean(true));
                bsEngine.put("y", new Boolean(false));
                boolAnswers = (List<Boolean>) bsEngine.eval("x & y; True | y;");
                printAnswers(boolAnswers);
        }
        catch (Exception ex)
        {
                System.out.println(ex.getMessage());
        }
}
```

The code puts the values of both x and y in the engine scope, then it calls the eval method on the engine to evaluate the BoolScript code. If you look at the ScriptEngine interface, you'll see that the eval method is overloaded with different parameters. If we call eval with a string as we did in Listing 12-7, the script engine will evaluate the code in its context. If we don't want to evaluate the code in the script engine's context, we have to supply the context we'd like to use when we call eval. Listing 12-7 shows how to use the eval method of the BoolScriptEngine class to evaluate BoolScript code. Next we'll look at how the eval method is implemented.

BoolScript Engine

Listing 12-8 shows the code in the eval method of the BoolScriptEngine class. The BoolScriptEngine class is the JSR 223 wrapper around the BoolScript language so that BoolScript language code can be hosted in a Java program the JSR 223 way. The eval method implemented in the BoolScriptEngine class is responsible for taking in BoolScript code as a string, parsing it, and evaluating it. As you can see from Listing 12-8, the eval method calls the static parse method of BoolScriptParser to parse BoolScript code. The result of the parsing is a list of BoolExpression instances. This is in line with what I mentioned earlier about the syntax of the BoolScript language. In the section where we looked at the grammar definition of the BoolScript language, we saw that a BoolScript program consists of zero or more expressions. It therefore shouldn't be surprising that I chose to use a list of BoolExpression instances to represent the result of the syntax parsing. Once a BoolScript program is parsed into a list of BoolExpression instances, evaluating the program becomes a matter of evaluating each BoolExpression instance. In order to do this, the eval method in Listing 12-8 needs a scope that contains necessary variable bindings. In Listing 12-8, we get a reference to the engine scope by calling the getBindings method on the context that's passed to the eval method as a parameter. Because more than one scope might be in a context, we indicate that we want to get the engine scope by passing the constant ScriptContex.ENGINE_SCOPE to the getBindings method.

Listing 12-8. The eval Method of the BoolScriptEngine Class

```
public Object eval(String script, ScriptContext context) {
        Bindings bindings = context.getBindings(ScriptContext.ENGINE_SCOPE);
        List<BoolExpression> expressions = BoolScriptParser.parse(script);
        List<Boolean> result = new ArrayList<Boolean>(expressions.size());
        for (BoolExpression expression : expressions)
                result.add(expression.eval(bindings));

        return result;
}
```

Listing 12-9 shows the code of the BoolExpression interface. The interface defines an eval method that's supposed to evaluate a BoolScript expression when called. In the BoolScript Eclipse project, you can find several classes such as AndExpression, OrExpression and VarExpression that implement the BoolExpression interface. Each of those classes will implement its own specific logic for the eval method defined in the BoolExpression interface. The eval method implemented in the AndExpression class takes the left and right subexpressions of a Boolean AND operator and does the evaluation by performing a logical AND operation. Listing 12-10 shows how the eval method is implemented in the AndExpression class.

Listing 12-9. The BoolExpression Interface

```
public interface BoolExpression {
        boolean eval(Map<String, Object> bindings);
        Set<VarExpression>  getVariables();
        String toTargetCode();
}
```

Listing 12-10. The eval Method Implemented in the AndExpression Class

```java
public class AndExpression implements BoolExpression {
        private BoolExpression left;
        private BoolExpression right;

        public AndExpression(BoolExpression left, BoolExpression right) {
                this.left = left;
                this.right = right;
        }

        @Override
        public boolean eval(Map<String, Object> bindings) {
                return left.eval(bindings) & right.eval(bindings);
        }

        //other methods omitted.
}
```

The VarExpression class represents variables in the BoolScript language. Because BoolScript code relies on the script context to provide variable binding, evaluating a VarExpression instance means retrieving the variable's value from the script context. Listing 12-11 shows the eval method implemented in the VarExpression class. The code in the eval method simply calls the get method on the parameter bindings, which represents the variable bindings in the scope of the expression evaluation. The code in the eval method looks up the variable's value by the variable's name in the bindings parameter.

Listing 12-11. The eval Method Implemented in the VarExpression Class

```java
public class VarExpression implements BoolExpression {

        private String varName;

        public VarExpression(String varName) {
                this.varName = varName;
        }

        @Override
        public boolean eval(Map<String, Object> bindings) {
                return (Boolean) bindings.get(varName);
        }

        //other methods omitted.
}
```

Finally, I am ready to explain why a script engine manager initializes a script engine by calling the engine's setBindings method: When a script engine manager calls an engine's setBindings method, it passes its global scope as a parameter to the method. The engine's implementation of the setBinding method is expected to store the global scope in the engine's script context.

Before we leave this section, let's look at a few classes in the scripting API. I said that a ScriptEngineManager contains an instance of Bindings that represents a global scope. If you look at the javax.script.ScriptEngineManager class, you'll see that there is a getBindings method for getting the bindings and a setBindings method for setting the bindings that represent the global scope in a ScriptEngineManager.

A ScriptEngine contains an instance of ScriptContext. If you look at the javax.script.ScriptEngine interface, you'll see the methods getContext and setContext for getting and setting the script context in a ScriptEngine.

So nothing prevents you from sharing a global scope among several script engine managers. To do that, you just need to call getBindings on one script engine manager to get its global scope and then call setBindings with that global scope on other script engine managers.

If you look at our example script engine class BoolScriptEngine, you won't see it keeping a reference to an instance of ScriptContext explicitly. That's because BoolScriptEngine inherits from AbstractScriptEngine, which already has an instance of ScriptContext as its member. If you ever need to implement a script engine from scratch without inheriting from a class such as AbstractScriptEngine, you'll need to keep an instance of ScriptContext in your script engine and implement the getContext and setContext methods accordingly.

Compile BoolScript Code

By now, we've implemented the minimum for our BoolScript engine to qualify as a JSR 223 script engine. Every time a Java client program wants to use our script engine, it passes in the BoolScript code as a string. Internally, the script engine has a parser that parses the string into a tree of BoolExpression instances commonly called an abstract syntax tree, then it calls the eval method on each of BoolExpression instances in the tree to evaluate the BoolScript program. This whole process of evaluating BoolScript code is called interpretation, as opposed to compilation. And in this role, the BoolScript engine is called an interpreter, as opposed to a compiler. To be a compiler, the BoolScript engine would need to transform the textual BoolScript code into an intermediate form so that it wouldn't have to parse the code into an abstract syntax tree every time it wanted to evaluate it.

If you recall, the DLR Hosting API provides functionality for compiling dynamic code. With the DLR Hosting API, once the dynamic code is compiled, we can execute it multiple times in different script scopes. With JSR 223, once the dynamic code is compiled, we can also execute it multiple times in different script contexts. This section will show you how to compile BoolScript code into JVM bytecode and execute the bytecode in different script contexts. Java programs are compiled into an intermediate form called Java bytecode and stored in .class files. At runtime, .class files are loaded by classloaders, and the JVM executes the bytecode. Instead of defining our own intermediate form and implementing our own virtual machine, we'll simply stand on the shoulder of Java by compiling BoolScript code into Java bytecode.

The construct JSR 223 defines to model the concept of compilation is javax.script.Compilable, which is the interface BoolScriptEngine needs to implement. Figure 12-12 shows the runCompiledBoolScriptExample method in BoolScriptHostApp.java that demonstrates how to use the compilable BoolScript engine to compile and execute BoolScript code.

Listing 12-12. Compiling BoolScript Code into Java Bytecode

```
private static void runCompiledBoolScriptExample() throws ScriptException,
NoSuchMethodException {
        ScriptEngineManager scriptManager = new ScriptEngineManager();
        ScriptEngine engine = scriptManager.getEngineByExtension("bool");
        CompiledScript compiledScript = ((Compilable) engine).compile("x & y;");
        Bindings bindings = new SimpleBindings();
        bindings.put("x", true);
```

```
        bindings.put("y", false);
        List<Boolean> result = (List<Boolean>) compiledScript.eval(bindings);
        for (Boolean boolValue : result)
                System.out.println("answer of boolean expression is: " + boolValue);
}
```

In Listing 12-12, the variable engine is an instance of BoolScriptEngine that we know also implements the Compilable interface. We cast it to an instance of Compilable and call its compile method to compile the code x & y. Listing 12-13 shows the implementation of the compile method in BoolScriptEngine.

Listing 12-13. The Compile Method of BoolScriptEngine

```
public CompiledScript compile(String script) throws ScriptException {
        BoolScriptCompiler compiler = new BoolScriptCompiler(this);
        compiledScript = compiler.compileSource(script);
        return compiledScript;
}
```

The compile method of BoolScriptEngine creates an instance of BoolScriptCompiler and calls its compileSource method. Internally, the compileSource method transforms the BoolScript code x & y into the following Java code:

```
package boolscript.generated;
import java.util.*;
import java.lang.reflect.*;

class TempBoolClass {
  public static List<Boolean> eval(boolean x, boolean y)
  {
    List<Boolean> resultList = new ArrayList<Boolean>();
    boolean result = false;
    result = x & y;
    resultList.add(new Boolean(result));
    return resultList;
  }
}
```

The transformation converts BoolScript code into a Java method inside a Java class. The class name and method name are hard-coded to be TempBoolClass and eval respectively. Each variable in BoolScript code becomes a parameter in the Java eval method. You can find the code that performs the conversion from BoolScript code to Java code in the compileBoolCode method of the BoolScriptCompiler class.

Transforming BoolScript code to Java code is just half the story. The other half is about compiling the generated Java code into bytecode. I chose to compile the generated Java code in memory using JSR 199, the Java Compiler API, a feature that begins to be available in Java SE 6.0. Details of the Java Compiler API are beyond the scope of this chapter's discussion.

The Compilable interface dictates that the compile method must return an instance of CompiledScript. The class CompiledScript is the construct JSR 223 defines to model the result of a compilation. No matter how we compile our script code, after all is said and done, we need to package the compilation result as an instance of CompiledScript. In the example code, I defined a class CompiledBoolScript and derived it from CompiledScript to store the compiled BoolScript code. Listing

12-14 shows the code of the CompiledBoolScript class. Because the purpose of CompiledBoolScript is to store the result of compiling BoolScript code, I defined a member variable in CompiledBoolScript called generatedClass. The member variable generatedClass references the in-memory Java class generated from compiling the input BoolScript code. Besides keeping a reference to the generated in-memory Java class, I also defined the varList member variable to keep track of the variable expressions in the input BoolScript code. This way, the eval method of the CompiledBoolScript class can retrieve the variables' values from the script context when it is invoked to execute the compiled BoolScript code. The eval method of the CompiledBoolScript class uses Java reflection to call the eval method of the generated Java class.

Listing 12-14. CompiledBoolScript Class

```
public class CompiledBoolScript extends CompiledScript {

  private BoolScriptEngine engine;
  private Class generatedClass;
  private List<VarExpression> varList;

  public CompiledBoolScript(BoolScriptEngine engine,
        Class generatedClass, List<VarExpression> varList) {
    this.engine = engine;
    this.generatedClass = generatedClass;
    this.varList = varList;
  }

  @Override
  public List<Boolean> eval(ScriptContext context) throws ScriptException {
    Class[] parameterTypes = new Class[varList.size()];
    Object[] parameters = new Object[varList.size()];
    for (int i = 0; i < parameterTypes.length; i++) {
      parameterTypes[i] = boolean.class;
      String varName = varList.get(i).getName();
      parameters[i] = context.getAttribute(varName);
    }

    Method evalMethod = getMethod(parameterTypes);
    Object result = invokeMethod(evalMethod, parameters);
    return (List<Boolean>) result;
  }

  private Object invokeMethod(Method evalMethod, Object[] parameters)
      throws ScriptException {
    try {
      return evalMethod.invoke(null, parameters);
    } catch (…) {
      //exception handling code omitted.
    }
  }

  private Method getMethod(Class[] parameterTypes) throws ScriptException {
    try {
      Method evalMethod = generatedClass.getMethod("eval", parameterTypes);
```

```
        evalMethod.setAccessible(true);
        return evalMethod;
    } catch (…) {
        //exception handling code omitted.
    }
}

//other method omitted.
}
```

Once the script code is compiled, the client Java program can repeatedly execute the compiled code by calling the eval method on the `CompiledBoolScript` instance that represents the compilation result of the source BoolScript code. When we call the eval method on the `CompiledBoolScript` instance that represents the compiled result of the BoolScript code x & y;, we need to pass in a script context that contains the values for variables x and y.

Run BoolScript Code as Invocable Function

The eval method of `CompiledScript` is not the only way to execute compiled script code. If the script engine implements the Invocable interface, we can call the invoke method of the Invocable interface to execute compiled script code too, much like we used Invocable to invoke Python and Ruby functions earlier in this chapter. In our simple example, there might not seem to be any difference between using `CompiledScript` and using Invocable for script execution. However, practically, users of a script engine will use `CompiledScript` to execute a whole script file, and they'll use Invocable to execute individual functions (methods, in Java terms) in a script. And if we look at Invocable's invoke method, distinguishing between `CompiledScript` and Invocable is not difficult. Unlike `CompiledScript`'s eval method, which takes an optional script context as a parameter, Invocable's invoke method takes as a parameter the name of the particular function you'd like to invoke in the compiled script.

Listing 12-15 shows `BoolScriptEngine`'s very simple implementation of the Invocable interface. The code simply uses the member variable compiledScript to keep a reference to the `CompiledBoolScript` instance that represents the result of compiling the source BoolScript code. Then in the invokeFunction method, the code creates a script context from the input args parameter and calls the eval method on the compiledScript member variable with the script context. The implementation of the Invocable interface in Listing 12-15 is very simple because all it does is store the result of compilation and use that result when asked to invoke a function. Practically, we should store not only the result of the `BoolScriptEngine`'s compile method but also the result of its eval method. This way, if a host Java program calls the eval method, the evaluated BoolScript code can be executed again by calling the invokeFunction method of `BoolScriptEngine`.

Listing 12-15. BoolScriptEngine's Implementation of the Invocable Interface

```
public class BoolScriptEngine
        extends AbstractScriptEngine
        implements Compilable, Invocable {

  private CompiledBoolScript compiledScript = null;

  @Override
  public CompiledScript compile(String script) throws ScriptException {
    BoolScriptCompiler compiler = new BoolScriptCompiler(this);
    compiledScript = compiler.compileSource(script);
```

```
    return compiledScript;
  }

  @Override
  public Object invokeFunction(String name, Object... args)
        throws ScriptException, NoSuchMethodException {

    List<VarExpression> vars = compiledScript.getVarList();
    ScriptContext context = new SimpleScriptContext();
    for (int i = 0; i < args.length; i++)
      context.setAttribute(vars.get(i).getName(), args[i], ScriptContext.ENGINE_SCOPE);

    return compiledScript.eval(context);
  }

  //other methods omitted.
}
```

Once we extend the BoolScriptEngine class to implement the Invocable interface, we can use it to execute BoolScript code as if the BoolScript code were an invocable function. Listing 12-16 shows an example of such usage of the BoolScriptEngine class.

In Listing 12-16, the variable engine is an instance of ScriptEngine that we know also implements the Compilable and Invocable interfaces. We cast it to be an instance of Compilable and call the compile method to compile the BoolScript code "x & y;". After the compilation, we cast engine to be an instance of Invocable and call its invokeFunction method. Invoking a compiled script function is much like invoking a Java method using Java reflection. You must tell invokeFunction the name of the function you want to invoke, and supply it with the parameters required by the function. We know that in our generated Java code, the method name is hard-coded to be eval. So we pass the string "eval" as the first parameter to invokeFunction. We also know that generated Java eval method takes two Boolean values as its input parameters. So we pass two Boolean values to invokeFunction as well.

Listing 12-16. Using BoolScriptEngine to Execute BoolScript Code as if It Were an Invocable Function

```
private static void invokeCompiledBoolScriptExample() throws ScriptException,
NoSuchMethodException {
        ScriptEngineManager scriptManager = new ScriptEngineManager();
        ScriptEngine engine = scriptManager.getEngineByExtension("bool");
        CompiledScript compiledScript = ((Compilable) engine).compile("x & y;");
        List<Boolean> result = (List<Boolean>) ((Invocable) engine).invokeFunction(
                "eval", true, false);

        for (Boolean boolValue : result)
                System.out.println("answer of boolean expression is: " + boolValue);
}
```

Summary

This chapter covered several major areas of JSR 223, such as the script engine discovery mechanism, variable bindings, and the Compilable and Invocable interfaces. One part of JSR 223 not mentioned in this article is Web scripting. If we implemented Web scripting in the BoolScript engine, clients of our script engine would be able to use it to generate Web contents in a servlet container.

We discussed and compared in a general way the dynamic language support provided by .NET and JVM, then we focused on a more in-depth discussion and comparison between JSR 223 and the DLR Hosting API. We saw that both JSR 223 and the DLR Hosting API have a mechanism for discovering script engines in a deployment environment. Both also define an API contract for interpreting or compiling dynamic language code. Furthermore, they both have a way to pass objects between a host program and the hosted dynamic language code.

Developing a non-trivial language compiler or interpreter is a huge undertaking, let alone integrating it with Java or .NET. Depending on the complexity of the language you want to design, developing a compiler or interpreter can remain a daunting task. However, thanks to JSR 223 and the DLR Hosting API, the integration between your language and Java or .NET has never been easier.

Index

Breinigsville, PA USA
10 December 2010
251075BV00004B/8/P